OCR
Sociology
A2

OCR and Heinemann are working together to provide better support for you

Carole Waugh
Peter Allen
Sue Brisbane
Stephen Gregory
Fionnuala Swann

www.heinemann.co.uk
✓ Free online support
✓ Useful weblinks
✓ 24 hour online ordering

01865 888080

Official Publisher Partnership

Heinemann is an imprint of Pearson Education Limited, a company incorporated in England and Wales, having its registered office at Edinburgh Gate, Harlow, Essex, CM20 2JE. Registered company number: 872828

www.heinemann.co.uk

Heinemann is a registered trademark of Pearson Education Limited

Text © Carole Waugh, Peter Allen, Sue Brisbane, Stephen Gregory, Fionnuala Swann

First published 2009

13 12 11 10 09
0 9 8 7 6 5 4 3 2 1

British Library Cataloguing in Publication Data is available from the British Library on request.

ISBN 978 0 435806 94 1

Edited by Jane Anson
Designed by Hicks Design
Typeset by Tek-Art, Crawley Down, West Sussex
Original illustrations © Pearson Education Limited 2008
Illustrated by Julian Mosedale and Tek-Art
Picture research by Lindsay Lewis
Printed in the UK by Scotprint, Haddington, Scotland

Websites

There are links to relevant websites in this book. In order to ensure that the links are up-to-date, that the links work, and that the sites are not inadvertently linked to sites that could be considered offensive, we have made the links available on the Heinemann website at www.heinemann.co.uk/hotlinks. When you access the site, the express code is 6941.

Contents

Acknowledgements

The authors and publisher would like to thank the following individuals and organisations for permission to reproduce material in this book.

Photos

Page 3 Sipa Press/Rex Features; page 15 AP/PA Photos; page 18 Picture Contact/Alamy; page 20 PYMCA/Alamy; page 39 Anthony Devlin/PA Archive/PA Photos; page 48 Sally & Richard Greenhill/Alamy; page 53 Adrian Sherratt/Alamy; page 64 Rob Walls/Alamy; page 67 Cultura/Corbis; page 81 Howard Barlow/Alamy; page 92 ITV/Rex Features; page 96 Alex Gitlits/Alamy; page 101 Simon Marcus/Corbis; page 120 Dave Hogan/Getty Images; page 125 Deutsche Press Agenture/PA Photos; page 140 Tony Kyriacou/Rex Features; page 155 Action Press/Rex Features; page 158 Homer Sykes Archive/Alamy; page 161 David Hoffman Photo Library/Alamy; page 173 Sion Touhig/Corbis; page 185 Justin Kase zthreez/Alamy; page 199 Panacea Pictures/Alamy; page 206 JUPITERIMAGES/i2i/Alamy; page 214 Bubbles Photo Library/Alamy; page 222 Raoul Minsart/Masterfile; page 228 Digital Stock; page 233 Punchstock.

Text

*Crown Copyright material is reproduced with the permission of the Controller Office of Public Sector Information (OPSI).

Page 10 *British Crime Survey, Home Office available at http://www.homeoffice.gov.uk/crime-victims/crime-statistics/; *Crime in England and Wales available at http://www.homeoffice.gov.uk/rds/pdfs08/hosb0708chap2.pdf; Pages 10–11 *British Crime Survey, Home Office available at http://www.homeoffice.gov.uk/crime-victims/crime-statistics/; Criminal Statistics, Ministry of Justice available at http://www.statistics.gov.uk/CCI/nugget.asp?ID=1661&Pos=5&ColRank=1&Rank=326; Page 11 *Statistics on Race and the Criminal Justice System available at http://www.homeoffice.gov.uk/rds/pdfs04/s95race2003.pdf; Page 26 *Youth Justice Board, Annual Workload Data available at http://www.yjb.gov.uk/Publications/Scripts/prodList.asp?eP=; Page 65 *Social Inequalities, Office for National Statistics available at http://www.statistics.gov.uk/cci/nugget.asp?id=1003; Page 71 *Attainment and Outcomes, Department for Children, Schools and Families available at http://www.dcsf.gov.uk/trends/index.cfm?fuseaction=home.showChart&cid=5&iid=32&chid=137; Page 72 *Focus on Gender, Office for National Statistics available at http://www.statistics.gov.uk/statbase/product.asp?vlnk=10923; Statistics from Universities and Colleges Admissions Service available at stats@ucas.ac.uk; Page 74 Statistics from Higher Education Statistics Agency available at http://www.hesa.ac.uk/dox/dataTables/studentsAndQualifiers/download/quals0607.xls?v=1.0; Page 75 *Ethnicity and Identity, Office for National Statistics available at http://www.statistics.gov.uk/cci/nugget.asp?id=461; Page 78 *Households Below Average Income, Department for Wages and Pensions available at http://www.poverty.org.uk/06/index.shtml?2; Page 94 Reproduced by permission of SAGE Publications, London, Los Angeles, New Delhi and Singapore, from Devereux, E. (2008) *Understanding the Media*, London: Sage. © Eoin Devereux, 2007; Page 98 *Family Spending, Office for National Statistics available at http://www.statistics.gov.uk/downloads/theme_social/Family_Spending_2006/FamilySpending2007_web.pdf; Page 107 Harcup, T. and O'Neill, D. (2001) 'What is news? Galtung and Ruge revisited', *Journalism Studies*, Volume 2, Number 2, pp.261–280 (Taylor & Francis Ltd, http://www.informaworld.com), reprinted by permission of the publisher; Page 110 BBC Royal Charter available at http://www.bbc.co.uk/bbctrust/assets/files/pdf/regulatory_framework/charter_agreement/royalchartersealed_sept06.pdf; Page 124 McRobbie, A. (2005) 'Cutting girls down to Victoria Beckham's size', *Times Higher Educational Supplement*, 14 October, permission granted by Angela McRobbie, Professor of Communications, Goldsmith University of London; Page 146 Adapted from Danitz, T. and Strobel, W. P. (1999), pp.158–168, 'Networking dissent: cyber activists use the internet to promote democracy in Burma', in Arquilla, J. and Ronfeldt, D. (eds) (2001) *Networks and Netwars: The Future of Terror, Crime, and Militancy*, Santa Monica: Rand; Page 192 *National Statistics Socio-Economic Classification, available at http://www.ons.gov.uk/about-statistics/classifications/current/ns-sec/cats-and-classes/analytic-classes/index.html; Page 193 *Social Trends 38, table 10.5, p.139, Office for National Statistics available at http://www.statistics.gov.uk/downloads/theme_social/Social_Trends38/Social_Trends_38.pdf; original source of data: General Household Survey 2006, table 4.12 available at http://www.statistics.gov.uk/downloads/theme_compendia/GHS06/GHS06chapter4-Housing&cd.xls; *Focus on Social Inequalities, Office for National Statistics available at http://www.statistics.gov.uk/focuson/socialinequalities/; Page 194 *Social Trends 38, table 6.6, p.84, Office for National Statistics, available at http://www.statistics.gov.uk/downloads/theme_social/Social_Trends38/Social_Trends_38.pdf; Department for Environment, Food and Social Affairs, Report on the Expenditure and Food Survey available at https://statistics.defra.gov.uk/esg/publications/efs/datasets/default.asp; *Focus on Social Inequalities, Office for National Statistics available at http://www.statistics.gov.uk/downloads/theme_compendia/fosi2004/SocialInequalities_full.pdf; *Evidence of Health Inequalities, Healthcare Commission available at http://www.healthcarecommission.org.uk/_db/_documents/04017601.pdf; Pages 194–5 Social background of MPs available at www.parliament.uk/commons/lib; Page 199 *Focus on Social Inequalities, Office for National Statistics available at http://www.statistics.gov.uk/downloads/theme_compendia/fosi2004/SocialInequalities_full.pdf; Pages 201, 202 Future Foundation (2006) *Middle Britain: Summary Report, Class Membership and Money in the 21st Century*, London: Liverpool Victoria; Page 209 Hutton, W. (1995) 30/30/40 Society available at http://www.jobsletter.org.nz/jbl03010.htm; Page 211 *Social Trends 38, table 4.2, p.48, Office for National Statistics available at http://www.statistics.gov.uk/downloads/theme_social/Social_Trends38/Social_Trends_38.pdf; Sealy, R., Singh, V. and Vinnicombe, S. (2007) The Female FTSE Report 2008, Cranfield: Cranfield School of Management; Page 212 *Social Trends 38, table 4.12, p.54, Office for National Statistics available at http://www.statistics.gov.uk/downloads/theme_social/Social_Trends38/Social_Trends_38.pdf; *Annual Survey of Hours and Earnings, Office for National Statistics available at http://www.statistics.gov.uk/pdfdir/ashe1107.pdf; Palmer, G., MacInnes, T. and Kenway, P. (2007) *Monitoring Poverty and Social Exclusion*, 2007, York: Joseph Rowntree Foundation and London: New Policy Institute, indicator 10, p.47, notes p.42; Page 213 *Attainment and Outcomes, Department for Children, Schools and Families available at http://www.dcsf.gov.uk/trends/upload/xls/5_5t.xls; Focus on Gender, Office for National Statistics available at http://www.statistics.gov.uk/statbase/product.asp?vlnk=10923; Page 214 *Social Trends 38, table 7.2, p.94, Office for National Statistics available at http://www.statistics.gov.uk/downloads/theme_social/Social_Trends38/Social_Trends_38.pdf; Page 218 Hakim, C. (2000) *Work-Lifestyle Choices in the 21st Century: Preference Theory*, Oxford: Oxford University Press. Reproduced with permission of Oxford University Press; Page 220 *Social Trends 38, table 1.5, p.5, Office for National Statistics available at http://www.statistics.gov.uk/downloads/theme_social/Social_Trends38/Social_Trends_38.pdf; Page 221 *Focus on Religion, Office for National Statistics available at http://www.statistics.gov.uk/downloads/theme_compendia/for2004/FocusonReligion.pdf; Equality and Human Rights Commission (2006) Facts about Women and Men in Great Britain available at www.eoc.org.uk. Copyright Equality and Human Rights Commission; Page 222 Business in the Community, Race for Opportunity, 'Facts and Stats', available at http://www.bitc.org.uk/workplace/diversity/race/facts_and_stats.html

Every effort has been made to contact copyright holders of material reproduced in this book. Any omissions will be rectified in subsequent printings if notice is given to the publishers.

Introduction

Sociologists would argue that individuals are not born equal. Consider, for example, the life chances of Prince William (born on 21 June 1982) compared with those of thousands of other children born on the same day but into radically different material and cultural circumstances. Clearly William's life chances and opportunities will differ from those of others born at the same time. Sociologists do not dispute the existence of social inequality and social difference, but they differ in their explanations of how these differences impact on opportunities and life chances.

Social inequality and differences are related to issues of power and control. In the contemporary UK, power is distributed differentially among individuals, organisations and social groups. Many sociologists propose that power in the UK is concentrated in the hands of a minority, albeit unfairly: such is the nature of a socially unequal society.

Social inequality and difference, and power and control are the core themes of A2 Sociology. You will study two units, which build on and extend the knowledge and understanding gained at AS Level.

- Unit G673 is called Power and control and explores four topics: Crime and deviance, Education, Mass media, Power and politics. You must study at least one of these in depth.

- Unit G674 is called Exploring social inequality and difference, and is related to the concepts of gender, social class, ethnicity and age which you studied at AS. At A2, however, your understanding will be tailored towards the core themes of social inequality and difference rather than socialisation, culture and identity. This unit also assesses your methodological understanding. It *builds on* what you covered at AS Level; *it does not replicate it*. It is *essential* therefore that you revisit your notes/AS text when preparing for this assessment.

The textbook is written to match the specification exactly, and contains a vast quantity of evidence to build on and sustain your sociological understanding. It adopts many of the same features as the AS text: it uses the same type of activities and weblinks; it has an Exam Café with practice questions, a student answer, and teacher and examiner tips, which will provide vital information for your assessment. There are also three new features that are specific to A2:

- a Methods Links icon is used to emphasise a study or piece of research that could be used to enhance your methodological understanding

- **Stretch and Challenge Activity**

  a Stretch and Challenge arrow is used for activities and ideas that will enhance your understanding and ability to think holistically as a sociologist

- finally, section summaries are provided which contain the main named theories in each section and key concepts. These key concepts all appear in the glossary (along with some additional methodological concepts) and to consolidate your understanding you are asked to write a paragraph summarising what you have learnt in that section using the selection of key words.

One final point about using this book and preparing for A2 Sociology: the skill of evaluation is more important at A2 than at AS level. Throughout the text we have offered evaluative points for the main theories but the more comfortable you become with the theories themselves the easier you will find evaluation within them and between them. For that reason, you are urged to 'think theoretically' and think 'holistically' as sociologists while you study the course.

Exam Café

The Exam Café provides a range of ideas to help with exam preparation. There is an Exam Café section at the end of each option in Unit 3 and at the end of Unit 4.

You can **Relax** because there's handy revision advice from fellow students.

Refresh your memory with summaries and checklists of the key ideas you need to revise.

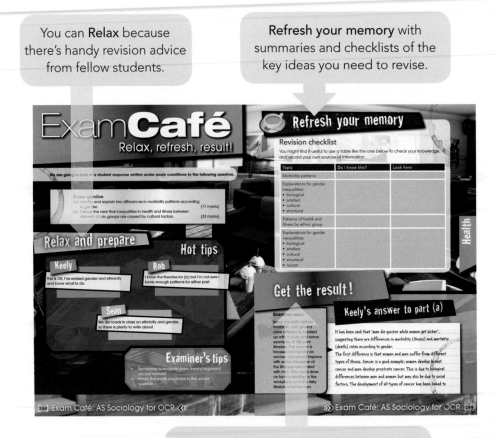

Get the result through practising exam-style questions, accompanied by hints and tips on getting the very best grades.

We hope that you will enjoy studying Sociology A2 Level.

Carole Waugh, Series Editor, January 2009

◆ Thank you to Paul, Alex and Ben for everything, to my sister Gill for her constant good humour, and to my Dad for always being there. *Carole Waugh*

◆ For my wife Ann and my sister Trish (and her little companions) for all their support and tolerance over the years; for Carole and Meena (and all at OCR) for their encouragement and confidence in me. *Peter Allen*

◆ Love and thanks to my wonderful sons Keir and Finlay for their encouragement, to Martin for his constant love and support and to my Mum for being there. In memory of my Dad who would have taken pleasure in the contents. *Sue Brisbane*

◆ Thanks to Charlotte and James for making me so proud of them, and Karen for her love and giving me time; to Andrew, Cath and Fionnuala for their support and encouragement. Last but not least, thanks Mum. *Stephen Gregory*

◆ For my sister, my best friend. And in loving memory of my Grandma, Ennyd Andrews – I wish you'd been able to see this. *Fionnuala Swann*

Unit 3

Power and control

- Sociology of crime and deviance
- Sociology of education
- Sociology of mass media
- Sociology of power and politics

Guidance on answering questions in Unit 3 (G673)

This unit is examined through two unstructured essays, out of a choice of three in each option. You are required to answer any two essay questions. You may answer questions from any option(s). Each essay is allocated 50 marks and you are advised to spend 45 minutes on each one.

Unstructured essays help to meet the requirements of synopticity. They are a chance for you to demonstrate your ability to target all three of the Assessment Objectives: knowledge and understanding (AO1), interpretation and application (AO2), and analysis and evaluation (AO3). All the essay questions begin with the phrase 'Outline and assess …', which means that you need knowledge and understanding to 'outline', interpretation and analysis to ensure that your selected knowledge is made relevant to the question, and evaluation skills in order to 'assess' the argument, theory or view stated in the question. At A2 Level, there are more marks available for the AO2 skills, so you must ensure that you focus particularly on these.

Assessment Objective (AO)	You can display Assessment Objectives by using terms such as:	
1 Knowledge and understanding: the studies, theories, concepts and contemporary examples you have learned throughout your course	• _____ argued… • A study by_____ explored… • The Marxists would explain this by… • A useful example is_____… • The concept of _____…	
2 Interpretation and application: how well you interpret the knowledge and apply it to a given question/point	• This means… • This shows…	• Therefore… • In relation to…
3 Evaluation and analysis: judgements, criticisms, appraisals and assessment of sociological knowledge	• However… • On the other hand… • A different view is offered by…	• This was criticised by…

Below are some general tips to help you answer the essay questions in Unit 3.

1   Spend a few minutes planning your answer to ensure that your essay follows a logical and fluent structure. Don't make this too detailed, as the plan will not be marked. Just focus on planning your answer around the view or theory expressed in the question.

2   At A2, your understanding of theory is important. Ensure that you fully explain what theories say in relation to the questions. Try to include the key concepts associated with each theory and explain them fully. For example, an essay question on Marxist theory of education or crime will probably include an explanation of the terms *ideology*, *false class consciousness*, *capitalism*.

3   In order to get into the top mark band for AO1 (knowledge and understanding), your answers need to contain depth as well as a range of knowledge. This means that you need to fully explain evidence and theory, not just list supporting studies.

Ask yourself 'Why am I including this theory/piece of evidence/sociological study?' Make it explicitly relevant by using phrases such as 'This shows that …'; 'This is significant because …'. By explaining *why* your selected sociological knowledge is relevant, you are targeting AO2 (interpretation and application).

Evaluation can be both positive and negative, and to get into the top mark band your response needs to be sustained. This means that you should try to develop an evaluative tone throughout your essay and when you are writing about alternative theories or evidence, make sure you are using them in a critical way. If you simply juxtapose one theory against another, you will only be awarded a maximum of half the available marks for evaluation. You should aim to make specific evaluation points by, for example, directly criticising a particular theory, study or methodological issue.

Sociology of crime and deviance

Pause for thought

1   What crimes do you think the police should prioritise?

2   Are the police and prisons the solution to crime and deviance?

3   Describe the type of person the police will be chasing and explain your answer.

Introduction

The issue of crime and deviance has fascinated sociologists for many decades. It has connections to many other topics, as many things may be defined as deviant. The topic is always in the news headlines, politicians seek to show that they have the solutions to the problems of crime and deviance and billions of pounds are spent on dealing with the issue. Sociologists play a crucial role in informing the debate and your study of this area will increase your awareness of the variety of ideas and debates.

The specification states:

'In this option, candidates explore issues of power and control through a detailed study of crime and deviance. The social construction of crime and deviance is emphasised and the role of agencies of social control and the law are explored. It aims to give an overview of different theoretical approaches to the study of crime and deviance.'

This option explores the following five key issues:

1   The definition and measurement of crime and deviance.

2   Trends, patterns and explanations of crime and deviance.

3   Patterns and explanations of victimisation.

4   The role of agents of social control in the construction of crime and deviance.

5   Solutions to the problem of crime.

(i) The definition and measurement of crime and deviance

Pause for thought

Give two examples of each of the following:

- something that is criminal in the UK but not elsewhere

- something that is now criminal but used not to be

- something that is deviant elsewhere but not in the UK

- something that is deviant now but used not to be.

At first glance the terms 'crime' and 'deviance' are easy to define. Crime is an activity that breaks the law and deviance is an action that is thought to be abnormal. However, as soon as we start to consider what is normal, we enter a minefield.

Social constructs

The idea of a **social construction** is a key concept in sociology. It is used to explain many aspects of social life. The important feature of social constructionism is the idea that the same thing can be interpreted in different ways. The interpretation we place on an action or event will depend on our point of view. An action or event is not deviant until it is defined as deviant. One person may think that men wearing skirts is deviant, whereas others may regard this as perfectly acceptable. As a sociologist, you should recognise that individuals do not operate in a vacuum, they are part of a society. Thus individuals may categorise something as deviant on the basis of their own norms and values. These values are a product of the social system – different societies will have different norms and values. What is deviant will also vary from time to time and place to place. The two key words that apply here are that deviance is *relative* and *subjective*.

The Native American Sioux practised a coming-of-age ritual known as the Sun Dance. This involved placing leather thongs or eagles' talons through the skin of the chest. These were then attached to a rope which was strung over an A-frame. The warriors would dance around the frame until they were exhausted and would then stand until they fell. The talons would rip the warriors' flesh and when this happened they were believed to gain magical powers. We may well look at this behaviour as deviant and abnormal. However, the Sioux regard the Sun Dance as perfectly normal. This is an example of how the same action may be regarded as normal or deviant depending on the society. The action is unimportant, but the interpretation is vital. The same is true with crime. Different socities define criminal behaviour differently and while the rule of law in the UK is supposed to apply equally everywhere, it is clear that different groups are treated differently by the law.

A good way to think about this is to see crime and deviance through the lens of Dr Who's TARDIS. The word TARDIS is an acronym (it stands for 'Time and Relative Dimensions in Space'). Crime and deviance are social constructs and thus vary over time and space (*between* societies); they also vary *within* a society, since there are different subcultures inside a society that possess different norms and values.

All this indicates that deviance is indeed a social construct. Many sociologists have developed this idea. As we shall see, theories like interactionism, **feminism** or Marxism hold different views about who or what has the power to construct deviance in a particular way.

An evaluation of the idea of a social construct

◆ On moral and ethical grounds it is difficult to follow social constructionism to its logical conclusion. The argument that no action is deviant or wrong and that deviance is to be found in the perception of those who interpret the action is flawed, because many would claim that some actions are clearly wrong. Thus to argue that the Nazis' treatment of the Jews is open to different judgements is to adopt a morally neutral view. This is clearly flawed as the murder of over six million Jews was morally wrong and this is a truth in all societies at all times.

Activity 1

Look at the examples below and explain how perceptions about each may vary over time, between societies or within societies.

- Drinking alcohol
- Crossing the road
- Being an unmarried mother
- Homosexuality
- Wearing no clothes

- Burping or belching in public
- Body piercing
- Using a mobile phone while driving
- Speaking in tongues

Now add your answers to the 'Pause for thought' on page 4 to this list, and put all your answers into a table like the one below.

Perceptions vary:	
over time	
over space	
within society	

Whilst the idea of cultural **relativity** can easily be seen to link to some less serious areas of deviance like smoking in public or burping, it creates large problems in serious criminal and deviant behaviours.

- By denying the reality of crime or deviance, real solutions to real problems are ignored. Social constructionism implies that crime is not real, and that if we change the definition of crime or deviance the crime or deviance will disappear. This may be true, but if we applied this to the case of an old woman who has just been assaulted and robbed, we may begin to wonder if this idea is useful. In order to help the old woman and stop further assaults, we need to recognise that she has been the victim of a criminal act. Only then can we begin to ask why this happened and search for solutions. Thus researchers who want to improve society would argue that we need to recognise that crime has a reality and is not just a label.

Methods for measuring crime

There are many methods which enable the collection of data on crime and here we will consider official statistics, victim surveys and self-report studies.

Official statistics

Weblink

You can use the Home Office website to look at the most recent trends in crime.

See 'Website', page ii.

There are two major sources of official statistics on crime. First, there are crimes that are recorded by the police and, second, statistics about those who have been convicted of offences. The detailed findings of these statistics can be found on pages 10–11. However, these statistics have received a great deal of criticism and many people now turn to victim surveys

such as the British Crime Survey (BCS) as more reliable sources of information. The state now carries out victim surveys and the results are published by the Home Office, which makes them official. Another source of survey data on crime and deviance is self-report studies, where people are asked if they have committed any crime.

The great advantage of the official statistics on crime and deviance is that they are cheap and readily available. The Home Office publishes them annually and anyone with internet access can download a mass of data easily. These statistics cover a large part of the population and as they are collected by the state they are seen to have a great deal of *validity*. They can easily be compared with previous statistics and their quantative nature allows trends and patterns to be established. The ability to go back and check the findings means that the data are *reliable*. Theories like functionalism have used official statistics to develop theories to explain patterns in the official statistics. Another advantage of using official statistics is that there are few ethical problems. Anyone engaging in observational research immediately has an ethical dilemma between the need to maintain the confidentiality of the person they are observing and the moral duty of the citizen to report crime. Other ethical concerns that are avoided are the issues of whether to obtain consent and the possibility of having to engage in immoral or distasteful activities. Finally, a real advantage of the statistics is that the sociologist does not have to engage in dangerous activities. This is a significant factor in the area of crime and deviance.

One disadvantage of official statistics for the sociologist interested in studying deviance is that the data may not be available.

Activity 2

Think about a topic you studied in your AS course. What statistics were used in this topic and what problems were there with these statistics? For example, why were things not reported or not recorded? Once you have written down a list of problems, think about why there may be similar problems with statistics on crime and deviance.

Marxists may use statistics to show how the ruling class engage in manipulation.

Feminism

Feminists would criticise the **patriarchal** nature of the statistics. This is similar to a Marxist critique in that the definitions and workings of the process of law-enforcement benefit the powerful. However, in this case the powerful are men and they can minimise their criminality through, for example, the limited punishments given in rape cases. In addition, gendered stereotypes are transmitted by the selective use of law-enforcement and punishment. Women who conform to gendered stereotypes are protected, whereas those who transgress them are punished.

Left realism

Left realists agree that the statistics on crime are flawed. They recognise that there are problems with describing most criminals as working class or black. However, they also argue that there is a reality to crime. They have used victim surveys to illustrate that some groups are more prone to becoming victims of crime than others, and they would argue that the level of crime increased from the Second World War onwards. Simply dismissing the large differences between groups of offenders as artefacts ignores the truth. People may be more willing to report crime now, but the changes in rates are so dramatic that they cannot be explained away by an increased willingness to report.

Activity 4

1 In small groups, choose one of the following theories: functionalism, Marxism, feminism and interactionism.

2 Spend five minutes writing a brief paragraph on what the proponents of the theory believe.

3 Now read your paragraph to the rest of the class. Explain what view you think your theory will take about the use or limitations of statistics.

4 As you listen to the other groups, think of a criticism from the perspective of your chosen theory.

Section summary

The main theories to consider in this section are functionalism, Marxism, interactionism, feminism and left realism.

Use the following words to write a paragraph explaining the key themes of this section.

- Social construction
- Relativity
- Criminal iceberg
- Criminalisation
- Crime
- Deviance

Stretch and Challenge Activity

The **government** has just announced that the crime figures for 2008 showed a reduction in street crime. It believes that this is a cause for celebration and a vindication of its policies. Write a newspaper editorial on the meaning of these figures. You may write from any of the perspectives above to develop a critique of the government's view.

Exam practice

1 Outline and assess the usefulness of victim surveys for measuring crime. (50 marks)

2 Outline and assess the view that crime and deviance are socially constructed. (50 marks)

Sociology of crime and deviance

Pause for thought

- Draw a picture or cartoon of what you think a criminal looks like.

- If you were the prime minister, what new law would you introduce – explain why you think there is a problem and how your law would solve it.

Trends and patterns related to crime

Think about what you believe about crime over the last decade. Has it got worse?

In general, crime over the last thirty years rose steadily and peaked in 1995. Since then it has fallen by 44 per cent, according to the British Crime Survey. This has not been a uniform fall, as crimes like burglary (down 59 per cent), vehicle thefts (down 60 per cent) exceed the average, while violent crime has fallen by 43 per cent.

The official figures for recorded crime show a slightly different picture. Figure 1.1 shows a fall of about 1 per cent between 2005 and 2006. What is clear is that even though crime is not increasing, people believe that it is.

Numbers of recorded crimes are affected by changes in reporting and recording practices. In April 1998, certain new offences such as common assault, possession of a weapon, assault on a constable and harassment were added to the recorded crime series. It is therefore not possible to draw direct comparisons between offences recorded before and after that date.

Activity 5

How might the statistics on crime be a social construct?

Gender and age

The statistics indicate that men are more likely than women to commit crime. In fact, in 2006, 80 per cent of offenders were men. However, it is

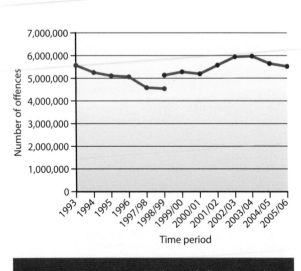

Figure 1.1: Long-term national recorded crime trend (Source: Crime in England and Wales, Home Office)

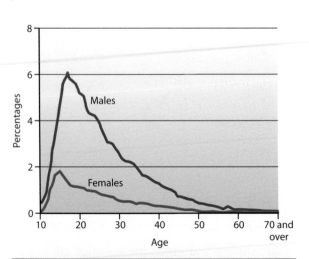

Figure 1.2: Offenders as a percentage of the population: by age, 2004, England and Wales (Source: British Crime Survey, Home Office; Criminal Statistics, Ministry of Justice)

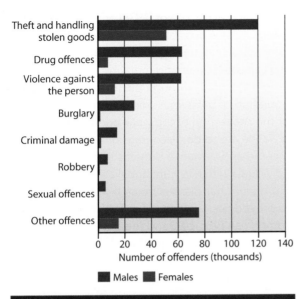

Figure 1.3: Offenders found guilty of, or cautioned for, indictable offences: by type of offence, 2004, England and Wales (Source: British Crime Survey, Home Office; Criminal Statistics, Ministry of Justice)

Activity 6

1 Look at the data in Table 1.1 and describe the gendered nature of crime. Which crimes are male crimes and which are female crimes?

2 What might explain the gendered nature of each crime you have identified?

Ethnicity

Table 1.1 indicates that crime is also affected by ethnicity. It is clear that our ethnic background has a bearing on our chances of being prosecuted.

Activity 7

Look at Table 1.1 and consider the following questions.

- Why might some sociologists argue that the terms 'white', 'black' and 'Asian' are inaccurate categories?

- How might the real level of criminality differ from the statistics for the prison population? Think about why the validity and reliability of the data can be questioned.

also important to note that crime is gendered in that there are male and female crimes (Figure 1.3 only covers general categories and hides this). The 2004 figures clearly indicate that crime is committed by young people. As people pass the age of 20 they start to drop out of crime (British Crime Survey).

Percentages	1996	1997	1998	1999	2000	2001	2002
Males							
White	86	86	86	86	86	85	84
Black	11	10	10	10	10	11	11
Asian	2	2	2	2	2	2	3
Chinese and other	1	2	2	2	2	2	2
Total male population (=100%) (thousands)	48.7	54.3	57.8	56.4	56.2	55.7	59.1
Females							
White	84	84	85	85	85	86	84
Black	13	13	12	12	12	12	11
Asian	1	1	1	1	1	1	1
Chinese and other	2	2	3	2	2	2	3
Total female population (=100%) (thousands)	2.0	2.3	2.6	2.7	2.8	3.0	3.5

Table 1.1: Prison population of British nationals: by ethnic group England and Wales (Source: Statistics on Race and the Criminal Justice System, Home Office)

One final pattern in the statistics on crime and deviance is that they show that there is a vast difference between the classes. The working class are much more predisposed to commit crime than the middle class. It is this pattern which most theories initially examined and it will be our starting point in trying to explain the patterns of crime and deviance (see pages 13–24). As you will see, the problems indicated by the earlier activities on gender and ethnicity also affect the statistics on crime and class.

The crime statistics clearly indicate patterns in crime. In other words, your chances of becoming a criminal are affected by whether you are middle or working class, a man or a woman, your ethnicity, age and geographical location (cities have higher crime rates than rural areas). Criminality is not an individual choice, if it were there would be no patterns. The relationship of these factors to criminal tendency are examined later in this section (see pages 13–30).

Sociologists are interested in explaining the different crime rates for different groups; they believe they can use these figures to tell us about society. However, what the rates tell us is a matter of great dispute between different perspectives. Similarly, different perspectives emphasise different crime rates: Marxists are particularly interested in social class, feminists in gender, left realists and new criminologists in ethnicity. As we shall see, functionalists attempt a more generic explanation of the patterns, trends and role of crime and deviance in society.

Functionalism

The functionalist approach to crime and deviance is not what you may expect. Functionalists believe that society is good and that order is necessary. From this viewpoint, crime and deviance would initially appear to be negative forces that disrupt social harmony. However, functionalists think that some crime and deviance is beneficial for the social system.

High rates of crime are negative because the social order benefits everyone, as anarchy would mean that the weak would suffer. In this sense functionalists draw on the work of Hobbes (1651) who argued that in a state of nature, life would be solitary, nasty, brutish and short. He believed that people were naturally greedy and selfish and the strong would prey upon the weak. In

the same way Durkheim (1938) argued for social order. Order is possible because people have a homo-duplex nature: they are naturally selfish but also capable of learning morality. Society controls people's instincts through the integration and regulation of behaviour. Social order is essential for the protection of the weak and crime and deviance are to be discouraged. The prevention of crime and deviance benefits society and the individuals within it. Functionalists would argue that disorder and crime mean that the weak can be preyed upon by roaming vigilante bands, women can be raped and the old abused. Social development and progress are limited and all suffer; thus crime and deviance need to be limited so that all can benefit.

This does not mean that deviance and crime are always a negative force. As long as the overall order is not challenged, some crime and deviance can have positive benefits. Functionalists point to a number of positive functions of deviance; these are described below.

- Crime and deviance can act as a warning device: some acts warn of problems that exist in the system. As a result, action can be taken to address the problem, for example, a child may skip school because they have problems at home, they may be being bullied at school or they may find school lessons unchallenging. As a result of the truancy the larger problems of abuse or cultural and material deprivation may be addressed and greater problems avoided.

- Crime and deviance may help society progress: today's deviants are tomorrow's innovators. People who challenge existing norms and values help to create new and better ways of living. Thus the deviance of Emily Pankhurst and the Suffragettes helped to create a more liberated society and votes for women.

- Crime and deviance provide employment. The criminal justice system employs judges, court officials, prison guards, builders, police officers, lawyers and cleaners, to name but a few. Thus it makes a significant contribution to the economy.

- Crime and deviance act as a safety valve: the release of a limited amount of anger or tension can mean that greater problems do not occur in the future. A married man who visits a prostitute is engaging in deviant behaviour, but functionalists would argue that it may be functional for his marriage as a long-term affair would be more likely to destabilise it.

◆ Crime and deviance may create social cohesion. People are sometimes bound together in the face of tragedy and loss: those individuals and society are strengthened and divisions that may have begun will be mended.

◆ Crime and deviance help to re-affirm the boundaries of what is acceptable: deviants can be made an example of and others may come to recognise what is and what is not acceptable. Thus if someone challenges a teacher in class they can be dealt with by the teacher and the rest of the class will learn about appropriate behaviour.

Activity 8

Think about a recent news story about a crime and outline the essential elements of the story. Who did what? Now discuss whether or not this deviance or crime was functional.

Durkheim and the inevitability of crime

Durkheim (1893) believed in consensus and the need for social order. He also believed that crime was inevitable. This was because he believed that crime and deviance were the product of a lack of attachment to the prevailing consensus over collective values. In society there are a variety of institutions and structures that affect our behaviour and people will have different experiences within them. It is therefore impossible for everyone to have the same values. As people's actions are the result of the norms and values they possess, they will act differently.

Durkheim believed that the speed of change in modern societies was likely to generate deviance and crime. This was because the modern world rapidly re-invents itself. Old traditions are lost and replaced by more modern ways of behaving and acting. The introduction of new economic processes and technology combined with social and geographic mobility leave people feeling unsure about their place in the world – think of the last time you saw an elderly person texting.

The result is that all are unsure of their place in the world; people lose a sense of what it is to be normal. They develop a sense of **anomie** (normlessness). In this situation crime and deviance are bound to increase. It is no surprise that after the fall of the Soviet Union, crime increased rapidly in Russia as the whole social fabric was transformed.

However, while crime and deviance are inevitable, society must control them in order to survive. Given the rapid pace of change, the potential for anomie that this creates and the increasing freedom in modern societies, the central problem is to maintain an attachment to collective values. Where this fails we have crime.

Weblink
You can read about crime theory on the internet (see 'Websites', page ii).

Merton

Merton (1938) agreed with Durkheim that crime is the result of people's different attachment to collective values. He tried to apply Durkheim's concept of anomie to US society in the 1930s and his ideas have influenced many later theories. They have been used to explain the preponderance of working-class youth in the statistics on crime and deviance.

Merton believed that while there is an overarching consensus, individuals in society are not equally capable of realising the goals of society. He argued that US society had, at its core, a commitment to the American Dream. This dream was the idea summed up by the story of Abraham Lincoln who, it is believed, came from a log cabin and became president. This story encapsulates the idea that anyone can achieve material success. The central values of **meritocracy** and materialism are summed up by the dream and the acquisition of material wealth is seen to be the goal of US society. People learn that they must achieve wealth by working within institutions like education and possess the right personal qualities like hard work. Crime and deviance emerge in the USA and the UK because too much emphasis is placed on the goal of wealth and not enough on the importance of the institutional means.

Individuals may react to this situation in a number of ways:

◆ They may conform – they strive for success in conventional ways. They are not deviant.

◆ They may innovate – they develop new ways of achieving success. They are likely to be working class, as they desire the goals of society but cannot achieve educational success. They turn to crime to become wealthy.

◆ They may engage in ritualism. Lower middle-class people have been socialised into the means of society but cannot achieve success. As a consequence they give up on the goals of success and this makes them deviant. They go through the motions and stick to the rules, but are not committed to the dream.

◆ They may retreat. Some may accept both goals and means but cannot achieve success. They may become mad or drop out and become homeless and withdraw from participation in society.

◆ They may engage in rebellion. These individuals will seek to replace the existing goals of society with new ones. They are truly deviant.

Merton believed that crime and deviance were caused by over-emphasis on the goal of wealth and the inability of some (particularly in the working class) to achieve this goal using legitimate means. Anomie was created by this strain.

Cohen (1955) agrees with Merton that anomie is a central problem in modern societies. However, he argues that those at the bottom of the system develop a subculture of criminality; they form a group with similar values. He also argues that much crime produces little material reward; in fact, crimes like vandalism and joyriding destroy property. This occurs because those at the bottom of the social system develop status frustration as they cannot achieve the goals of society. They realise that they cannot achieve the goals and begin to feel a lack of self-esteem. This problem is solved by placing value on destroying the things they cannot have. The better they are at joyriding and spraying paint on walls, the greater the prestige they receive. In a sense, working-class youth invert society's values. While Merton explains why some people steal lead from the church roof, Cohen is able to explain why others vandalise the building. Merton sees crime as an individual response, whereas Cohen sees crime as a group response – a subculture is formed.

The differences in crime and deviance between social groups can be explained by reference to our increasingly materialistic society. People's aspirations are ever higher. These dreams are bound to end in crime, as few can attain them through legitimate means. Those most excluded will turn to crime to attain those goals, or resort to vandalism to gain respect.

Hirschi fits into the functionalist model. He argues (1969) that we should focus on a different question from the issue of why criminals commit crime: we should instead ask why people do *not* commit crime. In this sense he says we should examine the controls placed on people and he argues that crime occurs when these controls are weakened or broken. These controls are linked to Durkheim's anomie and egoism (types of condition that produce suicide) and are products of deregulation. There are four types of control or social bond that produce conformity:

1 Attachment – people are under control if they are concerned about what other people think about them. If they do not care what other people think, they are free to deviate. Many see this as the most important social bond: people need to identify with their family and peers and develop strong emotional bonds with them.

2 Commitment – if people invest time in their education or business they are likely to suffer loss if they deviate, and hence are less likely to do so.

3 Involvement – if people are involved or busy in other activities they do not have the time or opportunity to get involved in crime or deviance. In this regard Hirschi has connections to opportunity theory.

4 Belief – people need to have a strong commitment to cultural goals. In this sense it is clear that control theory believes there is a common value system. They need to respect authority and law.

This theory has had an impact on policy in that it has encouraged the policy of public shaming. The criminal may be forced to walk down streets declaring that they are a criminal. Shaming is a way of keeping others in check as they realise the costs of deviance. The bonds of family and friends are more powerful, according to this theory, than the bonds of prison. However, the aim of reintegrative shaming is to allow the deviant back

Figure 1.4: A public shaming of suspected prostitutes in Shenzhen, China. Does this punishment stop or stigmatise the deviant?

into the community and thus there also need to be ceremonies that ensure forgiveness, apology and a de-certification of the deviance to allow the offender back into the community.

An evaluation of functionalism

◆ One major problem with Merton and Cohen's work is that they accept the validity of the official statistics. They clearly see crime as a predominantly working-class phenomenon, but this ignores the vast array of corporate or state crime. What of the crimes of the rich? The assumption is that all these crimes are accurately reported and recorded, but this may not be the case and crime may be spread throughout the system.

◆ Another problem with the work of the functionalists is that it fails to look at what is going on in the mind of the deviant. The deviant's thoughts and feelings are regarded as a consequence of the social structure, yet all working-class people do not respond in the same way. People are regarded as simply responding to structural forces rather than as being active, thinking human beings.

◆ A major problem for functionalist analysis is that it does not adequately account for the origin of law. Functionalists claim that the law

represents everyone's interests, but it is used by powerful groups to control weaker ones. Conflict theorists would point to the way in which the law may defend the interests of dominant groups rather than the weak.

The new right

The new right are no longer new, as their central ideas gained popularity in the 1980s. It might be argued that the key ideas of the new right can be traced back to the nineteenth century in the form of two differing doctrines: liberalism and conservatism (see pages 164–166). The new right is a fusion of these two philosophies and as such contains contradictions, in particular between an emphasis on the need for individual responsibility combined with the need for social control. Crime and deviance can be seen as having differing causes. In many cases, however, the new right would agree with functionalist writers' use of the concept of **cultural deprivation** and argue that some groups lack a commitment to the core values of society.

Murray (1994) argues that crime is a response to the generosity of the welfare state, which has come to dominate people's lives and denied them the ability to develop. A culture of dependency and crime has been passed on from generation to generation. This is what Murray calls the underclass: a group cut off from the rest of society. Marsland (1992) agrees with this notion and argues that individuals are deprived of the ability to make their own choices. The nanny state provides everything a person needs and there is no reason to work. On many estates, families without fathers proliferate as the state supports single-parenthood. In these families boys lack a strong role model and discipline, and crime is the inevitable result. The disciplines of work and family life are destroyed by the welfare state, but poverty is not a reason for crime. As Norman Tebbit argued, in the 1930s his father was out of work, but did not steal or riot. There was no real welfare state, so he got on his bike and found a job. The welfare state destroys individuals' initiative and self-reliance. In seeking to help people the nanny state prevents people from taking responsibility for their own actions. Individuals need to be free to reap the consequences of their own actions and the welfare system should be reduced.

According to the right realist Wilson (1975), the criminal engages in a rational calculation before engaging in crime. The criminal is encouraged to engage in crime because the punishments and alternatives to crime are too limited. Deterrence is important in reducing crime, and Wilson would argue that the sentences for some crimes are too lax. In other cases, the criminals' belief that they will not get caught means that they continue their behaviour. However, the largest problem in modern societies is a lack of community. People commit crime because they do not fear disgrace and social stigma as they would have done many years ago.

Both of the above views can be seen as part of a neo-liberal tradition that would emphasise people's rationality. However, the neo-conservatives would emphasise the lack of order and control. They argue that people are essentially irrational and selfish; they need control and guidance. The 1960s brought flower power and the era of the permissive society, where anything was acceptable and the destruction of tradition was important in the quest to build a freer and more tolerant world. These 'liberal' ideas were the philosophical backdrop to the new world. According to the new right, these ideas destroyed a safe and secure social world where order created freedom. However, the

seeds of the flower power generation have, in the 1980s, created new plants: the children and teenagers of that era now control the major political, legal and cultural institutions. On popular television soaps, single-parenthood, divorce and drug abuse are presented as part of normal life. Under-age drinking and promiscuity are encouraged. The culture of permissiveness has meant that people will accept minor acts of incivility. It is no surprise to the neo-conservatives that crime and deviance are increasing. In place of tolerance a new stricter morality needs to be encouraged and laws need to be strengthened.

An evaluation of the new right

◆ The new right ignore the impact of crime committed by the wealthy and powerful. Those at the top of society are not affected by the welfare state, yet they commit crime.

◆ In blaming the victim the new right draws attention away from the real causes of crime. Many homeless people are not homeless due to a lack of morality, but because of the social conditions they have encountered. They may have run away from abusive homes or have left the armed forces with psychological trauma. Indeed it may be argued that cuts in the welfare state are responsible for crime: people do not receive the care they need.

◆ The right realist view that crime is the result of rational calculation has come under attack from those who argue that this takes the emotion out of crime. Carrabine et al. (2004) identify a number of ways in which emotion rather than calculation is involved in crime. These include hate crime, crimes of passion, thrill-seeking, revenge and the desire to establish respect and self-esteem. This can be linked to Young (2007), who argues that these crimes have increased as individuals face greater uncertainty about who they are and a sense that the rewards of life are awarded chaotically.

Activity 9

Find out about homelessness. How far do your findings support the new-right view? Discuss with your group whether or not you would give money to a beggar.

Weblink

Look at the Shelter website for information about homelessness (see 'Websites', page ii).

Interactionism

Interactionists believe that people are not puppets of the social system. They believe that people behave in certain ways because of their beliefs about the world. People are not simply given these beliefs by the social system: they are conscious and reflect on the world. It is important to understand what people are thinking and feeling in order to understand their behaviour. This means that in order to understand crime and deviance, we need to understand the inner world of the criminal or police officer rather than focusing on the impact of poverty or the value consensus, and we need to establish *verstehen* with them. There are three themes within the broad church of interactionism:

1   A focus on the deviant and what makes them deviant.

2   A concern with those who define them as deviant.

3   A distrust of official statistics.

The real effects of labelling

Becker (1963) was one of the first to develop labelling theory. His starting point was that deviance was made by defining someone as deviant, so sociologists need to look at the reasons why some are called deviant and the effects of that definition. He argued that the police and other institutions may create more deviance by labelling them. A label is a judgement we make about someone before we know them; it may be based on stereotypes that we hold about certain groups. Such labels can be powerful; they can be regarded as a master status. This means that everyone treats the individual on the basis of that label and the label is the most important aspect of their identity. When individuals take on this identity, their deviance becomes a social fact: it is a self-fulfilling prophecy. This is different from a phenomenological view, which believes that facts about crime and deviance do not really exist and are a merely a classification.

This idea can be seen in Young's work (1971) on cannabis smokers in Notting Hill. He argued that initially some individuals occasionally smoked cannabis. It was a peripheral activity in their lives; however after they were caught and labelled by the police and courts their deviance became worse. Some lost their jobs and with that lost social networks. The only people who would associate with them were others who had been labelled as deviant. They were also drawn into the drug economy and harder drugs, as this became a source of income. In essence their drug-taking became central and their deviance was **amplified**. In effect the labelling process had created a deviant subculture.

A key idea behind Young's work and that of others who trace the deviancy amplification spiral is that of primary and secondary deviance. Primary deviance is seen as relatively small scale and limited. Secondary deviance is much larger and more significant. Lemert (1972) argued that secondary deviance only occurred because the primary deviance was labelled as deviant.

As you can see on page 132, this idea has been applied by sociologists of different traditions. It has also been applied to institutions other than the police.

The artificial nature of crime statistics

Phenomenologist writers take a slightly different approach to understanding crime and deviance. They belong to a slightly different theoretical tradition but can be classed as interpretivists as they focus on the importance of meaning and how those meanings are created. Phenomenologists are concerned with the way 'reality' is shaped by people's perceptions. In particular they believe that the social world is based upon the interpretations placed on events – in this case crime or deviance.

This approach is well illustrated by Atkinson's (1978) work on suicide. He argues that we can never know if someone has actually committed suicide. All we know is that the death has been defined as a suicide and all we can examine is how it came to be defined as such. We cannot explain why it happened. Previous explanations for suicide like Durkheim's are houses built on sand. Thus we should study the findings of those who categorise suicides and not the person who may or may not have taken their own life. The suicide rates are a product of subjective recording practices. Different countries and different coroners will have different ways of recording and defining suicide. This argument is also developed by Cicourel (1976) in his study of two Californian cities. The crime rates for these cities differed greatly, even though they had similar socio-economic circumstances. The reason for this was that the police in the different cities used different meanings and definitions. Different police forces will have different ways of reporting and processing criminals, which will affect the crime rates. In addition, individuals defined as criminals can present an image of themselves that will affect their chances of being prosecuted – they can negotiate their way out of the criminal justice system. Thus the statistics lack an objective reality and sociologists cannot produce explanations of social reality. Phenomenologists seek to explain how phenomena are categorised rather than explaining the causes of deviance by examining the social structure.

The predominance of ethnic minorities, men or the working class in criminal statistics may say more about the police and courts than about the groups themselves. Increases in crime and deviance over the last thirty years are explained primarily in terms of greater sensitisation and the changing meanings of crime and deviance in addition to the greater scope for reporting and recording crime.

An evaluation of interactionism

◆ Interactionism is criticised for being too deterministic. This means that some regard labelling and the self-fulfilling prophecy as an inevitable process. There are no other options for the person who is labelled than to conform. However this criticism is unfair: interactionists are keen to point out that an individual can react in a number of ways to the label they have been given. In Young's study the cannabis smokers are not all condemned to a life in the drug underworld, and Young is keen to point this out.

◆ Another criticism of interactionism is that in focusing on the consequences of labelling (the secondary deviance) it is likely to underplay or ignore the initial or primary act of deviance. Thus, in Young's study, why did the individuals choose to smoke cannabis in the first place? Structuralists would be keen to develop the idea of structural forces like poverty or culture to explain this.

◆ Another problem with this approach is its reliance on the secondary effects of labelling. Conflict theorists would argue that labelling is a useful insight, but interactionists fail to examine the wider context of labelling. In particular they fail to explain why particular labels are given to particular groups at particular times. To conflict theorists, labelling is not an individual act but a process controlled by powerful groups. Labelling is used by the powerful to maintain their position; groups that may oppose the powerful are labelled deviant or criminal. You can read more about this on page 20.

◆ The phenomenologist's argument that crime and deviance are just labels ignores the reality of much crime and deviance. While the examples looked at by the interactionists are relatively trivial, ignoring crimes like murder means that real solutions to these problems will not be developed.

Weblink

The British Medical Association (BMA) website examines the debate over legalisation (see 'Websites', page ii).

Figure 1.5: To **criminalise** or not to criminalise? That is the question

Marxism

Marxist sociologists argue that in order to understand crime and deviance we need to understand the nature of capitalist societies. They believe that capitalism is an exploitative economic system in which the bourgeoisie or ruling class exploit the proletariat or working class. This exploitation drives the working class into poverty and creates a conflict of interest. Workers have an interest in reducing and ending the exploitation, whilst the capitalist class must exploit their workers in order to maintain profitability. Eventually there will be an inevitable revolution and the ruling class will be removed. However, this revolution has been delayed as the capitalist class have used ideology to create false consciousness amongst the working class. All crime and deviance can be understood in this context. Marxists take slightly different views. Some seek to explain working-class criminality, others point to the crimes of the rich and powerful, while others focus on how crime is defined and measured for the benefit of the ruling class.

Marxists argue that crime is the result of poverty and is generated by the capitalist system. People steal because they are materially deprived and this deprivation results from the poverty wages paid by the ruling class. Even the minimum wage does not protect against wage slavery. Working for the minimum wage will not be enough to support a family. Students may be happy to work for low pay, but for people with bills to pay, low wages are a cause of crime. This is why many statistics show that the working class engage in criminal behaviour. The ruling class have little motivation, as they already have the essential elements of success. In this sense Marxists are much more likely than functionalist writers to develop the idea of **material deprivation** to explain crime.

A second strand of the argument is that capitalism generates crime. Capitalist companies need to generate profit by selling goods to customers. Capitalism generates greed and avarice. It does this through the media. Advertising creates the illusion that happiness can be bought and fosters the values of materialism. People believe that buying the latest shoes or computer games will bring them happiness. This is falsehood as the happiness is temporary. The root cause of their misery is capitalism, but this is hidden. Indeed, by buying into the mirage of materialism they sustain the beast that is destroying them. The capitalists may use television programmes like *The Apprentice* to maintain the illusion that everyone should strive for material success. The Lottery tells us that 'It could be you'. Capitalism also generates a selfish mindset that means that people have little regard for the interests and feelings of others. These feelings help to create crime, as people put themselves first. This competitive culture can be found in the media and also in structures like the education system, where students learn that helping others is cheating. Chambliss argued that the capitalist system fosters crime at all levels within the system. Everyone is exposed to ideology and crime occurs in the corporate boardrooms where millions can be gained. People have different methods of attaining wealth, but they are all motivated by an insatiable desire for it and crime is built into capitalist societies. People begin to see products, rather than human relationships, as their goal in life, and these products become divorced from the conditions in which they are made. In Marx's words, people within capitalism develop commodity fetishism.

The neo-Marxist Hebdige (1988) argued that crime and deviance amongst the working class can be seen as signs of resistance and rebellion. To understand this process he combined Marxist insights with semiology in order to reveal the hidden messages in the clothing and fashions which people use. He argues that working-class communities in the East End of London were being destroyed by re-development. The word 'development' suggests progress, but Hebdige argues that property developers were bulldozing traditional housing in order to make a large profit. Old terraced housing was bought cheaply and replaced by expensive developments that the poor could not afford. The sole motivation was profit and the consequence was the destruction of people's past, present and future. Houses occupied by the same families for generations and friendship ties built up over years were pulled apart, causing anger and resentment. The working-class youth of these areas developed a subculture that tried to resist the destruction of their way of life and adopted some elements of their traditional community. They shaved their hair, they wore Doc Martens, jeans and braces – all a re-creation of a traditional life that had been lost. He also applied a similar analysis to other groups like Rastafarians and punks, when he argued that their resistance to capitalism could be seen in their clothing and style.

Figure 1.6: Yob or working-class fighter?

A final element of Marxism is its analysis of the nature of law. Unlike functionalists who believe that the law benefits all and represents everyone's interests, Marxists argue that the law defends the interests of the ruling class. This is because the state represents the interests of the ruling class. It does this in a number of different ways. First, the ruling class ensure that they are rarely defined as breaking the law, because the law defines the actions of the working class as crime while the ruling class's crimes are not defined as such. To a Marxist, the ruling classes steal from the workers every day by paying them less than the value of the goods they produce. In a sense, they take money from the working class to which they are not entitled. It should be a crime for people to be able to buy their own private island and eat caviar while others starve to death, yet this is not defined as criminal. Next, the capitalist class ensure that their interests are protected, thus most laws (according to Chambliss (1976)) are based around the protection of private property. As capitalists control the media they can help to destroy politicians, and the ruling class are also able to dis-invest in a country and cause economic turmoil. Furthermore, the ruling class ensure that if any laws do define their actions as criminal,

then they will not carry harsh punishments. If a capitalist does actually reach the court, they can afford to hire the best lawyers to ensure either a lenient sentence or an acquittal. As Miliband (1969) argued, the Judiciary are from the same background as the ruling class and are likely to side with them. Slapper and Tombs (1999) argue that the activities and immunity from prosecution of large transnational companies in developing countries illustrate their power and influence. The Bhopal disaster in 1984, which caused mass death and sickness for poor Indian workers and their families, without what they would regard as justice, illustrates the Marxist view. Such events do not occur only in the developing world: in 2007 the UK government put pressure on the police to stop investigating British Aerospace's arms deals with the Saudi government, when even the OECD had serious concerns about bribery.

Weblinks

Corporate behaviour is examined at several sites on the internet (see 'Websites', page ii).

An evaluation of Marxism

The law may represent interests other than those of the capitalist class. Functionalists would argue that it represents everyone's interests, feminists would argue that it represents men's interests and Weberians would argue that the state represents its own interests.

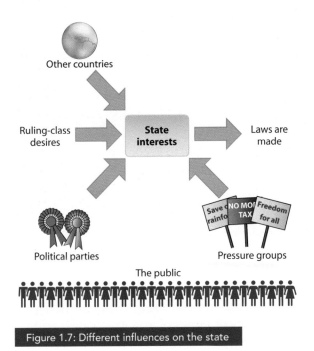

Figure 1.7: Different influences on the state

◆ Crime may not be caused by material deprivation. It may well be that poor socialisation creates crime and deviance. Merton would argue that crime is a result of over-socialisation into goals rather than means, and the new right would argue that crime stems from the welfare state and permissiveness.

◆ The representation of crime as political rebellion is a denial of the real harm caused by that crime. It also ignores the way in which the victims of crime are the working class. Most crime is directed at the poor and the young. Being beaten up on a Saturday night is not about the redistribution of wealth or a challenge to the capitalist system.

The new criminology

The new criminology was developed in the early 1970s by Taylor, Walton and Young (1973) and was new in the sense that it attempted to redevelop Marxist approaches. In this sense, it is a form of neo-Marxism. It maintained that crime was best understood in the context of capitalism and the inequalities that are generated by capitalism. The new criminologists argued that individuals choose to commit crime; people are not just puppets of the economy. They also argued that many crimes were politically motivated – theft is an attempt to redistribute wealth and deviants are struggling against capitalism and helping to bring about social change. The drug-taker is rejecting the materialism of capitalism and the vandal is literally kicking back at capitalist society. They also argued that sociologists should examine who has the power to make and enforce the rules of society. Deviance needs to be understood by reference to the social conditions of a capitalist society, like exploitation, poverty and materialism. The final theme that they developed is that a complete theory of deviance should also examine the consequences of being labelled. Amplification may be just one possible response and in order to understand deviance we must examine the social reaction of society and the outcome of the social reaction.

Activity 10

Consider the following study and explain how it may be used to criticise the Marxist view of crime and deviance.

Jamieson and McEvoy (2005) argue that modern states try to hide their criminal activities by using other agents and proxies to conduct their crime. States fund paramilitary organisations, assist rebels and use special forces to provide training and intelligence to achieve their objectives. In many cases these organisations are immune from prosecution, but this is not true in every case. A contemporary illustration of this can be found in the US company Blackwater, which attracted much controversy for its operations in Iraq as it was engaged in firefights on the streets of Baghdad. Until 2008 it was immune from prosecution in Iraq.

Thus this theory can be seen as an attempt to bring together Marxist approaches and interactionist concepts.

An evaluation of the new criminology

◆ Many feminist writers have argued that in focusing on capitalism the new criminologists have ignored the impact of crime on women. They would argue that the act of rape is not a challenge to the capitalist system but about men wanting to establish their power over women.

◆ In focusing on crime as rebellion and portraying theft as the action of Robin Hood, the new criminologists ignore the impact of crime on the working class. The working class are much more likely to be the victims of crime, and stealing from them cannot be portrayed as redistribution of wealth from the rich to the poor.

Subcultural theories

Many theories employ the concept of a subculture. It means that in a society there is a dominant culture to which most people subscribe. However, some groups may possess some of the mainstream culture but also have their own way of life. A culture is composed of elements like language, dress, food, values and norms. A subculture will involve people within the group displaying different elements of this culture.

Activity 11

Think about three subcultural groups that you are familiar with. How do they differ in terms of their culture from the rest of society? Goths, for instance, may have different ways of dressing and speaking, and enjoy particular types of music.

Miller (1958) argued that working-class males possess a distinctive subculture that was part of the working-class way of life. It stemmed from the boredom and insecurity of working-class jobs and pushed working-class youth into crime and deviance. It is seen as a way of explaining high rates of criminality amongst the working class. He argued that working-class youths develop a set of focal concerns, the key aspects that produce delinquency. They are:

◆ Smartness – being able to think on your feet and engage in witty banter.

◆ Excitement – being focused on the buzz and adrenaline.

◆ Toughness – an ability to face down others and a willingness to use force to achieve your goals.

◆ Autonomy – being in control and not letting others tell you what to do.

◆ Fate – being unable to determine your own future and affect what happens in the future.

◆ Trouble – being willing to accept that trouble is a feature of life and should not be hidden from.

These concerns have been used to explain the greater likelihood of working-class youth being found guilty of crimes of assault, joyriding and most recently binge-drinking. Miller saw the working class as being cut off from the rest of society's values and their criminality as a result of conforming to their distinctive subcultural values. In studies of health and education, many sociologists have used the concepts of cultural deprivation, and others such as Lewis (1959) have talked about a culture of poverty. These ideas are closely related to the idea of a distinctive working-class subculture.

It is worth noting, however, that different perspectives have different views about the origins of subculture. They employ different concepts to explain the origins of these subcultures. Table 1.2 should act as a review of the material you have already covered.

Perspective	Concept	Study
Functionalism	Dysfunction	Cohen
New right	Underclass	Murray
Marxism	Resistance	Hebdige
Interactionism	Labelling	Young

Table 1.2 An overview of theories and concepts

Add extra concepts and studies to Table 1.2 to extend the depth of your awareness of these themes.

Them and us, us and them?

The concept of subculture has received a great deal of criticism. The most common theme of its critics is that there is no evidence to support it. Most young people want the same things as the rest of society.

One of the strongest critics of subcultural theory is Matza (1964). He argues that it is difficult to divide society into 'them' and 'us' as a great deal of subcultural theory does. He argues that many deviants are like everyone else. We can see this because many criminals engage in techniques of neutralisation that help to make what they have done seem excusable. In using these techniques they also show that they feel guilt at having broken the morality of society. In seeking to excuse their actions they are confirming their commitment to the moral order they have broken. This shows that these people are like the rest of us and that their deviance is temporary – people drift in and out of deviance. It is not a permanent feature of their lives. Look at the techniques below and think about whether you have ever used them.

- Denial of responsibility – 'It's not my fault there's nothing to do round here.'

- Denial of injury – 'I was having a laugh, it wasn't serious' or 'They are insured and will get their money back.'

- Denial of wrongdoing – 'The shop deserved it because they charge rip-off prices.'

- Condemnation of the rule-makers – 'The real problem is the police who pick on me because I'm from…'

- Appeal to higher loyalties – 'My child needed some trainers and I couldn't afford them.'

Left realism

Left realists are politically left-wing but they reject Marxist ideas and believe that the capitalist system can be changed to help the working class.

They reject the Marxists' argument that crime is a construct of the ruling class, and believe that there is a reality of crime. White-collar and corporate crime may be underestimated by the statistics, but they argue that the working class are real victims of working-class crime. This makes them particularly critical of the new criminology. They clearly influenced New Labour and Tony Blair's promise to be tough on crime and the causes of crime.

Lea and Young (1984) argue that the post-war rise in crime was due to three processes: relative deprivation, subculture and marginalisation. Relative deprivation means that a group feels deprived if it cannot achieve its expectations. Thus as advertising has increased expectations, all groups, including middle-class ones, experience frustration, which produces theft. A group that feels deprived will begin to develop its own subculture, but this response is not always criminal. Some Afro-Caribbeans turned to religion, for instance. Finally, marginal groups who have no commitment to other groups through things like unions or pressure groups will develop resentment.

The left realists developed their analysis into what might be called the square of crime. This involves dealing with four elements:

1   The state: the way the police deal with crime will affect crime itself. Military-style policing may produce a more confrontational situation and drag in people who would not normally participate in crime. Investigating minor drug offences means that less time can be spent on domestic abuse and racist attacks, and this will build resentment.

2   The offender: why do offenders offend, what is the impact of society and what informal rules govern their behaviour?

3   Society: crime can be tackled by providing better job prospects, better housing and projects that build a sense of community cohesion.

4   The victim: victims will report or not report crime due to a number of factors. Do they fear the offender? Do they know the offender? Do they think the offence is serious enough? To fully understand crime, we need to understand these issues and what makes a person more likely to be a victim. You can read more about this on pages 31–33.

Each of these elements is important, but their importance will vary from time to time and place to place.

An evaluation of the left realists

◆ Although they argue that we should deal with four elements, they tend to focus on the victim. They do not spend enough time looking at the offender.

◆ By adopting a subcultural view, left realists fall into the problem of believing that there are distinct groups of deviants and non-deviants. Many of the criticisms found in the earlier section on subcultural theory (page 23) can be used here.

◆ The theory of relative deprivation is useful for property crime, but it becomes more difficult to apply this to things like rape or violent assault.

◆ The left realists have mentioned the impact of corporate crime, but do not deal with it in any depth.

As left realism looks to combine approaches, many of the criticisms could be found in earlier sections. For some, it combines the strengths of previous approaches, whereas others would argue that it combines their weaknesses. In his more recent work, Young (2002) argues that a sense of relative deprivation has increased immensely and we are developing into an exclusive society where some feel a sense of economic security whilst many experience economic insecurity. Those at the bottom are trapped into poverty. Even the middle class fear that they may lose their social position, envy the perceived lifestyle of the underclass that appears free and unrestrained, and express outrage at the wages of those undeserving footballers above them. As a result, crime spreads through society and changes its focus. It is now directed at domestic as well as commercial property and hate crime has risen significantly.

You have looked at two types of realism. It is worth noting that they are both called realists because they agree that crime is a significant problem affecting many people. However, they differ in what they see as the cause of the problem; they also disagree on its solution. Whilst left realists stress solutions based on reducing inequality and changing police priorities, the right would stress a return to traditional morality and a greater use of the criminal justice system. More details of the right realist approach can be found on pages 15–16.

Feminism

Early theories of crime and gender put differences in offending down to biology. Today some still argue that genes explain the difference in offending between men and women. Some argue that hormonal imbalances may make women commit crime.

Smart (1979) argued that previous theories of crime and deviance have ignored women. In particular they have ignored women's treatment by the criminal justice system and crimes committed by men against women. Carrabine et al. (2004) have argued that feminist ideas have also forced sociologists to look at the specific nature of male offending. In general, feminists have sought to explain the reasons for the under-representation of women in the statistics. Some see the statistics as fact, while others believe they are constructed.

The statistics as facts

Those who believe the statistics are facts argue that women are less likely than men to commit crime because of the patriarchal controls placed on women. This begins at an early age when girls are taught to be less adventurous and see their mothers passively conforming. These cultural traits are learnt and not a product of biology; we know this because women act differently in different times and places while their biology remains static. This socialisation is continued through school, where girls are more likely to take subjects like food technology and health and social care. In the media girls are exposed to images that sustain this passivity: there is a focus on looking good and getting a man. Heidensohn (2002) argues that women are controlled as they attain adulthood. As housewives they are unlikely to be in places that allow crime and their role gives them little time to commit crime. They are unlikely to go out at night for fear of rape and developing a reputation. At work they are likely to experience sexual harassment, which intimidates and controls them.

At least I don't have time for anti-social behaviour.

Figure 1.8

This cultural argument is used by Adler (1975) to explain the rise in female crime over the last few decades. She argues that women throughout the western world are committing crime as a result of the impact of feminism and women becoming more involved in traditionally male spheres. This theme has been taken up recently in the concern over the development of the 'ladette' culture that involves young women drinking excessively and engaging in antisocial behaviour. It is seen to be a consequence of teenage girls adopting masculine characteristics and culture and their new-found empowerment. However, as Heidensohn argued (2002) in response to Adler, middle-class girls are more likely to be affected by feminism, and they are least likely to be criminal. Women's poverty is more likely to be a factor in increasing their criminal activities, as welfare has been cut. Prostitution is not driven by women's liberation but by economic need.

Crime is, according to the statistics, gendered. Women are much more likely to be convicted of shoplifting and prostitution, whereas men are much more likely to commit crimes like theft and GBH. These can be explained by the different processes of socialisation and the different controls placed on women.

Males are more likely to commit crime. This has been of growing interest in modern sociology as a result of feminist concerns. While not all the writers in this area are feminists, they have developed a focus on male offending as a result of feminist interest in women. They have come to recognise the importance of gender as a dimension of crime that had been relatively unexplored. Some early sociologists did look at male offending, but this was not their primary concern. Cohen's (1955) work was focused explicitly on boys and Miller (1958) also developed his work by reference to males. It is worth reminding yourself about their explanation for male crime (pages 14 and 22). Modern writers have begun to focus their attention on male criminality.

Messerschmidt (1993) argues that men are not just puppets of their biology or socialisation, but that they have different masculinities, different ways of thinking and acting as a male. However, while they can choose to enact particular masculinities, their opportunities to do so are limited by social constraints. Different men in different social contexts will commit crime in response to achieving masculinity when other methods have failed. Middle-class boys will be successful at school and in sport (an accommodating masculinity) but still commit crime because they have given up things like independence and control whilst they are at school. Out of school they may drink and commit acts of petty vandalism (an oppositional masculinity) to help assert their male identity. Working-class boys engage in aggression (oppositional masculinity) inside and outside school as they cannot achieve educational success. Lower-working-class ethnic-minority boys are unlikely to be academically successful or get a good job, and use violence and gang warfare as a way of asserting masculinity. Sometimes rape is used to assert their power over women, sometimes it may be asserted through consensual sex.

Activity 14

Explain how the phrase 'boys will be boys' may reflect a plurality of masculinities.

Winlow (2001) argues that the nature of male crime and violence has changed as a result of the de-industrialisation of areas like the north east and the process of globalisation. Male work – heavy industry – has reduced and the economy has become, in part, a night-time one. At the same time the global media have created mainly American images of masculinity. Men were unable to sustain the traditional image of the man who could maintain a wife and family; they had to develop a new identity. This combined elements of the past and the new. Men were paid to act as doormen or bouncers, and used this as an opportunity to get involved in selling drugs or cheap imported beer. They also got involved in protection rackets. Violence became a mechanism for earning a living rather than a way of gaining status.

Weblinks
You might like to look at the Justice for women site (see 'Websites', page ii).

Statistics on crime as flawed

Many of the earlier views we have examined on gender have accepted the statistics as truth. They believe that men are more criminal and women have only recently started to become like men. However, we have seen that statistics on crime may be thought to be a social construct, and the same is true in the case of statistics on gender and crime.

Pollack (1950) argued that this was a result of the attitudes of the law enforcers and the deviousness of women. Men are socialised to be chivalrous and are likely to punish women less than men. Women also learn to be devious as they learn to conceal their emotional state during sex (they can 'fake it') and hide their bodily state from men during menstruation. The first part of his argument is the one that has been developed by later researchers. It has become known as the **chivalry thesis**. Many self-report studies have indicated that women commit more crime than is suggested by the

official statistics (Flood-Page, 2000). Women have a reduced risk of being caught and when caught they have a reduced risk of being prosecuted. It is argued that male police officers and male judges don't believe that women would be capable of criminal acts and even when guilty, they are treated more gently than men.

However, there are areas where the law operates against women. The first of these is in the way that feminists argue that the law fails to protect women against rape, sexual assault and domestic violence. Walklate (1998) argues that women who have been raped are put on trial and that despite the introduction of new police procedures for dealing with rape victims the original claims are not dealt with effectively. Even David Cameron (hardly a notable feminist campaigner) argued in 2007 that over the last few years the number of rape crisis centres had fallen and the successful prosecution rate of just 5.7 per cent of reported rapes was a failure of the system. The second area where the law operates against women is that women who commit crimes that transgress gender roles will be punished more heavily. Thus women who commit murder, particularly child murder, are likely to be punished more severely. They are punished for the crime and they are also punished for breaking traditional expectations about their maternal role: they are doubly deviant.

According to figures from the Youth Justice Board, girls aged between 10 and 17 committed 59,236 crimes in 2006–7, a 25 per cent increase from 47,358 in 2003–4. However, researchers have argued that there are dangers of creating a moral panic over the crime that girls commit. Eagle (2008) has argued that the rise in female offenders can be explained by two factors. The first is an increase in the number of girls compared to boys. In 2001, 1.3 per cent of the young female population committed an offence, whereas in 2005, 1.5 per cent of girls committed an offence (Youth Justice Board). A second factor to consider is the greater willingness of the public to report disturbances by girls and the authorities' greater willingness to prosecute.

Thus the crime statistics do not represent the reality of crime for men and women.

Activity 15

Create a poster using some recent headlines on girls' criminality. Include reasons why we may question the headlines and the statistics.

An evaluation of the feminist analysis of crime and deviance

◆ The law may now serve women's interests rather than men's. This is the view of groups like Fathers for Justice, who argue that divorce law is now heavily weighted against men.

◆ Women and men's traditional socialisation has now changed. Many feminist accounts have ignored the way women can now participate in many areas of life and are free from control.

◆ Feminist explanations have ignored or underplayed the extent of crimes committed against men by women. Women are not just victims of domestic abuse; they also inflict abuse on their partners.

Geographical location

It is clear from the official data that crime rates vary according to location. Many of these trends may be explained by some of the theories that we have examined. Marxists may point to the poverty present in many cities, while functionalists may argue that there are greater chances of status frustration developing. However, a group of sociologists known as the Chicago School argue that there is something distinctive about cities which produces high crime rates.

Shaw and McKay (1942) developed a concentric zone model of city development that plotted crime according to the location of the offender. They argued that the city could be divided into five concentric zones. In particular they argued that zone two was prone to high levels of delinquency and that this was the result of a different value system emerging. Zone two was where many immigrants came to live as housing was

cheap. These immigrants moved out as they became more successful and were replaced by the next group. The result of this is that the zone of transition experiences a high degree of social disorganisation and there are fewer controls on the people who live there. There is little chance of strong collective bonds and shared values developing. Shaw and McKay later redeveloped this idea to argue that the distinctive values were passed on from generation to generation by a process of cultural transmission (despite a high population turnover) where younger boys learn specific techniques and values from older boys. They argued that these values did not develop in other areas as children in wealthier neighbourhoods were subject to much greater control.

◆ These ideas have been influential and it is possible to see them in the work of a variety of writers. For instance, Baldwin and Bottoms (1976) argue that some council estates are prone to a process of 'tipping'. They argue that if an estate starts to develop an antisocial group within it, those who can will leave, while families of those who are antisocial will be attracted to the estate by their family ties and connections. The informal controls on people will start to break down and the estate will have been tipped – it has become a problem estate. Sampson (1997) has argued that violent crime is the result of the community's inability to achieve its objectives and a failure to establish trust and shared expectations about intervention when order is threatened. This occurs in neighbourhoods where poverty, family instability and high mobility occur.

Ethnicity and crime

According to the statistics, some ethnic minorities are more predisposed towards criminality and are also more likely to be victims of crime. A variety of models are used to explain this. In recent years attention has shifted from Afro-Caribbeans towards Asian criminality. The approach used in explaining the figures is also useful in this area. Some argue that crime is a real problem and others that there are problems with the statistics.

Crime as a real problem

Some early functionalists argued that crime and deviance could be understood by examining the culture of ethnic minorities. In particular they developed a host–immigrant model of ethnic relations, which argued that conflict was temporary. In particular it was argued that immigrants brought their own culture with them. Their distinctive values and norms represented a challenge to the culture of the host society, which meant that there would be conflict as people act according to their values and beliefs. An example of this can be found in the argument of a chief constable in 2008 that drink-driving was becoming a problem because East European immigrants thought it was acceptable to drink and drive. However, according to functionalists like Park (1950) these conflicts will disappear as the immigrant culture becomes absorbed into the host culture. There is a slight modification of the mainstream culture, but the major change occurs in the immigrant culture, which becomes assimilated. This means that immigrants lose their distinctive values – the source of conflict. Within this model there are two elements. The first is that this is a process that will happen as ethnic minorities come into contact with the mainstream culture – they shop, go to school and find jobs in the host society, and this means they will change, sometimes over generations. In addition to the first aspect of this model, which emphasises 'will', there is also a 'should'. In essence there is an expectation that ethnic minorities *should* lose their distinctive traditions and identity. The Irish community is held up as evidence here. They came to Britain in the 1800s and encountered many problems and racism. However as generations have passed so too has a sense of the Irish community in the UK. Occasionally we hear echoes from the past in the form of racist jokes about 'stupid' Irish people, but much of the discrimination they faced has died and so too has their own distinctive (deviant) behaviour. This model fell out of favour and politicians began to espouse multiculturalism. Many policies were developed to celebrate cultural difference and diversity in a climate of tolerance and respect. However, there are signs that many politicians are abandoning multiculturalism. The home-grown nature of British Islamic **terrorism** (2005) and the riots of 2001 have created calls for ethnic minorities to be assimilated rather than accepted as different. However, there are a number of problems with this approach:

1 The model presents a unified image of the host culture, but one may ask what British culture is. What is it that ethnic minorities are supposed to be absorbed into?

2 In focusing on the immigrant culture, it neatly sidesteps the problems created by the host culture. Many ethnic minorities may wonder why they are expected to conform to a culture that emphasises drunkenness and its effects in major towns and cities every Friday and Saturday night.

3 This model tends to emphasise the problems created by the immigrants rather than examining the racism in the host society. As we shall see, this racism may well provoke conflict and create anger amongst ethnic minorities.

Activity 16

In pairs, write down what you think are the five most important things that make someone British. Discuss your list with the rest of the class.

Marxists reject the cultural arguments put forward by functionalists. They argue that conflicts over race are caused by the capitalist system and that capitalism generates racism. According to Castles and Kosack (1973) this is because the capitalist class can use ethnic minorities as cheap labour; racism serves to justify their low wages and poor living conditions. At the same time, racism means that white workers who are unemployed or paid low wages, unable to get a good school for their child or adequate care when they are sick, blame ethnic minorities: they direct their anger at the 'other'. Their anger is misdirected: the real source of their low wages and poor life chances is the exploitation created by the capitalist class, whose dominance is maintained by racist ideologies perpetuated in institutions like the media and schools. In some ways this model attempts to explain the victimisation of ethnic minorities, but later writers have also developed an explanation of black criminality.

Hall et al. (1979) argue that capitalism is prone to booms and slumps. Ethnic minorities are made redundant in the slumps. If they are lucky they get the worst jobs in the labour market. Turning to crime is motivated by economic hardship, and hustling, dealing drugs or prostitution are ways of making money. Lea and Young, left realists, argue that crime is the result of relative deprivation and marginalisation (1984).

Activity 17

Create a set of montages illustrating the concepts of relative deprivation and marginalisation.

This argument is a challenge to those who argue that ethnic minority crime is a reaction to racism and the idea that crime is part of a political struggle against the white oppressor (Gilroy, 1983). This challenge is sustained by the fact that much ethnic minority crime is directed at ethnic minorities rather than the white colonial oppressor. However, Desai (1999) has argued that Asian crime has increased in recent years. This is due to groups of Asian males who are willing to move outside their own cultural group in a way their parents did not. They are more willing to stand up against racism, sometimes aggressively, to defend their community and fight for their families and friends. Their violence may be seen as a defence against a society that has marginalised them.

Abbas (2005) argues that the current climate of Islamophobia has the potential to make Asian crime and victimisation much worse. He argues that there have been more attacks on Asians since 9/11 and that many policies have continued to send out negative images to the Asian community. The danger is that the increased stereotyping of Islam as a negative force will have a negative impact. In particular the marginalisation that ethnic minorities face will create a spiral of deviance and conflict. The more Asians are stigmatised and the greater 'the War on Terror', the more they will be pushed into the arms of the terrorists. Indeed, this may well be one of the terrorists' aims.

Activity 18

As class, research recent policies towards ethnic minorities and debate whether we should enforce assimilation or pursue multiculturalism.

Weblinks

You could look at the role of religion through research conducted by Andrew Holden, see 'Websites', page ii.

Problems with the statistics

The idea of over-representation of ethnic minorities is that the statistics on crime and ethnicity are flawed. A number of issues need to be examined. The two most important are the idea of a moral panic and the nature of the criminal justice system.

Hall et al. (1979) have argued that Afro-Caribbeans were labelled as criminal by the media. They were portrayed as being involved in robbings, knifings and murders. This was a media exaggeration, but it was believed. The panic over this new crime wave was sustained by comments by politicians, judges and police. Mugging came to be seen as a black crime, due to the coverage in the media. Hall et al. found no evidence that violent crime was either black or rising. The panic was created due to the needs of the capitalist system. At the time, capitalism was undergoing an economic crisis as inflation and unemployment were rising, and also there was a crisis of legitimation or hegemony. The focus on black crime was able to justify greater police powers over the whole population. This greater attention focused police resources on mugging and more trouble was found. Hall et al. argue that there is a reality to some crime, but their work is a useful illustration of the idea that our images of ethnicity and crime are affected by the media. The idea of a moral panic is discussed in more detail in a later section (see pages 34–36).

The notion that there is a moral panic about ethnicity can also be seen in the work of Alexander (2000). She argues that there are media concerns about Asian and in particular Muslim youth. However, she argues that while there were conflicts between Asian and black youth, the idea of an Asian gang is inaccurate, because locality and individuals were more significant than the group and the group did not treat all black men as the same. She argues that there is fragmentation and diversity in the group and that media portrayals were inaccurate.

There is also evidence that ethnic minorities are more likely to be treated differently by the criminal justice system. The Macpherson inquiry (1999), set up after the murder of Stephen Lawrence, found the police to be **institutionally racist**. The police were likely to stereotype ethnic minorities as criminal, which will affect the way they deal with ethnic minorities. Phillips and Bowling (2002) argue that the situation has changed little, because ethnic neighbourhoods are over-policed and the police use military-style methods. A study conducted by Mhlanga (1999) found that the CPS was more likely to terminate a case involving ethnic minorities. This may be an indication of the willingness of the police to put forward cases involving ethnic minorities. Hood (1992) found that the courts were more willing to give a black man a custodial sentence than a white man, and black men were also given longer prison sentences. Asian men were likely to be given even longer prison sentences than black men. Finally, self-report studies conducted by the Home Office also show that black and white people commit similar amounts of crime.

Activity 19

1 Create a table with the two headings below and place the different theories and ideas you have covered under the headings. It is possible to place a theory under both headings.

The statistics reveal the truth	The statistics are constructed

Functionalism   Interactionism   Studies of ethnicity
Marxism   New right   Subculture
Left realism   Feminism   New criminology

2 Explain your table to the rest of the class.

U3
1

Sociology of crime and deviance

Section summary

The main theories to consider in this section are functionalism, new right, interactionism, Marxism, new criminology, subculturalism, left realism and feminism.

Use the following words to write a paragraph explaining the key themes of this section.

- Anomie
- Cultural deprivation
- Labelling
- Criminalised
- Material deprivation
- Chivalry thesis
- Institutional racism

Stretch and Challenge Activity

From your awareness of today's society, identify a modern deviant culture that may produce crime and deviance. Examine this group in relation to the theories you have learnt about and discuss how effectively the theories would explain this group.

Exam practice

1 Outline and assess the Marxist theories of the relationship between social class and crime. (50 marks)

2 Outline and assess sociological explanations for the relationship between geographical area and crime. (50 marks)

30

(iii) Patterns and explanations of victimisation

Pause for thought

- Who do you think are the victims of crime? Is there a typical victim?
- What do you think are the consequences of being a victim? Are those consequences confined to the victim?
- Should victims have a role in deciding the punishment of offenders?

Much research has been directed towards explaining and analysing the offenders. Sociologists have also begun to consider the patterns of victimisation. It is clear that your chances of becoming a victim are not randomly distributed. In the first six months of 2008, 18 young people were killed by knives in London. You have already considered many issues connected to victims, but it is worth considering victims in a discrete section. Look at the work of left realists and feminist analysis of crime in the previous section, as many of their arguments are relevant here.

Left realism (Lea and Young (1984))

- The victims of crime are mainly working class and black.
- They are victims due, in the main, to the actions of other working-class and black people.
- These groups are also the victims of racist police practices.
- The police should change their practices to help and assist local communities and victims.

Feminism (Walklate (2007), Walby and Allen (2004))

- The female victims of crime are largely ignored or hidden.
- Their victimisation is connected to the patriarchal nature of society.
- Police and court procedures serve to discourage women from reporting crimes that have been committed against them. These procedures need to be reformed.

There are patterns indicated by the official statistics, but there are also problems with these statistics. The explanations for these patterns will be affected by the sociologists' own priorities and interests.

The major sources of data on victims are surveys like the BCS; this is also combined with data on offences recorded by the police. It is worth remembering the problems of victim surveys and thinking about what crimes and therefore which victims they ignore. The victims of murder, for instance, cannot be revealed by victim surveys. These surveys have indicated that there are four major patterns to victimisation.

1. The working class are most likely to be victims of property crime. This is one of the central features of the left realist argument against those who believe that crime is an act of rebellion.

2. Age is another dimension to victimisation. Those at greatest risk of being murdered are children under the age of one. Teenagers are most at risk of assault and harassment. Few such incidents are reported to the police, who tend to concentrate upon youth offending rather than victimisation. Child abuse and elder abuse are rarely reported and it is clear that the extent of this pattern of victimisation is hidden by the figures on crime.

3. Gender is another dimension. Men are more likely to be victims of violent attacks in public spaces. They are also more likely to be victims of injury in the workplace or as a result of their employment – being a bouncer is more dangerous than being a secretary. However, women are much more likely to be victims

Sociology of crime and deviance

of domestic abuse. According to Walby and Allen (2004), 36 per cent of women report an experience of domestic violence, sexual victimisation or stalking. This indicates that it is dispersed. A small number of women suffer multiple attacks and in this way victimisation is concentrated on a few women.

4   Ethnic minorities are at greater risk, but there are significant variations between different minority groups, offences and locations. However, the Macpherson Report (1999) found that institutional racism was prevalent within the Metropolitan Police and this meant that ethnic minorities were not treated equally; this applies to victimisation as well as offending. Walklate (2007) argues that while elderly females are most concerned about becoming victims, they are actually least at risk. Females appear to have a greater sense of the impact of crime, but in practice males are most likely to be victims.

The problem when looking at these data is that they are very much influenced by the type of victimology adopted. Karmen (1990) identified three major ways of viewing the victim. These views have consequences for how victimisation is explained.

1   The conservative strand believes that crime is visible, that people should be accountable for their actions, and that most victims are known about. People should be self-reliant and justice should be based on **retribution**. This view is closely linked with the new right, and believes that there is something in the victim's lifestyle that makes them likely to become a victim and that victims can and should take precautions. This idea has attracted some support, but has provoked criticism when applied to victims of rape.

2   The liberal tradition extends the conservative approach and argues that many victims are hidden. Victims of **corporate crime** or fraud are unaware or unwilling to admit that they have been a victim of this type of crime. The consequences of this type of crime go beyond the boundaries established by those on the right. The victims of corporate crime need to be helped and the damage they have suffered needs to be made good.

3   The radical or critical tradition develops this analysis further. Crime embraces malnutrition

and poverty alongside state crime like false imprisonment and state-sanctioned murder. The crimes of the powerful are hidden, therefore their victims are also hidden. This type of analysis tends to stress the need for the empowerment of victims by giving them political and social rights. Some in this tradition argue for **zemiology** rather than criminology.

Thus it can be said that the study of victimisation illustrates the idea that crime is a social construct. Who we regard as a victim will depend on our values and beliefs. Marxists will stress that the working class are victims of crime and would seek to transform capitalism to aid the victim, while radical feminists would see women as the victim of patriarchal power and treat men as the problem. It is also true that people's values and attitudes will affect how victims are treated.

Carrabine et al. (2000) point to a hierarchy of victimisation: some victims enjoy a higher status than others. In effect, some victims are stigmatised while others are idealised. The ideal victim is an elderly woman or a child (vulnerable and weak); young men or homeless people are not ideal victims. This hierarchy affects the way victims of crime are treated. Only certain types of women are thought to deserve protection from the law and there are victims who in some ways are culpable and others who are innocent. For some feminists this is tied into the idea of **victim-blaming** and patriarchal justice.

Activity 20

1   Read these two quotes.

'Women who say no do not always mean no.' (Judge Wild, 1982)

'It is the height of impudence for any girl to hitch-hike at night.' (Judge Bertrand Richards, 1982)

2   In groups, discuss the quotes. Do you agree with the judges? Would a female judge have the same views? What effect might these attitudes have on the willingness of victims to report rape?

A new development in the criminal justice process is the emergence of victim movements. This means that victims should be given a voice within the courtroom. They should be allowed to make victim impact statements and their views should be taken into account in decisions on things like bail or sentencing. Thus the family of a murder victim get the opportunity to explain their loss to the court. This idea is different from the idea of reconciliation, which is being tested by allowing victims and offenders to meet, under controlled conditions, in an attempt to establish greater understanding on the part of the victim to the question 'Why me?' and an attempt to make the criminal recognise the harm their actions have caused. As well as focusing on the needs of the victim, this model of justice fits into the idea of justice as being about re-integration and restoring the wrongdoing, rather than a more punitive approach.

Section summary

The main theories to consider in this section are feminism and left realism.

Use the following words to write a paragraph explaining the key themes of this section.

- Corporate crime
- Victim-blaming
- Retribution

Stretch and Challenge Activity

1   Find some recent newspaper stories about victims. What do these stories tell you about the hierarchy of victimisation?

2   Discuss how this portrayal and the treatment of victims in the criminal justice system may help or hinder their recovery from being a victim.

3   How might this link to the treatment of victims of bullying within school? Prepare a view to be presented to your school or college council.

Exam practice

1   Outline and assess feminist explanations for the relationship between gender and victimisation. (50 marks)

2   Outline and assess sociological explanations of the overrepresentation of young males as victims of crime. (50 marks)

Pause for thought

- When did you last hear a politician talk tough about crime or deviance? What was the issue and were there any other media stories on this theme?

- What do you think military policing and community policing are, and how might they affect crime and deviance?

- How might the interpretations of the judiciary and the police affect the official crime rates?

Moral panic and the media

Cohen (1972) was the first sociologist to use the term 'moral panic'. This idea illustrates the media's role in generating crime and the fear of crime. It is used to indicate that the fear is exaggerated and out of proportion to the reality of crime. Cohen drew from concepts found in interactionism and functionalism.

He based his study on the media reaction to two youth groups: the 'mods' and the 'rockers'. He argued that the media over-sensationalised the nature of these groups and that this had consequences for the rest of society. This powerful idea has been used to explain many events since his original study, and is well worth considering even though it is an old idea.

The two groups visited Clacton, a town on the Essex coast, on the Easter Bank Holiday in 1964. These groups were loosely knit, as many youths did not see themselves as mods or rockers, but were more likely to define their identity along regional affiliations. There were no clearly drawn lines between the two groups, but some minor disturbances did break out. The events were so minor that the local newspapers did not mention them on their front pages. The events were not covered by the national newspapers and were not considered significant. However, the national media did eventually pick up on the story.

When this happened, they exaggerated the extent of crime and violence. Phrases such as 'day of terror' were used to convey an impression of anarchy and havoc created by conflict between two rival gangs. The consequences of this can be categorised in two ways.

First, the establishment began to demand greater police action against these groups. Judges were asked to consider longer sentences and the groups were placed under closer surveillance. Once the police began to look at this group, they found more crime, not because the reality changed, but because more was reported and recorded. The figures appeared to confirm the initial media concerns.

The second consequence was the reaction of the groups themselves; they began to define themselves in opposition to one another. Loathing and images of the alleged fights between the groups **polarised** what were initially disparate groups: a self-fulfilling prophecy had been created. These rivalries would play themselves out on the streets for many years, but would not have reached such a pitch if the media reporting had not been so sensationalised. These further conflicts were reported and a **deviancy amplification** spiral had been created. The reporting of deviancy makes that deviancy worse.

Activity 21

This argument is based, in part, on a study of the media. This is known as content analysis. What are its strengths and weakness?

Cohen argues that the media create these panics in response to rapid social change. At the time, Britain was undergoing many social upheavals as traditional working-class communities were being transformed, youths were developing spending power and consumerism was emerging. Many of the established patterns of behaviour were being undermined. This generated a sense of anomie. People were unsure of right and wrong and their place in the world. The creation of **folk devils**, groups that represent a challenge to the moral order, help to create a symbol of all that is wrong and a symbol that can be easily challenged and criticised. Another significant factor in the creation of a moral panic is the need of the media to sell newspapers and attract ratings. They can achieve this by over-reporting and sensationalising.

This idea has been used to explain many aspects of crime and deviance. Football hooliganism, drug abuse, vandalism and mugging have all been examined using this concept. A recent study of hoodies illustrates the continued relevance of this idea.

Fawbert (speaking on Radio 4 in 2008) analysed coverage of hoodies in the media. He argued that although shopping centres such as the Trafford Centre had banned hoodies, they had not attracted press interest. It was only in May 2005 when the Bluewater shopping centre banned them that the moral panic surrounding hoodies began to be created by newspaper headlines. Fawbert argued that media reports were driven by the desire for greater readership. Before the ban at Bluewater, the word 'hoodie' had not been used in the media in the previous three months and had only been used once in the last year. The headlines created a false picture of criminal youth. Between 1993 and 2003 there had been a 26 per cent fall in youth crime, but 65 per cent of people believed that crime had increased and many thought that youth crime was much greater than it was. Politicians and police demanded greater punishment. One chief constable called for longer sentences if a criminal was caught wearing a hoodie. Fawbert argued that the panic declined as the media began to run out of new sensational headlines and in fact towards the end of the media concern, stories praising hoodies began to appear.

Activity 22

1   Conduct some research on media presentations of Islam.

2   Write a recommendation for the Department of Justice. Explain your concerns about the nature of recent media coverage of Islam and the Muslim community and explain some possible consequences of the coverage for British society.

An evaluation of the idea of a moral panic

The idea of moral panic has been influential within sociology and has been used by writers from a number of different traditions. It is now widely employed outside the discipline of sociology, although it is often used inaccurately.

However, the idea of a moral panic has invited a number of criticisms, many of which attack the theoretical roots of the idea. Many of them should be familiar to you, as you have looked at these ideas in theories of crime and deviance.

◆   One major problem with the idea of moral panic is that it focuses on the consequences of the media exaggeration and ignores the initial act of deviance. There is no account of the reason for the disturbances in Clacton or why those wearing hoodies were violent in the first place. In a sense, the reality of the initial act is denied.

◆   Many radical Marxists and feminists would argue that the concept of a moral panic created as a response to the need for profit or anomie ignores the actions of the powerful. Moral panics may be used to whip up support against groups that the powerful consider a threat. The general panic may be used to legitimate a clampdown in society against all, as the increased power of the state is used to repress any dissent. This idea is developed by Hall (1978) in his analysis of mugging as a black crime (see page 29). It is difficult to see how minority and weak social groups have the ability to stir up moral panic, and an account of media influence that does not recognise the power of dominant groups is bound to be flawed.

- Another problem of the idea of moral panic is its **determinism**. The self-fulfilling-prophecy element of the amplification spiral sees people as passive dupes. The audience are injected with a message and they simply respond. The real world is not like this. People have many different responses to the media. For instance they may be horrified by what they see and hear, which may have the effect of reducing crime and deviance rather than amplifying it as they turn away from these portrayals.

- Postmodernists would argue that the idea of moral panic is outdated. In today's media-saturated world it is more difficult to establish a moral consensus. People can create their own stories and accounts and show them to the world on the internet. Dominant groups do not have exclusive access to the media and media professionals draw from a variety of sources. In this sense, there are no dominant groups. It is hard to establish a discourse of derision against the 'deviants', as many of the deviants have an effect on the content. For instance, there may have been an attempt to create islamophobia in the media, but as soon as this happened others began to create positive images of Muslims – there was no single story of the Muslim community. In effect the media cannot create a single story; this is what is meant by the phrase 'the death of the **meta-narrative**'. In addition, people are media literate and aware: they are unlikely to accept what is given to them.

- The theory of moral panics does not explain how these panics end. It is clear that the media do not continue to create images about groups and we move on to other panics. The theory focuses too much on the effects of the panic and not enough on the reasons for its decline.

The police and courts

The media are not the only agents who can construct crime and deviance, other groups include the police and the courts. You have already examined many of the ways in which the police and the courts are involved in this process. Look back at the previous sections and note down how the following factors or theories are relevant. Try to use studies to help you. Griffith (1997) has something to say about judicial background, for instance. There are also many other relevant theories and concepts.

- Judicial background
- Police background
- Coughing and cuffing
- Military policing
- Interactionism, feminism and Marxism

You need to pull together work from a number of different sections to understand how crime and deviance may be affected by the agencies of control.

Section summary

The main theories to consider in this section are functionalism, postmodernism, interactionism (labelling) and Marxism.

Use the following concepts and theories to write a brief summary of how different agents of control can construct crime and deviance.

- Folk devil
- Amplify
- Patriarchy
- Polarisation

Stretch and Challenge Activity

1 Consider two topics you have considered so far in your course.

2 Explain how each of the structures you have examined may create or limit the deviance of particular social groups.

(v) Solutions to the problem of crime

Pause for thought

- Do you think some people deserve to feel pain and suffering as a form of punishment?

- What sorts of people do you think have the power to inflict punishment on others? Do they have the right to do this?

- Should women who kill their husbands have their punishment reduced if they have been abused by their partners?

- Is punishment the most effective way of controlling crime?

There have been many different views on the solutions to crime. These views reflect different theoretical positions. The work of sociologists in this area has been applied by governments, but it is too simplistic to put particular theoretical positions into the framework of party policies.

Left realism

As we have seen, left realists believe that crime is produced by relative deprivation and marginalisation. Thus the solutions to crime are most likely to be found in reducing these problems. They will involve ensuring that there are not vast inequalities, and left realists would criticise the shift to a market economy and general reductions in welfare. They would also like to see better leisure facilities, improvements to housing and better employment prospects.

The principal aim of these policies is the creation of cohesive communities where people feel they belong. Many politicians have been influenced by this argument in their repeated calls for the development of a sense of community. A central argument is that crime is prevented by changing social conditions rather than spending money on policing. **Crime prevention** is best undertaken by improving the conditions in which people live rather than strengthening surveillance. These politicians would also like to develop a number of specific proposals for changes to the system of policing. They believe that amongst some ethnic minority groups in particular, trust has broken down between the community and the police. This results in a reduction in the supply of information, which the police need in order to solve crime. In a vicious cycle the police are then led into military policing, which further extends feelings of alienation and resentment across the community. Thus a central policy suggestion from left realists is the development of local, democratic control of the police which would direct police priorities. In addition 'stop-and-search' tactics should be abandoned, as they foster a great deal of resentment and do little to solve crime. Finally they make a plea for the police to focus on racial attacks, corporate crime and domestic abuse rather than, for example, minor drug offences. Many of these policies have been adopted in the UK. For instance, the police now employ neighbourhood policing, which demands that the police hold regular consultations with the local community and discuss priorities. There has been a vast increase in the number of police community support officers, who are drawn from the local community and are intended to act as the 'eyes and ears' of the police.

The major political party to have been influenced by left realism has been the Labour Party and government. The slogan 'tough on crime, tough on the causes of crime' put forward by ex-Prime Minister Tony Blair is a clear indication of the type of influence this thinking has had. New Labour have supported people back into work via the New Deal, tax credits and investing in inner cities, and they have limited welfare for those they have deemed as abusing the system. They have also brought in antisocial behaviour orders (ASBOs) to try to curb teenage delinquency. Left realists would probably be less happy with this last policy and it is worth noting that New Labour does not directly equate to left realism.

Activity 24

Invite a local representative of the police to come and talk to you about what they see as the role of the police in your local area and the effectiveness of community support officers.

Evaluation of left realism

1   A key limitation of left realism in the eyes of Marxists is that it tends to focus on managing capitalism. The key problem is capitalism and suggesting modifications is only a 'sticking plaster' to cover the serious and endemic problems of capitalism.

2   There is a tension between arguing for local control and then suggesting police priorities. What happens if the local community demands a focus on the crimes which the left realists see as less significant?

3   As we shall see in the next section, left realists would be criticised for ignoring the need for greater control and harsher punishment. They focus too much on deprivation and not enough on returning to traditional values.

New right

The new right would seem to have an affinity with the Conservative Party, and it has certainly influenced that party's thinking and policy suggestions. However it has also found a sympathetic hearing within New Labour and has policy consequences in both the UK and the USA. In particular the new right argues that rising crime is linked to moral decline and lenient punishments, and its suggestions stem from this.

Like the new left, the new right argues that the collapse in community is a major problem of modern social life. It breaks down the controls that limit deviance and crime. More emphasis needs to be placed on preserving the order and stability of social life, as each crime that is committed undermines people's faith and trust in the community. The new right argues that we never see a building with one broken window. As soon as a window is broken in a disused building, others are smashed. The building and area around it become a focus for more incivility. If the first window were not broken the others would not follow. Thus they argue for the theory of **broken windows**: stopping minor acts of crime will reduce more serious crimes. This policy was pursued in north-east England after the introduction of the policy of zero tolerance in New York. It has been claimed that New York was transformed from one of the murder capitals of the world into a relatively safe city by keeping drugs, tramps and prostitutes off the streets. New Labour has introduced ASBOs to combat minor acts of criminality and to give people the confidence to challenge delinquent youth. The collapse in community is also underpinned by a collapse in

Figure 1.9: The modern **panopticon?**

traditional family structures. It follows from this that the new right sees the support of nuclear families as a priority. This would involve support for the nuclear family by making divorce more difficult, by imposing cooling-off periods and tax support like a married couple's allowance. In addition, welfare support for unmarried mothers needs to be reduced in order to stop women from getting pregnant so that they can receive benefits.

The new right would also argue that the punishments for offences are far from clear and that prison works. Criminals, they believe, make a rational calculation about whether a crime is worth committing. **Incarceration** is a way of removing crime from the streets and acts as a deterrent to further criminality. Hence in the USA the policy of 'three strikes' was introduced as a clear message to anyone thinking of committing a crime. On their third

offence, a person would be sent to prison for a lengthy term, regardless of the nature of their offence. In California, for instance, those who have stolen golf-clubs or pizzas have been sentenced to between 25 years and life if they have had previous convictions for more serious offences. It is clear from this policy that many on the right do *not* believe that prison is useful for rehabilitating offenders. The function of punishment is to stop further offences taking place by deterring others. A second function of punishment is incapacitation: removing criminals from the streets removes their ability to commit crime; this is what a Conservative home secretary meant when he said that 'prison works'. According to Newburn, some of the most recent developments of this theme concern sex offences. High-risk offenders, repeat offenders and the like are subjected to curfews and surveillance once they have been released. Some countries practise surgical castration while others use chemical castration. In addition, greater funding for the police and more visible policing make it more likely that criminals believe they will get caught and the new right would be keen to improve the resources available to the police. The introduction of CCTV into many areas of social life is designed to make criminals think that they will be caught and thus helps to act as a deterrent as well as improving the chances of catching those who do commit crime.

Weblinks

The government website on crime reduction provides a good insight into current government thinking and research (see 'Websites', page ii).

A useful source of information on prison reform is the Howard League for Penal Reform (see 'Websites', page ii).

Another way that the new right argues that we can reduce crime is by making it more difficult to commit crime. The new right have championed target-hardening. This involves a variety of measures such as improving car security to stop cars being stolen, and the introduction of plastic glasses to limit the potential weapons available in a pub brawl.

A final criticism of **rehabilitation** as a function of sentencing is the new right's belief in retribution, which can be defined as 'an eye for an eye, a tooth for a tooth': a murderer deserves to be executed. Thus many (though not all) within the Conservative Party have campaigned for the death sentence. The theory of just deserts influenced the 1991 Criminal Justice Act, which attempted to grade punishments into three groups on the basis of their seriousness.

Evaluation of the new right

It is clear that the new right has had a great deal of influence over government policy, even under New Labour. The theory has produced many practical solutions to the issue of crime, but there are a number of problems with the approach.

Activity 25

Situational crime-prevention strategies believe that crime can be reduced by changing the situations in which crime occurs. In New York, public washrooms were seen as places where drug-users, homeless people and deviants gathered. As part of the attempt to design crime out of the environment, these were adapted to create washrooms that discourage crime.

Copy the table below and fill in suggestions for the missing problems and solutions.

Toilet feature	Before the change	After the change
Ceiling panels	Removable	
Attendants		Present
Lighting		Bright and secure
Walls	Easy to write on	
Nooks	Present	
Sink size	Six users	

1 The approach tends to ignore crime that develops as a consequence of poverty and deprivation. The collapse of community is primarily created by poor housing and a lack of job opportunities rather than a decline in the moral order. The collapse in values, if it occurs, is a result of poverty.

2 It is argued that many of the policies do not work. For instance, the fall in crime in New York might have been the result of criminals moving elsewhere. It is argued that CCTV simply moves the problem of crime to locations where there are fewer cameras, and does not address the root causes of crime. The use of ASBOs may have unintended consequences: youths may come to see them as a badge of honour, or being defined as a delinquent may have stigmatising effects.

3 The move towards greater surveillance and increased police powers has led many to fear the development of a trend towards a totalitarian society where the state tracks and categorises everyone's movements. People will lose their privacy under the eye of the state. It is interesting to note that David Davies, a Conservative shadow cabinet member, resigned in 2008 to fight a by-election on the issue of identity cards. Some liberals within the new right are opposed to the surveillance society, which may lead to the theory being inconsistent.

4 Many of the policies focus on street crime and burglary. They tend to be silent on issues like corporate crime and domestic abuse.

5 Who is to be incapacitated by sterilisation is a difficult and ultimately arbitrary judgement. At what point does one become a repeat or habitual offender? Is there a difference between someone who commits ten crimes over a two-month period and someone who commits crimes over a five-year period? A second problem lies in punishing someone for a predicted crime that they have not yet committed.

6 In order to assign retribution, equivalence needs to be established. In other words, if a murderer deserves to be killed, what is the proportionate punishment for shoplifting? Should the shop owner come and take something from the offender's home? This principle also ignores how far the circumstances behind the crime should influence policy.

Restorative justice

In a move away from deterrence, **retribution** and incarceration, a new model of justice is rapidly developing. It was first pioneered by Christie, who argued that traditional models of crime and justice ignored the victim and the rest of the community. Traditional models have failed to prevent crime and taken crime away from the victim and the offender. Moving crime into the formal criminal justice system makes it remote and benefits only the lawyers. There are three elements to restorative justice: it seeks to put right the harm that has been done, it seeks to balance the need of the victim with the need for accountability of the offender and it seeks to ensure that the victim is involved in the decision-making process. According to the Home Office, the process is based on the three Rs:

◆ **Restoration** – offenders should apologise and make amends for the harm done.

◆ **Reintegration** – offenders should be brought back into the community after they have paid their debt.

◆ **Responsibility** – offenders take responsibility for the consequences of their actions.

The principle of restorative justice has influenced many policy initiatives such as victim-offender mediation, citizen panels and community boards, sentencing circles, conferencing and court-based schemes.

Weblinks

A variety of information on restorative justice is available on the internet (see 'Websites', page ii).

Feminism

Feminist writers have brought a great deal of insight into the relationship between gender and crime. They have also put forward a number of policy suggestions. It is difficult to categorise each of these policies, as different feminists have different priorities. However, there are some policies that most feminists would advocate.

Activity 26

In 2008 the actress Helen Mirren suggested that not all victims of date rape should expect to take their case to court. She also said that a woman who was engaging in sexual activity with a man and then said no should not expect to take the man to court if he raped her.

In groups, discuss this argument.

Feminists are concerned about rape and many policy suggestions arise from this. They would campaign for safer streets by ensuring adequate street lighting. They would also encourage women to carry rape alarms and take self-defence classes. But they have been critical of advice such as 'don't go out alone at night,' 'don't travel on public transport at night,' 'don't use alleyways,' and so on, as this seeks to limit women's freedom and independence (Newburn, 2007). However, they do not believe that most rape is conducted by strangers. They think that too many women are silent victims of rape by someone who is known to them. They believe that women should be encouraged to speak out against their abusers and would campaign for changes to the treatment of women within the criminal justice system. They think that police need to be better trained to deal with victims and that there should be more specialist centres to help women give their accounts and better recording of the forensic evidence. There are now more rape examination suites and cases are now more personally dealt with by female officers. Feminists believe that a woman should not be put on trial when she enters the court, and would like to preserve victims' anonymity when possible. In addition they argue that there should be more rape crisis centres and domestic abuse centres to help female victims of male crime. As Newburn argues, there has been a decline in the number of rape crisis centres, whilst there has been a massive increase in the number of reported rapes. Feminists have also campaigned to extend what is defined as an illegal act. For instance, legislation on sexual harassment at work and equal pay have allowed women greater freedom in the workplace and reduced the discrimination they used to face. And since the 2004 Domestic Violence, Crime and Victims Act, arrests can be made for common assault.

Activity 27

On separate pieces of paper, write out as many policies as you can that deal with the issue of crime and deviance. Place the pieces of paper in a hat and pass it round your class. Students take out a piece of paper and explain what that policy is, who would support it and why it is seen as necessary.

Section summary

The most relevant theories to consider in this section are left realism, right realism (and the new right) and feminism.

Use the following words to write a paragraph explaining the key themes of this section.

* Broken windows

* Incarceration

* Crime prevention

* Restorative justice

* Re-integrative shaming

Stretch and Challenge Activity

Marx once argued that while philosophers had tried to understand the world, his task was to change it. Discuss how far you think sociology should be used to guide government policy.

How desirable is a move towards mass incarceration as a means of reducing crime?

Exam practice

1   Outline and assess the impact of crime prevention strategies as solutions to crime. (50 marks)

2   Outline and assess left realist theories about the solutions to the problem of crime. (50 marks)

ExamCafé
Relax, refresh, result!

Exam question
Outline and assess the role of the mass media in the social construction of crime and deviance.

(50 marks)

Relax and prepare

Ben

I have learnt a lot about the role of the media in the social construction of crime. I have so much information that I will need to look carefully at how to structure my response.

Hot tips

Freddy

I enjoyed studying the role of the mass media in the social construction of crime. I particularly liked looking at the contemporary examples of moral panics, which will be relevant to this essay.

Julie

This is a tricky question. I must remember to focus on the social construction of crime and deviance and not just the media. Also, I need to include sociological theory as this is key to gaining a top grade at A-Level.

Examiner's tip

This whole unit is examined through you writing answers to two unstructured essay questions. They are worth 50 marks each and you should spend 45 minutes on each one in the exam. You are assessed on all three Assessment Objectives, so it is important that you target each of these. It would be helpful to focus your revision for this unit around writing essay-style questions. Try writing 5-minute plans with the main for and against debates and then build up to writing timed responses. Look back at page 2 for general advice on answering essay-style questions. You could then ask your teacher to mark them and offer some constructive criticism.

Revision checklist

You might find it useful to use a table like the one below to check your knowledge, and record your own sources of information.

Topic	Studies	Do I know this?	Look here
Defining and measuring crime and deviance			
Trends, patterns and explanations of crime and deviance			
Victimisation			
The role of agents of social control in the social construction of crime and deviance			
Solutions to the problem of crime			

Get the result!

Student answer

Outline and assess the role of the mass media in the social construction of crime and deviance.

(50 marks)

Deviance is defined as being any behaviour that is disapproved of in society. However, as interactionists believe, it is not a fixed concept, and it differs both between and within societies. Thus, our perceptions of both crime and deviance are affected by the media and our culture. There are many forms of mass media, notably television, radio, books and newspapers. The public show an increasing hunger for crime coverage in the media, although many sociologists believe that it is not becoming more prevalent.

Examiner comment:

This is a general introduction which would be awarded some knowledge marks, though more could have been made of the concept 'social construction'.

The most obvious presentation of crime in the media is in the news. While all newspapers feature articles on crime, Reiner noted that more crime is featured in the more down-market newspapers, i.e. there is more crime in The Sun than the Independent. This may be because of the differences in the newspapers' audiences. However, newspapers and television do not necessarily present an accurate view of crime and deviance. Dobash et al. commented on how TV crime programmes primarily focus on crimes such as murder, armed robbery and rape, as obviously viewers find these topics more interesting.

Examiner comment:

There is relevant evidence discussed here, although it becomes rather assertive and simplistic towards the end of this paragraph and starts to drift away from the idea of social construction.

News and newspapers have been criticised for deliberately giving certain impressions of particular social groups. For example, Chibnall commented on how, when discussing corruption within the police force, the officers involved are always presented as individuals rather than the police as a whole, whereas this is not always the case for other groups. A classic example of this is referred to by Ray Pawson with the newspaper headline 'Girl guide, 14, raped at Hell's Angels convention'. This is an example of text encouraging a particular reading and creating a particular impression. This is a classic example of the 'innocent victim / wicked perpetrator' pair, which creates the impression of two extremes. Other forms of media, such as crime fiction and films, also focus on similar themes to crime news stories. Reiner notes that media fiction focuses on murder and violent crime and offenders are mainly portrayed as middle-aged, middle-class as opposed to the young, working-class males in official statistics and self-report studies.

Examiner comment:

This is a good paragraph, explaining relevant knowledge in the form of studies, examples and concepts. AO2 skills are explicitly demonstrated in phrases such as 'This is an example of…'.

Examiner comment:

However, this student focuses too much on the media at the expense of the social construction of crime, which should be the main focus of this essay.

The idea that the media help to create 'deviance' and its definition is held by those supporting the interactionist viewpoint. Interactionism was described by Blumer as maintaining that people's perceptions are constantly changing, and that it is people who

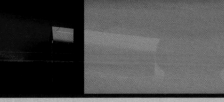

Examiner comment:

Some clear knowledge and understanding of interactionists, but undeveloped in terms of the link between media and social construction of crime. Some of it is underdeveloped; for example, Becker needs further elaboration.

Examiner comment:

This is a good paragraph. It contains explanation of a key study with some depth and a good conceptual understanding and a contemporary example.

Examiner comment:

This is a good, explicit and direct evaluation, although it is underdeveloped in parts; for example, the Marxist critique could have been developed further.

Examiner comment:

This is a useful conclusion which is both summative and evaluative in tone. Overall, this answer displays a wide range of knowledge and understanding. It focuses on several themes, including the presentation of crime in the news, the impression of social groups, and the theory of interactionism. Some studies, contemporary examples, theory and concepts are mentioned. It does, however, lack depth and detail in parts and some points made are underdeveloped. The whole notion of how the media socially construct crime and deviance needs to be made more central as it is often only implied. There is, however, some direct and explicit evaluation which goes beyond simple juxtaposition. Overall, this is a high-level response, but not the very best that could be achieved at this level.

create society. Becker's labelling theory goes further to explain how the mass media may create perceptions of deviance; that there is no innate deviance and it is society that creates it as norms and values develop. The mass media today may be contributing to the creation of morals and norms and are often blamed for providing people with bad role models as well. It has been said that films with violence, or gangsta rap music, could lead to copycat violence. Theories such as Cohen's subcultural theory and Miller's lower-class culture theory, where people create their own subcultures with norms and values such as excitement and aggression, could well be affected by media that increasingly glamorise behaviour that would traditionally be considered 'deviant'.

Cohen also dealt with the media's effect on the social construction of crime and deviance. He called it deviancy amplification and claimed that the media exaggerate crimes and deviant behaviour to make them appear more interesting. He interviewed 'mods' and 'rockers', groups who in the 1960s were often accused of getting into large fights and violent disruptive behaviour. However, he found that many of them had never considered themselves as a type of a subculture and had not been involved in the violent acts that were focused on by the media. This supports Cohen's theory that deviance has been amplified, or made worse, by the media. Cohen also claimed that this led to a downward spiral where the crimes were even more focused on by the media. A more contemporary example of this might be Fawbert's 2008 study of the moral panic over 'hoodies', where newspaper headlines sensationalised an event and turned 'hoodies' into folk devils.

The good thing about Cohen's theory is that it takes into account the news values which newspapers employ to increase readership. It also explains who might have the greatest influence in the actual creation of deviant labels, that is, the media. However, Young criticises this interactionist theory for not taking crime more seriously and for underestimating its true extent. Marxists also criticise interactionists for failing to consider who has the power to define certain acts as deviant and criminal. Why, for example, do newspapers not report more on corporate and white-collar crime?

In conclusion, the mass media can be said to be responsible both for the creation of crime and deviance and for shaping the public perception of crime and deviance. The media's representations of some social groups may even create stereotypes relating to crime. This may be explained through the media's choice of which crimes to focus on. As a vastly prevalent force in society, the media are both the main constructor and informer of what crime and deviance are, and how they should be handled.

Sociology of education

Pause for thought

1   How would you describe your education from the ages of 4 to 16?

2   Are there any similarities/differences between your experiences of school and the image in the picture below?

3   In your view, what should education do for individuals?

Introduction

Education is important for three reasons. First, formal education takes up a vast amount of young people's lives: all children aged 5 to 17 in the UK have to receive formal education. In this sense, it is a major agency of secondary socialisation and it can be a powerful influence on shaping people's beliefs and moral values. as well as developing new skills and passing on knowledge. Second, a significant proportion of public expenditure in the UK is spent on education, which means that education policies receive a great deal of scrutiny for their economic benefits. Third, education is seen as playing a key role in an individual's life chances, as educational achievement opens so many doors to social improvement. In this sense education raises issues of social inequality, power and control, which are the core themes of A Level Sociology.

The specification states:

'In this option, candidates explore issues of power and control through a detailed study of education.'

This option explores the following five key issues:

1　The structure and organisation of the education system

2　The role and function of education in society

3　Differential educational achievement

4　The relationship between education and the economy

5　Education and social policy.

(i) The structure and organisation of the education system

Pause for thought

Most of you have already experienced at least twelve years in the education system; you have spent approximately 17,550 hours in school and have attended at least two different types of school.

1　Think about the variety of education you have had, the types of schools. How did they differ in terms of size, structure, and organisation?

2　What do you think the purpose of education is (a) for individuals and (b) for society as a whole?

Developments in the structure and organisation of education

If you study the history of the UK education system, you will find both continuity and change. Formal compulsory state-organised and funded education began in 1870 and continues to the present day. Since this time, schooling has expanded; in 1880 education was made compulsory up to the age of 10. Today, it is compulsory to 16. By 2013, young people will be required to stay in school, training or workplace training until the age of 18. Since 1870, successive governments have increased expenditure on education and have built more schools, although it was not until after the Second World War that the government took more central responsibility for the organisation of education. Before this time, most schools were run by private or church authorities under the supervision of local government boards.

The New Labour government has embarked on an ambitious school-rebuilding programme. Building Schools for the Future (BSF) is the biggest-ever school buildings investment programme. The aim is to rebuild or renew nearly every secondary school in England.

Carry out some research into the BSF programme. Have any new secondary schools been built under this scheme in your area? What are the aims of the project? Has it been successful? Have there been any criticisms?

Weblinks

You might like to look at a useful account of the tripartite system and its faults (see 'Websites', page ii).

Education pre-1988

After the Second World War, there was a desire to create a fairer society, so free state-run secondary education became available for all. It was thought that different types of children would benefit from secondary education in three different types of school, collectively known as the **tripartite system**. This consisted of three levels of school, catering for students of different abilities as determined by a test called the 11+, which was taken at the age of 11 and determined the type of school a child would attend.

If the child passed the 11+ they could attend a grammar school; if they failed, they went to a secondary modern school or a technical college. Grammar schools offered a higher level of education, a broader range of subjects and more academic prospects. At the time, the rationale behind this system was that it embraced the notion of *equality of opportunity*, as all students were equally entered for the 11+ exam. This system was, however, deemed unfair because the education received was governed largely by the results of a test taken at the tender age of 11. Increasingly, many local education authorities abandoned the idea of the 11+ as it was so unpopular, and, from 1965, the then Labour government asked local education authorities to reorganise their secondary schools as **comprehensive schools** to serve a local area and cater for students of all abilities with more of a focus on *equality of outcome*.

However, many educationalists and especially those from the **new right** argued that comprehensive schools did not cater well enough for the more or the less able and tended to teach to the middle of the ability range. After being elected in 1970, the Conservatives opposed the comprehensive programme and allowed the continued existence of some grammar schools. The co-existence of comprehensives and grammar schools continues to this day. From the mid-1970s onwards, there was increased criticism of comprehensive schools. Some believed that schools and teachers were given too much choice in what they taught, how they taught it and how children were assessed. This had created an education system where there were differences in the quality and quantity of education children were receiving. Furthermore, there was no way in which a child's progress could be measured nationally against other children in the same age group, as most children were only formally assessed for the first time at the age of 16. In addition, most young people left school at 16 and entered the workplace or were placed on youth training schemes (YTS) with little prospect of enhanced employment opportunities.

Carry out a survey of people who have experienced comprehensive schools. Choose a method and find out what their experiences were of the comprehensive education system. What were the advantages and disadvantages?

The 1988 Education Reform Act

The Education Reform Act of 1988 was the most far-reaching legislation since the 1944 Education Act. It was the 'jewel in the crown' of new right thinking and was a way for the state to achieve centralised control of the curriculum and assessment, so that progress and performance of schools could be monitored year on year while giving spending control to schools and choice to the parents on where they sent their children to school. This balance between state control and individual freedom ran through the new right thinking. This, it was argued, paved the way for education to become more businesslike, for the school system to become like a marketplace, and for the education system to become dominated by a culture of target-setting and a performance culture (Ball, 1990). This was a huge departure from the earlier, more liberal ideas, which believed that schooling should encourage free thinking and creativity, catering for individual needs. The Act introduced the following measures:

1   A National Curriculum – established for 5- to 16-year-olds in state schools. Originally, the core subjects of English, Mathematics and Science were to occupy 30–40 per cent of teaching time. Seven foundation subjects, including Technology and a foreign language (secondary schools) were to be taught. The list has since changed; it has largely been slimmed down, although the subject of Citizenship has been added.

Weblinks

From 2008, the Key Stage 3 National Curriculum has changed. Look at the subjects that are now included (see 'Websites', page ii).

2   Standard Attainment Tests (SATs) and league tables – tests in English, Mathematics and Science at the end of each Key Stage were introduced to check if the attainment targets had been reached by pupils. These results were published in league tables to encourage schools' effectiveness and to give parents enough information to enable them to make an informed choice of school. In 1993, the Office for Standards in Education (Ofsted) was set up to inspect schools in England and Wales. Its reports provided further information for the assessment of schools.

3   Grant-maintained (Opt-out) schools – state schools were allowed to opt out of local authority control if enough parents voted to support this move. These grant-maintained schools were funded directly by central government. The idea was to free schools to specialise in particular subjects or types of students, with the aim of offering diversity and choice for parents and encouraging schools to compete against each other in the educational marketplace.

4   City Technology colleges – located in inner-city deprived areas and funded by central government and private industry with the aim of bringing more IT and links with business into their curricula.

5   Local Management of Schools – more power was given to head teachers and governors in the way a school spends its money, thus restricting the influence of local education authorities.

6   Open enrolment – parents were given the right to send their children to the school of their choice. This would encourage schools to compete and improve their results, arguably creating a sense of **parentocracy**.

7   Formula funding – the financing of schools was largely based on the number of students on roll. This was intended to reward successful schools which attracted large numbers of pupils, while giving less successful schools an incentive to improve.

1   Table 2.1 describes the education system pre-1988. Using the information above, draw up a similar table for the post-1988 education system.

If you know anyone who went to school before 1988, ask them their views on what changed in 1988.

	Pre-1988 Education Act
Curriculum	Schools could decide what subjects they taught, although all would offer the core subjects.
Assessment	Only at 16, through O Levels for the more able or CSEs for the less able. A Levels were taken only by a minority of students and few post-16 vocational courses were available. There were no league tables, so parents had no way of comparing schools' performance.
School funding	All funding came from local education authorities, which played a large role in determining how individual schools spent their allocated money.
Specialist schools	There were no specialisms, other than grammar schools for the most able, or private schools for those who could afford them or were awarded grants.
Parental choice	There was no parental choice: children attended the school in their local area, unless their parents paid for private education or they passed the 11+ and went to a grammar school.

Table 2.1: The education system before the 1988 Education Act

2   Taking each feature of the 1988 Education Reform Act in turn from Table 2.1, explain how it contributed to either promoting fairness and democracy and/or employability and economic efficiency.

3   Can you match each of the criticisms listed in Figure 2.1 to a specific aspect of the 1988 Education Reform Act?

KEEPING DETAILED PROGRESS RECORDS OF EACH CHILD AT EACH KEY STAGE TAKES TIME AWAY FROM CLASSROOM TEACHING AND LESSON PREPARATION.

TEST RESULTS COULD LEAD TO CHILDREN BEING LABELLED AS HAVING MORE, OR LESS, POTENTIAL FROM AN EARLY AGE, WHICH COULD BE DIVISIVE.

PRESSURE FROM LEAGUE TABLE PERFORMANCE MIGHT MEAN THAT SCHOOLS TRY TO SELECT MORE ABLE STUDENTS; THIS IS AGAINST THE COMPREHENSIVE PRINCIPLE.

AT KEY STAGE 4, ATTENTION WAS FOCUSED ON THE '5A*-C' PUPILS; VERY HIGH- AND VERY LOW- ACHIEVING PUPILS WERE NEGLECTED (GILLBORN AND YOUDELL 2000).

SOME PARENTS STILL HAVE MORE CHOICE THAN OTHERS AND CHILDREN FROM THE MIDDLE CLASS ARE MORE ABLE TO 'CHOOSE' BETTER SCHOOLS.

AN LEA IS LESS ABLE TO ACHIEVE BALANCED PLANNING IF MANY SCHOOLS IN THE AREA OPT OUT OF ITS CONTROL.

EDUCATION HAS BECOME MARKETISED, WHICH MEANS THAT A MATERIALISTIC, COMPETITIVE ATMOSPHERE PREVAILS AND EDUCATIONAL PRINCIPLES ARE INCREASINGLY FORGOTTEN (BALL, 1990).

Figure 2.1

The structure and organisation of education since 1988

Many of the changes introduced in the 1988 Education Reform Act have continued to the present day and you will be able to recognise many of the features which have been discussed. The National Curriculum, testing, league tables and Ofsted remain key features of the current education system, but there have also been new developments in both its structure and organisation. Current educational policy is discussed in more detail in section v, but the main changes are listed briefly below.

Changes to post-16 education

Changes to post-16 education began with Curriculum 2000, which was an attempt to introduce a broader range of A Levels and introduce a new AS Level qualification. In addition, key skills qualifications in communication, IT and number aimed to ensure that students continued to develop the basic skills valued by employers. In 2008, further changes were made to A Levels with the reduction from six to four units, elimination of coursework in many subjects, the introduction of the extended project and the introduction of an A* grade. A new diploma is also being introduced from 2009 (see below – The Tomlinson Report).

The Tomlinson Report 2004

The government adviser Mike Tomlinson recommended a major overhaul to the system of 14–19 education. The main proposal was the

Figure 2.2: Breakfast clubs were set up with the aim of helping to improve children's performance at school

abolition of GCSEs, A Levels and vocational qualifications, to be replaced by a diploma accessible at four levels. Students would specialise in academic or vocational subjects or a combination, but those choosing a vocational route would spend some time with training providers outside the school environment. The intention was to implement the Tomlinson proposals over a decade and new diplomas for 14- to 19-year-olds are being offered from 2009 in five areas including Construction and the Built Environment, Creative and Media, and Engineering. However, there is currently no plan to abolish A Levels, so Tomlinson's recommendations are not being implemented.

Education Action Zones (EAZs) and Excellence in Cities (EiC)

From 1998, additional funding was given to disadvantaged areas to set up breakfast clubs, homework clubs, summer literacy and numeracy schemes, and to pay for a range of extra-curricular activities in response to locally identified needs. Some schemes are sponsored by industry as well as by central government.

The more recent EiCs programme steadily replaced EAZs. It aimed to improve attainment levels of pupils from low-income backgrounds. The main initiatives of EiC were special programmes for gifted pupils, city learning centres with IT facilities, learning mentors and low-cost leasing for home computers.

Activity 6

1   What educational benefits do you think children particpating in EiC programmes receive?

2   Can you think of any criticisms of the scheme?

Activity 7

1   Carry out some research into the differences between state and private schools. Consider factors such as cost, facilities, curriculum, exam results and the culture/ethos of the school. You may want to investigate aspects of the **hidden curriculum** and the formal curriculum (for a discussion of the hidden curriculum, see page 58).

2   You could debate the proposal that 'Private education should be abolished'. Prepare and present an argument to support or refute this view.

Different types of schools and their purpose in society

As the 'pause for thought' section on page 48 pointed out, you have experienced at least two different types of schools and you may even have found yourself thinking about the purpose of education. This section will consider the various types of school and their purpose.

1   Private schools

Private, or fee-paying, schools have been a permanent feature of the British education system. Today, around seven per cent of the school population are educated at these independent schools, which are attended largely by the children of wealthy upper-middle- and upper-class parents. The public schools are a small group of independent schools belonging to what is called the 'Headmasters' Conference'; these are long-established private schools such as Eton, Harrow and Rugby, which charge thousands of pounds a year. Today, the state provides free education for all in an attempt to create a **meritocracy**, but the existence of private schools is seen by some sociologists as a way of passing on privilege. This view is rejected by the new right, who see public schools as an important aspect of choice and parentocracy in our society.

2   Faith schools

There are over 7000 faith primary and secondary schools in England and Wales, the vast majority of which are Church of England or Roman Catholic. Tony Blair's New Labour government actively encouraged the establishment of new faith schools in areas where there is clear local agreement, as they believed that they improve educational standards. A previous education secretary, David Blunkett, said he wanted to 'bottle' the ethos of faith schools which, he argued, contributes to edcuational success. Faith schools are publicly funded; the state pays 85 per cent of capital costs and the government says it is considering raising this to 90 per cent; it also pays the teachers. All faith schools have to teach the National Curriculum. For religious education, around 57 per cent of faith schools (voluntary-aided) teach their own faith. The remaining 43 per cent (voluntary-controlled or foundation schools) teach the locally agreed religious education syllabus, which has a more multi-ethnic approach.

Admissions policy is determined by the school governors, but in many cases the local education authority is also involved. A school can insist that children come from a particular faith background, but it is bound by the Race Relations Act. Popular schools may insist on proof of baptism and regular church attendance. The Church of England urges schools to take account of the local community and make sure that wealthier parents from outside the area do not push out local people. A report by Lord Dearing for the church suggests that some places should be reserved for children of other faiths and of no faith. However, this decision rests with the governors.

Activity 8

Research the debates around faith schools. Focus on debates around admission policies and equality of opportunity, divisive communities and religious segregation. Write a summary in four bullet points, summarising the criticisms levelled against faith schools.

3 Specialist schools and city academies

Specialist schools receive extra funding for giving priority to a particular subject and involving other schools in projects relating to it, for example a school could become a specialist language college, a technology college or a performing-arts specialist. City academies are publicly funded schools, to which private sponsors contribute financially in exchange for a say in the curriculum, ethos and staffing. They are encouraged to specialise, so they are allowed to select up to 10 per cent of students with aptitude for the specialist subject. They have sometimes replaced 'failing' comprehensive schools in disadvantaged areas and have met with a mixed reception. Supporters argue that the academies cater for local communities and a large proportion of children receive free school meals (a measure of deprivation). Local stakeholders also feel a sense of hope when a failing school is closed and a new academy is built. However, critics argue that once the academies are oversubscribed, they start selecting students on ability to boost their results. Other critics are concerned about the influence of sponsors. For example, the evangelical Christian Sir Peter Vardy sponsors an adademy in Gateshead which teaches creationism alongside evolutionary theory in science lessons (Tomlinson, 2005).

Section summary

Use the following words to write a paragraph explaining the key themes of this section.

- Equality of opportunity
- Equality of outcome
- Meritocracy
- Parentocracy
- Marketisation

Stretch and Challenge Activity

Apply some of the concepts you have learnt about in this section to your own educational establishment. Can you find examples of the hidden curriculum at work? In what ways does it affect students? Is there evidence of equality of opportunity? Carry out some interviews with teachers on their views of equality of opportunity in school/college.

Exam practice

1   Outline and assess the view that the existence of different types of schools helps to create a more meritocratic education system. (50 marks)

2   Outline and assess the impact of the 1988 Education Reform Act. (50 marks)

(ii) The role and function of education in society

Pause for thought

- Should education be used to benefit certain social groups?

- Do all schools teach the same sorts of things?

- Should education help to create unique and special individuals?

- Should racist students be excluded from school?

There are many debates amongst sociologists about the role of education. Some focus on how the system operates at the moment, while others focus on what more education should do (we will look at the suggestions for educational change later). Many of the debates go to the heart of power and control, about who has power and how far they can use it to control others, and who benefits from the use of power.

This section will consider the different theoretical approaches to the role and purpose of education.

Functionalism

Functionalist writers argue that education is a positive force in today's society, and that it benefits both individuals and society as a whole. They believe this because they think that all social structures must make a positive contribution to the other parts of the social system and that individuals are relatively powerless against the pressures that society can place on them. They argue that formal education developed out of the needs of modern societies. There are four key functionalist writers who argue that education plays a positive role, the first of these is Durkheim (1925).

Durkheim argued that education had a key role in modern societies, which had developed from traditional societies in which institutions like the church and family could help to create a moral order that would control crime and deviance. However, as people began to become geographically mobile, societies were less likely to be bound together by the power of these institutions, and so the education system must ensure that everyone has similar norms and values. This is what Durkheim described as cultural homogeneity. Societies depend on shared values for their survival; if people value different things they will clash, social breakdown will occur and both individuals and society as a whole will suffer as a result. Education is necessary to create commitment to society and to control each individual's selfish desires. People are happiest when they share common interests; they can also cooperate much more successfully. Durkheim thus saw education as a key institution in secondary socialisation. In essence, the function of education is to create social harmony.

Durkheim believed that the most important subject within the school curriculum was History, because it gives individuals a sense of shared interests and belonging. It gives them a common identity and a sense that they are part of a community; it creates social solidarity. Thus, part of British history are the events of 1066, 1918, 1944 and 1966 (ask a football fan about the last one). The dates, and figures from the past, such as Churchill, come to represent some special characteristics of 'Britishness'. The power of this sentiment can be felt at times of national sporting success, or failure, when the team's achievements become ours: it is our team which has won or lost; it is our team which makes us cry or shout for joy. These emotional responses reflect our commitment to something greater than ourselves, and this is only possible because education has given us this commitment. In a sense, it is worth considering the teaching of Citizenship in schools as a Durkheimian project to create a moral understanding and to understand the nature of society.

Durkheim also believed that schools act as a social microcosm: they act like smaller versions of society. In education we can learn to mix with others; this is a vital skill, as in the modern world we frequently need to interact with people who are new to us. We must learn to socialise beyond the family, as we move from one place to another. In addition, education is where individuals learn to obey and conform to the social rules. Children need to be disciplined and to be punished if they disobey. Punishment must not be arbitrary, however, as children have to understand the reasons for it. They also have to understand that rules exist for everyone's benefit and that they should control their urges for the benefit of everyone.

Activity 9

In groups, discuss whether schools should have the right to ban students who come into school with dyed Mohican haircuts or flout the uniform rules.

Another role of education for Durkheim is the creation of a skilled workforce. A pre-industrial economy needs relatively unskilled workers. Parents in such an economy can teach their children what they need to know, for example basic agricultural skills like milking cows or sowing crops. There is no need for formal education. However, modern societies are more demanding: there are many more tasks and those tasks are much more complex. This means that numerate and literate workers have to be trained by teachers and the role of education is to create these workers.

Parsons (1961) argued that the school was a vital institution in modern societies, because modern societies are organised on meritocratic principles. Individuals are treated equally by the education system, regardless of their background, and what they achieve is a result of their own efforts rather than parental privilege. Students from different backgrounds receive the same teaching and materials, and the role of education is to help foster equality of opportunity. In addition to this the school helps to transmit the values of achievement and equality of opportunity. This is important because to prevent disorder everyone (even the

poor) needs to feel that the system is just and legitimate. Thus the education system has a key role in creating a **value consensus** in society. The creation of a value consensus can be seen every day in US schools, where individuals from a variety of backgrounds pledge an oath of allegiance to the flag.

Another aspect of Parsons' argument is that education must ensure that there is effective role allocation. In other words, the school system must ensure that occupations are filled by those most suited to them. This argument was also developed by Davis and Moore (1945). They believed that it was possible to identify the functionally most important occupations in society, and that education should select the talented and allocate them to the most important positions. This would benefit everyone, including the less talented, since the social system would be able to progress as it would be led by the best. Those who were sick would be treated by talented doctors, and businesses would be able to compete, ensuring jobs and prosperity.

Overall it is clear that functionalism offers the idea that the education system has three central functions:

◆ the transmission and creation of a common culture

◆ the transmission of important skills for the economy

◆ the creation of a meritocratic social order.

An evaluation of the functionalist view

Functionalism has helped to show that education is connected to the economy and that it has an effect on society. However, it has also received a number of criticisms.

1 Functionalist writers assume that individuals will passively respond to the education system. They do not recognise that pupils may develop a separate set of ideas from those taught by the education system. Pupils smoke, play truant and do not hand in homework, despite the demands placed on them by the education system. (The idea of anti-school subcultures is dealt with later.)

2 Functionalist writers argue that education transmits a common set of values, but we

must question whether there is a common set of values in contemporary society. As you will see, there are Marxist and feminist writers who would argue that these values are an imposition on people, they are a form of brainwashing which suits powerful groups.

3   There is a great deal of evidence to suggest that the education system is not meritocratic. There are vast differences in attainment between class, gender and ethnic groups, and critics would argue that education selects and allocates on the basis of background rather than ability.

The desirability of a meritocratic order is questioned by those who believe that in a meritocracy those at the bottom are constantly engaged in a battle to reach the top and compete against those at the top. Those at the top are constantly looking over their shoulders for the competition from below. This is not a happy and harmonious society and causes alienation and psychological trauma.

Marxism

Marxists adopt an approach to education which emphasises the way in which education serves the interests of the ruling class. Marxists believe that the ruling class exploits the proletariat and that education helps in this process by helping the ruling class pass on wealth and privilege and also by justifying the vast inequalities that develop under capitalism. This approach can be seen in the work of Bowles and Gintis (1976).

Bowles and Gintis believe that education has a number of important roles. They begin by arguing that education has a close correspondence to work. In particular, the education system must produce a subservient workforce that will work long hours for little pay. It is a workforce which, when told to jump by the boss, will simply ask: 'How high?' Education is able to achieve this because alongside the formal curriculum there is a hidden curriculum. This is a set of values and habits that the schools teach by the way they are organised. The hidden curriculum has many facets.

◆   Schools teach a respect for hierarchy and authority. When teachers walk into a room many schools expect students to stand up, teachers tell students what they will be

studying and decide on the way lessons are organised. This mirrors the world of work where workers have to defer to the authority of the employer.

◆   The education system also teaches workers to accept motivation through external reward. Students are taught that they should study not for the joy of learning but for exam certificates. They come to accept that school is boring and to be motivated by extrinsic rewards – rewards from an external source. This mirrors the world of work, because capitalist employment is repetitive and boring. Workers need to learn to accept that they should accept the reward of the pay packet rather than the joy of the job itself.

◆   Students also develop a passive and dependent personality as a result of the hidden curriculum. High grades are given to those who are punctual and to those who persevere, rather than to those who are independent and free thinkers.

◆   Students also learn to accept that they should only be responsible for a small part of the production process. This allows the owner to simplify tasks and reduces the power of the worker. In turn this also means that workers can easily be replaced and their ability to bargain for higher wages is vastly reduced. The school deliberately fragments subjects into categories like History, Science, Art and so on. It is perfectly possible to develop a common theme to the subjects studied in schools, but this does not happen and knowledge becomes fragmented as work is fragmented. Students learn to accept this fragmentation.

It must be remembered that this is an education for the working class. Members of the ruling class experience a very different form of education. They are trained for leadership and control; they are groomed for the positions of power which they will occupy as they become older.

Weblink
There is a good source of information on public schools on the internet (see 'Websites', page ii).

Education has another role, connected to the reproduction and legitimation of inequality. This is illustrated by Bowles and Gintis' findings that IQ has little connection to educational attainment. The most important factor in determining educational success is parental background. As you will see in section iii, students from poorer backgrounds face many obstacles to success. In addition to this, Bowles and Gintis found that IQ did not significantly affect earnings and occupation. The most significant factor in determining a person's position in the labour market was their class background. In other words, education did not create a meritocratic system, instead it maintained inequality and privilege. There is reproduction of inequality as the wealthy are able to pass on their wealth to their children (normally male) and the poor remain poor. The class system is reborn generation after generation and meritocracy is a myth. However, while the system maintains inequality it also justifies it by creating the illusion that everyone has an equal chance, the same opportunity. Everyone appears to have the same teachers and textbooks, and they all take the same exams. This means that poor people who fail believe that their failure is their own fault, and that the rich deserve their wealth, since they have worked harder and are smarter. However, this belief is an ideological one. It means that workers accept poor pay while capitalists can enjoy great wealth. In a sense the education system individualises failure and makes the inequalities appear natural and just. Vast inequalities are justified and maintained by the education system, which is a gigantic myth-making machine.

The argument that education benefits the ruling class is also developed by Bourdieu (1973), who believes that education helps to maintain the wealth of the ruling class by ensuring the educational success of the wealthy. He argues that the ruling class possess **cultural capital** – the values, knowledge and skills of the ruling class. The education system is based on cultural capital as it tests the values and knowledge of the ruling class and teachers use language that is familiar to the ruling class rather than the working class. The system assumes prior knowledge, the knowledge of the ruling class. Working-class culture is devalued by the education system and the proletariat will never be able to compete in the educational race. The children of the wealthy will always win and therefore will gain the power and wealth of their parents. Middle-class students will do better than working-class students because

their culture is closer to the ruling class. In his later work Bourdieu develops the idea of **habitus** – the cultural environment that each of the different classes inhabits. They develop different ideas about common sense and this affects their views about what is likely to happen to them in the future. Common sense refers to the way in which people see the world, what they think is acceptable or not acceptable and what is possible or not possible. This affects the decisions they make within education. It also shows in the development of different class tastes. These different tastes in art, literature, music and other aspects of culture will affect education because they will affect teachers' judgements about students.

Boudon (1974) argues that there is much greater pressure on middle-class students to succeed. They risk social demotion and will lose friends if they are demoted, whereas working-class students are more likely to lose contact with their friends if they are successful. It costs working-class students to choose success, and thus their cultural position means that they will be much more likely to fail; they are much less likely than middle-class students to choose higher education.

An evaluation of the Marxist view

Marxism has been useful in pointing to the ways in which education can be used to benefit some groups rather than others. In this sense it acts as a useful alternative to functionalist notions that education helps everyone equally. However, there are a number of problems with the Marxist view.

1   Marxism has a narrow focus that concentrates on class inequalities. It is limited in its focus on gender and ethnic inequalities and has little to say about the reasons for underachievement related to gender or ethnicity. In addition it is limited in exploring the ways in which education may promote ideologies that may disadvantage groups other than class.

2   Marxists tend to take a 'mug and jug' approach to education. They see students as passively waiting to be filled by capitalist ideology. The capitalists are the jug and the students the mug. However, students may not believe the ideologies that are presented to them, and they may reject the controls placed on them.

3   Many aspects of school promote critical students. Over the last few years Critical

Thinking has been introduced as a subject area to help students look at arguments and beliefs in a critical manner. Many other subjects also show that capitalism has negative effects, for example in Geography, students are likely to learn about global warming. In a world where capitalists control the curriculum it is difficult to imagine a justification for Sociology and you may have encountered teachers with left-wing views that make you challenge the official views given to you at other times.

Social democracy

The social democratic view of education was particularly significant during the 1960s. It has declined in authority but is still a significant influence on the thinking of the major parties. The key themes of social democracy are a desire for meritocracy, but with a recognition that the system as it stands is unable to deliver. Unlike Marxists, social democrats believe that it is possible to work within capitalism to create a fairer system and that democratic governments can work in the interests of those who elect them rather than the capitalist class. They would also argue that some inequality of outcome is desirable and inevitable. This is because they believe that some people are naturally more talented and intelligent than others. Social democrats like Halsey argued that the grammar-school system disadvantaged working-class

Emile Gintis is a confused young man. Look at the ideas he is developing inside his head. Help him by creating a table with the two headings below to sort his ideas into categories.

Functionalism	Marxism

U3
2

Sociology of education

children. The 11+ exam tested middle-class culture and falsely labelled working-class children as less intelligent; this label was believed by the working class and then acted on. Social democrats believed that the tripartite system of education needed to be abolished and replaced by the comprehensive system, where everyone would receive the same opportunities and working-class children and middle-class children could mix. Today there are just 162 grammar schools. Social democrats would agree with functionalists who argue that education has a key role in creating a skilled workforce. Creating a meritocracy would release more talent into society and the economy could compete with economies in the rest of the world. In addition the movement away from manufacturing industry and relatively unskilled jobs means that workers need to be trained for white-collar occupations, and education has a key role in ensuring the competitiveness of the British economy.

An evaluation of social democracy

1   While the education system has been transformed, inequality of opportunity remains. Many more students are gaining better and better results, but the gap between the attainment of the rich and the poor remains as fixed as it was in the 1960s. Changing education has not created a meritocracy and the social democrats' initial focus on the education system as the source of inequality seems misplaced. Today, social democrats focus on modifying social and economic inequalities in the wider society rather than on changing the education system.

2   The belief in the need for vocational education indicates a shift in the direction of education away from knowledge to work-based skills. Many governments are convinced that education is the major route for maintaining the UK's competitive edge in the world. However, there are also concerns that we may be over-educating the population. There are many unemployed graduates and Switzerland, for example, spends less money on education than other countries, yet it is one of the richest (Woolf, 2002). The link between high levels of education and economic success is not an inevitable one on either an individual or society-wide level.

Interactionism

Interactionist theories of education move our attention from the impact of society, the needs of the ruling class or the needs of the economic system towards looking at what goes on inside education. As you will see in the section on differential educational achievement (pages 64–79), many studies suggest that an understanding of what goes on inside schools is important for understanding behaviour and attainment in the school. The central theme of interactionist work is the idea of the self. Interactionists argue that we hold ideas about ourselves and that these ideas affect our behaviour.

As interactionism is a micro-theory, interactionists are not focused on the effect that education has on other institutions. They want to know how individuals shape and are shaped by the education system. The key to understanding how individuals make sense of the world is to understand the meanings they hold about it. A meaning is an understanding that we hold about the world and those in it, it is our view of ourselves and it exists in our consciousness and thoughts. Thus we are not simply products of the social system but active individuals with our own thoughts and feelings. We do not passively react to what we encounter: we think, we are more than just rocks and atoms.

U3

2

Sociology of education

Activity 11

If you wanted to find out what students and teachers thought about education and what went on in schools, what methods do you think interactionists would favour and why do you think they would use these methods? Explain two possible criticisms of these methods.

Becker (1977) argued that teachers develop an image of each of their students in a very short period of time. This is based on the student's initial appearance and is built up within the first five minutes. It includes ideas about a student's ability and behaviour which may be completely false, but the assumptions are made. Becker argues that some students are defined as 'ideal', because they closely resemble the teacher's middle-class view of what the perfect student is like. This image becomes a **label,** a definition of that student. There are a variety of responses to this label. Interactionists have been associated with the idea of the self-fulfilling prophecy, as developed by Rosenthal and Jacobsen (1968), who argue that a teacher makes a prediction about a student and that this prediction becomes true only *because of* the initial prediction. In effect, the student internalises the label, they come to believe it. However, interactionists may point to a variety of other responses to labelling, such as rejecting the label. In addition, these labels are negotiable and can thus be changed. We shall examine these ideas in the section on differential educational achievement (pages 64–79).

An evaluation of the interactionist view

Interactionism has brought attention to what goes on inside the classroom and helped to provide some practical suggestions for improving the practice of teachers and schools. However, there are a number of problems with the interactionist arguments.

1   By focusing on the school, interactionists ignore the wider social context. Who controls the school and what goes on inside it? What is the impact of material and cultural deprivation?

2   Many interactionist studies are qualitative in nature, they are small-scale and subjective.

3   Interactionism has been accused of determinism, as it appears that students cannot escape the self-fulfilling prophecy. However, this is based on a misunderstanding of interactionism. Following the self-fulfilling prophecy is one possible reaction to being labelled, but as individuals they believe are active interactionists would be keen to point out, there are a variety of other possible reactions.

New right

The new right combine two different elements and their views often pull in contradictory ways. The neo-liberal tradition believes that individuals are rational and should be allowed to make decisions about their own futures. The neo-conservatives believe that people need guidance and that their choices need to be limited. These two opposing elements are clearly seen within new right views on education.

In some ways the new right agree with the functionalist position in that they argue that some people are naturally more able than others, in the same way that some are born faster, some slower, some more intelligent and some less intelligent. They believe that education should create a meritocratic social order where the best will prosper. This is why many recent prime ministers have talked of a classless society. They also argue that the education system should help to create a united and integrated society by creating a common national culture and identity. Thus, a key role of education is to socialise. However, the new right also believe that the current education system is failing to achieve these goals and needs to be transformed. There are two key reasons for this. The first is that education is a state monopoly and as such is likely to become inefficient. There is no competitive edge and no reason to improve. They do not need to take into account the demands of the consumers (parents and children) in the provision of their service (education). Indeed, the education system becomes dominated by, in the words of one ex-minister, a secret garden. Few people can get into the garden, few people control education. In fact it is those who produce education who come to dominate the decision-making process. They dominate it in their own interests and not the interests of the parents and children. For many in the new right, the solution is to break down the walls of the garden and unleash the power of the market: let the consumer decide what constitutes appropriate education. In other words, the new right want to take power away from the state bureaucrats and teachers and give it back to parents and create a parentocracy. This idea will be looked at in the section on education policy (pages 83–87).

The new right are also concerned that education has moved too far in the direction of trying to create equality, and that the focus should be on standards. This was the motivating force behind the 1988 Education Act. At this point it is worth noting that the standards agenda was seen to run in conjunction with market forces. The creation of an educational market where parents would have the power to choose which school their child would attend, would force schools to raise their standards and focus on raising attainment. The contradictory forces in the new right can also be seen in their policy, as they showed a distrust of local power and parental power by imposing a National Curriculum.

A final effect of the educational elite's control over education is that a primary purpose of education is lost. In particular, the new right argue that many of the UK's economic problems stem from a narrow focus on academic education and knowledge for its own sake. They argue that in a global economy the UK needs a skilled workforce that has the essential skills to enable it to compete with other countries. Without this, businesses will not be able to win contracts, companies will suffer and jobs will be lost. In effect, schools should have a greater focus on work-based skills and less of a focus on raising cultural awareness. However, again there are those in the new right, who from a neo-conservative position would desire greater teaching of classic literature and British History.

An evaluation of the new right view

The new right have been very influential and their policy agenda has had an impact. Indeed, it has been adopted by New Labour in many but not all respects. However, it has also received a great deal of criticism.

1   The new right stress the importance of market forces, but as we shall see, the operation of the market has the effect of disadvantaging working-class students. This is against the meritocratic dreams of their classless society. It also acts to limit the pool of talent available to a competitive economy.

2   The idea that ability is a fixed and natural biological characteristic is questionable. It ignores the impact of material, cultural or educational process that may alter a person's ability.

Section summary

The main theories to consider in this section are functionalism, Marxism, interactionism, social democracy, new right.

Use the following words to write a paragraph explaining the key themes of this section.

- Meritocracy
- Labelling
- Hidden curriculum
- Parentocracy
- Value consensus

Stretch and Challenge Activity

Many of the theories emphasise the role of education in creating social cohesion. Explain why some people might find that this idea threatens an individual and democratic society, and discuss whether or not you agree with their fears.

Given the diversity of schooling in the UK (described in section i) today, do you believe it is possible to create theories about the whole of the education system?

Exam practice

1   Outline and assess functionalist theories of the role of education in society. (50 marks)

2   Outline and assess the view that the role of the education system is to justify and reproduce social inequalities. (50 marks)

(iii) Differential educational achievement

Pause for thought

- Do you think that the education system should treat everyone the same, regardless of their background?

- Did anything apart from natural intelligence affect your AS grades?

- How far does misbehaviour in school stem from the failure of the school?

Differential educational attainment refers to the significant differences in educational success and failure. Your success may appear to be the result of your hard work and natural ability and the failure of others may be the result of their own shortcomings, however, this misses an important sociological truth, which is that there are patterns to success and failure. Individuals may think that their actions are the result of their own choices, but the data show that there are clear and significant differences between social groups. Some genetic explanations of success and failure might suggest that some people are born naturally more intelligent or hard-working.

However, the existence of these patterns suggests that an individual's DNA is not the most significant element in their attainment.

Attainment is greatly affected by a person's social characteristics. The other element to consider is that these patterns are subject to change. Social groups have had different patterns of attainment at different times. It would be difficult to argue that men or women have undergone a significant biological change over the last few decades, yet their examination results have. The change has occurred because of changes in society, not biology, and this would indicate that social

Figure 2.3: They may have won this race, but who will win the race for qualifications?

factors are more significant than biological ones. Sociologists agree that society is more important than biology in explaining behaviour.

However, the precise cause of differential attainment is the subject of considerable debate, and different sociologists will stress the importance of different elements. As you will see in the section on educational policy, many of these theories and the evidence have influenced governments. Gorard (2008) makes an interesting point about the statistics that many take at face value: they are based on judgements made by researchers and forms completed by people. Both these elements cause problems for accurately describing patterns of attainment. He develops an analysis of the figures for participation in higher education and argues that the figures are not straightforward, since there are problems such as:

◆ Where to position the social class of someone with parents in two separate classes?

◆ The census is only conducted every ten years, but is used to describe the population. This is inevitably an outdated measure of the composition of the population used to compare participation rates. Furthermore, not everyone answers the questions on class or class background.

◆ Different definitions of class are used by different agencies, for instance the census and UCAS use different definitions.

◆ With regards to ethnicity, the 'missing' category is the second largest group after white students. This category is larger than all other ethnic groups. ('Missing' refers to those unable or unwilling to categorise themselves by ethnic group.)

Thus, it is difficult to judge accurately from the statistics the extent of participation in education and by implication it is also difficult to accurately plot attainment rates between different groups. It is well worth bearing this in mind when you look at the statistics. Gorard argues that part of the changing patterns of participation may be affected by a willingness to complete forms rather than a real change, and that patterns of class attainment ignore the increasing numbers of middle-class families in relation to working-class families.

However, this argument has the implication that the statistics are nothing more than social constructs and that there is little we can say or do about real inequalities.

Education and class

Parental and family circumstances impact on GCSE attainment. In 2002, 77 per cent of children in Year 11 in England and Wales with parents in higher professional occupations gained five or more A*–C grade GCSEs. This was more than double the proportion for children with parents in routine occupations (32 per cent; Office for National Statistics).

Like attainment at school, participation in further or higher education is strongly influenced by social and economic background. In 2002, 87 per cent of 16-year-olds with parents in higher professional occupations were in full-time education. This compares with 60 per cent of those with parents in routine occupations, and 58 per cent with parents in lower supervisory occupations (Office for National Statistics).

One other important element to note about examination performance and class is that, while all exam results have improved, the difference between social classes in terms of relative attainment has not changed. In other words, although everyone is improving their qualifications, relatively, they are in the same position they were in before the improvement.

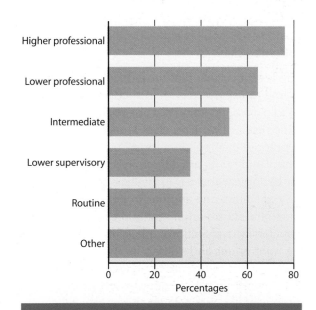

Figure 2.4: Exam results differ by social status: attainment of five or more GCSE grades A* to C: by parental NS-SEC, 2002, England and Wales (Source: Office for National Statistics)

An important study by the Sutton Trust in 2008 found that class differences in attainment were significant. They argued that many of the differences occurred as a result of factors in the early years of a child's life. If a student from a poor background made it into A Levels, their chances of obtaining a university place were the same as students from more affluent backgrounds. They did, however, also note that if a student from a private school had the same A Level results as a state-school pupil, they were more likely to gain a place in the more prestigious universities.

Activity 12

In groups, note down all the factors that you think influence attainment, apart from natural intelligence. Discuss your answers with the rest of the class.

Functionalism

Functionalists begin with the view that a meritocratic social order is desirable. Meritocracy is not just important on the grounds of fairness and equality. A social system that excludes the talented from the highest positions is an inefficient system, and a system that has the potential to degenerate into conflict due to ascribed status is difficult to defend. Thus, functionalists believe that education should create social mobility and allow those from the bottom to climb to the top.

However, it is clear that the working class are unable to achieve the same success as the middle class. Functionalists believe that this is the result of working-class families failing to prepare their children for school. As the school and home are interconnected (look at the biological analogy in your theory notes) they will affect one another. In essence, functionalists are arguing that the working-class family dysfunctions, it fails to transmit the right values and skills to its children. This is why functionalism has been associated with the concept of **cultural deprivation**. Culture is a way of life and includes things like values, norms and language. This theory argues that the working class lack these things and that as working-class children lack cultural support from

the home they will not succeed in school. Many studies have been used to support the general theory, however you should also note that the studies we will look at here are not specifically functionalist studies; they would tend to support the cultural deprivation argument.

Hyman (1967) argued that working-class families possessed a distinctive sub-culture that was passed on through the generations. While it was not true of all working-class families, Hyman argued that many members placed a limited value on education and gaining a high-status job such as a doctor or lawyer. This argument has similarities to Sugarman (1970) who argues that the working class develop a culture based on fatalism, immediate gratification, present-time orientation and collectivism. Working-class jobs are monotonous and boring; workers have no control over their lives as they are told what to do and when to do it. They develop a culture in response to these jobs; they feel they have no control and become fatalistic; they develop immediate gratification (seek pleasures now rather than wait for later rewards), they live in the present and they are loyal to their group. Middle-class professions, however, encourage workers to plan for the future (future-time orientation and deferred gratification) and also emphasise individualism where people see themselves as more independent. This cultural difference explains differential attainment as schools are based on middle-class values rather than working-class values.

One of the most significant pieces of research to have been conducted in this area is Douglas's longitudinal study *The Home and the School* (1964). It clearly showed that IQ was not the significant factor in educational success and failure. Rather home background was, as working-class children left school earlier and with fewer qualifications. Douglas argued that the single most important factor was parents' interest in their child's education, and that middle-class parents were much more likely to talk to their children about education, provide them with a range of activities and attend parents' evenings. Feinstein conducted a similar study in 2003 and found similar results in that parental interest and support were crucial in providing an environment where children could be motivated and effectively disciplined.

Activity 13

Hyman and Sugarman used interviews and questionnaires to find out about the values and norms of the classes. Why might these data be flawed?

Douglas also used a longitudinal study. What are the problems with this method?

Figure 2.5: Are all children going to be as confused as this one?

One of the most significant arguments used to support the theory of cultural deprivation is that of Bernstein (1961). He argues that his theory is one of difference rather than deprivation, but his study has been used to support the arguments of the cultural deprivation theorists. He argues that there are two types of language code or ways of speaking: the elaborated code and the restricted code. There are many differences between the two, but features of the codes include the following.

The elaborated code is full of complex sentences; there are explicit meanings (everything is explained) and a large vocabulary. The restricted code uses much shorter sentences; it relies on shared meanings and a more limited vocabulary. These language codes are learnt primarily in the home and middle-class students develop access to the elaborated code and the restricted code while the working class only develop access to the restricted code. It must be noted that middle-class students do learn the restricted code; they can speak it, whereas the working class can only use the restricted code.

Working-class students will be disadvantaged because the education system is based on the elaborated code. When they enter school they are spoken to in elaborated code, the books are written in elaborated code, and they are expected to give answers in class using the elaborated code. When they come to the end of education and are expected to write examination answers, they are expected to use elaborated code. Middle-class students can do all these things, whereas working-class students are disadvantaged and also feel uncomfortable in this environment. It is no surprise that working-class students fail when education is based on a linguistic system to which they do not have access.

An evaluation of functionalist views

The theme of cultural deprivation has been a powerful one. Functionalist and social democratic views have endorsed it. There have also been many policies based on the idea that some groups lack culture (you will examine programmes of compensatory education and other schemes later). However, this view is also subject to a great deal of criticism.

1   The theory is criticised for ignoring the impact of poverty on attainment. You will see later that a lack of money rather than values may be responsible for educational failure. In addition it could be argued that the values of the working class may be a product of their poverty. They may not value education because they have to earn money for their family, or they may recognise that few escape poverty and they may just be being realistic.

2   The theory also ignores the impact of the school. As we shall see, the school and what goes on inside the classroom may affect

working-class students negatively. Focusing on the home and the parents neatly sidesteps issues about the importance of teachers in affecting students' performance.

3   Many of the studies have a questionable methodology and findings. Douglas used attendance at parents' evenings to judge parental interest and commitment, but there may be material reasons for lack of attendance. Labov (1973) argues that black, poor students in Harlem have very complex language use and are capable of developing difficult ideas. He argued that differences in response from students may be a result of the different social characteristics of the researcher.

4   Labov's findings are also connected to the idea that there is a cultural difference rather than cultural deprivation: one way of speaking is not superior or inferior. We shall develop this idea when we examine theories of cultural capital.

5   The theory tends to emphasise the differences between the cultures. This is problematic because distinctions of class are notoriously difficult to judge. What is a working-class person and what is a middle-class person? Even if one could create objective categories, there are still problems because the cultural similarities between the classes may be greater than the differences.

Marxist views

Marxists tend to develop two distinct sets of arguments. The first relates to cultural factors while the second relates to material factors. Again, while the following arguments are employed by Marxists, it should be noted that many non-Marxists are willing to employ the concepts and ideas developed in this section of the book. Before you begin this section you should look again at the work of Bowles and Gintis (pages 58–59) to remind you of their arguments.

Marxists are critical of the functionalist view because they believe that the idea of cultural deprivation blames working-class people for their failure when the failure of the working class is connected to the operation of the capitalist system. This idea is developed by Bourdieu, who argues that the education system

is based on ruling-class culture. The ruling class have the power to define what is counted as knowledge within the education system. Thus, the education system is based on their knowledge and skills. It will test these things and this gives the ruling class an advantage, which begins when a child enters primary school and continues through the child's education. It ensures academic success and it also means that these children will occupy the top positions in society.

Education is not about creating a meritocracy; it is about transmitting privilege and wealth from one generation to another. This is the notion of cultural capital, that the culture of the ruling class can be turned into wealth and power. The working class are not culturally deprived; they do not lack values and norms; rather they are in a rigged race. We should look to those who have the power to control the race rather than the individual athletes, to explain failure.

This concept has been used by writers other than Marxists to provide reasons for the failure of the working class. Gewirtz et al. (1995) argue that a parent's cultural capital can explain attainment. They argue that there are three types of parent:

◆   Privileged skilled choosers. They know about the school system and have the time and money to support their child's education.

◆   Semi-skilled choosers. They are concerned for their child's education but lack awareness of how to choose the best schools.

◆   Disconnected choosers. They are concerned for their child but do not see their choice of school as being a determinant of educational success. They also lack the material resources to choose a good school.

The privileged skilled choosers are likely to be middle class. They have the cultural awareness and skills to enable them to make a choice and they also have the resources to get into that school. The implication of this study is clear. The more parents are given choice, the more middle-class students will become concentrated in what are thought to be the best schools, and the greater their academic success will be. The development of choice means that social class differences in education will increase. This idea is developed in the section on education policy (pages 83–87).

Sullivan (2001) also supports the theory of cultural capital. She argues that the school has a limited effect on the culture of the child. Rather, parental background is the most significant factor. Cultural capital is transmitted via things like reading classic books, quality newspapers and the type of television programmes watched: middle-class children are more likely to watch factual documentaries and arts review programmes. This enables the development of a more sophisticated vocabulary and ultimately examination success. Musical skills and knowledge were not deemed to be significant factors affecting GCSE performance. However, she is keen to point out that material factors are also highly significant.

While Werfhorst and Hofstede (2007) agree that cultural capital is a significant factor in explaining ability levels, they argue that it is important to draw on the work of Boudon to explain aspirations. They argue that students' choices about their education are dependent on the risks associated with downward mobility, and that while higher education has expanded, working-class students are less likely to continue than the middle-class students who risk social demotion if they do not. They describe this as the core of relative risk-aversion theory.

The second feature of the Marxists' argument is a stress on material factors. Again this is not an exclusively Marxist view; many social democrats would also subscribe to the view that poverty has an impact on attainment. Marxists believe that poverty is not accidental. The working class are in poverty because the ruling class, in their drive to increase their profits, will seek to pay workers as little as possible. Poverty occurs because people are paid too little. The results of poverty have been well documented and advocates of this view say that **material deprivation** rather than cultural deprivation is the cause of poor educational performance.

Smith and Noble (1995) argue that poverty means that parents are unable to afford school uniform, trips and things like computers. They are unable to afford housing in the catchment area of a good school.

Activity 14

In groups, use the following bullet points to develop the ways in which poverty links to educational failure. Develop your ideas in a presentation to the rest of the class. While you listen to others' presentations, try to think about how you would criticise each point they develop.

- The costs of free education (Bull). Think about things like music tuition.
- The impact of staying on after 16 (Heath).
- The impact of part-time jobs.
- The choice of schooling and the idea of selection by mortgage.
- Overcrowded and unsatisfactory housing.

Weblinks

You might like to get a feel for the latest campaign to address child poverty (see 'Websites', page ii). Pay close attention to the page entitled 'The facts'.

Figure 2.6: The ladder of opportunity is only used by some

An evaluation of Marxist views

The ideas of Marxism have influenced sociological thinking in education. The strength of their ideas can be seen in the adoption of some key ideas by other sociologists of a non-Marxist view. Ideas like cultural capital have become an accepted part of thinking about educational advantage. The idea that material deprivation is an influence on attainment has led governments to introduce **Education Maintenance Allowance (EMA)**. However, their ideas have also been subject to much criticism.

1   The idea that some groups are significantly deprived is strongly rejected by new right thinkers. They argue that in a period of growing affluence and the welfare state, poverty is an outdated concept and its consequences need not be damaging.

2   The idea that the ruling class control the education system is criticised by pluralists, who would argue that there are many influences on government policy, not least the electorate in a democratic state.

3   The focus on factors external to the education system and what happens inside the classroom means that the effect of teachers on their students is ignored. This idea is developed in the next section.

Interactionist views

You have already briefly examined the interactionist view of education in section ii, and we will now consider in more detail the ways in which schools may affect the attainment of working-class pupils. It is worth looking back at your notes on interactionism.

Activity 15

In pairs, develop an explanation of labelling and then present it to the rest of the class.

The idea of labelling is a powerful one. A key study that illustrates the power of the label is the self-fulfilling prophecy. Rosenthal and Jacobsen (1968) administered a test to a class and told teachers that one group of students was much more intelligent than the other; in fact they were no more or less able. However, when the researchers returned a year later, the students who had been labelled as 'spurters' had, generally, increased their test scores against the rest of the class. It is argued on the basis of this test that students will internalise teachers' labels of students. They assumed that teachers had reacted differently to students on the basis of the label that had been given to them.

What ethical issues are involved in dealing with school pupils and why may the issue of harm be significant? Why is the researcher's absence from the classroom a cause for concern in this particular piece of research?

Teachers' labels can have other effects. Keddie (1973) argues that the creation of teacher labels and perceptions of ability creates a different process from that of the internalisation of the label. She argues that in schools where streaming exists, working-class students are placed in lower streams and middle-class students are placed in higher streams. This was crucial because those in the lower streams were denied the knowledge which they needed to succeed; they were unable to gain access to the information that would produce success at the end of the course. It is possible to see this process at work in today's schools. In GCSE there is tiering of qualifications and some A Level courses such as Mathematics may demand a higher-tier GCSE. In effect, a pupil will be denied the opportunity to study this subject at a very early age and will not be taught the appropriate knowledge. Gillborn and Youdell (2001) argue that setting is based on teacher perception of ability and that middle-class students are placed in the top sets while working-class students find themselves in the lower sets and denied access to the knowledge they need to gain the top grades.

Activity 16

In groups, discuss whether it is good to classify someone as gifted and talented and provide a different type of education for them.

Cicourel and Kitsuse (1963) argue that this process affects the advice working-class students are given on what university and what course to apply for. They are given different advice about courses and careers, all based on their class background. Working-class students are classified negatively due to their clothes, language and demeanour.

Hargreaves (1967) argues that labelling can have a different effect. He argues that labelling students as worthless can result in anti-school sub-cultures. Those in the bottom streams, in his study, were multiple failures because they had failed the 11+ and had been placed in the lowest streams: they had been written off by the school; they had been denied status. In an attempt to overcome this lack of status they inverted the values of the school, turning its values upside down. Thus smoking, fighting, truancy were seen as badges of honour, and from being at the bottom they were suddenly at the top of the status hierarchy. Academic achievement was not on their list of priorities and educational failure as well as deviant behaviour was the result of the school and its actions.

An evaluation of interactionist views

Interactionism has had an impact on the way teachers have been trained and has brought an awareness of what happens inside the classroom. The new right also believe that good schools can create success in areas of deprivation and that schools make a difference. This is the justification for league tables. However, interactionism has also received a great deal of criticism.

1   The idea of a label is much disputed; it suggests that teachers do not know what they are doing. They have many years of training and experience and it may be that some children are much brighter than others. In other words, teachers' judgements may be facts.

2   Linked to the above it may be argued that performance at school is the result of the home rather than the school. Labelling ignores the impact of cultural and material factors. The new right would argue that a major reason for poor behaviour in schools (particularly amongst boys) is the growth of single-parenthood.

3   The idea of the label may be a partial one as it does not explain who controls the label. Focusing on one teacher's label does not explain why there are general patterns to the labels, why it is working-class pupils who are labelled as failures? We need to look at macro power structures to explain these patterns.

4   The idea of the self-fulfilling prophecy is too deterministic.

Gender and education

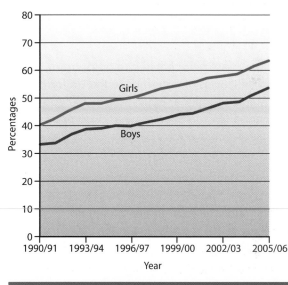

Figure 2.7: Students achieving five or more GCSE grades A*–C or equivalent: by sex (Source: Department for Children, Schools and Families)

Activity 17

So far, you have looked at the process of differential attainment through a focus on theory. Make a copy of the table below to restructure your awareness, placing studies or concepts in the appropriate spaces.

	The home	The school
Material factors		
Cultural factors		

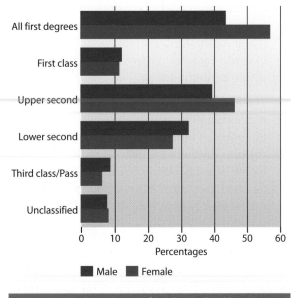

Figure 2.8: Achievement at first-degree level by sex: UK, 2005/06 (Source: Focus on Gender, Office for National Statistics)

On the whole, girls continue to outperform boys at all levels of education in the UK from Key Stage 1 to higher education. In 2005/06, 64 per cent of girls in their last year of compulsory education achieved five or more GCSE grades A* to C, compared with 54 per cent of boys.

Figures from the Universities and Colleges Admissions Service (UCAS) show that more women than men are entering full-time undergraduate courses: in autumn 2006, a total of 390,890 gained places, of whom 210,334 (53.8 per cent) were women.

Sociological explanations of gendered attainment

A variety of explanations have been put forward for the improvement in female attainment. For the feminist movement as a whole, it is a vindication of their campaign for equal treatment. This is particularly true of the liberal feminists who have consistently argued for the possibility of evolutionary change working within the existing institutions. However, it must be noted that the improvement in female attainment has not produced equality in earnings. Women still earn 80 per cent of what men earn and there is still a glass ceiling. Within education it is clear that subject choice is gendered and there are still boys' subjects and girls' subjects, but girls' subjects have a lower status.

In trying to explain the differences in attainment between boys and girls and the changes which have taken place over the last twenty years, sociologists have focused on two areas. The first is why girls have done well and the second is why boys have done badly. It is worth noting that the poor attainment of boys is relative. Boys are doing better than they were, and both genders' exam results have improved, but girls' improvement has been faster.

Girls' attainment has been dramatic and is clearly the result of social process rather than biological change. It supports the feminist view that biology is not destiny. A number of reasons have been put forward to explain the change.

One of these is a massive cultural change in the attitudes of girls. In a classic study in 1976, Sue Sharpe clearly showed that girls' priorities were love, marriage and children. She followed this up in 1994 with another study and found that girls' priorities were developing a career and supporting themselves financially. The rising divorce rate and their experiences of marital conflict in their own homes meant that girls placed less trust in the notion of the male as provider. They saw women making their own way in the labour market and achieving financial independence. The impact of equal opportunities legislation has meant that many career opportunities have opened up for women and many of these require qualifications. Girls who want to be lawyers need A Levels and degrees. There has also been a general shift in the economy towards service-sector jobs which are seen as requiring greater communication skills – the skills possessed by girls. The changed attitudes are part of a larger cultural shift which, liberal feminists would argue, has meant a decline in **patriarchal** attitudes. In the media there are more positive role models for girls to aspire to and girls now see a career as an option open to them. Mitsos and Browne (1998) argue that the improvement in rights for women and women's increasing self-esteem are the result of campaigns by the feminist movement. While many young women are unwilling to classify themselves as feminists, they are, without knowing it, the beneficiaries of the feminist movement. However, girls have not become too radicalised. There is also evidence of a 'bedroom culture' among girls, which means that girls are more likely to invite friends round to their houses and chat in their bedrooms. This encourages verbal skills which boys do not get the chance to develop.

In a survey of 1310 Year 5 pupils in 21 primary schools, Gray and McLellan (2006) found that at this early age pupils had gendered responses to school. Girls are more positive and enthusiastic about school than boys, who were more likely to be disengaged and disaffected. They did note, however, that it is too simplistic to see girls as pro-school and as boys as anti-school. A significant number of girls (9 per cent) were anti-school and some boys were pro-school. A significant number fitted into other categories such as 'moderately interested but easily bored' and 'committed but lacking self-esteem'. Gray and McLellan did not examine whether class or gender were significant factors in the emergence of these groups.

Activity 18

Gray and McLellan used a large-scale questionnaire of primary school pupils. What advantages would this method have over small-scale qualitative research? What problems might the researchers have in accessing this group and in the wording of questions? How might the issue of operationalising concepts be significant in this research?

However, it is not only changes within society as a whole that have raised female achievement. Schools have also changed and are no longer patriarchal institutions. It is argued that the introduction of coursework has benefited girls, because girls like to work in a methodical and organised way while boys are more disorganised. Coursework suits those who are organised and persistent. In addition to this a variety of initiatives have been introduced in schools, such as Girls into Science and Technology, which have produced changes in teaching to develop girls' attainment and participation. Teachers are more likely to see girls as more academic than boys, and this affects the way they react to girls. Teacher training from the 1970s has changed and teachers believe that it is important to develop girls in a way that would have been unthinkable a few years ago. It is also argued that many of the teaching materials have changed from the past. Examination questions, textbooks and classroom language have changed to include and recognise girls, so that girls now see education as an institution for them.

Activity 19

In groups, look at some modern textbooks and reading schemes for primary school children and compare them with books your parents may have used. You could ask your parents if they have any, or ask at a local primary school.

However, focusing on girls ignores the underperformance of boys. For some, the idea of boy's underperformance is a moral panic. Boys are doing well; they are not failing as their results have improved. It is also important to note that middle-class boys have continued to perform well. However, this does sidestep the issue of why girls have outperformed boys in recent years. A number of reasons are given for this.

There has been a reduction in manual work over the last twenty-five years. The employment opportunities for boys have reduced as opportunities for girls have increased. Working-class boys may see little point in working at school if there are few job opportunities when they leave. In addition Jackson (2006) argues that the threat of losing their traditional identities has led boys to develop laddish behaviour in an attempt to re-develop their sense of male identity. Another factor is that boys are more likely to overestimate their ability. This produces an overconfidence in boys which means that they will not work as hard as girls. Girls, on the other hand, feel less confident and work harder to overcome their anxieties. Boys are more likely to be socialised into activities that involve little talking, such as sport or computer games, and hence do not develop the same communication skills as girls.

According to the new right, boys are at much greater risk from the negative consequences of single parenthood; they often lack a strong disciplinarian (as 90 per cent of single-parent families are headed by a woman) and will not be forced to sit down to complete their school work. They also lack a male role model who goes out to work. In addition there is evidence which shows that boys perform better in families where fathers read to their children. Without a male role model, boys come to see reading as an activity performed by girls, and this adversely affects their educational performance. Another factor is that it has been argued that primary schools have become feminised: the majority of non-teaching and teaching staff are women; the parents who wait at the school gate are overwhelmingly women, and this can create the impression in a young boy's mind that education is a feminine environment. Educational success is for girls rather than for boys. Finally, boys are more likely to be seen as less able than girls. They are seen as more disruptive and teachers are more likely to expect more from girls.

Kane (2006) develops Willis's idea (1977) that working-class boys actively participate in creating their identities and in so doing come into conflict with the school. Willis argued, from a Marxist-influenced position, that the lads he studied partially penetrated capitalist ideology and did not simply accept the values transmitted by schools. They kicked back against the system but in so doing re-created the failure of their parents. In Kane's study of four schools in Scotland where heavy industry had all but finished, working-class boys were excluded for general and persistent disobedience. This was the result of different and not similar reasons. Some of the boys lacked self-control while others were very much in control of their own actions. It appears that all excluded boys are part of an oppositional subculture, but this may not be the case. Kane argued that some of the boys sought well-paid jobs, but because of a lack of knowledge about university and the financial burdens involved, none of them had considered it. They were actively responding to their situation in different ways. The higher rates of exclusion for boys are closely linked to the impact of class, as middle-class boys are less likely to be excluded.

Girls' subjects		Boys' subjects		Not gendered	
A Level*	Degree†	A Level	Degree	A Level	Degree
Biological sciences	Biosciences	ICT		Geography	Medicine and dentistry
Psychology	Social, economic and political sciences	Computer studies	Computer science	History	Agriculture
Communication studies	Library and information sciences	Maths	Maths	Business studies	Business and business admin
Media, film and television	Subjects allied to medicine	Physics	Physical sciences	Chemistry	Humanities
Home economics		Economics			Creative art and design
Foreign languages	Languages		Architecture, building and planning		
English and English literature	Education Teacher training		Engineering technology		

*Calculated from A Level entries 2002–3.
†Calculated from numbers studying for first degrees in 2003.

Table 2.2: Girls' and boys' subjects (Source: Higher Education Statistics Agency)

Gendered subject choice

Activity 20

Use Table 2.2 to describe what is meant by 'gendered subjects'. In groups, create a poster explaining the different types of pressures within schools and outside schools that lead to the creation of gendered subjects.

An evaluation of explanations of gendered attainment

The explanations of the different attainment of girls and boys have been useful in creating an awareness of the process at work in attainment. However, many feminists see the debate about male underachievement as a moral panic which deflects attention away from the continuing inequalities in subject choice, while others would argue that we need to focus on measures to improve the boys' attainment. There are also some specific criticisms of the explanations you have encountered.

1   Most jobs that women have are part-time and temporary. Typical examples are cleaning and catering. Women earn about 80 per cent of what men earn, all of which indicates that employment opportunities for women are limited. There is still a glass ceiling.

2   The effects of the changed media are questioned by radical feminists, who would argue that the media have not changed significantly. Lara Croft may be an action figure but she is ultimately fashioned by patriarchal ideologies of the body.

3   Primary schools may be feminine but the males who enter teaching dominate the top positions.

3   Factors like the introduction of coursework imply biological aspects of behaviour which many sociologists would be sceptical of. Biologists have yet to find a coursework gene.

5   Boys may develop anti-school sub-cultures but these are nothing new and they also tend to be working-class. Middle-class boys continue to perform well, suggesting that class may be more significant than gender.

Ethnicity and attainment

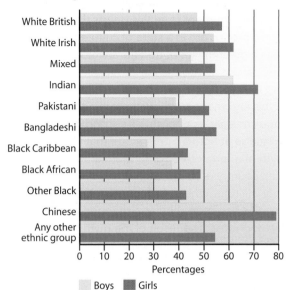

Figure 2.9: Students achieving 5 or more A*–C grades at GCSE/GNVQ: by sex and ethnic group, 2004, England (Source: Office for National Statistics)

Activity 21

Look at Figure 2.9.

1   Which two ethnic groups have the highest attainment?

2   Which two groups have the lowest attainment?

The patterns of attainment for ethnicity are complex. To simplify the patterns it is clear that in general, ethnic minorities perform worse than the white population, but this covers wide variations between groups. In particular Indian and Chinese students outperform white students, while Pakistani, Bangladeshi and Afro-Caribbean students do worse than the white population. Any account of attainment must therefore attempt to explain the differences between ethnic minorities as well as the general patterns.

There are a number of cultural explanations. Some of them seem to blame the culture of the ethnic minorities for their own failure. They see Afro-Caribbean culture, for instance, as pathological. The culture of the minority ethnic group is a culture that creates failure. There is a high rate of male desertion so Afro-Caribbean boys lack role models, will be vulnerable to peer-group pressure and become drawn into an aggressive version of masculinity (Sewell, 1997). Another argument from this view is that some ethnic groups are in a state of culture shock. They have a different set of traditions which means that they cannot fit into the conventions of schools and thus find it difficult to adapt. Other elements of this argument are that ethnic minorities lack linguistic skills as English is a second or third language at home. Some argue that there is a myth of return: ethnic groups are attached to their country of origin and believe that one day they will return there. Bolognani (2007) argues that this has intensified and changed as a result of Islamophobia. The result of the myth of return for education is that students with family in Pakistan will be more likely to take long holidays to Pakistan and miss large chunks of the school year. Others feel that a commitment to religion resulting in extra time out of school or a lack of study time will affect results.

However, it is possible to see the culture of some ethnic groups as a resource and the statistics are not as clear as they may first appear. Briggs et al. (2006) argue that ethnic groups improve more while they are at school than the white population and that looking at bare GCSE figures hides this improvement. This improvement is a consequence of high aspirations and positive attitudes towards educational success. It is worth noting that many individuals from ethnic groups stay on in education after compulsory schooling. Archer and Francis (2006) argue that cultural factors are very significant in explaining the success of British-Chinese students. In particular they argue that educational success is part of British-Chinese identity, and even when boys engage in laddish behaviour they still maintain a commitment to educational success. Parents continually talked to their children about their future educational choices. They also invested time and money in supporting their children, even when they had little money to spend. Parents would be happy to push their children and were critical of white British parents who were seen as allowing failure to develop. Thus British-Chinese students in poverty were able to outperform other groups in poverty. It is worth noting some negative points from the research: many British-Chinese felt insecure about their ability (even when they were top of the class), many found the idea of Chinese cleverness constraining, and it is clear that educational success did not guarantee success in employment.

An evaluation of cultural models

1   Arguing that failing ethnic minorities are culturally deprived helps to scapegoat these groups. It is a victim-blaming theory, which makes them responsible for their own failure. In doing so it avoids looking at the education system or those who control it. It also distracts attention from the impact of poverty on ethnic minorities.

2   Many of the studies accept definitions of ethnicity and regard this as unproblematic. However, when one stops from being of a particular ethnic tradition is clearly a matter of opinion. Does one stop being of Afro-Caribbean descent after two, three or four generations? Or does it never stop? It is not an objective or clear-cut category. Haynes et al. show that some schools enter ethnic background on the basis of perceptions of teachers. As previously noted, the work of Gorard (2008) shows that the second largest ethnic group in higher education is the 'missing' group, in other words, respondents did not know or were unwilling to enter their ethnic background. This group clearly poses a challenge to the usefulness of the statistics.

Activity 22

Ask your parents or grandparents if their parents were immigrants. Talk to them about whether or not they feel part of an ethnic group and what this means to them. Do they see their ethnic ties becoming weakened in you? Discuss this in class. What about families of mixed descent? Which ethnic group do they (or do you) belong to?

The impact of the school

Rather than focus on the culture of the home, many sociologists have drawn attention to the way in which the school acts against ethnic-minority students. They employ many of the concepts and ideas you have looked at in interactionism, such as labelling, but there are also some significantly different insights into the way schools operate.

Studies like Wright (1992) found teacher **racism**. Teachers held labels of students that meant that they believed Asian students would have a poor grasp of English and left them out of discussions or spoke to them in simple terms. Gillborn and Youdell (2000) argue that teachers' racist assumptions led them to believe that Afro-Caribbean students would cause trouble and that teachers would see the behaviour of these students as challenging. Teachers would confront this behaviour and this would build resentment and escalate problems. Later theorists have argued that the introduction of league tables has adversely affected ethnic-minority students as schools exclude more and more pupils in a bid to drive up their results.

In a report in 2007, Channel Four used the Freedom of Information Act to uncover the extent of racist attacks in schools. It found that over 100,000 incidents had been documented and that there had been a significant increase recently. Mirza argued that this clearly indicated that there was a significant problem within schools and that the figures were an underestimation of the problem. Pupils who are subjected to a barrage of bullying are likely to underperform in their education.

Weblinks

The details of the Channel Four report are available on the internet (see 'Websites', page ii).

Activity 23

In groups, discuss what should be done to students who perpetrate racist attacks. Do you think they should be punished for the bullying and punished more for the racist element of the bullying?

Strand (2008) argued in a talk to the British Educational Research Association that schools were institutionally racist. He found that teachers were less likely to enter Afro-Caribbean students for higher-tier tests at 14 in Science and Mathematics; this had a knock-on effect on which

GCSE they were entered for. The reason for this was that teachers developed a perception of Afro-Caribbean students as disruptive and then made an inaccurate judgement on their ability. This echoes the findings of a study conducted by the CRE (1992) which found that Asian students were put into lower sets because teachers' judgements were used to decide which GCSE sets students would be placed in. They were placed in lower sets, even when they had the same assessment scores.

Another example of **institutional racism** can be found in the work of Coard. He developed the idea that the school curriculum was ethnocentric. This means that the curriculum is based around one particular cultural viewpoint while ignoring others. Thus white history and white literature come to dominate the curriculum. Teachers are dismissive of non-standard English as a way of speaking and these sometimes hidden and sometimes overt messages are transferred to students. Their culture is devalued and they are devalued. White students also pick up on this and the resulting racism is dealt with ineffectively by the school.

Sewell rejects the idea that schools are universally racist and that teachers are the problem. He argues that disruptive black students need to be excluded and removed so that other students, including ethnic-minority students, can progress: the idea of institutional racism helps to provide black youth with an excuse. In a sense he is arguing that black misbehaviour is a fact and not a social construct, that the problems stem from outside the classroom and not inside the classroom.

In a study of students of white and black Caribbean descent by Haynes et al. (2006) it was argued that students of mixed heritage are often misunderstood by schools and teachers. Teachers believed that these students had identity issues and low expectations. All these fed through to how they treated this group. This operates in addition to socio-economic disadvantages this group faces and helps to explain their relative failure and high level of exclusion.

The impact of the organisation on the way in which schools are organised will also have a consequence for ethnic-minority students.

Discuss what you think the impact of parental choice will be on ethnic-minority students.

An evaluation of the impact of the school on ethnic minorities

1   Ethnic-minority students will not just accept the labels given to them. Studies by Fuller (1984) show that students labelled as failures may become more determined to succeed, in order to prove the teacher wrong.

2   It is difficult to call all schools and all teachers racist. Many schools treat racism very seriously and actively promote equal opportunities. There are many opportunities for you to get involved in this.

Weblinks

You could use the 'Show Racism the Red Card' website to help organise a red card day in your school or college (see 'Websites', page ii).

3   While research shows that Indian and Pakistani students perform very differently, it is difficult to believe that a racist education system or racist teachers would be able to differentiate between these two groups.

4   Research like Wright's is based on observations of classrooms, which will be thought by some positivists to be subjective and biased.

5   Focusing on the school ignores the impact of poverty.

The impact of poverty

You have already examined the impact of material deprivation on the working class. Poverty is also a key feature of the life of many ethnic minorities and affects their attainment.

One central theme of the materialist argument is that Figure 2.10 clearly indicates differences within ethnic minority groups and that these differences closely match the differences in attainment between ethnic groups. Swann (1985) argued that at least 50 per cent of ethnic attainment differences can be explained by social class. Platt (2007) argues that this poverty stems from a variety of factors like low qualifications, discrimination in the workplace and limited savings. The effects of this may be seen in a variety of consequences such as poorer health, homelessness, overcrowding, poorer diet and limited choices in education.

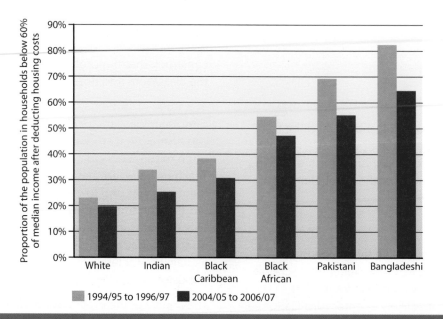

Figure 2.10: More than half of people from Bangladeshi and Pakistani ethnic backgrounds still live in low-income households (Source : Households Below Average Income, Department for Wages and Pensions)

Weblinks

You could use the Joseph Rowntree Foundation website to find some contemporary research on ethnicity and poverty (see 'Websites', page ii).

Activity 25

Create a poster explaining the links between material deprivation and ethnic failure. Use the previous section on class and material deprivation to guide you.

A final thought

There is a very important debate about the cause of educational failure. Different theoretical traditions will emphasise different causes. Marxists will tend to emphasise the material conditions of people's lives, whereas functionalists would focus more on people's values. Interactionists would argue that the school is the place where success and failure are determined. Social democratic views would focus on the importance of establishing a meritocracy

and the new right would highlight in particular the role of parental choice (see section ii). These debates are important to anyone who wants to see children able to succeed on the basis of their own ability and efforts. It is also important for determining what policies should be pursued by the government in its bid to create a meritocratic system. In reality it would be unwise to adopt a mono-causal explanation, given the variety of groups that are affected by differential educational attainment. Tackling class inequality may do little to help the inequalities between boys and girls. An indication of the complexity of the issue of attainment is that in 2008 Strand found that white British were the most polarised social group. While white middle-class boys were amongst the most successful groups in education, white working-class boys were amongst the least successful, with 85 per cent of this group failing to gain five A*–C grades at GCSE. Archer et al. (2007) examined the position of girls within education and argued that a policy focus on failing boys ignored the failure of girls from minority ethnic groups and the working class, who were still subject to many disadvantages that were not being addressed. It is interesting to note that while educational policy concentrates on raising the attainment of boys, the issue of girls' attainment seems to be unproblematic despite the moral panic over the emergence of the ladette. This was due to a one-dimensional policy approach which meant that teachers simply concentrated on boys.

However, it is clear from Gillborn and Mirza (2000) that class is a much more significant influence on attainment than gender (5x) and that ethnicity is also more significant than gender (2x). In an era when choice and individuality are supposed to reign supreme, the social structure still has a role to play in people's lives.

Section summary

The main theories to consider in this section are functionalism, Marxism, interactionism and feminism.

Use the following concepts to explain the key themes of this section. Develop three themes around ethnicity, class and gender. When you get into the exam, start to panic and feel your heart race, remember ECG.

- Material deprivation
- Cultural deprivation
- Labelling (a concept from section ii)
- Institutional racism
- Patriarchy

Stretch and Challenge Activity

Using the concepts listed in the Section summary, develop a paragraph of criticisms of this explanation. Make sure you use theories and concepts.

Exam practice

1   Outline and assess the view that social class inequalities in educational attainment are caused by factors outside the school. (50 marks)

2   Outline and assess the view that ethnic inequalities in educational achievement are caused by teachers and processes inside schools themselves. (50 marks)

U3

2

Sociology of education

(iv) The relationship between education and the economy

Pause for thought

- Should schools just teach the things that employers need?

- How did you decide which which type of post-16 course(s) to follow, and what factors did you consider in making your choice?

- How do you think your experience differs from students following a purely vocational course?

You have already seen in the section on the role and function of education how different theories think about education. This section will try to pull out clearly some of the links between education and the economy and the views held by the different theories.

For functionalists it is clear that the development of a formal system of education, which takes place in institutions separate from the home, is a development of modern society. In agricultural societies, where skills are relatively simple and status is normally ascribed, there is little need for a formal system of education. However, the development of a large-scale industrial economy (**industrialisation**) with a higher level of mobility (both geographic and social) necessitates the emergence of an education system. In the medieval period few children went to school, but with the passing of Foster's Education Act (1870) and in 1880 (towards the end of the industrial revolution), mass schooling was introduced.

Marxists see the development of education connected to very different process. They argue that as capitalist economies grew, capitalists needed a mechanism to control the working class. The ruling class was worried about the newly emergent working class: they had seen revolutions spread throughout Europe in the early to mid-nineteenth century, and were anxious about this revolutionary fervour spreading to the new working classes living in poverty in the industrial cities and towns.

Activity 26

Make a copy of Table 2.3 and explain what is meant by the ideas in the boxes, using the material from the section on the role and function of education (pages 56–63).

Functionalism		Marxism	
Parsons	Selects and allocates occupational position	Bowles and Gintis	Creates a subservient workforce
Durkheim	Creates a skilled workforce	Bourdieu	Creates illusion of equality to enable happy workers
Davis and Moore	Allocates people to the right positions		

Table 2.3: The role of education

Education was seen as a way in which the working classes could be deflected from **radicalisation**. In this perspective education is about control rather than the development of individual freedom, the creation of a skilled workforce enjoying fulfilling employment and the creation of a meritocratic social order.

Thus, the different perspectives see the role of education very differently.

The difference between these ideas about the nature of the education system can be seen in their views of the role of **vocational education.** This is a focus for contemporary debates about the link between education and the economy. Functionalists would argue that vocational education is an important element of education which benefits individuals and society. It is connected to Durkheim's argument about the creation of a skilled workforce. Marxists see vocational education as training workers for exploitation and creating a pool of cheap labour while artificially reducing the unemployment figures. The new right and social democratic perspectives agree that vocational education is important. The Labour government began a debate about the need for vocational education in the 1960s and 1970s. This was picked up by

later Conservative governments. Both parties see vocational education as a panacea for the UK's economic woes and a step towards creating a skilled and competitive economy.

A number of schemes have been introduced under the umbrella of vocational education. Governments have argued that vocational educational was and is necessary to help provide young people with the skills they would need in the workplace. It was argued that the UK was losing its **competitive** edge, unemployment was rising and young people needed to leave school with much better skills. If they did leave school without work-based skills, then colleges should provide courses that would give them the right skills for the job market. The government has now extended the school-leaving age. It is clear that many of those who would have left education at 16 will follow the vocational qualifications rather than an academic route.

One of the most significant programmes under New Labour was the **New Deal**. This was aimed at unemployed young people who were given full-time education or training for a year, or work for six months in the voluntary sector or with the environmental task force, or a job with training. There was also the possibility of

Figure 2.11: Do different horses need different courses?

help in the development of self-employment. There was compulsion involved, as anyone who refused to take part in the programme would lose benefits. This programme summed up many of the debates about vocational training. The Government claimed that it helped to reduce unemployment and got people off welfare. Others argued that the scheme helped little, the jobs that were created would have been created anyway, the compulsory nature of the schemes gave employers too much power over the trainees and the schemes did not really provide valuable skills.

Weblinks

The new deal was extended to groups other than young workers. You can find about these schemes on the internet (see 'Websites', page ii).

Activity 27

In groups, design an advert for an office job and present this to the class. Focus on what you think are the important skills required by the job.

After you have done this, pick out some common skills required by most jobs, and talk about your own work experience. How far does it fit in with the aims of vocational education? Did it really prepare you for the world of work?

Vocational GCSEs have been attacked as being introduced by schools to improve their positions in the league tables. De Waal (2008) has argued that the new vocational qualifications do not teach vocational skills of any use. The qualifications, equivalent to five GCSEs, are used to ensure that those who are likely to fail the academic GCSEs will pass government targets. However, these qualifications do not really help the students, but are really about occupying their time and have little value in the outside world. She argues that this damages the value of real vocational education. This is particularly true with the introduction of vocational education at 14.

Another concern that De Waal developed was that the present system may re-create the old tripartite system. Middle-class students will follow an academic curriculum which is valued whereas working-class students will follow a less valuable qualification. The students' futures will be decided early in their lives as a result of the different value of these qualifications. This concern has been a perpetual concern with the academic–vocational divide. For instance, there were concerns in the 1990s that vocational education of the time perpetuated the social divisions between the educated and the trained (Lees et al., 1990). The government hopes that its new Diplomas will overcome this divide and create qualifications with equal perceived value, but many governments have had this hope. According to Hoelscher (2008), those with vocational qualifications are more likely to choose one of the universities formed in 1992 than one of the more traditional universities, and it was clear that vocational qualifications affected the choice of subject at university. Both of these factors had a consequence for employment after university.

In a talk in 2002, Evans argued that the quality of much of the training offered in vocational education was poor. This was because many low-skilled workers received little training, while the well qualified normally received more. In addition, much of the training failed to reflect many of the changes in the new economic environment and the need for time to develop effective vocational skills. These concerns are connected to the concerns of people who believe that vocational education in schools is about making tea or photocopying rather than learning anything valuable.

In a paper on vocational education for 14- to 16-year-olds, Davies and Biesta (2007) argue that students get very varied experiences. This is probably a useful insight into the nature of vocational education. At its worst it is dull, repetitive and unrewarding. Some employers may be tempted to use students on vocational schemes as **cheap labour** who will generate profits for the business while gaining nothing themselves. It is also an extremely useful way of massaging the unemployment figures, which do not include people on training schemes. However, at their best they can be an invaluable method of giving people important skills that will enable them to gain good jobs and promote the economy.

(v) Education and social policy

Pause for thought

- Do you think Education Maintenance Allowance (EMA) is a good idea?

- Should governments try to reduce class or ethnic inequalities in education? They would have to do this by taxing the wealthy to spend on the poor.

- At what age should someone be able to leave school?

- Should universities make lower admissions offers to working-class students?

In many ways you have considered the central aspects of educational policy in previous sections. A number of significant changes have been introduced into education since 1988, to deal with different problems identified by governments. The problems that the policies were intended to address have been classified in four ways by Machin and Vignoles (2006).

1   Falling standards in secondary education.

2   Limited participation post-16.

3   Poor basic skills.

4   Unequal participation in higher education.

These have been the common concerns of both New Labour and the new right, and they have both been involved in attempts to address these issues. However, it must also be said that the new right have been more concerned by points 1 and 3 than 2 and 4. Social democrats would see point 4 as a major issue for concern as it links into their notions of social justice.

It might be useful to consider these areas, in which social policy has been drawn up to influence education.

Raising standards in secondary education

The 1988 Education Act, as you have seen, was introduced by the new right because they believed that greater parental choice and competition would bring about increasing standards as schools competed for students. This idea was endorsed by New Labour, who continued to develop a system that produced more choice and diversity. Thus, we have academies, faith schools and specialist schools. However, the impact of these policies is unclear. Those who believe that the changes have been successful might point to the improving GCSE results caused by better teaching due to the pressure of market forces in state education and also the increasing participation in further education. However, critics might argue that increasing exam success is due to factors other than the impact of marketisation. In addition, there has been a great deal of concern that the result of choice is greater inequality, as middle-class parents use their cultural and material advantages to help their children gain places in better schools. Ball (2008) argues that the ability of individuals to choose produces social segregation. In some areas of England, councils have scrapped parental choice and instead allocate places at oversubscribed schools on the basis of a lottery.

Increasing participation post-16

There have been two major ways in which students have been encouraged into further education by the new right and more recently and specifically by New Labour. The first has been the development of vocational courses like GNVQs, and modern apprenticeships and diplomas (there are to be some academic diplomas, according to the latest thinking). Vocational courses were also directed at improving the perceived skills deficiencies of British workers compared with those in other countries. According to Ball (2008), around 40 per cent of students will take vocational qualifications. This concern with dividing students reflects a historic concern, in the UK, with separating children into categories (see page 50), but it also reflects a concern amongst New Labour with the development of the **knowledge economy**. For Ball, a great deal of education has now been geared to the knowledge economy and education is becoming dominated by its subservience to the needs of the economy. (Indeed the schools themselves are becoming more businesslike in their operation and staff are motivated through incentive schemes.) This is at a time when most jobs that are being created are in the service sector rather than in science and technology. The post-16 diplomas are an indication of government thinking on this. However, as you saw in the section on education and the economy, the value of these schemes is variable and there is also evidence that they are creating or reinforcing divisions of class and ethnicity.

U3
2

Sociology of education

Activity 28

Sort the following statements about the lottery system into strengths and weaknesses.

It prevents the middle classes from getting into the best schools by buying houses in the catchment areas (supply and demand mean that house prices rise in areas with good schools)	Less time would be spent appealing as the decision is difficult to challenge. This will save money and time, and should also reduce stress on pupils who do not know which school they will be going to
Children will be separated from their friends – local people should go to a local school	It might reduce house prices in some areas and this would be unfair
Parents should have a right to choose the school that they feel is best for their child	It makes access to popular schools much fairer
It stops people lying about where they live or renting a flat (but not living in it) just to get into a good school	It will help to ensure that there is a proper social mix in schools and prevent the emergence of working-class sink schools

Another element of recent government policy associated specifically with New Labour has been the development of the idea of the personal learner, otherwise known as **personalisation**. This development is occurring in all levels of education. The learner is mentored and given individual learning plans in the hope that this will create active learners who will become self-reliant and capable of continuous change and improvement. Thus, individuals should be given individual meetings with staff and decide on individual targets to enable their individual development. For some it is a feature of contemporary society which prides itself on the creation of an individualistic society. However, discordant voices argue that such a system will only serve to entrench the power of dominant groups as they use their cultural and economic advantage to benefit from the system. It is directly tied into the demands of the flexible labour market and the need to create a competitive economy. It looks as though individuals are becoming empowered, but in reality they are being tied into the economic system.

The other major mechanism by which students are encouraged into further education has been EMA introduced by New Labour. Machin and Vignoles argue that the impact of the scheme has been positive and that it has increased disadvantaged students' participation in further education. It has been designed to help those who suffer from material deprivation. The scheme has been criticised by some for not targeting the poor, as some wealthy students are able to get EMA. In addition, there are concerns that although working-class students may be participating in further education, they are not taking the same subjects as middle-class students.

Improving basic skills

Both the new right and New Labour have tried to tackle the lack of basic skills. The new right government introduced the National Curriculum as part of the 1988 Education Reform Act. The New Labour government also introduced national literacy and numeracy hours in primary schools. The impact of the National Curriculum is difficult to judge, given that it was a national strategy and therefore there is little scope for undertaking comparative work. The literacy and numeracy hours seem to have had some limited effects. Machin and McNally (2004) argue that the literacy strategy has had a positive effect on reading and English attainment; they also argue that the literacy hour has helped to reduce gender differences in reading scores, as boys who took part in the hour improved their reading. This would appear to support the view that schools can make a difference to their students' results if the right strategies are adopted. They did not, however, look at class differences in attainment.

Widening participation in higher education

The government has attempted to introduce schemes into higher education to widen participation. This is why it is inaccurate to describe New Labour policy as simply adopting new right policy, because while there are elements of neo-liberalism (marketisation), New Labour has retained a social democratic interest in creating a more meritocratic social order and spent a great deal of money trying to achieve this aim. However, the introduction of student loans may have the reverse effect, although the evidence of the impact of fees and loans is unclear. The gap in participation between the classes has not been reduced in recent years, but is a product of problems in the mainstream education system. In other words, working-class students rarely get the grades to get into university and this appears to be the source of the problem rather than students getting the grades and choosing not to apply. In response to this there have been moves to introduce positive discrimination into the university admission process. This could take the form of universities requiring lower A Level and GCSE grades from working-class students. A second response was to develop EAZs and the EiC (look at pages 53–54 if you are unsure what these mean). The evidence from McKnight et al. (2005) indicates that there were some small improvements in Key Stage 3 results and attendance.

Some policies have been introduced which have aimed to tackle a number of social problems, including problems in education, and it is therefore worth considering the effect of schemes like Sure Start, a scheme designed to tackle issues like health inequalities and crime. It is also designed to improve the attainment of the poorest groups in society, and can be seen as an educational policy. In many ways it follows in the footsteps of other **compensatory education** schemes. The scope of Sure Start is very large: the government spent over £3 billion between 2004 and 2008, and by 2010 it aims to create 3500 Sure Start centres. These will have a significant degree of autonomy, as local schemes are designed to tackle local problems.

Weblinks

You might be interested to look at the Sure Start programme, or to see the legacy of compensatory education in action (see 'Websites', page ii).

Activity 30

Invite a speaker from a Sure Start centre near you to talk about the work their centre does.

Research about the effectiveness of Sure Start is still being undertaken and in many ways the results will be difficult to judge as they may not be felt for many years. However, a report by the University of London (NESS Team) in 2008 indicated that 3-year-olds who had been on the schemes showed better social development, more positive social behaviour, and greater independence and self-reliance than others who had not been on the schemes. In part, this was as result of better parenting derived from the scheme: children had received more immunisations and suffered fewer accidents and injuries. This is in contrast to an earlier report, which showed that the scheme had a limited impact. Different reasons for this change have been proposed. It has been argued that there was a greater exposure to the programme as the children grew up, and that the programmes were delivered in a more effective manner. Others have argued that previous compensatory

schemes did not target the right social groups, or that material inequalities cannot be addressed by schemes based on cultural deprivation theory. Marxists would see schemes like this as ideological window-dressing and an attempt to hide the inequities generated by capitalism. These arguments are similar to those related to a US scheme called Operation Headstart, which involved spending billions of dollars in a war on poverty and focused on cultural change amongst deprived groups. Its effects are still unclear.

Over recent years and in response to the Crick Report, the government has been developing Citizenship in schools, with the aim of developing students' awareness of the political and social environment and making them feel that they can participate in their community. This is something that all students should be exposed to and the aim is to create legions of active citizens who are empowered to participate in modern democratic society. It also aims to create an understanding and tolerance of diverse communities and make a step towards community cohesion. However, critics of this approach argue that:

◆ The creation of faith schools serves to divide communities.

◆ The impact of marketisation is to divide communities.

◆ Social cohesion is based around the creation of a common culture which ends up imposing one set of values and crushing ethnic and cultural differences.

◆ It does not work. Schools and teachers are ill-prepared to discuss these issues and most young people are more concerned about the newest ipod than political empowerment.

◆ It is dangerous to give the state the right to dictate the values that people should adopt: for some it is a step towards the development of a totalitarian society.

◆ Thus, some question the effectiveness of the policy while some question its desirability. Critics can be divided into those who see the policy as a positive development which needs refinement, and those who would question its whole basis. This is something that you should consider at the end of this section: what should education be about and how can this best be achieved?

Sociology of education

Section summary

The most important theories to consider in this section are the new right and New Labour ideas.

Use the following words to create a summary of the major educational policies of the last few years.

- Compensatory education
- Knowledge economy
- EMA
- Marketisation
- Material deprivation
- Cultural deprivation

Stretch and Challenge Activity

Discuss whether it is possible for education to compensate for the impact of society on attainment and behaviour.

Exam practice

1   Outline and assess the view that educational policies since 1988 have led to an improvement in educational standards in the contemporary UK. (50 marks)

2   Outline and assess New Labour's strategies and theories of educational social policy. (50 marks)

U3

2

Sociology of education

ExamCafé

Relax, refresh, result!

Relax and prepare

Hot tips

Stacey

This question seems a straightforward one on the role of the education system. I have learnt a lot about the different sociological theories on the role of the education system, but I must make sure that I focus on functionalism.

John

I must remember to include sociological theories when answering this question.

Alice

I really enjoyed applying sociological theories to a study of the role of education. It meant that I was able to understand the theories much better as it wasn't so abstract. Concepts such as meritocracy and the hidden curriculum are now easy to understand.

Examiner's tip

Sociological theories are made explicit on the specification for each of the power and control options, so it is not unlikely that you will be asked an essay question on a specific sociological theory. It is important, therefore, that you understand and revise all of the theories named in the specification in preparation for this. It is a good idea to ensure that you have knowledge and understanding of the general theory as well as how it is applied in the context of education. A useful tip for understanding theory is to try to explain it to someone else. When revising for this unit, ask your family if you can explain functionalist theory to them – the clearer the explanation, the more likely they are to understand it.

Refresh your memory

Revision checklist

You might find it useful to use a table like the one below to check your knowledge, and record your own sources of information.

Topic	Studies	Do I know this?	Look here
The structure and organisation of education			
The role of education in society			
Differential educational achievement			
The relationship between education and the economy			
Education and social policy			

Revision hint - making the links

There is a lot of overlap in the study of education. You could create some mind maps showing the links between the topic areas above and sociological theories. For example, there are links between functionalist theories of the role of education and functionalist theories of the relationship between education and the economy. There are also links between the structure and organisation of education (see the table above) and education and social policy.

Get the result!

Below is a student's response written under exam conditions to the following question:

Student answer

Outline and assess functionalist explanations of the role of the education system. **(50 marks)**

Functionalist explanations for the role of the education system concern three broad ideas: socialisation, skill provision and role allocation.

First, socialisation within the school is a form of secondary socialisation. Durkheim, a functionalist sociologist, states that through secondary socialisation within the school, key values are passed down from generation to generation. Also, the division of labour is taught through socialisation in schools. Both these functions of socialisation prevent chaos and confusion and help to obtain social order. Durkheim goes on to argue that social solidarity is a key part of secondary socialisation. Social solidarity reflects the idea that in order to survive in society we must have essential similarities. Durkheim's ideas of essential similarities were originally very complex, linking with democracy and education inequalities. However, more recently, functionalists have linked the similarities with school uniforms, sports teams and school assemblies. These ideas link similarities and therefore bind people in society together. Durkheim also stressed that all social beings must be loyal to society as a whole. This illustrates that we must have a sense of belonging to something wider than our immediate situation. School subject choice is a perfect example of not only having a sense of belonging but also binding people in society together. The Welsh language as a subject is compulsory in Welsh schools, as it must have a Welsh dimension. Through the Welsh language we expand our knowledge of Welsh culture. This can be done through the Welsh celebration, Eisteddfod, where poems, literature and songs are all shared. From this, we get a sense of belonging to a wider group, that is Wales.

However, Hargreaves criticises the functionalist view that examinations and competitions are good for society. Instead, he argues that they cause people to be set into groups of failure and success. Those less able students as result become alienated, forming anti-school subcultures which prevent social order.

Parsons, another functionalist, sees the socialisation of children through the school as a microcosm of society. Also, the school acts as a bridge between childhood and adulthood. In childhood, within the family, we obtain an ascribed status which we do not have to work for: we are a daughter, sister, etc. However, through education, we obtain our achieved status, based on our talents and abilities. For example, someone may achieve the status of head girl at school.

Examiner comment:

This is a very short introduction and while it is useful to pinpoint exactly the main features of the functionalist argument, this student has lost the opportunity to pick up some interpretation and application marks by putting the debate into its wider sociological context.

Examiner comment:

This is an excellent paragraph. It is conceptually strong and contains depth of knowledge on this particular function. The examples are relevant and contemporary.

Examiner comment:

This is explicit, direct evaluation, although it could have been explained in a little more depth.

Examiner comment:

There are some good concepts here, although again it is a little undeveloped. For example, it doesn't explain how education is a microcosm.

Skills provision is an aspect that functionalists also consider. Durkheim stated that in today's industrial society, skills needed in order to succeed have become more complex in recent years. Skills such as IT and computing are needed in some way in most jobs and are therefore crucial. Durkheim therefore concludes that the school's core function is to teach these skills in order for students to fit into a successful job. Vocational courses have become highly popular in schools and colleges. This is because students learn skills and train to aspire to their chosen career. However, Tumin argues that the link between skills and rewards are questionable. It seems it is not necessarily the skills we are qualified in which promote us into our adult jobs. Many university graduates end up in jobs that do not reflect their level of education. There is also a debate about the relationship between talent and reward. Some jobs are very functionally important, for example street cleaners, but they are not rewarded with high pay. Another criticism of the functionalist view can be reflected through the old-boy network. The upper class obtain well-paid jobs which for other classes demand highly skilled people, yet the upper classes still obtain top jobs with or without skills. The social closure within the upper class shows it's not always what you know, but who you know that counts.

Role allocation is another core function of education, according to functionalists. Davis and Moore argue that within the school, children are assigned to their future roles based on abilities and talents. Those with the greatest ability and talents are given the most functionally important jobs in society. Functionalists see role allocation as a fair system because everyone in education has the opportunity to obtain important jobs based on ability and hard work. This is called meritocracy.

Bowles and Gintis, both Marxists, agree with the functionalist view that schools reflect society. They argue that what goes on in schools is reflected in what happens in the workplace. This is called the correspondence principle. For example, students learn the idea of hierarchy at school and this is then transferred to the workplace hierarchies.

In contrast to the functionalists, Althusser offers a Marxist interpretation of the role of the education system. He believes that education is an ideological state apparatus and working-class children are socialised to accept their failure. Neo-Marxist Willis argues that schools prepare working-class students for their place in society where they will be doing working-class jobs. He studies a group of working-class lads who actively created their own school failure, but this in itself meant they were preparing themselves to be failures in the workplace too.

Overall, functionalists have a very positive view of the education system, but they fail to recognise the clear inequalities which exist. Most evidence does not support the idea of schools being based on meritocracy and therefore the theory is not backed up with evidence.

Sociology of the mass media

Pause for thought

1 How important do you think the media are in society?

2 Think about ways in which the media may have a positive impact on audiences.

3 Think about ways in which the media may have a negative impact on audiences.

Introduction

From your AS Sociology course, you will have learned about the media as an agent of secondary socialisation and their role in shaping our culture and identity. The mass media also play a powerful role in society because media companies make millions of pounds every year and so have the potential to exercise economic influence.

The increasing prevalence of the mass media in our lives has led to the term 'media-saturated society' being applied to countries like the UK, where media institutions, products and technologies have grown to such an extent that they form a large part of our daily experience, providing us with a constant flow of information and entertainment, and are a fundamental element in the functioning of society.

The specification states:

'In this option, candidates explore issues of power and control through a detailed study of the mass media. The core A2 themes can be explored through studying media institutions and processes; candidates are encouraged to reflect on their own experience of media consumption in the light of the concepts of power, control, inequality and differentiation. This option aims to give an overview of different theoretical approaches to the study of the media.'

This option explores the following five key issues:

1. Defining and researching the mass media
2. Ownership and control of the media
3. Social construction of the news
4. Media representations of social groups
5. The effect of the media on society

(i) Defining and researching the mass media

Pause for thought

- What does the term 'mass media' mean?
- What issues do you think researchers investigate when studying the mass media?
- What methods do sociologists use to conduct research into the mass media?

Sociologists are interested in the ways in which the media exercise control over our lives by shaping our identity. McQuail (2000) sees the mass media as of great significance in relation to culture and contends that the mass media provide people with their image of 'social reality' and that it expresses their 'shared identity'. He explains this by pointing out that the mass media is the main 'leisure time interest' in society and provides people with more of a 'shared environment' than any other institution.

The extent of the media's effect on our lives is difficult to measure and is the subject of much discussion between sociologists. Some are concerned that audiences could become more violent as a result of what is seen, read and heard in the media, while others believe that the media have little effect on audiences. Sociologists also study other ways in which the media may have control, including the extent of their influence over powerful people and institutions in society.

Mass media

When sociologists refer to the 'media' they are generally using a short-hand term for what is actually the 'mass media'. Early studies of the **mass media** in the 1920s and 1930s used straightforward definitions that referred to ways of communicating to large audiences that involved cinema, magazines, newspapers and radio. Definitions of the mass media have become increasingly complex as the range, role and scope of media products develop and change. New media including satellite television, WAP mobile phones and the internet, for example, allow information to circulate around the world almost immediately and result in the world becoming what McLuhan (1971) described as a 'global village'. McCullagh provides us with a basic definition of the mass media: 'the mass media are simply the means through which content, whether fact or fiction, is produced by organisations and transmitted to and received by an audience' (McCullagh, 2002, page 5).

Activity 1

Make a list of as many types of media as you can think of. Include new forms as well as more traditional areas such as television and cinema. Create a media diary for a week, in which you list the different media products or processes that feature in your life. As you keep the diary, record the approximate time frame (how long you were online, etc.) and whether you discussed media themes with other people. For example, did you discuss a TV programme with a friend? Your findings could be presented in the form of a table. Discuss the results of your research with others in your class to judge the extent to which your exposure to media resembles or differs from that of your contemporaries.

Devereux (2008, page 13) contributes a useful analysis of the mass media in their social context by identifying a number of key aspects that help us to develop a more detailed understanding of their role:

◆ Mass media as means of communication between 'senders' and 'receivers'.

◆ Mass media texts as cultural products with social, cultural and political significance.

◆ Mass media as industries or organisations.

◆ Mass media as agents of social change and globalisation.

◆ Mass media texts as commodities produced by media industries.

◆ Mass media as agents of socialisation and powerful sources of social meaning.

Activity 2

Discuss Devereux's points as listed above, then write a sentence explaining each in your own words.

Activity 3

Using the information you have learnt so far in this subsection, devise a clear definition of the mass media and make a poster illustrating this definition.

Determinism

As you will see from different subsections of this topic, the power and influence of the media are widely debated. Some commentators see the media as a beneficial institution that educates, informs and entertains and gives the audience diversity and range from which to exercise choice. Others are concerned that the media have a negative and controlling effect on audiences. These concerns are founded on the view that the audience uncritically receives the messages being transmitted. Such a view is based on the concept of determinism, which sees human behaviour as a fixed consequence of particular events or experiences and denies or minimises the possibility of free choice.

In using the term 'media determinism', McLuhan (1964) argues that the media, and in particular new media technologies, have a determining influence on social change. He believes that the widespread and ever-changing use of the media has a fundamental effect on how people experience life, society and the world.

Censorship

Censorship of the media refers to ways of regulating and controlling the media that involve preventing or removing material from reaching its audience or restricting the audience being reached. The process takes a numbers of forms and is applied in a variety of situations. Censorship can be used by the government and regulatory bodies and can be brought about by the decisions and judgements of media professionals, known as self-censorship. Media owners might also be seen as exercising censorship when they seek to control content. (This issue is discussed in sections iii and iv.) Governmental censorship includes use of the Official Secrets Act and DA Notices (official requests not to publish an item) to prevent the reporting of certain events on the grounds that it could damage national security. Regulatory bodies, known as 'watchdogs', like the Press Complaints Commission and the British Board of Film Classification, aim to keep a check on media content. Other forms of censorship include the use of a watershed (on television) to restrict content broadcast before a specific time. Censorship can be seen as formal and informal. Formal censorship includes regulation by official bodies such as the government. Informal censorship is exercised by media professionals based on mutual agreements and informal discussion. The effectiveness or desirability of censorship is the subject of great debate, with some theorists contending that censorship is unnecessary as the media's effect on their audience remains unproven. Others argue that free choice should be protected unless harm can be proven. Those supportive of censorship claim that it is an important means of protecting vulnerable members of society and believe that the media can have a significant effect on their audience and on society.

Activity 4

1 In groups, research the ways in which censorship operates in the British media including methods used by government, regulatory bodies and less formal forms of censorship.

2 Construct a list of both formal and informal methods of censorship.

The effect of the media on society is explored on pages 126–135.

Methods of researching the mass media

A variety of methods can be used when researching the mass media:

◆ content analysis

◆ semiology

◆ experiments.

Content analysis

You may have considered the method of content analysis in your AS studies. **Content analysis** is used to analyse the content of media products such as newspapers and magazines. It is often used to quantify a particular aspect of media content by counting or measuring it. For example, Lobban (1974) and Best (1993) used content analysis to examine gender representations in children's reading schemes by counting the numbers appearing in particular categories, such as heroines and heroes. This type of content analysis is part of the quantitative approach to research.

Problems with content analysis:

◆ The general problems associated with using secondary data (such as the possibility of bias or error on the part of the original researcher).

◆ The meaning of the content to the audience is not explored. For example, it does not tell us how the audience was affected by the content.

Figure 3.1: There are many ways of researching the media.

- The intentions of the producer of the message are not addressed.

- Both of the last two points mean that there are issues with validity.

Further content analysis activities appear on pages 108, 112, 117, 119, 120, 121, 122, 125, where we consider media representations of social groups.

Problems with semiology:

Problems with semiology:

- The analysis relies greatly on the researcher's interpretation of the content.

- It presents an analysis of the researcher's reading of the text but does not refer to the way the audience receives the message.

- It lacks reliability.

Some researchers, such as the Glasgow University Media Group, combine both quantitative content analysis and semiology to produce data that measure content and seek to uncover meanings and as such can be seen as both reliable and valid. They have gone further and have incorporated audience-reception analysis to complete the process of research.

Activity 5

Using newspapers or magazines and the stages listed below, conduct a content analysis concerning the portrayal of young people. Count the number of articles representing them in positive and negative ways. Write a brief report of your findings.

1 Choose an appropriate text.

2 Break the text down into smaller units, e.g. paragraphs, sentences, words, images.

3 Decide on the relevant categories and give them headings.

4 Analyse the units according to the categories.

5 Count how often each occurs.

6 Analyse your findings in terms of the frequency and any patterns.

Semiology

Semiology is a research method that involves analysing the meaning of signs and codes within their cultural context. These signs can be found in written texts and visual representations in the media, and the task of semiology is to uncover the message being conveyed. Some sociologists use semiotic analysis to uncover what they believe to be ideological messages. An example can be found in section iii where we consider the research of the Glasgow University Media Group into construction of the news. Feminists also use semiology to analyse messages related to gender-role ideology. Semiology has been defined as a science, but it has been argued that, since it rests on the interpretations of the researcher, it falls more within a qualitative approach to research.

Figure 3.2: Models influence perception of size in young people

Use semiology to analyse the meanings of some media messages in relation to representation of gender. You can do this using both written text and visual images. In written text you could focus on the words and language used in relation to males and females. In visual images, consider the underlying meaning being conveyed by signs such as the setting, posture, lighting, camera angle.

Present your analysis to your group.

Experiments

The use of **experiments** to study the media is influenced by the methodology of the natural sciences. For example, natural scientists conduct experiments in a laboratory in order to exercise control over the variables involved and to measure effects. While some social scientists, such as psychologists, have used laboratory experiments, sociologists tend to favour experiments that move beyond this environment into what is called the 'field'. Field experiments

occur in a more natural social environment where researchers hope to observe behaviour that is less explicitly affected by the research process. In this situation, researchers may still choose to manipulate the environment, depending on the theoretical perspective they adopt and the topic of their study, for example they may use collaborators to take on a particular role in a situation. Field experiments are more likely to be found in studies of media effects where variables might be manipulated to examine their influence.

Problems with experiments:

◆ There are significant ethical concerns about possible effects on the participants and about issues of informed consent.

◆ The artificial environment of the experiment means that the validity of the results can be called into question.

◆ Researcher effect may be an issue in influencing the behaviour of the participants where they are aware of their involvement in the experiment. This is known as the Hawthorne Effect.

Section summary

Using the key terms below, write a paragraph summarising the main points you have learnt about defining and researching the mass media.

• Mass media

• Determinism

• Censorship

• Content analysis

• Semiology

• Experiments

Stretch and Challenge Activity

Conduct further research into the use of content analysis, semiology and experiments to study the media and construct a list of strengths and weaknesses for each method.

Exam practice

1 Outline and evaluate the research methods used by sociologists when studying the media. (50 marks)

2 Outline and assess the view that censorship of the media is unnecessary. (50 marks)

(ii) Ownership and control of the media

Pause for thought

- Who owns the media?
- Does it matter who owns the media?
- Who controls the content of the media?

The figures, from government research, that appear in the box below show that the media are a large part of our daily lives and have the potential to exert great influence over us. In this section we will explore the trends and patterns in media ownership and control, look at who owns and controls the media, and study the theoretical explanations offered by different sociological perspectives. These explanations examine the role of audiences, media professionals and media owners in exercising control over the content of the media.

Media use in 2006:

- 71 per cent of households had a satellite, digital or cable receiver and 83 per cent of households with children had a satellite, digital or cable receiver, compared with just 66 per cent of households without children

- 67 per cent of households owned a home computer

- 59 per cent of households had an internet connection

- 83 per cent of households owned a DVD player

- 80 per cent of households owned a mobile phone.

(Source: Office for National Statistics)

According to the Audit Bureau of Circulations, an organisation that provides data about media readership, the *Sun* has a daily circulation of almost three million, the *Daily Mail* has a circulation of over two million and *The Times*'s circulation is over half a million copies per day.

Circulation figures relate to the number of copies distributed each day, so it is likely that readership figures will be higher than this; some estimates suggest they are at least three times higher.

Weblinks

For information on newspaper circulation, see the Audit Bureau of Circulations website (see 'Websites', page ii).

Activity 7

1. Carry out research to find out about media use by people in your class, based on the kind of media products referred to in the data above.

2. Find out how much time is spent using different media products.

3. Present your findings to your group.

Trends and patterns in media ownership and control

In order to understand issues of power and control in the mass media, it is important to know who owns and controls the media, and to explore the direction media ownership is taking in the twenty-first century. The media are subject to frequent development as technology advances and wider social changes make an impact, for example the effect of globalisation. A prominent pattern is that the most powerful companies are battling to expand their business both across continents and beyond their existing media areas: trying to dominate new media products by buying up companies involved with new technologies like internet service providers, search engine companies and telecom companies.

Within this overall pattern of media ownership are a number of trends that give some indication of the factors shaping ownership now and into the future:

◆ concentration
◆ vertical integration
◆ horizontal integration
◆ transnational ownership
◆ diversification
◆ synergy.

Concentration

Concentration is a trend towards the media being owned by a smaller number of organisations. In other words, ownership is *concentrated* in fewer hands. Media companies have become larger by buying up smaller companies or merging with others. Rupert Murdoch, for example, owns a number of newspapers including *The Times* and the *Sun* in the UK and the *New York Post* in the USA. Some theorists are concerned that the process of concentration in media ownership represents a threat to democracy, as it leads to a narrower range of views being expressed, and that those views are those of the rich and powerful.

Vertical integration

Vertical integration is a trend towards all the stages in production, distribution and consumption being owned by one company. This might involve the purchasing of a number of companies, ranging from those that produce the paper used to make magazines and newspapers through to the transport organisations that deliver them for sale and the newsagents' shops that sell them. This trend is seen as significant because it increases control and cuts costs. Vertical integration is evident within the Disney empire, with its ownership of film and distribution companies, television networks, radio stations, publishing companies, magazines, record labels, theme parks and resorts and shops selling Disney merchandise.

Horizontal integration

The trend towards **horizontal integration** involves the takeover or merger of companies in the same section of the media. This process reduces competition and gives owners greater control of the market for the product in question. An example of horizontal integration can be seen in Rupert Murdoch's News Corporation, which owns a range of television networks including FOX News in the USA, BskyB in the UK and FOXtel in Australia.

Transnational ownership

The trend towards **transnational ownership** is linked to the process of globalisation, which means that companies can operate in a global market. Media ownership is increasingly globalised, with the larger companies taking over smaller ones around the world and creating organisations that cross national boundaries. An example is Viacom, which markets itself as a 'global entertainment content company' and owns a number of film companies and over 150 television networks around the world. According to its website, its brands are represented in more than 561 million households in 161 countries and territories, offering media products in 33 different languages.

Diversification

Diversification is a trend in media ownership towards owning a variety of media products or even branching out to take over businesses outside of the media.

The largest media companies have developed in this way and are known as 'conglomerates'. This means they are made up of companies from a number of areas of the media and outside it. The biggest media company in the world was created when America Online (AOL) and Time Warner merged in 2001. AOL Time Warner owns organisations including television and film companies, record labels, theme parks and sports teams.

Synergy

The recent trend of **synergy** links to vertical integration and diversification. Large media companies can now bring together various aspects of their business to develop a range of connected products. For example, Time Warner owns the rights to the comic character Batman and as a result has produced a film that was advertised in its magazines and released a soundtrack on its record label. Both these products were promoted in its cable and television networks, and it has also made a range of Batman merchandise including children's toys. All these media products based around one theme have resulted in maximising the company's profits.

Look at the six trends discussed above and make a list of the strengths and weaknesses that you think there are for each. Record your findings in a table like the one below.

Trends	Strengths	Weaknesses
Concentration		
Vertical integration		
Horizontal integration		
Transnational ownership		
Diversification		
Synergy		

The process of synergy has led some commentators to argue that in some cases films have become mere vehicles for the surrounding products, created with the associated products in mind: for example, their translation into video games.

These six trends in media ownership can be difficult to see as completely separate developments, since they are part of a larger process of change. For example, horizontal integration can be linked with transnational ownership when an organisation buys companies in the same section of the media but in other countries and so expands the original organisation across the globe.

Stretch and Challenge Activity

Find further research that has been produced on these trends in media ownership. Try to evaluate this evidence in terms of its strengths and weaknesses. Be aware of the source of any data you use and the possibility of bias in the information provided.

Weblinks

For further analysis of trends in media ownership, consult the website on global issues (see 'Websites', page ii).

For additional information about the work of the Campaign for Press and Broadcasting Freedom, visit its website (see 'Websites', page ii).

A range of concerns has been expressed about the trends in media ownership. The Campaign for Press and Broadcasting Freedom (CPBF), an organisation that campaigns for diverse, democratic and accountable media, is worried that these trends will undermine the diversity of both media content and ownership. For example, it fears that the internet will change from being an open means of global communication to one that functions to serve the commercial interests of powerful companies. It is concerned that the lack of regulation of new media technologies will mean that quality and range of content will not be protected in the way that they are with more traditional forms of media. The CPBF is also worried that massive databases of information on internet users will be created when companies merge and that this will raise issues about protection of privacy.

Bagdikian (2000, page xvii), in considering vertical integration, notes concerns 'that corporations which have control of a total process, from raw material to fabrication to sales, also have few motives for genuine innovation and the power to seize out anyone else who tries to compete.'

Limited diversity and choice, reduced quality, concentration of power and the threats to democracy that this may bring, as well as the erosion of regional cultures, are seen as key problems with the way that media ownership is developing to create huge global media empires headed by powerful owners sometimes called 'media moguls'.

Theoretical explanations of ownership and control of the media

There are a number of theoretical explanations about ownership and control of the media and each offers a different view on who is in control:

◆ Marxism

◆ neo-Marxism

◆ pluralism.

Marxism

We will consider the views of both traditional **Marxism** and **neo-Marxism**.

Traditional Marxists believe that power and control in the media lie with the ruling class (the bourgeoisie), including the state and the owners of the media. The media are seen as serving the powerful in society. Marxists use the term 'ideology' to explain the way in which the ruling class establishes a set of ideas that maintain its interests but which people in society accept as natural and fair. Marxists argue that ruling-class ideology comes to be seen in this way because it is reinforced as the norm by social institutions like the education system, religion and the media. Traditional Marxists believe that media owners directly intervene in the running of their organisations to ensure that their views are put across and to promote the profitability of their businesses.

Miliband (1969), in his book *The State in a Capitalist Society*, wrote from a Marxist perspective and argued that the ruling class uses the mass media to control society by creating a false picture of reality that presents capitalism in a positive way. The media legitimate the inequalities in society caused by the way capitalism works, by making them seem inevitable and justifiable. In doing so, people accept capitalist values and, in Marxist terms, live in a state of false class-consciousness. The proletariat accept the values of the capitalist system, even though these values are not in the interests of their class.

Miliband believed that owners directly intervene in the day-to-day running of the media companies they own. Owners act as a group with shared interests and are part of the ruling class.

Drawing on Marx's ideas on religion, Miliband regarded the mass media as the new 'opium

Figure 3.3: Is television the opium of the people?

of the people'. He saw the media as having replaced religion as a drug that numbs the senses and produces an illusion of happiness that is not real happiness. The media divert the proletariat's attention away from the exploitation and oppression of the capitalist system and allow the ruling class to dominate the working class.

Contemporary evidence can be used to support the Marxist view. There are well-documented examples of interventions of owners, such as Rupert Murdoch. For example, journalists working for him have complained that they were prevented from reporting critically about Israel because of Murdoch's business dealings there and his friendship with the then prime minister, Ariel Sharon. Murdoch is reported to have intervened to try to prevent publication of a book by the British politician Chris Patten that was critical of China, at a time when Murdoch was seeking to negotiate with the Chinese government about the introduction of cable networks into China. Murdoch's attempts to influence the British government, for example his alleged threat to former prime minister Tony Blair that the *Sun* would switch its allegiance from Labour to the Conservative Party if the Labour Party did not follow a more critical stance on Europe, have led to him being known as the 'Phantom Prime Minister'.

Marxists are concerned about the trends in media ownership described above. They see these trends as strengthening the control of owners and giving them a much wider range of power covering diverse areas of the media in countries across the globe. Murdock and Golding (1973) investigated the trend towards concentration of ownership in a range of media industries in the UK including print, film and recording. They found that ownership was concentrated in fewer and fewer hands and that the top five companies dominated each sector of the media.

Marxists argue that globalisation has made it increasingly difficult to constrain the power of media owners as they build huge business empires that do not acknowledge national boundaries.

Evaluation

◆ It is argued that traditional Marxists present an overly conspiratorial view of the role of owners, whose main aim is to provide the audience with what they want so that they will buy their products.

◆ Owners' main aim is to make a profit and this may bring them into conflict with other owners. This calls into question the idea of owners being a united group that seeks to impose a singular ideology.

◆ Marxists are criticised for failing to take account of the role of media professionals in constructing the news. For example, John Pilger, an investigative journalist, has been able to create many influential media products (films, newspaper articles and books) that provide in-depth critical analyses of contemporary events that run counter to mainstream political ideas.

◆ Pluralists, commentators who believe that there is more of a balance of power between audiences, owners, media professionals and others involved, would argue that Marxists ignore the range of views offered in the media, including those that criticise the powerful. For example, writers like the environmental campaigner George Monbiot are regularly given space to present alternative views that challenge the capitalist system.

◆ Negrine (1989) offers a number of criticisms:

  ◆ He argues that the evidence to support the view that media ownership equals control is anecdotal and cannot be generalised.

  ◆ He questions whether owners can be seen as a group that share common interests, since their main concern is likely to be the survival and success of their business.

  ◆ He contends that, since media owners are business people, their main concern is likely to centre on commercial success.

  ◆ He sees it as unlikely that individual owners would be able to exercise control of huge global companies operating in a diverse range of media areas.

Sociology of the mass media

1 Using a selection of broadsheet newspapers, identify stories that might be seen to challenge the status quo. George Monbiot's column in the *Guardian* might be a starting point.

2 Using content analysis, assess how much space is given over to stories of this kind and discuss the impact such stories are likely to have in the overall approach of the newspaper.

3 Undertake the same process for the stories making the headlines.

4 Record your findings in a brief written summary.

Neo-Marxism

Neo-Marxism seeks to update traditional views and to respond to perceived weaknesses of the traditional Marxist approach. For example, neo-Marxists extend their analysis of social inequalities beyond social class to cover other disadvantaged groups, including those based on gender, ethnicity and sexuality. Neo-Marxists are interested in examining the role that culture has to play in maintaining inequalities in society and so have conducted research on the mass media.

While neo-Marxists accept that the ruling class exercises power and control in society, they are particularly interested in the ways in which the culture of the ruling class is dominant in society and shapes the activities of people in society. The term **hegemony** is used in neo-Marxism and refers to the dominance of a particular set of ideas. Hegemony is spread through different institutions in society including education and religion. The media are seen as having a key role to play in reinforcing hegemony, since they have such a wide reach within society.

Neo-Marxists look beyond the role of owners to examine the control exercised by media professionals. They see media professionals as being products of institutions, like public schools, that strongly reinforce capitalist hegemony. Neo-Marxists are interested in the way the background of media professionals influences the choices they make and approaches they take when creating media products. They contend that most media professionals are white, middle-class men who come from similar educational backgrounds and so share a similar worldview. This worldview will be present in the films, books, news reports etc. that they produce. Alternative views will be neglected, presented as odd or ridiculed because they go against prevailing norms and values.

Neo-Marxists have produced a considerable amount of research on the way in which the news is constructed by editors and journalists and this is explored in the next section.

Hall and his colleagues at the Centre for Contemporary Cultural Studies at Birmingham University contributed to neo-Marxist ideas. They analysed ways in which media professionals create media products that reflect and reinforce the power structures of society without much overt influence or control from media owners. In a book entitled *Policing the Crisis* (Hall et al., 1995), they described the ways in which the media supported the role of the police and other legal structures at a time when many people were beginning to ask questions about their role in society. The way that policing was described in the media seemed to ignore such questioning.

Fairclough developed some of these ideas in a study of a TV programme called *Crimewatch* (Fairclough, 1995). This programme seemed to describe an ideal world in which the police and the public worked together to catch criminals, but it did not refer to any of the concerns of those members of society or communities who felt alienated from the police. Such questioning did not occur in the programme and it seemed as if challenging questions could not be asked. Fairclough contended that media professionals had created a type of discourse, or language, that affects the way people think, in which only some ideas were given consideration. The neo-Marxist view is that such discourses seem 'natural' to the media professionals who create them, since they themselves are immersed in a hegemonic worldview that does not acknowledge the credibility of alternatives to this worldview.

When considering trends in media ownership, neo-Marxists are critical of these for many of the same reasons as traditional Marxists. They are also concerned that the rise of transnational companies has led to cultural domination by American-owned companies that promote western norms and values, and erodes the uniqueness of regional cultures.

Evaluation

Many of the criticisms of traditional Marxism apply to neo-Marxism, but there are also specific criticisms.

◆ It can be argued that it fails to recognise the growing number of media professionals who are women and/or from ethnic-minority backgrounds.

◆ The development of new technologies can be seen as increasing the representation of a wider range of views. Personal computers and the availability of publishing software have enabled individuals to produce professional-quality media products. Access to the internet and video-sharing websites like YouTube have offered individuals the opportunity to reach a wider audience. Media phenomena like the online encyclopedia Wikipedia can be said to have democratised access to knowledge by opening the production of knowledge to those who wish to be involved with it.

Activity 10

Discuss the issues raised by neo-Marxist research. Can you think of examples from contemporary sources of the media that support the neo-Marxist view? How much impact can individuals make when using new media products like Wikipedia and YouTube to express themselves?

Stretch and Challenge Activity

Develop your knowledge by finding other examples of media products and/or services that provide people with an audience for the expression of their views. Evaluate how successful these products and/or services are likely to be in giving people a voice to be heard by as wide an audience as possible.

Pluralism

Pluralism is a view usually supported by media professionals, but there is little empirical research to cite when considering this perspective. The view argues that there is diversity and choice of media products. Media professionals are regarded as making professional judgements and acting responsibly to produce good-quality media products. They are seen as operating in a market situation where they must ensure that the work they produce attracts as large an audience as possible. Media producers compete for consumers of their products and this competition ensures quality and diversity. Media audiences come from a range of backgrounds and there will, therefore, be a range of media products to suit their various requirements.

In terms of issues of control, pluralists see the audience as having power because the success of media products lies in the hands of those consuming them. The audience uses the media to fulfil its needs and desires in a 'free market' – a situation of supply and demand where media consumers are supplied with what they demand. Whale, a former newspaper reporter, supports the pluralist position and argues that 'the broad shape and nature of the press is determined by no-one but its readers' (1980, page 85).

The concept of the **Fourth Estate** has been used by pluralists to describe the positive role that the media can have in protecting democracy. Some pluralists see the media as acting as a check on the other three estates, or powers in society – government, parliament and the judiciary. Investigative journalism, for example, can act to expose problems within these powerful institutions in society.

Where Marxists are critical of the trends in media ownership, pluralists believe they can bring positive benefits to the consumer. The concentration of ownership, for example, can bring the resources to enhance the quality of media products and the finance to invest in developing new products and services. The pluralists Collins and Murroni (1996) contend that 'large size tends to bring the resources required for comprehensive high quality reporting' (page 75).

Evaluation

◆ Pluralists are criticised for failing to address the narrow background of media professionals. Neo-Marxists argue that media institutions are dominated by those who represent the interests of the powerful in society and that, as a result, there is restricted diversity of views.

◆ Marxists argue that pluralists ignore the role of owners in shaping the content of the media.

◆ Diversity and choice may be limited by the power of advertisers. In the contest to attract advertising revenue, media producers must deliver large audiences. This may restrict the production of less mainstream media products that serve minority audiences but do not have widespread appeal.

Activity 11

Make a mind-map for each theoretical explanation, identifying key supporting evidence and criticisms in each case.

Stretch and Challenge Activity ➤

Add to your mind-map by including any counter-views to the criticisms you have identified. Can you extend your evaluation by referring to strengths and weaknesses of the methods used to gather the supporting evidence?

Section summary

The main theories to consider in this section are Marxism, neo-Marxism and pluralism.

Using the key terms below, write a paragraph summarising the main points you have learnt about ownership and control of the media.

- Trends and patterns in media ownership and control
- Concentration
- Vertical integration
- Horizontal integration
- Transnational ownership
- Diversification
- Synergy
- Marxism
- Neo-Marxism
- Pluralism
- Hegemony
- Fourth Estate

Stretch and Challenge Activity ➤

Conduct research into recent developments in media technology, like the internet, and assess the extent to which they have given audiences greater control of the media. Add this to your section summary.

Exam practice

1 Outline and assess the view that audiences determine the content of the media. (50 marks)

2 Outline and assess neo-Marxist views on ownership and control of the media. (50 marks)

(iii) Social construction of the news

- What is 'the news'?

- How do we get to know about what is in the news?

- Who decides what is news?

Some people think of the news as a window on the world, which provides the audience with a factual account of events, but sociologists look beyond this view to find out how news is made. This section will examine factors involved in the production of the news, and explore the influences from within the media and from wider society that are involved in the process of constructing the news. We will look at the role of journalists and editors, owners and the state.

News can involve a number of aspects:

◆ reports in the media (television, radio, newspapers etc.) about a recent event

◆ new or updated information about a recent event or issue

◆ information about a person or occurrence that is thought to be of interest.

Sociologists are interested in investigating who decides what is worthy of being reported as news, how such decisions are made and who writes the reports. News is shaped by a number of factors including economic considerations involving costs and profits. Williams (2003) identified other influences including the power of media professionals (the people who work in the media like journalists and editors), organisational factors, including the time and space available, and the culture of society.

Journalists

Journalists are trained media professionals who report on events and issues for print and broadcast media. In doing this they construct news stories from events that have happened. A factor influencing the selection of a story is whether it is seen as newsworthy. When deciding what to report, journalists use a range of criteria

known as **news values**. News values reflect the beliefs and attitudes journalists hold, some of which are unconscious, which shape the way the news is constructed. These beliefs will influence the stories that are selected and the way they are written. News values play a part in the decision-making process for journalists as they select stories to report. Galtung and Ruge (1965, cited in Harcup and O'Neill, 2001) analysed international news stories and identified news values that were present in stories that reached the top of the news agenda. Some of the key news values identified by Galtung and Ruge appear in Table 3.1.

Activity 12

1 Using newspapers, television or radio reports, choose four stories and decide which news values from Table 3.1 may have led journalists to select these stories.

2 There may be more than one news value evident in each story. Briefly explain your reasons for identifying these news values in a short summary about each story.

There are a number of criticisms of Galtung and Ruge's news values.

◆ Vasterman (1995) argues that they are mistaken in believing that journalists actually report events: 'But news is not out there, journalists do not report news. They construct it, they construct facts, they construct statements, they construct a context in which these facts make sense. They reconstruct "a" reality'.

Key term	Definition
Frequency	an event that fits with the frequency of the broadcast or publication is more likely to be selected than one that unfolds over a longer timescale
Threshold	the size of an event: a story with greater drama or intensity is preferred
Unambiguity	the easier a story is to explain, the more likely it is to be selected
Meaningfulness	stories that are geographically close to the audience are seen as more newsworthy. Also, stories that are more culturally close to the audience are more likely to feature, e.g. stories about events in the western world rather than the developing world
Consonance	a story is more likely to be selected if the journalist can construct a mental image of the event. To do this the story must connect with the journalist's way of understanding the world
Unexpectedness	events that are unexpected have more value than those expected to happen
Continuity	an ongoing story with updates on developments that keep it in the spotlight
Composition	some stories are included to give balance to the newspaper or broadcast, e.g. a relatively unimportant foreign story may be included if the foreign news section is in need of filling, or a story may be included because it reinforces another issue being reported
Reference to elite nations	stories about dominant countries are seen as more newsworthy
Reference to elite people	stories about important and/or powerful people are preferred
Reference to persons	stories about people have human-interest value. There is current concern that this type of reporting has increased in relation to well-known people and has led to the development of the cult of celebrity and to dumbing down
Negativity	bad news is more likely to feature than good news

Table 3.1: Key news values (Source: Harcup and O'Neill, 2001)

◆ Hall (1981) cited in Harcup and O'Neill (2001) commenting from a Marxist perspective, argues that Galtung and Ruge's list of news values fails to shed light on the ideological factors underlying them.

◆ Harcup and O'Neill still see a value in Galtung and Ruge's work, but believe that their list must be updated to reflect contemporary trends in news reporting. For example, they propose that a news value of 'entertainment' be added, as their research found this to be a factor found in all newspapers (Harcup and O'Neill, 2001).

Editors

The issues relating to news values discussed above also apply to **editors**. Editors are trained media professionals who supervise journalists' work and who can select, make changes to and rewrite stories. Editors are the media professionals in news organisations who have the final say in what appears in news reports. Case studies have noted the influence of editorial intervention and the self-censorship that journalists employ in an attempt to please their editors (Curran and Gurevitch, 2005). Journalists may include material that they believe will meet with the editors' approval and so increase the chances of their stories remaining intact. Sumpter (2000) comments on the editors' role and suggests that they keep a close eye on audience figures and make decisions on what stories to include on the basis of concerns about increasing audience size. This can be seen, in some cases, as conflicting with the factors that influence journalists when writing their stories.

Both journalists and editors are **gatekeepers**. A gatekeeper has the power to select the content of the news in print and broadcast media. In this respect, gatekeeping can be seen as a form of censorship. A similar process involved in selecting the news is agenda-setting. An agenda is a schedule or list of matters to be addressed. In news production, **agenda-setting** involves the shaping of a news story, including the focus given to particular issues within a story. The processes of gatekeeping and agenda-setting mean that some events and issues are not reported and brought to the attention of the public. Editors and journalists are involved in both these processes, but editors have greater power and control than journalists as they can change content or decide that a story will not be included. Some sociologists believe that gatekeeping and agenda-setting are influenced by wider ideological influences; this view is discussed later in this section.

Stretch and Challenge Activity

Daily newspapers contain an editorial section. Read four editorials from a range of different newspapers on any one day and answer the following questions.

1 Can you detect a particular bias in the tone of the section?

2 What factors do you think have influenced the comments being made by the editors?

3 How much influence do you think these editorial pages are likely to have on the readers?

Hierarchy of credibility

The concept of the 'hierarchy of credibility', introduced by the interactionist sociologist Becker (Marshall, 1998), has been applied to the processes involved in the construction of the news. It has been argued that journalists and editors give more value and credibility to the views of those in society who have greater status, influence and power and will seek access and give prominence to their views when reporting a story. This means that the views of those lower down the social system may be marginalised and denied access. For example, when reporting on youth and gun crime, journalists often include comments from police officers but not from young people living in the area involved.

Activity 13

1 Watch television news broadcasts covering one evening's viewing.

2 Using the research method of content analysis, note down the various stories making the news that day and the roles of the different people contributing to each story: for example, a police spokesperson or a government minister.

3 Estimate where they fit in the hierarchy of credibility.

4 Are there any other people who could have been consulted but weren't?

5 Discuss your findings with members of your class.

Other factors have been identified as influencing journalists' and editors' roles in the construction of the news.

The news diary

Schlesinger (1987) referred to the importance of the news diary in shaping the content of the news. Much of the news that is reported is recorded in advance in a news diary of forthcoming events such as royal birthdays, the launch of an innovative product or a meeting of heads of state. Journalists will have organised their schedules around these events and space will have been allocated to the reporting of them.

Sociology of the mass media

U3
3

Economic considerations

The process of constructing the news is also affected by economic considerations involving costs and profits. Most organisations involved in the reporting of news are profit-making companies and need to be aware of the costs involved in their work. Non-profit-making organisations are also accountable to financial regulators and must be seen to be financially responsible in the way that they operate. This has led to the use of news agencies that collect and assemble reports and sell them to newspapers and broadcasters. The use of news agencies can reduce the costs involved in constructing a story, including expensive flights and accommodation for media professionals and their equipment, but it also means that some control over content is lost as stories are put together outside the organisation.

The point in the financial year in which news items arise will influence how they are reported. If the end of the financial year is approaching and money in the budget is running out, coverage of the story will be affected.

Factors influencing the way journalists and editors construct the news may be separated into two categories:

◆ Cultural – values that reflect the background and attitudes of the journalist writing the story. Cultural news values are also influenced by the style and political standpoint of the newspaper.

◆ Bureaucratic – the practical aspects of news production including the timing of going to print or going on air and the amount of space or time available to report the story.

Owners

Owners strive to ensure that their organisation is as profitable as possible and able to compete effectively with other media companies. Owners employ media professionals, including journalists and editors, to write and report news stories. However, there is no general agreement about the role that owners play in news construction. Some sociologists believe that owners leave it to the media professionals they employ to construct the news, while other sociologists argue that owners seek to exert influence over the content of the news. This may be because they have a particular viewpoint that they wish to be expressed or because they want to maximise profits. For example, it has been suggested that owners are responsible for the greater emphasis in the news on personalised stories about celebrities because they believe them to be popular and therefore profitable. These differing views are discussed later in this section when we explore theoretical explanations.

Activity 14

Using the factors involved in constructing the news referred to so far in this section, draw up a list of those that you think are influenced by cultural values and those influenced by practical issues. Note down your findings in a table like the one below and discuss with your class.

Factors	Cultural	Practical
Newspapers' support for a particular political party	✓	
Space available for international news		✓

The state

The state refers to institutions that govern society including the government, the civil service, the royal family and the military. The government, in particular, has a role in the control of the media and can influence the construction of the news in a number of ways:

◆ Laws – certain stories can be censored or banned through the use of laws like the Officials Secrets Act, the Terrorism Act 2006 and through the use of Defence Authority Notices, which are official but voluntary requests to news editors not to publish items on specified subjects on the grounds of national security.

◆ Spin doctors – there is increasing concern that government officials are getting involved in managing the flow of information to the media and manipulating it in a way that benefits the government. They place a particular 'spin' on a news story that conveys a message in the way they want the public to receive it. Such government officials can be known as 'spin doctors', although the term extends to other non-government media spokespeople. Another spin technique involves delaying the release of bad news until a time when it will do least damage. On the day of the 9/11 bombings in the USA, a British government press officer, Jo Moore, sent an email stating that this was a good day to release news that the government wanted to bury.

◆ Constitutional constraints – the BBC is a state-owned public service broadcaster. The BBC Royal Charter, which was renewed in 2007 for a period of ten years, sets out the public purpose of the BBC:

  a sustaining citizenship and civil society

  b promoting education and learning

  c stimulating creativity and cultural excellence

  d representing the UK, its nations, regions and communities

  e bringing the UK to the world and the world to the UK

  f in promoting its other purposes, helping to deliver to the public the benefit of emerging communications technologies and services and, in addition, taking a leading role in the switchover to digital television.

The BBC is required, under the terms of the Charter, to maintain an independent approach: 'The BBC shall be independent in all matters concerning the content of its output, the times and manner in which this is supplied, and in the management of its affairs' (BBC Royal Charter, 2007).

Weblinks

For full details of the BBC Royal Charter, or to look at further examples of spin, see 'Websites', page ii.

Activity 15

Write a newspaper article explaining to the public the factors that shape the news they receive. You may wish to write this as a sensationalised story that aims to stir up an emotional response, or one that seeks to be more neutral and factually based.

Theoretical explanations

This subsection will examine the different sociological explanations for social construction of the news. It will consider the four theories explored in section ii, and it would be useful to refer back to them:

◆ Marxism

◆ neo-Marxism

◆ pluralism

◆ postmodern views.

Marxism

We will consider the views of both traditional Marxism and, below, the neo-Marxist approach. Traditional Marxists believe that power and control in the media lie with the ruling class, including the state and the owners of the media. Owners form an alliance with powerful politicians as they share an interest in maintaining power and promoting their interests and, in the case of owners, increasing their profits. As a result they manipulate the content of the news to maintain the status quo and so protect their position of power. Traditional Marxists believe that news is constructed under the control of owners to present capitalism in a favourable light and to prevent the working class from seeing the true inequality that lies at the heart of capitalism. In this respect, the news is used to maintain false class-consciousness.

Tunstall and Palmer's research (1991) into media owners in the UK, France, Germany and Italy provides evidence of the power of media owners to influence the news in relation to political events. They studied the role of owners in affecting the way that people vote in national elections and found that owners used their television channels and newspapers to 'deliver partisan support at national elections' (page 107).

Contemporary evidence supports the Marxist view that owners directly intervene in the construction of the news. Evans (1983) refers to Rupert Murdoch's active and detailed control of the content of his newspapers by, in some cases, phone calls to editors to direct the form that the front page should take. Thussu (2007) conducted research into Star News, a news channel owned by Rupert Murdoch's News International. He argues that Murdoch seeks to maximise his profits by shaping the news agenda to reflect what he believes will attract audiences and, in turn, advertisers that bring in revenue. Thussu argues that Murdoch promotes a news agenda that emphasises 'an obsessive interest in glamour, crime and celebrity culture' (page 599).

Evaluation – also see criticisms of Marxism in section ii (page 102).

◆ Traditional Marxists can be regarded as presenting an overly conspiratorial view of the role of owners. They see them as acting as a united group concerned with maintaining capitalist ideology. It is argued by pluralists that owners' main aim is to provide the audience with what they want so that they will buy their products and so increase the profits of the companies they own.

◆ Marxists are criticised for failing to take account of the role of media professionals in constructing the news.

◆ It is said that Marxists ignore the range of views offered in the media, including those that are critical of the powerful in society.

Neo-Marxism

Neo-Marxists share some of the views of traditional Marxists, but focus less on the view that media owners deliberately seek to brainwash the audience into believing capitalist ideology. Neo-Marxism sees the media as reinforcing hegemony, a dominant set of ideas, through the culture of the media professionals involved in the construction of the news. Journalists and editors are seen as coming largely from a white, middle-class background and so they share white, middle-class norms and values which govern their outlook on the world and what they see as 'normal'. In this sense they reinforce the views of the powerful in society because they have been socialised into these views. This shapes the decisions they make when constructing the news, including the stories to be selected (gatekeeping), the views to be included and the way stories are presented (agenda-setting). Because of this, the media are seen as representing the ideas of the ruling class and ignoring, ridiculing or criticising alternative views that do not fit with those of the media professionals. The process, however, is unconscious in that it is the product of the media professionals' worldview rather than a deliberate attempt to manipulate the audience.

Research undertaken by the Glasgow University Media Group (GUMG), using the research method of content analysis, has investigated news stories covering industrial action by trade unions and the reporting of war stories. Its research has found that television news is constructed in a way that reflects the outlook of the journalists involved and gives a biased picture of the world. News stories are selected and constructed from a particular outlook, which connects with, and supports, those in authority and presents them favourably. When referring to those who challenge the powerful, reports portray them negatively. This is done through the language used to describe them and their actions and by the camera angles employed. The situation is presented from the point of view of the powerful and gives the viewer an insight into this perspective.

More recently, the GUMG has developed its work using audience research and concluded that the audience perceives the media in a number of different ways. The concept of a 'circuit of communication' is used to describe issues related to production, content and the way that messages are received. Philo and Miller (2005) identify four elements in the communication process that interact with each other: social and political institutions, the media content, the public and decision-makers. However, the Group points out that the different parts of the circuit do not have equal degrees of influence and that the public has less power than the other three elements.

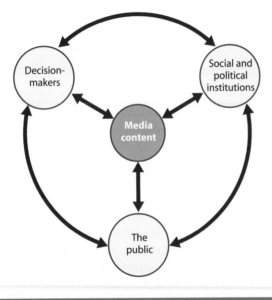

Figure 3.4: The circuit of communication, in which the different parts affect each other although they do not have equal amounts of influence

The GUMG concludes that there are clear agendas framing the construction of the news, but that the audience can be critical of the messages delivered by being active in the way that they use the media.

Philo (1999) found, from his research into audiences and the reception of messages, that three important factors determine whether media messages are accepted or rejected.

◆ First, the audience member's direct experience of the issue in question has an impact on the way the message is received.

◆ Second, the use of logic in coming to an understanding of the issue, for example identifying contradictions in the account given, influences how the message is received.

◆ Finally, the value systems of the audience affect the way they receive the message.

Activity 16

1 Using content analysis, examine three current news stories from television, radio or newspapers from a neo-Marxist perspective.

2 Try to identify ways in which the story has been constructed that support the status quo, for example the language used, the issues highlighted and photos or camera angles used to present images.

3 Using the same three news stories, think about how you received them. What factors were involved in you coming to an understanding of the content, for example, were you aware of your own experience in relation to the stories?

4 Present your findings to your group.

Neo-Marxists also see the state as exercising considerable control over the content of the news through a range of formal and informal controls. Formal controls include the power of UK governments to grant media franchises or to determine the size of the BBC licence fee. Informal controls include the increasing power of government spin doctors to determine the access of news media to government ministers and officials.

Evaluation – also see criticisms of neo-Marxism in section ii.

Many of the criticisms of traditional Marxism apply to neo-Marxism. In addition:

◆ Neo-Marxists are criticised for failing to recognise the growing number of journalists and editors who are women and/or from ethnic minorities, and who bring a different perspective than that of white middle-class men.

◆ The large number of digital news channels that now exist can be said to have broadened the range and type of stories being covered.

◆ The internet provides the opportunity for a wide range of views to be aired. For example, a number of websites offer alternative news stories.

- Pluralists argue that journalists are trained professionals who bring objectivity and a sense of responsibility to the work that they do in reporting the news.

- On his website, Shaun Best offers a range of criticisms of the work of the GUMG. He argues that it approaches its research with the answers already decided in advance because of the theoretical viewpoint it comes from. He believes that the Group's positivist approach in using content analysis assumes that there is a logical basis for the way they measure media content, which other theorists would contest.

Weblink

For further information about the Glasgow University Media Group and its research, or to read Shaun Best's criticisms in more detail, see 'Websites', page ii.

Pluralism

The pluralist view is often expressed by media professionals. It argues that the media operate in a market situation where media professionals must ensure that the work they produce attracts viewers, listeners and readers. Pluralists believe that journalists and editors work autonomously as skilled professionals, although they will be aware of their audiences' interests and will respond to these when constructing news stories. Media professionals therefore are alert to issues of supply and demand.

According to **pluralism**, any bias in media content comes about from the media representing different viewpoints from which the audience can make a selection. Media bias also comes from technical and bureaucratic factors, such as the limited time and space in which to present information, that can result in the more complex elements of stories being left out. This can also lead to more complicated news items that would require detailed explanation being absent from newspapers and broadcast reports.

As professionals, journalists and editors bring news values, such as those discussed earlier

in this section, to their work. Some pluralists argue that the work of media professionals, when writing and reporting news stories, is governed by objectivity and a sense of social responsibility.

Evaluation – also see criticisms of pluralism on pages 104–105.

- Critics of this view would argue that the media represent a quite limited range of viewpoints because they are dominated by white middle-aged, middle-class media professionals who share broadly the same norms and values which shape their decisions when selecting and constructing news stories.

- Another factor that may be seen to limit the range of viewpoints in the news is the increasingly widespread use of news agencies. News agencies are organisations that gather news stories and sell them to broadcast and print media companies. This means that the same stories are being sold to a number of newspapers and television news channels. The Campaign for Press and Broadcasting Freedom (CPBF) found that in the case of internet news, consumers are offered the illusion of information diversity and an endless range of perspectives, when the reality is concentration, not diversity. One search engine claimed to use 4500 news sources from around the world, but a CPBF investigation revealed that it relied on just four: three news agencies and the BBC.

- Marxists argue that media professionals are constrained by a number of factors. The news stories that appear do not simply reflect the professional judgements of journalists and editors and the demands of the market, but are also shaped by the influence of owners, the state and advertisers.

Weblink

For additional information about the work of the Campaign for Press and Broadcasting Freedom, visit its website (see 'Websites', page ii).

Postmodern views

Postmodern theorists believe that we live in a media-saturated society where the media play a central role in defining our culture. The media transmit a variety of views and are characterised by diversity and choice in both the content and the range of media products available. In relation to the news, the media blur the boundaries between the global and local world. Television news broadcasts can transmit images almost immediately across the globe, leading to talk of the world becoming what McLuhan described as a 'global village' (McLuhan and Fiore, 1971) where we have access to world events and can easily gain knowledge of world communities. This can also lead to the domination of news stories by the USA and the UK as two of the most powerful countries in the western world. This has led to concerns that globalisation becomes a means of expanding the domination of the world's most powerful nations, as their news becomes the central focus and news from other countries is increasingly controlled by those with the greatest power. This process is heightened by the use of news agencies, since the most successful and widely used news agencies tend to be from the USA or the UK.

A key idea in **postmodern** views of the media that is relevant to an understanding of the social construction of the news is the concept of 'hyperreality'. The idea, derived from the sociologist Baudrillard (1988), is that in the postmodern world, the media create images or symbols that the audience can confuse with reality. Just as postmodernists see boundaries being blurred between different forms of social identity such as masculinity and femininity, so too are boundaries blurred between reality and media constructions of reality. Audiences come to experience neither reality nor illusion, but a confused mixture – 'hyperreality'. An example of hyperreality might be a place like Disneyland, which exists and can be visited but is actually a carefully constructed fantasy world. Baudrillard provocatively suggested that certain major events did not, in fact, take place as described in the media. For example, he suggested (1995) that the first Gulf War in 1991 (when American forces attacked Saddam Hussein's Iraq, following its invasion of Kuwait) did not take place. He explained that while 100,000 people died, very little actually changed (for example, Saddam Hussein remained in power) in the ways that the concept of a war would suggest. It was the media that helped to create a simplified confusing image of these events as a war. In this instance, the idea of the first Gulf War is not a reality but a hyperreality, in which the boundary between fact and image is blurred. Another hyperreal news story might be a report about a celebrity, such as David Beckham, whose life with Victoria Beckham in Beckingham Palace is real but the media portrayal is hyperreal, in that it is difficult or impossible to tell where reality ends and fantasy begins.

According to Baudrillard, the blurring of boundaries between image and reality and global and local issues can lead to uncertainty about truth and morality. Traditional beliefs become less strictly adhered to and people pick and mix from the range of views they are exposed to, to create their own truth. This truth, in turn, is less fixed and certain and is open to frequent modifications. This leads some postmodernists to believe that we are living in an era of the 'end of meaning'. News then becomes a matter of story-telling rather than reporting of fact. This process has led to the development of the term 'infotainment' to describe the way in which news reporting can be seen as a form of entertainment.

Activity 17

In pairs, think of your own examples of Baudrillard's concept of hyperreality. Present these to the class using posters or storyboards to illustrate the difference between reality and hyperreality.

Stretch and Challenge Activity

Develop your understanding of postmodern views of the media by finding two additional studies by postmodern theorists. Summarise the key points and note down three strengths and/or weaknesses of the data.

The postmodern explanations of news construction are complex and present contradictory views. On the one hand, the media are seen as diverse and offering choice to their audience in terms of both the range of products and content. On the other, they are seen as a sinister and powerful institution that can manipulate the audience and distort reality. The media can blur global boundaries and so enrich cultures and promote mutual understanding, but also have the potential to increase the influence of already powerful nations.

Evaluation

◆ Critics claim that postmodern views lack empirical evidence.

◆ Marxists argue that the focus on diversity and choice ignores the persistence of the control of the media by the power of the state and media owners.

◆ Hegemonic Marxists claim that media professionals come from a narrow range of backgrounds and that this also limits the diversity of viewpoints presented in news stories.

Section summary

The most relevant theories to consider in this section are Marxism, neo-Marxism, pluralism and postmodern views.

Using the key terms below, write a paragraph summarising the main points you have learnt about social construction of the news.

• Journalists
• Editors
• Owners
• The state
• Marxism
• Neo-Marxism
• Pluralism
• Postmodern view
• News values
• Gatekeepers
• Agenda-setting

Stretch and Challenge Activity

Add a paragraph to your section summary that assesses the extent to which journalists, editors, owners and the state have control over the construction of the news.

Exam practice

1 Outline and assess postmodern views on the social construction of the news. (50 marks)

2 Outline and assess the role of owners in the construction of the news. (50 marks)

(iv) Media representations of social groups

Pause for thought

- What are the main stereotypes used by the media to represent males and females?
- Do the media present a balanced view of young people?
- Which ethnic groups are presented most negatively?
- What stereotypes do the media use when referring to social class?

As an agent of secondary socialisation the media are likely to have an important influence on the way we view different groups in society, including those based on gender, ethnicity, age and social class. Because the media cannot represent the full range of characteristics evident in the various groups in society, they tend to use stereotypes when referring to these groups. Since a stereotype presents an oversimplified image that draws on generalisations about a particular social group, it may contain some aspects that are accurate but can also present a distorted view. Some theorists have expressed concern that the media have the power to create damaging stereotypes, while others contend that it simply reinforces views of social groups that are held more widely by society.

This section will explore the ways in which gender, ethnicity, age and social class are represented in the media. We will also examine theoretical explanations that seek to promote understanding of why these social groups are represented in the way that they are.

Gender

An analysis of **gender** representations in the media is not straightforward. Early research produced in the 1960s, 1970s and 1980s found that portrayals of men and women were distinct and different, with women in a limited number of roles as housewives, mothers and sex objects and men taking the leading roles with a wider range of mostly strong, dominant characters. Recent studies acknowledge a shift from the 1990s onwards towards a more varied range of representations of males and females. However, the picture is complicated by the fact that the media products being commented on by earlier researchers are still frequently recycled on satellite and cable television networks, making them a feature of current representations. Therefore, audiences are exposed to traditional stereotypes alongside contemporary, more varied images of gender. Another complication relates to the variety of media products that contain representations of gender. These range from red-top tabloids to television programmes and films that can present very different images of gender and explore a diversity of masculinities and femininities. Any examination of media representations of gender, therefore, needs to recognise these contradictions and variations and be aware that there is not a simple line of development that leaves traditional stereotypes in a past era.

Gauntlett (2008) notes evidence of a shift from the 1990s onwards away from more traditional gender roles across a range of media products. Using content analysis, his research into prime-time television in this period found that gender roles seemed to become increasingly equal and non-stereotyped (2008). Using the example of the television sitcom *Friends*, Gauntlett contends that the characters were equal but different, with males and females adopting more modern characteristics that moved beyond traditional roles.

In evaluation, while Gauntlett (2008) believes that representations of gender on television have 'turned a corner', it is suggested that trends towards equality may have reached a plateau as evidence shows that the ratio of men to women on television has hardly changed in a decade. Leading roles in dramas still tend to be played by men, many television series centre on male characters, and discussions about politics continue to be dominated by men.

Sociology of the mass media

U3

3

1 Watch an episode of *Friends* and conduct a content analysis of the main male and female characters.

2 Identify ways in which the main male and female characters may be seen to be equal but different.

3 Is there evidence of equality and inequality in their roles and the way they are presented?

4 Are there ways in which the characters conform to more traditional gender stereotypes?

5 Discuss your views in class.

Gauntlett's (2008) analysis of gender representations in films since the 1990s shows men and women as having similar skills and talents to each other. He refers to films like *Spiderman 3*, *Knocked Up* and *Fantastic Four: Rise of the Silver Surfer* as examples of modern films that present a challenge to conventional masculinity by showing more traditional masculine behaviour to be fundamentally flawed. Females in these films are more assertive.

However, Gauntlett notes that men still tend to take the leading roles, act as heroes to save women, and are more likely than women to be lead characters as they get older, for example Sean Connery, Harrison Ford and Bruce Willis.

1 Use content analysis to consider three contemporary films that you have seen recently.

2 What roles did the males and females take, including lead characters?

3 What skills and talents did they have in the films?

4 Compare the differences and similarities between the male and female characters and list these.

5 Present your findings in the form of a film review.

Watch the film *Knocked Up* and discuss the gender representations within the film.

Stretch and Challenge Activity

1 Using semiology, identify the signs and codes used to convey particular messages about gender roles.

2 Find further examples of research into the use of stereotypes. Note down the key points and any evaluative comments you can make.

3 Evaluate the extent to which *Knocked Up* demonstrates a shift in representations of gender. Can you identify aspects of hegemonic gender roles within the film?

Other research into media representations of gender is less optimistic than Gauntlett's; this will be discussed later in the section when we consider feminist explanations of media representation.

Ethnicity

Media representations of **ethnicity** vary across different ethnic groups, with some groups being represented more negatively than others. As with gender, the representations also vary across media products. There are, for example, satellite channels dedicated to specific minority ethnic groups and the representations in programmes from these sources will differ from those from more mainstream sources. For example, there are channels that offer representations of ethnicity that reflect the lived experience and culture of minority ethnic groups. These channels present representations that are appreciated by their target audience but may be less engaging to groups outside of this ethnicity. In addition, the emergence of hybrid identities within minority ethnic groups adds a further layer of complexity when considering media representations, since such identities may challenge assumptions about the experience of some ethnic groups.

For example, fusion music that combines two or more genres drawn from minority ethnic groups can be difficult to categorise.

Research into representations of ethnicity in the media tends to find that minority ethnic groups are presented in a limited range of stereotypical roles, are under-represented and are often seen in roles constructed from a white perspective, usually because they are produced by white media professionals. It has been argued that, in terms of media representations, minority ethnic groups have been stereotyped, marginalised or excluded.

Moore et al. (2005) identify five stereotypes commonly used to portray black people in the media:

- as criminals, for example the word 'black' is often used in descriptions of criminals but 'white' is not generally used in this way. Hall's study *Policing the Crisis* (Hall et al., 1995) discusses the use of this stereotype

- as a threat – for example tabloid scares about immigrants and asylum seekers taking jobs and using the resources of the welfare state

- as abnormal – ways in which the media present the cultural practices of minority ethnic groups as odd, for example arranged marriages

- as unimportant – for example the way in which priority is given to the reporting of issues affecting white people

- as dependent – images of less developed countries tend to focus on what has been described as 'coup–war–famine–starvation syndrome' with little discussion of their exploitation by western countries.

The view that the media adopt a negative approach to representing minority ethnic groups is supported in a classic study by van Dijk (1991). He found evidence of unconscious racism in media reporting of minority ethnic groups. Van Dijk argued that the negative language used and lack of reference to quotes from minority ethnic sources resulted in biased reporting that demonstrated a white perspective on news stories.

Malik (2002) is concerned that contemporary media do not accurately reflect the ethnic reality of the contemporary UK.

Activity 21

'The reality of a lived multiculturalism is not represented on British television and the media in general can by no means be seen as ethnically neutral. Although it is now common to see Black and Asian people on British television who do not necessarily function to solely "carry" the race theme, the repertoire of imagery still remains limited. We rarely see strong Asian women ... or Black factual commentators outside sports programmes, and there are still too few Black people actually reaching the industry's boardrooms. Television is still far too "White"; an admission made by the BBC's newly appointed Director General, Greg Dyke, following his visit around BBC departments (Dyke said this in a speech delivered at the CRE's Race in the Media Awards in April 2000) (Malik, 2002, page 366).

1 List the concerns expressed by Malik about the British media.

2 Do you agree with Greg Dyke that television is still far too 'White'? Construct arguments for and against this view.

Stretch and Challenge Activity

What do you think Malik means by 'a lived multiculturalism'? Can you think of examples of films or television programmes that represent the reality of 'a lived multiculturalism'?

Barker (1999) notes developments but also sees ambiguities in the representations of minority ethnic groups in the soap opera *Eastenders*. The drama can be seen as representing a multi-ethnic community, since a range of black and Asian characters take up significant roles. However, the series has been criticised for using stereotypes by casting Asians as doctors and shopkeepers. Barker also refers to the way the programme can be seen as failing to engage with wider structural forms of racism by presenting it as the product of an individual character trait. Finally, he draws attention to the criticism that the black and Asian characters take a more marginal place in the drama and that the central characters are white.

U3

3

Sociology of the mass media

1 Identify the characters in *Eastenders* who come from a minority ethnic background.

2 How far do characters from minority ethnic backgrounds conform to ethnic stereotypes?

3 Are they central characters in the programme?

4 Are issues of ethnicity and racism considered? If so, how are they dealt with?

Draw up a list of the stereotypes that you think are most likely to be used to represent young and old people. Discuss which group is most likely to be negatively represented and the reasons why this might be the case.

Overall, research points to some change in media representations of ethnic groups, with a greater diversity of roles and more positive images being portrayed. However, these changes are not accepted uncritically and there are concerns that minority ethnic groups continue to be presented in stereotyped and marginalised ways. It is also important to be aware that representations vary across different ethnic groups and can also be seen to respond to wider social factors, for example it is argued that the impact of the events of 9/11 has changed representations of some Asian groups.

Further evidence to support the view that media representations of ethnic minority groups are problematic can be found later in this subsection when we consider the neo-Marxist explanation of media representations.

Weblinks

@

Useful information on the experience of minority ethnic groups and discussion of media representations of such experience can be found in web-based resources and, in particular, in blogs that allow the exchange of ideas, including blogs on 'ethnicity' and on 'hybrid identity' (see 'Websites', page ii).

Age

Research into media representations of **age** tends to focus on two particular aspects: representations of young and old. Representations of young people are also addressed on pages 34–36 and 133–134, where moral panics are considered.

As with media representations of gender and ethnicity, research into age has found the use of stereotypes across a range of media products.

Representations of youth in the early 1950s offered positive images that reflected and celebrated the relative freedom and prosperity being enjoyed by young people. More recently, youth culture is frequently represented in the media as a problem: young people are seen as deviating from society's norms and values and as a threat. Dominant images of young people tend to link them with binge-drinking, drug-taking, knife crime and other violent incidents.

Osgerby (2002) studied the shifts in media representations of youth in the second half of the twentieth century, although he noted a recurring theme of 'youth-as-trouble', a phrase coined by Hebdige (1988). Osgerby contends that shifts in media representations of youth reflect wider cultural developments and mirror the spirit of the times. He illustrates this view by referring to the way in which the media represented youth positively in the 1950s and early 1960s in a post-war mood of hope and prosperity. This contrasted with darker images of teenage violence in the 1970s and 1980s, which seemed to reflect concerns about growing lawlessness and social breakdown.

Research into older age groups similarly indicates a changing scene. Researchers note a shift away from narrow stereotypes of 'grumpy old men' and 'doddery old codgers' towards more varied images that acknowledge changes in ageing and the social trend towards older and younger groups sharing leisure interests.

Biggs (1993) identifies trends in the representations of ageing including:

◆ older people appearing in considerable numbers in soap operas

◆ negative portrayals of old age in sitcoms

◆ a move towards a more active view of older people, in which old people are portrayed as participating in leisure activities and in society as a whole.

U3

3

Sociology of the mass media

Figure 3.5: Music as a form of communication where older and younger members of the audience share leisure interests

Activity 24

Drawing on the studies by Osgerby and Biggs, identify contemporary examples to support their findings.

Social class

What research there is on media representations of **social class** tends to focus on the working class and, in particular, traditional working communities like those portrayed in the television programmes *Eastenders* and *Coronation Street*. Such representations often adopt a nostalgic view of a working-class community life that is no longer experienced by most working-class people. Other representations of working-class people link them to social problems related to striking, scrounging from the welfare state or living on the fringes of criminality. Representations of the underclass do this in a more overt way and mirror new right views of underclass lifestyle. The middle class tend to be portrayed as unproblematic and living a lifestyle that represents the 'norm' in British

society. There is less media engagement with the upper class, perhaps because the effect of **social closure** means that there is little knowledge and understanding of this group on which to base representations. Fictional portrayals tend to take the form of period dramas harking back to an era when there was little challenge to the power of the upper class in society.

Activity 25

1 Identify and list television programmes and characters from programmes that represent social class in the way described above.

2 In groups, discuss how realistic you believe these representations to be.

Devereux (2008) sees media representations of the working class as falling into two main categories. There are positive portrayals of 'happy' and 'deserving' poor people that contrast with the negative images of those on welfare benefits. Devereux also refers to research that examines the way that certain groups, such as 'chavs', become the target of media-generated moral panics.

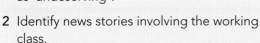

1 Drawing on your list from the activity above, which of the characters fall into the category of 'deserving poor' and which can be seen as 'undeserving'?

2 Identify news stories involving the working class.

3 Using content analysis or semiology, analyse these stories and the representations of those from the working class.

4 Use your results to make a poster illustrating your key findings.

Weblinks

For more information about chavs, look at websites devoted to an understanding of chavs (see 'Websites', page ii).

Theoretical explanations

Marxism

Marxism views media representations as supporting the interests of the ruling class. Traditional Marxists focus on social class divisions in society as the fundamental inequality. As a result, they are concerned with the ways in which the media function to control society through ideology and media representations. However, because they are interested in the economic base of society, much of their research focuses on issues discussed in sections ii and iii concerning ownership and control.

Evaluation

◆ Neo-Marxists and feminists have been critical of traditional Marxists for failing to address social inequalities beyond social class.

◆ Neo-Marxists also contend that the traditional Marxist focus on economic power neglects other power structures in society, such as the media's role in creating negative stereotypes of some social groups.

◆ Pluralists would argue that Marxists ignore the range of views offered in the media, including those that offer a positive representation of disadvantaged social groups.

Neo-Marxism

Neo-Marxist concerns about social inequality extend beyond the social class focus of traditional Marxists who see other inequalities as a product of the fundamental social class divisions in society. As we have seen in other subsections, neo-Marxism uses the term 'hegemony' to explain how ruling-class norms and values are maintained in society. A further aspect of this hegemony relates to media representations of social groups. For example, Hall has studied the way in which these representations create and reinforce a dominant ideology. In an influential study published in 1981, Hall argued that the media operated with three overriding stereotypes of black people: the native, the entertainer and the slave (Hall, 1981). Later, he identified a development in media representations where a more diverse range of images was presented. However, Hall sees such diversity as existing within a framework that is constructed by the powerful in society and does not present any challenge to their dominance.

1 Using examples from contemporary films and television programmes, draw up a list of representations of minority ethnic groups.

2 Assess how diverse the range of representations is, taking into consideration factors such as status and power and whether the representations are positive or negative.

3 Summarise your findings in a paragraph.

Stretch and Challenge Activity

Evaluate Hall's arguments using evidence from your findings from Activity 27 and elsewhere.

Sociology of the mass media

Overall, neo-Marxists would argue that media representations of social groups reinforce the hegemony that supports the ruling class in society. This analysis can be applied to representations of gender, ethnicity, age and social class, where the images used will maintain dominant norms and values. Challenges to these norms and values will be presented as a threat or as a joke, or will be ignored.

Activity 28

In groups, look at a variety of media representations of gender, ethnicity, age or social class. Construct a list of examples of representations from within that social group that can be seen to present a challenge to social norms and values. Discuss the ways in which these more alternative representations are presented.

Evaluation

◆ Neo-Marxism has been criticised for ignoring the evidence that shows significant improvements in the representations of social groups.

◆ Critics also point to the increasing number of media professionals coming from varied social backgrounds who bring a different perspective to the media products they are involved with.

◆ It is argued that the increasing number of media products available means that there is greater opportunity for variations in media representations, including access to programmes and channels dedicated to particular social groups.

◆ The development of new technologies can be seen as increasing the representation of a wider range of views. Personal computers and the availability of publishing software have enabled individuals to produce professional-quality media products. Access to the internet, blogs and video-sharing websites like YouTube have offered individuals the opportunity to present more varied representations.

Pluralism

Pluralism regards media representations of social groups as reflecting both the diversity evident in society and the demands of the audience. According to the pluralist view, media representations will develop to reflect changes in society as the media respond to meet society's needs. Pluralists argue that media professionals are alert to the responsibility they have to represent social groups in a fair and balanced way, and are guided by professional values.

Evaluation

◆ The pluralist view ignores the negative impact that media representations can have on social groups, particularly those that are more marginalised in society.

◆ Pluralists are accused of ignoring issues of power and control in the way that media representations are constructed.

◆ Pluralists are criticised for failing to address the narrow background of media professionals. Neo-Marxists argue that media institutions represent the interests of the powerful in society and there is limited diversity of representations.

◆ Marxists argue that pluralists ignore the role of owners in shaping the content of the media.

◆ Diversity and choice may be limited by the power of advertisers. In the contest to attract advertising revenue, media producers must deliver large audiences. This may restrict the production of less mainstream media products that serve minority audiences but do not have widespread appeal.

Feminism

Feminism is a theory that encompasses a number of strands. In general, feminists are united in opposing patriarchy, but the various strands within feminism offer different overviews on gender inequalities, including those that pertain to representations in the media.

Liberal feminists tend to be more optimistic about the possibility of change and would contend that there is evidence of greater equality in media representations of gender. They argue that increasing numbers of women are employed as media professionals and this contributes to changes in the way gender representations are conceived and produced. Liberal feminists also point to the wider variety of roles being played by women in film and television, including more dominant characters like *Buffy the Vampire Slayer*, the female lead, Ripley, in the *Alien* films, and Ugly Betty.

Radical feminists see little change in gender representations in the media. They would argue that traditional stereotypes are ever-present in advertising and that the media still degrade women by presenting them as sex objects for men. According to radical feminists, culture, including media products, continues to be dominated and controlled by men and they still occupy the key positions of power in society. Men set the agenda and the media reflect a 'malestream' perspective.

Marxist feminists link media representations of gender with both capitalism and patriarchy. According to Marxist feminists, it is in the interests of these two, or dual, systems of power to maintain gender inequalities. Since the media function as a capitalist industry dominated by male owners and male media professionals, nothing much will change until both systems have been overthrown. Marxist feminists see the media as reinforcing hegemonic gender roles by promoting an ideology of femininity and masculinity that conforms to conventional norms and values.

More generally, recent feminist research into the media contends that traditional stereotypes persist and some theorists believe that there is evidence of a backlash against feminism.

Whelehan's (2000) study of men's magazines such as *Loaded*, *FHM* and *Maxim*, argues that such magazines attempt to challenge feminism by promoting a world where women are seen as sex objects, and changes in gender roles can be dismissed with an ironic joke.

Gauntlett (2008) criticises Whelehan's analysis as superficial and he argues that she adopts an overly pessimistic view about the influence such magazines have on men's identities. He believes that men's magazines do not deliver just one message and that often they offer contradictory views that acknowledge changing gender roles and the diversity of masculinities in the contemporary UK.

The feminist McRobbie has conducted a number of studies of girls' and women's magazines using qualitative methods including content analysis and semiology. Over the years (her research spans four decades) McRobbie has come to different conclusions about the impact of these magazines on femininity and identity. In her early research she suggested that magazines had a significant influence on their female readers' identity. Later, McRobbie accepted the criticism by Frazer (1987) that her view on the influence of girls' magazines was overly deterministic (Frazer's own research found that girls read the magazines critically and were likely to laugh at their content). More recently, McRobbie seems to have returned to her earlier concerns about the impact of the media on women's identity. She has expressed worries about the negative effect on young women of celebrity magazines such as *Heat* and *Closer*.

Activity 29

Using a table like the one below, list as many contemporary examples as you can from a range of media to support each of the different feminist views.

	Summary	Contemporary examples in support
Liberal feminism		
Radical feminism		
Marxist feminism		

'Such publications trap their readers into cycles of anxiety, self-loathing and misery that have become a standard mark of modern womanhood. "Normative discontent" about body image, about never being beautiful enough, about success and fear of failure, about not finding a husband at just the right moment in the life cycle, about keeping to rules of dating, about the dire cost of breaking the rules: such values become all encompassing, invading the space of other interests and other activities. The girl becomes a harshly self-judging person.' (McRobbie, 2005)

1 According to McRobbie, what values do magazines such as *Heat* and *Closer* encourage in young women?

2 What effect does McRobbie see these magazines having on young women?

3 In groups, design and conduct your own research to find out the attitudes of young women in your class towards the impact of these magazines.

4 Discuss your findings in class.

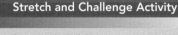

Stretch and Challenge Activity

Evaluate McRobbie's view expressed above by considering whether you think it is overly deterministic or not. What evidence can you find to show that young women do not take such media products seriously? Write a paragraph evaluating feminist concerns about the impact of the media on women.

Feminist research has analysed a wide range of media products including films, television programmes, magazines, advertising and more recently the internet. Most conclude that much still needs to be changed before it can be claimed that there is equality in media representations of gender.

Evaluation

◆ Feminist views on gender representations in the media provide a challenging set of ideas. Liberal feminists produce evidence of change, but this is contested by radical and Marxist feminists who regard any change as superficial and lacking in substance.

◆ Radical and Marxist feminists would argue that while the variety of roles for women may seem greater, the characters often contain aspects associated with traditional femininity. The women in these roles conform to conventional images of attractiveness and aspects of their physical appearance are focused on.

◆ Some feminists are criticised for failing to acknowledge women's ability to resist the ideology of femininity that comes across in women's magazines.

Using resources including textbooks, the internet, and/or articles, identify some earlier studies (from the 1970s or early 1980s) into media representations of gender. Note down the name of the researcher and the key points of the study, and then assess whether you think the evidence is still valid today. This can be used as evidence of change, or to support the view of radical and Marxist feminists who believe that traditional gender stereotypes still dominate media representations.

Weblinks

A useful source for research into contemporary feminist thinking including discussion of media representations can be found in web-based resources, particularly blogs. The 'fword' website contains useful web-based material and blogs, as does the 'feminist reprise' website (see 'Websites', page ii).

Postmodern views

Postmodernists see the boundaries between social groups blurring as distinctions between them become less clear and there is interplay between groups. The media have been fundamental to this process by representing a variety of images from which people can pick and choose. Postmodern views refer to the process of globalisation and its impact on broadening the range of identities and lifestyles that are available.

Figure 3.6: In what ways does this image of Madonna blur boundaries?

Activity 32

1 In groups, use content analysis to study television adverts portraying gender, ethnicity, age and social class. Each group should analyse one of the social groups.

2 Draw up a chart of products being advertised on a mainstream television channel during one peak-time slot.

3 Identify and quantify the kind of roles being played.

4 Assess whether the adverts reflect traditional stereotypes.

5 Write a report summarising your findings.

6 Compare and discuss findings with other groups.

Weblinks

Look at David Gauntlett's site for further analysis of media representations (see 'Websites', page ii).

Evaluation

◆ Postmodern theorists are accused of ignoring the continuing influence of social class, gender, age and ethnicity in media representations.

◆ Critics also argue that postmodernism exaggerates the power of media representations to blur distinctions and create choices.

◆ Critics claim that postmodern views lack evidence for their view of media representations.

◆ Marxists argue that the focus on diversity and choice ignores the continued control of the media by the state and media owners.

◆ Hegemonic Marxists claim that media professionals come from a narrow range of backgrounds and this influences the way they represent social groups.

Section summary

The most relevant theories to be considered in this section are Marxism, neo-Marxism, pluralism, feminism and postmodern views.

Using the key terms below, write a paragraph summarising the main points you have learnt about media representations of social groups.

• Gender

• Ethnicity

• Age

• Social class

• Marxism

• Neo-Marxism

• Pluralism

• Feminism

• Postmodern views

Exam practice

1 Outline and assess feminist views of media representations of gender. (50 marks)

2 Outline and assess the view that the media use negative stereotypes when representing some social groups. (50 marks)

(v) The effect of the media on society

Pause for thought

- In what ways might the media influence audiences?

- Which groups are most likely to be affected by the media?

- What kind of effect might the media have on society?

The effect of the media on society is a much debated issue within the sociology of the media and a range of responses have emerged that contribute to the discussion. Some theorists argue that the media have a powerful and immediate effect on audiences, while others see the effect as occurring over a longer period of time such that it becomes part of the audience's way of experiencing the world. There are those who regard the media's influence as beneficial to society and others who are concerned that the media have a negative effect. This section will examine these different views. The theoretical explanations of the influence of the media on their audiences are discussed together with the effects of the media on wider society, so that a fuller understanding can be gained.

Influence of the media on audiences and on wider society

A useful distinction when exploring the different viewpoints is to examine those that see a direct effect and those that see the effect as indirect.

Direct theories

Direct theories are based on the view that the media have an immediate and powerful influence on their audience. Such theories see the audience as unable to resist media messages and believe that these messages flow from the media directly through to the audience. Much of the concern about the media having a direct effect centres on the issue of imitation of violence and, in particular, their influence on children, young people and other more vulnerable members of society.

A classic direct theory is the 'hypodermic syringe model' associated with Packard (1957) and also known as the 'magic bullet theory'. Packard argued that the media were like a syringe that injected messages into the audience. Packard was directing his view towards the impact of advertising, but it has been applied more widely to explain the influence of the media on their audience. The effect is seen as immediate and powerful and the audience is regarded as passive and uncritical. The theory does not acknowledge differences between members of the audience and, therefore, the audience is seen as homogenous.

Around the same time that Packard was discussing the hypodermic syringe model, Bandura was conducting research that he believed demonstrated that children imitated violence shown on television. One of Bandura's now famous 'bobo doll' experiments involved showing pre-school children a film clip of a large inflated toy, known as a bobo doll, being hit by a child (1963). The children were then led to a laboratory and on the way shown attractive toys that they were told they were not allowed to play with. The children were left alone in the laboratory with toys, including a bobo doll, and their behaviour was observed through one-way mirrors. A control group of children were not shown the film clip. The study showed that the children who had seen the film clip acted aggressively towards the bobo doll.

Concerns about the imitation of violence in the media have persisted and scenes from particular films like *The Matrix*, *Scream*, *Natural Born Killers* and *Child's Play 3* have been associated with acts of violence. More recently, there has been discussion in the media about a possible link between lyrics from Emo music and incidence of self-harm and suicide among its followers. Some researchers have also expressed concerns about the negative effect of video games. The game *Manhunt* was banned in several countries and has been linked to a murder in the UK. As well as violent games being accused of causing aggression in their users, there have been claims that they contribute to poor communication skills amongst players and increased levels of childhood obesity. Critics argue that these concerns are fuelled by media hype and remain unsubstantiated and unproven.

The concept of catharsis confirms that that the media can have a direct effect, but it challenges the fears that are founded on such theories. Field experiments such as that conducted by Feshbach and Singer (1971) involve real-life situations: they used two groups of participants, one exposed to media violence and one not, and found that the group that viewed non-violent images displayed more aggression than the other group. Such findings propose that watching violence in the media can have a direct effect in providing a safe means of release for

aggression, known as catharsis. Stack (2000) suggests that music may also have a cathartic effect, in that listening to it may decrease depression and reduce suicidal tendencies.

Evaluation

The popularity of direct theories has declined over the years since they were conceived. Critics argue that the research that established them is limited because it only measures short-term effects. In addition, laboratory experiments are criticised on the grounds that they do not reflect real-life situations. Field experiments conducted in real-life settings tend to find weaker effects than laboratory experiments. It is also difficult to measure direct effects because of the problem of isolating all other influences that can lead to particular kinds of behaviour. Gauntlett (1995) criticises direct theories for blaming television for problems such as crime while ignoring other possible causes such as social inequality.

A further contribution to the discussion comes from research by Gamson into the factors involved in shaping people's views on political issues. Using focus groups, he found that while people draw on the media, they also use their own experiences and their understanding as these are shaped by popular knowledge of issues. He concluded that people read messages in complicated and sometimes unpredictable ways (Gamson, 1992). Direct theories do not tend to acknowledge much complexity in the process of media effects.

Indirect theories

Indirect theories acknowledge that the media have an effect on audiences, but see this as the product of interaction between different factors. Such theories look beyond a simple one-way effects process that sees the media conveying meaning to the audience, and looks at the way audiences receive media messages and the factors shaping this reception.

An early indirect theory known as the Two-Step Flow Model sees the effect of the media coming through the interaction between people. Katz and Lazarsfeld (1955) identify the role of an opinion leader in influencing the views of others. The opinion leader is an individual who has more exposure to media views on a particular topic through, for example, reading newspapers or watching television, and comes to be regarded by their social contacts as something of an expert on this topic. The influence of the media reaches the audience through two steps: the opinion leader takes in the media messages and passes them on within the context of social relationships. The process of social interaction is an important element in media influence in this theory.

Another approach to understanding the effects of the media on audiences comes through the Cultural Effects Theory, which argues that the media affect the attitudes and behaviour of different social groups in different ways depending on their cultural background. The effect of media messages will vary according to the gender, social class, ethnicity and age of the audience. For example, a news report about binge-drinking will be viewed differently by younger and older audiences, and violent films will not affect men and women in the same way. Research by Stack et al. (1994) into suicide among heavy-metal music fans suggests that followers tend to come from lower social class groups and that this may be a relevant factor in their suicide. According to the Cultural Effects Theory, media effects, though significant, are not direct but are shaped by the norms, values and experiences of the audience. This approach links with the research of some theorists from both neo-Marxist and interpretivist perspectives discussed below.

Another approach, the 'drip-drip' model, sees the media as shaping the norms and values of the audience. The process happens gradually over long-term exposure to the media. For example, some commentators are worried that publications like *Sugar* and *Bliss*, two top-selling teenage lifestyle magazines for young women, when read regularly, come to shape identity and behaviour. Gauntlett (2008) suggests that such magazines become a habit for their readers by feeding into teenage concerns. They also pattern behaviour which is then followed into adulthood with the reading of women's magazines. The concept of desensitisation is also associated with the drip-drip model. It describes the way the audience's norms can be altered by viewing particular images, for example those of a violent nature. It is claimed that over time the audience

stops finding such images disturbing and violence becomes more acceptable. The concept of desensitisation has also been applied to the effect of media images of famine and poverty in developing countries.

Evaluation

Indirect theories share some of the criticisms of direct theories. It is difficult to measure the media's effect on the norms, values and attitudes of the audience. Audiences are likely to be affected by a range of factors and it is almost impossible to isolate the impact of the media in this complex web of influence. While indirect theories see greater complexity in the way that the media affect audiences, their analysis tends to look more at the issue from the point of view of the media impacting on the audience. Recent research has shifted its focus from the effect of the media on the audience to the way in which the audience receives media messages. Audience-reception theories, discussed below, do not deny the power of the media to affect the audience, but acknowledge that the audience is active in its interaction with the media.

A criticism of both direct and indirect theories of media effects is implied in the Uses and Gratifications approach. This model argues that audiences use the media for their own purposes and to satisfy their needs. According to McQuail (1972), individuals are active in their approach to the media and use them in a number of ways, including as a form of escape, as a means of gathering information, to form personal relationships and in constructing personal identity.

Marxism

The views within traditional Marxism tend to agree with direct theories and see the effect of the media on audiences and on society as a one-way process that has the power to exert a significant influence. Marxists believe that this power comes from having control of the economy. Murdock (1982) sees media owners, who are part of the ruling class, as having the power to control and manipulate media messages and so, in turn, influence media audiences. The media functions to support capitalism by producing 'false class consciousness' in audiences, which results in them accepting ruling-class values.

In relation to the effects of the media on wider society, Marxists regard social class as the dominant inequality in society, and they focus almost exclusively on the power of the ruling class to control and influence the working class. Marxists see the media as a powerful institution that acts as a form of social control and promotes capitalist ideology. The media represent the interests of the ruling class and help to maintain false class consciousness in the working class by presenting capitalism as fair and reasonable. Marxists also see the media as an important social institution for supporting capitalism by promoting a consumer culture that increases the profits of capitalist companies. They do this by presenting consumer culture as an attractive and desirable lifestyle and, more directly, by providing a vehicle for the advertising of products and services.

Neo-Marxism

Neo-Marxism also sees the media as having a powerful effect on audiences. Both forms of Marxism agree that the media are used to promote capitalist values by influencing audiences. A major difference between Marxism and neo-Marxism is that neo-Marxists look beyond the role of owners in influencing media messages. Media professionals are seen as key agents in creating and shaping the culture of society. They see the media as an important social institution that plays a complex role in winning and maintaining support for capitalism.

Gramsci saw the media as a site for the battle for hearts and minds that had to be continuously alert to the need to keep the audience on the side of capitalism. He used the term 'hegemony' to discuss the way capitalist ideas were presented as 'common sense' and seen as natural. The audience must consent to these ideas and the media had an important role in gaining this consent. According to neo-Marxists, media professionals have an important role in promoting hegemony and they are able to do this effectively because it reflects their own worldview.

Adorno coined the term 'culture industry' to describe the way popular culture can be seen as similar to a factory that produces culture. Adorno believed that the media prevent audiences from thinking for themselves by filling their time with entertainment that stops them seeing the inequalities of the capitalist system and revolting against it. The media dull the senses by feeding the audience a constant diet of popular culture.

Hall (1980) created a useful model with which to understand how media professionals affect the way in which their audience interprets the world. He argued that media professionals 'encode', or construct, their messages in ways that support the power structures of society. He suggested that media audiences 'decode' these messages in various ways according to their background and experiences, and that media professionals cannot completely control this. Hall argues that the media have a powerful and dominant effect on their audience, but that the audience are able to oppose media messages in the light of their experience and background.

More recently, the neo-Marxist Glasgow University Media Group has widened the focus of research beyond examining the role of the media in influencing the audience to analysing the process by which audiences receive media messages. Through the use of focus groups, it has found that audiences can be active in their use of the media, but that the media also have an important influence in shaping people's views. Audiences bring their own experiences and values to bear when interacting with the media, but the media construct the overall framework within which audiences participate. According to Kitzinger, 'the media help to define what counts as a public issue, organize our understandings of individual events, shape suspicions and beliefs, and resource memories, conversations, actions and even identities.'(Kitzinger, 2002, page 279).

Activity 34

Drawing on the neo-Marxist views above, discuss the following question in pairs and then bring your answers to a wider discussion involving the whole class.

To what extent do the media shape the following:

- suspicions
- beliefs
- memories
- conversations
- actions
- identities?

Think of examples to support each point.

Stretch and Challenge Activity

1 Discuss what you think Adorno meant when he talked about the media 'dulling the senses'.

2 What evidence can you think of to support the claim that the media dull the senses?

When examining the effect of the media on wider society, a key feature of neo-Marxism is its greater attention to the media's role as a powerful institution that is more than just a mouthpiece for the ruling class but increasingly functions as a source of influence in its own right. According to neo-Marxism, the media constitute an important social institution in promoting hegemony and this affects the way society views particular social groups like women, minority ethnic groups and young people. A significant effect of the media on wider society is that they help to maintain inequalities and prevent social change by

representing alternatives to the hegemonic view as extreme, ridiculous or laughable. In this sense, the media can be seen as repressing some social groups.

As well as dulling the senses of the audience, neo-Marxists are concerned that the media play a part in 'dumbing down' society as a whole by focusing on personalities and gossip. Political and social issues are trivialised and shaped by the values of those employed in the 'culture industry'.

Althusser referred to the media as an **ideological state apparatus (ISA)**, an institution whose main purpose is to maintain hegemony by shaping society's ideas and values. Like other neo-Marxists, he moved away from focusing on the power of the economy to control society, to look at the power of dominant viewpoints. The media help to create the illusion that society is free when in reality it is controlled by social institutions like the education system, another ideological state apparatus, and by the media themselves. According to Althusser, if the ISAs fail to maintain hegemony, **repressive state apparatus (RSA)** like the army and the police can be used by the ruling class to more overtly prevent opposition to capitalism.

Stretch and Challenge Activity

Carry out some research into the work of Adorno, Gramsci and Althusser and summarise their main arguments about the effect of the media.

Interpretivism

Interpretivism focuses on the way audiences receive media messages and tends to see the audience as active in this process as opposed to the passive audiences discussed by some other explanations. Early research by Klapper (1960) suggests that media messages have to pass through three filters before they can have an effect:

◆ Selective exposure – the audience chooses which media to use on the basis of a number of factors including their interests, educational background, work commitments.

- ◆ Selective perception – the audience may see media messages in different ways.

- ◆ Selective retention – the audience will keep some messages and not others.

The effect the media have depends on the way the messages are received by the audience.

Fiske sees the power of the audience to interpret media messages as stronger than the power of the media to send messages to their audiences. He argues that the audience is not an homogenous group but rather is made up of a variety of individuals who have changing tastes and come from a range of social backgrounds. They interpret the media in the context of their own individual situation. His views directly contradict Adorno's concept of the 'culture industry'. Fiske (1989) argues that culture is a live and dynamic process that cannot be imposed from above. He sees the audience as active in producing popular culture in the process of interacting with the media. As a result, some media products will be unsuccessful because the audience has chosen not to like them.

A further dimension to the interpretive approach comes through the concept of 'preferred reading' which sees the audience as active in interpreting media messages but also acknowledges the power of the media. The media give messages a dominant meaning that most of the audience is likely to accept. Some elements within the audience may interpret the message differently, depending on their background and experience. In some respects this idea can be seen as similar to Hall's work on encoding and decoding discussed above (page 129).

Stretch and Challenge Activity

Review the ideas of neo-Marxism and interpretivism on audience reception and identify any similarities and differences between them. You can use your findings when analysing and evaluating these approaches.

Interpretivism tends to focus on the audience and the way it receives media messages. This can be extended to explain wider social effects. For example, Fiske believes that the media can promote diversity by responding to audiences' demands for new and different products. He also believes that the media present people with the opportunity to think through issues, and that this might ultimately lead to social change. In this sense the media can be viewed as an empowering institution for both individuals and social groups in society.

Postmodern views

Postmodern views on the media cover a range of issues and some thinkers see media effects as unproblematic. They see the media as characterised by diversity and choice and offering a range of products. From this, audiences create their own meanings. The media promote consumer culture where identities are in a state of constant review and change and can be 'picked and mixed' and remodelled. Other postmodern thinkers have a darker view of the effect of the media on audiences. Diversity and choice are seen as resulting in fragmented identities where audiences lose a sense of who they are and their connection with others around them. For example, social networking sites and video-sharing media like YouTube have provoked worries about their effect on younger people. The widespread use of the media and the new technologies available to media producers also means that there is a blurring of the distinction between reality and media images, which leaves audiences confused about what is real and what is media-created. Reality-television programmes like *Big Brother* show real people in a media-created environment responding to media-manipulated situations and presented to the audience in a heavily edited form.

Critics argue that postmodern views ignore the persistence of traditional identities and the role of the media in maintaining these identities. Research into media representations of gender, ethnicity, social class and age, as discussed on pages 116–126, indicate that diversity and choice can be restricted by hegemonic media representations of social groups.

Some research challenges postmodern views on fragmented identities. Gauntlett (2007) produced an interesting study about identities in which he asked participants to build a model that represented their identity using Lego pieces. He found that the models that they produced demonstrated unified identities that were not fragmented in the way that postmodern views suggest. He also found that the participants felt that the media had little influence on their identity.

Postmodern views on the effects of the media on wider society are drawn from their belief that society is now characterised by diversity, choice and media saturation. Media institutions, products and technologies have grown to such an extent that they form a large part of our daily experience, providing us with a constant flow of information and entertainment and are a fundamental element of the functioning of society. The concept of incessant choosing is used by postmodern thinkers when referring to the effect of the media on the culture of society, which shifts between the variety of constantly changing products and lifestyles available. Programmes like *Big Brother* can be seen to reflect and promote diversity in society. Gauntlett (2008) refers to the way in which contestants on the show frequently have identities and relationships that cut across traditional social divisions like class, gender, ethnicity and age. Society appears to support this diversity; during *Celebrity Big Brother*, in 2007, there was social outrage at the seemingly racist remarks made by some contestants towards Shilpa Shetty, a Bollywood film star.

Some postmodern views see new media technologies as bringing benefits to society. For example, the internet and digital television have encouraged a greater sense of global awareness. They have also empowered people by enabling them to voice their views through a medium that can reach a global audience. Vattimo (1992) refers to the way in which subcultural groups can use the media to find new and exciting ways of communicating their views The developments in media technologies have increased the range and variety of media products available and this has promoted an eclectic approach where ideas can be drawn from a diverse range of sources. As a result, society's way of life can be seen to have been enriched.

However, according to some views of postmodern society, such developments can mean that people have a much-reduced involvement with the real world outside of the media. They can come to see the world through the images and perspectives that the media present. The diversity of media products can help to create a confusing array of choices and meanings that result in a society where shared norms and values are less and less clear. Criminals have used the media to commit acts of fraud across the globe and there are concerns about the use of global communications to assist terrorist activities. The internet has also been used as a vehicle for pornography, sexual deviance and other forms of deviant behaviour. Concerns have been expressed about the way in which websites, including those involving social networks and video-sharing, have been used to promote violence, self-harm and suicide.

Activity 35

In groups, draw up two lists, one relating to the influence of the media on audiences and one on their effects on wider society. Identify positive and negative influences and effects. Circulate the lists around the class to be added to. When you have finished the lists, display them on the wall and draw mind-maps showing the key issues.

Stretch and Challenge Activity

Undertake additional research into postmodern thinkers like Baudrillard and Vattimo and summarise their views on the effect of the media on audiences and on society.

Deviancy amplification theories

Deviancy amplification theories seek to understand the role of the media in strengthening and magnifying deviance

The Daily Herald

'Britain's beaches invaded by hoodies'

Figure 3.7

in society. This may happen in two ways: first, through heightening public awareness and concern about an issue and second, through escalating the problem by increasing participation in it. Deviancy amplification has been studied by a number of sociologists, including those from Marxist and interactionist perspectives.

Marxists argue that deviancy amplification is used as a form of social control to support capitalism, while interactionists explore the process of defining and labelling deviance.

Moral panics

The term '**moral panic**' refers to the way the media react to particular social groups or activities that are seen as a threat to society's norms and values. It is important to be aware of the moral dimension involved – there are frequent panics expressed in the media that do not necessarily refer to moral concerns, for example, about shortages of fuel or food safety.

Cohen (1972) identified the stages of development of a moral panic. First, the media use sensational, stereotypical and exaggerated language in stories and headlines about a particular event or group. This results in public anxiety, which is fuelled by influential commentators like bishops and politicians. This puts pressure on the authorities to intervene and can lead, for example, to greater police involvement. The increased social awareness of the problem can also lead more people to participate in the activity. Cohen's well known study of moral panics used interactionist methodology. He observed seaside fights between two youth subcultures, the mods and rockers, and examined the media's response. He argued that the media labelled the mods and rockers in a negative and stereotyped way and as a result they came to be seen as 'folk devils' (a threat to society's values and interests). Cohen highlighted the role of the media in defining the situation and argued that they had created a greatly exaggerated picture of the conflict between mods and rockers.

Some moral panics arise from media products themselves. The film *Juno*, which was released in 2007 in the USA, was reported in the media as glorifying teenage pregnancy when 17 girls in an American high school became pregnant in one year. Opponents of this view argue that the high rate of pregnancies in the school was more to do with social factors affecting the town than the influence of the film. This did not stop the media from coining the term the 'Juno Effect' to describe the film's impact on teenage pregnancies.

Activity 36

Choose a social group or activity that has been the subject of a moral panic and make a poster to show, step-by-step, the process that creates a moral panic as outlined above.

Later research by Goode and Ben-Yehuda (1994) rejected Cohen's view that a moral panic went through a series of stages that have a beginning, middle and end. Instead they described five elements present in a moral panic:

◆ Concern – heightened public concern that the behaviour of a particular group is a threat to social order.

◆ Hostility – an increased hostility in the media towards the group that leads to its members being seen as 'folk devils'.

◆ Consensus – influential people, known as moral entrepreneurs, lead a campaign against the group that leads to general agreement about its behaviour.

◆ Disproportionality – the reaction is out of proportion to the harm caused by the group.

◆ Volatility – moral panics come and go quickly as interest moves on to another issue.

Interactionists are interested in the way in which groups and events come to be defined as deviant through the process of stereotyping and labelling involved in moral panics. They use the concept of the 'deviancy amplification spiral' to illustrate the effects of labelling and the self-fulfilling prophecy on those identified as deviant. Jewkes (2004) refers to the way in which rising social reaction to an event results in the 'deviants' involved becoming increasingly marginalised and, in turn, drawn to further criminal behaviour (see page 17).

Critics of interactionism argue that it fails to explore the power relations behind the labelling process. Neo-Marxists see a need to investigate who has the power to define deviance and to explain why some groups come to be identified as folk devils in the first place.

Writing from a Marxist perspective, Hall et al. (1995) believed that moral panics serve an ideological function to support capitalism. Referring to the emergence of the use of the term 'mugging' in the UK, he argued that it was applied to young working-class black men to cause division between black and white members of the working class. In addition the moral panic took attention away from economic problems caused by capitalism and allowed laws to be introduced that could be used to repress other groups that opposed capitalism.

Such Marxist views are criticised for failing to acknowledge that moral panics can be the product of real concerns in society. They are also seen to take an over-conspiratorial view where members of the ruling class get together and decide on a course of action that creates a moral panic when there is no evidence of this having occurred.

Activity 37

In groups, conduct further research into moral panics and present your findings to the class.

Section summary

The most relevant theories to consider on this section are Marxism, neo-Marxism, pluralism, interpretivism and postmodern views.

Using the key terms below, write a paragraph summarising the main points you have learnt about the effect of the media on society.

- Direct theories
- Indirect theories
- Marxism
- Neo-Marxism
- Interpretivism
- Postmodern views
- Effects of the media on wider society – theoretical explanations
- Deviancy amplification theories: moral panics

Stretch and Challenge Activity

Add a paragraph to your section summary that evaluates the main arguments of the theoretical explanations referred to.

Exam practice

1   Outline and assess the view that the media have a slow and gradual effect on audiences.
    (50 marks)

2   Outline and assess sociological explanations of the effects of the media on wider society.
    (50 marks)

ExamCafé
Relax, refresh, result!

Exam question
Outline and assess the view that the media have an indirect influence on their audience.

(50 marks)

Relax and prepare

Hot tips

Finn

I've found it really interesting to study the media. It's such a big part of my life but I'd never really stopped to think about who's in charge of it and how it might affect me. I need to use these ideas when it comes to revision to help me plan for the exam.

Emily

There are so many different views to consider. I've been making mind-maps and writing some essay plans to help me organise all the evidence that I've learned about.

Dylan

I've been preparing some revision notes on theories and studies. We're going to need to know these to write detailed answers in the exam. I've added a section in my notes headed 'How will I use this evidence?' to help me focus on how I will apply this to the questions.

Examiner's tips

- Think theoretically when planning the evidence to include in your answer.
- Consider why particular studies might be useful to include and how they will help you to answer the question set.
- When you are evaluating evidence it is important to explain the precise criticisms being made. For example, when you state that a theorist disagrees with a concept, study or theory, explain why they disagree. If you state that a study is outdated, explain why, perhaps by referring to social changes that may have affected its relevance.

Refresh your memory

Revision checklist

You might find it useful to use a table like the one below to check your knowledge, and record your own sources of information.

Topic	Studies	Do I know this?	Look here
Methods of researching the mass media • content analysis • semiology • experiments			
Theoretical explanations of ownership and control of the media • Marxism • neo-Marxism • pluralism			

Get the result!

Student answer

Outline and assess the view that the media have an indirect influence on their audience. **(50 marks)**

Examiner comment:
This is a good introduction that indicates that the writer understands the question and has selected relevant evidence to answer it. It also shows an awareness of the counter-views. The paragraph introduces the issues involved in answering the question and sets the scene for the rest of the essay.

Examiner comment:
This is a good starting point to examine indirect effects. The answer could have been more detailed about the role of opinion leaders. The student uses effective wording to show how the model helps answer the question and will gain marks for interpretation and application here. The evaluative comment about the media having a direct effect on the opinion leader is well thought out. The explicit evaluation point about the evidence being dated could be developed to explain why the research is less relevant today.

Examiner comment:
This paragraph shows a good understanding of Cultural Effects Theory and Hall's view, but could be further developed. The next paragraph makes evaluative comment and also flags up the next issue to be discussed.

There are a number of studies that support the view that the media have an indirect influence on their audience. Some research looks at how social interaction can have an impact on the way the media affect their audience while other evidence suggests that the social class, gender, ethnicity and age of the audience will mean that media messages affect different social groups in different ways. On the other hand, there are views that argue that the effect of the media is much more direct or even that there is little effect at all.

The two-step flow model shows that the media have an indirect effect on their audience because of the influence of opinion leaders. The effect the media have takes two steps, as the first step involves the media influencing the opinion leader and the second step happens when the opinion leader influences other people during interaction with them. This effect the media have is indirect because it passes through the opinion leader before influencing others, although it could be argued that the effect on the opinion leader is a direct one. However, the research on this was done by Katz and Lazarsfeld in the 1950s and may not be relevant to society now as the media have changed so much.

Other evidence looks at the background of the audience and argues that this will impact on the way the media influence their audience. The Cultural Effects Theory argues that the effect the media have will vary depending on the social class, gender, ethnicity and age of the audience. This shows that the media have an indirect effect because it is filtered through the cultural background of the members of the audience. The Neo-Marxist Stuart Hall agrees that audiences, when receiving media messages, decode them in different ways depending on their background and experiences.

Although Cultural Effects Theory and the work of Stuart Hall see the media's effect as indirect, they both seem to regard the media as having a significant influence. Other researchers have argued that that audiences play a more active role in the way that they receive media messages.

According to Klapper, media messages pass through a series of filters before there is any effect. He refers to the concept of selective exposure and makes the point that the audience chooses which media to use. He also talks of selective perception where the audience sees media messages in different ways. Finally, he mentions the idea of selective retention to suggest that the audience only

Examiner comment:

This paragraph is strong on analysis and evaluation in the way that it contrasts Klapper and Fiske but the reference to Fiske is rather brief and could have more detail about how the audience create the media.

Examiner comment:

The student has selected appropriate evidence but the evidence could be explained in more detail. The answer could give further contemporary examples to reinforce the point that there continues to be concern about the direct effect of the media. Marxist theory could also be used to show the view that the media manipulate and brainwash their audience. This paragraph could draw a distinction between laboratory experiments and field experiments and add evaluation. There are many criticisms of direct theories that could be included.

Examiner comment:

The student does well to link the uses and gratifications approach with postmodern views. The evaluation point at the end could be further developed by including some examples and there are other criticisms that could be discussed.

Examiner comment:

The student draws the evidence together with a concise and balanced conclusion which refers back to the wording of the question. The final paragraph highlights a key problem involved in measuring media effects. It would have been useful if this and other problems had been discussed more fully in the body of the essay. Overall, though, this is a well informed response that shows a very good level of knowledge and understanding and an ability to analyse evidence.

holds on to some messages and forgets others. The different filters that media messages go through mean that the effect is indirect and depends on the way the messages are received by the audience.

Fiske takes the idea of the audience having an active role a step further and argues that audiences have more power than the media. He believes that audiences actually create the media and have the power to determine whether a media product will be successful or not. However, there is evidence that argues that the media are very powerful and have an immediate and direct influence on their audience.

The Hypodermic Syringe Model describes the media as injecting the audience with their messages and sees the effect as immediate and direct. According to this model the audience is passive and uncritical in its relationship with the media. This view is supported by the bobo doll experiments that Bandura conducted on children. He found that children who were subjected to the media displayed more aggression than those who were not. Bandura's research indicated a copycat effect and more recently this has been discussed in relation to concerns about the effect of video games like 'Manhunt'.

Other evidence suggests that the media have little effect and see the audience as in control. The uses and gratifications approach argues that audiences use the media for their own purposes and to satisfy their needs. McQuail believes that individuals use the media in many different ways including to create their identities, as a kind of escapism, to become better informed and to establish personal relationships. The uses and gratifications approach links to postmodern views that discuss diversity and choice within the media. This diversity and choice contribute to consumer culture that gives the audience a range of ideas and products from which they can select and create their own identities. However, such views don't acknowledge the ways in which traditional identities continue to be passed on through agents of socialisation including the media. In this sense, the media can be seen as having a significant effect in shaping our identity.

In conclusion, there are many different views about the effect the media have on their audience. Some research shows an indirect effect because there are factors that get in the way of the media having a direct effect, such as the role of opinion leaders and the social characteristics of the audience like their social class, gender, ethnicity and age. However, this view is challenged by evidence that sees the media's effect as immediate and direct. Such research is concerned that the media can have a powerful and negative influence and that the audience can end up copying behaviour viewed in the media. On the other side of the argument is the view that audiences are active and use the media for their own purposes. There are problems with each point of view and it is difficult to decide which is more accurate. A major problem concerns how to measure media effect as opposed to other factors that may be involved. Until this is established, it is difficult to come to a conclusion about whether the media have an indirect, direct or, indeed, any effect at all.

Sociology of power and politics

Pause for thought

1 Which war do you think these demonstrators are trying to stop?

2 Why are they demonstrating in this particular part of London?

3 How successful do you think demonstrations like this are in bringing about change?

Introduction

Whether we like it or not, our lives are shaped by issues of power and control. Every day, television and newspaper reports show how the world is affected by politics – from the individual to the international level. People respond in various ways, and voting every few years is only one of them. The modern world is increasingly complex and fast-changing: today, political action is frequently channelled through social movements that use direct-action methods, and the political ideas that inform such movements are changing too. An understanding of these issues will offer future generations a chance to make the world a better place.

The specification states:

'In this option candidates explore issues of power and control through a detailed study of political action, new social movements and theories of power. The role of ideology is emphasised, as well as an explanation of where political power lies in society. It aims to give an overview of different theoretical approaches to the study of political action and new social movements.'

This option explores five key issues:

1 Defining and exploring political action in society.

2 Participation in and emergence of new social movements.

3 The changing patterns of political action.

4 Political ideologies and their relationship to political action.

5 The nature and distribution of political power in society.

(i) Defining and exploring political action in society

Pause for thought

- Do you think politics has much effect on your everyday life?

- How important is it for people to vote in general elections?

- Would it be a good idea to reduce the voting age to sixteen?

Activity 1

In a social group, there were four people named *Everybody*, *Somebody*, *Anybody*, and *Nobody*. There was an important job to be done and *Everybody* was sure that *Somebody* would do it. *Anybody* could have done it, but *Nobody* did. *Somebody* got angry about this, because it was *Everybody*'s job. *Everybody* thought *Anybody* could do it, but *Nobody* realised that *Everybody* wouldn't do it. In the end, *Everybody* blamed *Somebody* when *Nobody* did what *Anybody* could have done.

Think about life in a real, modern-day society. Something important needs to be done:

1 If *Nobody* is doing anything about it, why can't *Everybody* get on with it?

2 Is it always true that *Anybody* could do what *Everybody* wants done?

3 In what way(s) could *Everybody* choose *Somebody* to get it done?

4 If *Nobody* likes what *Somebody* does for *Everybody*, how can *Anybody* let them know about this?

Have you ever heard someone say (or yourself said) 'Why don't *they* do something?' Often, it may not be obvious who 'they' are – the government, our local council, teachers or parents, perhaps. What all these groups have in common is that because we expect them to do something on our behalf, they are assumed to have some sort of power and control – perhaps 'over' us, but at least to act on behalf of those who have less power and control. The notion of power and control is a central topic in sociology, and within A Level Sociology it forms two of the core themes – indeed, it inspired some of the founders of the subject to develop their theories. As such, it has various definitions, although there are some key similarities in each definition.

'Power' may be defined as the ability of a person/ people to make others do something they want them to, even when those others may not themselves want to do it. In other words, power is the ability some people have to control what happens under particular circumstances. Power can be exercised in different ways: the most obvious way to make others do what they may not want to is coercion (force); another is to use influence (persuasion); or yet again, authority could be used, where those without power do as they are told because they accept the right (legitimacy) of those who do possess it. (Weber (1922) wrote that authority was of three different types – traditional, charismatic or legal.)

'Politics' involves the exercise of power in all its shapes and forms, but mostly legal. Many people feel that politics 'doesn't interest them' and 'doesn't affect them'. However, politics is not some formal activity that is played out by 'politicians'; it concerns almost every member of the community, as Blondel (1963), author of *Voters, Parties and Leaders*, wrote. In a modern democratic society, we are all likely to engage in politics to some extent, whether through political parties or pressure groups, direct or **indirect action**, or – increasingly in the age of the internet – cybernetworking.

In this sense, democratic politics has come a long way from its origins. The ancient Greeks invented politics – in fact, the word comes from *polis*, the Greek word for city. In the fifth century BC, Greece was made up of different city states. One of these, Athens, was governed by an assembly of all its citizens (adult males, that is – women, children and slaves were not classed as citizens), and

was a true **democracy** in the sense that people (*demos*) rule (*kratos*) prevailed. Another, Sparta, was governed by a small group (elite) who made all the decisions themselves, and this gave rise to **oligarchy** – rule (*archia*) by the few (*oligos*).

Ancient societies were small enough to permit 'people power' to prevail, but modern societies are simply too big. Today, direct democracy has given way to representative democracy: citizens vote in elections from time to time and so choose representatives to act on their behalf in decision-making. In the UK today, these representatives are known as Members of Parliament (MPs), and (almost) everyone over the age of eighteen is eligible to vote at least once every five years in choosing theirs. In theory, this process gives MPs the authority to pass laws regulating the lives of the population – that is, power and control over the sixty million people who live in the UK.

Like the UK, many other countries in the world are 'liberal democracies' in which power is seen to be exercised over their populations in a **legitimate** (legal) way. This is by no means true of all countries – a number are ruled by authoritarian governments, or even dictatorships, and their people are denied basic political rights. However, even in a liberal democracy such as the USA – in 1863, described by Abraham Lincoln as government 'of the people, by the people, for the people' – some commentators worry that ordinary people's political rights are not quite what representative democracy portrays them to be.

In his classic sociological study *The Power Elite*, Mills (1956) examined power and control in the USA in the 1950s. He concluded that ordinary people's lives were often shaped by forces over which they had little or no control. The nature of modern society denied them control of their lives, which were instead shaped by social pressures beyond their control, leaving them powerless and feeling that life lacked purpose – something Marx called **alienation**. In contrast, a small group of people – a 'power elite' – possessed the power to control ordinary people's lives and to take the big decisions that affected them all.

Clearly, whether people will accept having power and control exercised over them depends on whether they regard it as legitimate. Ironically, it is in the very liberal democracies where power may be seen as most legitimate that ordinary people seem to be most disillusioned with it today. This tendency has given rise to what some sociologists call a 'paradox of democracy' – the fact that the governments of individual countries are too small to deal with big political issues and yet too big to deal with the little political issues in the modern – or postmodern – world. It seems a plausible explanation for many political trends apparent today.

Political parties

In the UK today, the membership of political parties is in decline. **Political parties** are groups of like-minded individuals who come together in an attempt to win elections and get into government so that they can put their policies into effect. By no means do all members of political parties aim to become MPs, even though they are all members of organisations that have that aim. Parties have a range of policies (published in a manifesto) which members accept as a 'package'. During most of the twentieth century the government of the UK alternated between two main parties, the Conservative Party and the Labour Party, each with its own distinctive policies. In 1997, New Labour won power by promising to govern according to a 'third way', but many commentators feel that the two main parties' policies are now too similar.

Pressure groups

Traditionally, another way for individuals to get their voices heard in British politics has been through pressure groups. **Pressure groups** also comprise groups of like-minded individuals, but in coming together their objective is not to win power but only to shape the formulation of policy in regard to one or a narrower range of specific matters. Trade unions can be seen as pressure groups, concerned with protecting their members' interests with regard to employment law. As a pressure group to represent management, the Confederation of British Industry was formed in 1965. Both were a valuable part of the democratic process for three decades after the Second World War, but by the 1980s these (and other pressure groups) began to lose influence with government. Trade-union membership in the UK peaked at 13.2 million in 1979 and is only around half that figure today. Other pressure groups include the Child Poverty Action Group and the League Against Cruel Sports.

New social movements

The postmodern world has witnessed the rise of social movements of a different kind. **New social movements (NSMs)**, unlike older social movements, tend not to have links with institutionalised government. Indeed, they may have no leaders as such, no formal organisation nor any sort of hierarchy – instead, they often take decisions on the basis of full participation by their members. Their concerns may well be much broader in scope than those of even the largest pressure groups. NSMs vary considerably in size – perhaps from a hundred to maybe millions of people – and they may transcend national boundaries. NSMs seem different from earlier groups in terms of what drives them and how they operate – they often act *outside* the realms of established political activity, as witnessed by the protests of the worldwide anti-capitalist movement.

Direct and indirect action

The growth of NSMs can be seen as evidence that ordinary people have not lost sight of the role of politics in their everyday lives. Rather, they have become disillusioned with the more conventional ways of pursuing their political concerns. The use of indirect action – where people believe in representative democracy and trust politicians to act on their behalf – has given way to **direct action**. Whilst in the past there was an emphasis on following more formal and bureaucratic methods in order to achieve goals, today the emphasis is on more informal and less bureaucratic methods. Because national governments seem less able to respond to people's concerns in the twenty-first century, people may increasingly take matters into their own hands, as anti-road-building campaigners have done on numerous occasions in recent years.

The methods used to deal with political matters will also change. Pressure groups relied on indirect action, such as **lobbying** MPs (writing to and meeting MPs – originally in the lobby of the House of Commons) with a view to influencing their views. If a more urgent need was felt, pressure groups have used tactics such as demonstrations (as the Peace Women did at Greenham Common) or **strikes** (as the Miners' Union did in the mid-1980s) – although neither of these groups succeeded in the face of a government determined to defeat them (Margaret Thatcher's Conservative government of 1979–90). Although traditional methods are still used by groups with money and prestige – like the National Farmers' Union (NFU) and British Medical Association (BMA) – it is perhaps understandable that things have changed.

Weblinks

You might like to look at the following websites:

- The official site of the Greenham Women's Peace Camp, with BBC radio links
- BBC news items about the Greenham Women's Peace Camp, 1981–2000
- BBC news items – *The Miners' Strike* slideshow with audio and archive images
- Video and soundtrack about the Birmingham Pub Bombings in November 1974
- BBC news bulletin about the IRA bombing of the City of London in April 1993
- Video and soundtrack about the *Battle of Trafalgar (Square)* in March 1990
- BBC news bulletin about the London Poll Tax Riots on 31 March, 1990
- BBC news bulletin about Scottish Coalfield strike/events on 12 March, 1984.

(See 'Websites', page ii.)

Terrorism, riots, demonstrations and lobbying

Of course, the use of direct action is not unique to NSMs. In the past, terrorism and riots have been used to try and influence government (although they usually proved counter-productive). **Political terrorism** involves the use of violence by groups that are opposed to an established government – usually because they are not recognised in their own right. In its campaign to achieve a united Ireland, the IRA resorted to terrorism (including some infamous bombings of civilian 'targets'). Such violent direct action was unacceptable to most people in a democratic society, but terrorists portray themselves as 'freedom fighters' battling against repressive political regimes. In some

circumstances violent revolutionaries do bring about regime change, as in Russia in 1917.

Riots are acts of public disorder that involve crowd violence, such as damage to property and clashes with the police. In its opposition to the 'Community Charge', the Anti-Poll Tax Federation organised mass gatherings, some of which turned into riots, and this played a significant part in Thatcher's resignation in November 1990. **Demonstrations** also involve large crowds of people in public meetings, but they do not normally descend into violence – people express their views in more passive protests such as marches, banner-waving and sit-ins. The police may become involved, but only to remove the protesters: the famous Aldermaston Marches organised by the Campaign for Nuclear Disarmament (CND) every Easter were usually relatively peaceful.

Lobbying involves groups of people in organised attempts to influence those in power. Members of the public are able to lobby their MPs to try to influence their votes when changes in the law are being discussed in Parliament, for instance. However, recent years have witnessed the rise of the professional lobbyists who are paid because they are close to MPs and have specialist expertise in relation to the law. Many MPs act as consultants and are paid to lobby on behalf of companies, giving advice and making speeches. These forms of lobbying can sometimes overstep the mark and cause scandals such as the 'cash for questions' affair, in which MPs allegedly accepted payments in return for raising issues in Parliament.

Today's NSMs include pressure groups and other political organisations that can trace their roots back over several decades – including the civil-rights and feminist movements. Where they differ is that they are more concerned with social than economic issues, but they have in common a belief that direct action is more useful to their causes than reliance on party politicians. NSMs more readily resort to street politics, such as those associated with the worldwide alliance of anti-capitalist and anti-globalisation movements, which have been involved in violent protests at meetings of international governments such as the G8 (Group of 8) at Seattle in June 1999.

Sociology of power and politics

Can you link each of the methods 1–5 with its appropriate definition a–e?

1   Lobbying

2   Demonstrating

3   Striking

4   Rioting

5   Terrorism

a   Members of a trade union vote not to go to work until their employers agree to give them a pay rise.

b   A group of car salesmen take their local MP out for a business lunch and discuss reducing taxes on used-car sales.

c   The residents of a street being used as a short cut past a busy town centre sit in the road and demand that the government lowers speed limits.

d   Members of a fundamentalist religious sect try to get the law on abortion changed by bombing abortion clinics.

e   A group of people opposed to the building of a new airport runway break through the perimeter fence and smash construction machinery.

Cybernetworking

Arguably, the single most important factor in the growth of new social movements of all kinds is the growth in global electronic communication. The creation of the internet has resulted in what is termed **cybernetworking**: the use of the internet to develop global networks of individuals who share concerns about social and political issues. In a far-sighted study entitled *Cyberocracy is Coming*, Ronfeldt (1992) argued that new information technologies offered opportunities for grassroots activists with computer access to be empowered and to challenge undemocratic political regimes. In this way, a new form of internet democracy – **cyberocracy** – would arise, and citizens would become 'netizens'.

Burma – a case study

Burma – a country in southeast Asia bordered by India, China and Thailand – hit the headlines on 2 May 2008 when it was struck by Cyclone Nargis, but it had been in and out of the news for 46 years by then. In a coup d'état in 1962, a military junta had seized control of the country and turned its back on the rest of the world. So it was shocking but no surprise to many observers that the country's authoritarian and oppressive government attempted to block foreign aid to Burma in the aftermath of the 2008 cyclone, even though 2.4 million of its inhabitants faced starvation and disease, having lost their homes and livelihoods.

The cynical junta had held elections in 1990, but when the opposition National League for Democracy won 80 per cent of the seats, its leader was placed under house arrest whilst the military junta's State Law and Order Restoration Council (SLORC) pursued a policy of forced labour and displacement of the Burmese people. Those who could, fled; many settled in the USA and began communicating information about life in Burma via the internet. In 1993, they set up BurmaNet, featuring English-language stories of human-rights abuses in Burma taken from Thai newspapers.

Burmese exiles around the world found that they now had the means to communicate with one another about their homeland. The internet allowed them to create a virtual community and growing numbers subscribed – though not in Burma itself, where under a law passed by SLORC in 1996, anyone caught using the internet faced a prison sentence of seven to fifteen years. However, encouraged by student sympathisers in the USA, in 1995 exiled Burmese activists organised a Free Burma Coalition that was able to coordinate international action via the internet.

A selective purchasing campaign was started in Massachusetts, aimed at banning US companies that did business in Burma from obtaining business contracts at home – and it worked. Major US companies like Hewlett-Packard, AppleCorp, Motorola, Liz Claiborne and Eddie Bauer began to withdraw from Burmese investments rather than lose more lucrative domestic business contracts.

U3

4

Sociology of power and politics

Students from the prestigious Harvard University next joined in. They had just heard that the university's million-dollar dining contract, which was up for renewal, was going to be awarded to PepsiCo, which also invested in Burma (Pepsi had opened a bottling plant in Rangoon in 1990). However, the students had other ideas and began a massive internet campaign against PepsiCo. The firm's shareholders were lobbied and the Harvard student body was mobilised to block the contract, which Pepsi subsequently lost. In January 1997, PepsiCo announced that it was terminating its business investments in Burma.

This was not a complete victory for 'cyberocracy'. In June 2000, the Massachusetts boycott was ruled invalid by the US Supreme Court (although the USA banned all imports from Burma in 2003). What is significant is that the Harvard students were sure that without 'cybernetworking', their movement would not have been nearly as successful. Of course, it is not without its shortcomings – Ronfelt (1992) says that cyberocracy does not only promote democracy or totalitarianism, but may also lead to more extreme forms of both; moreover, Putnam (2000) warns that it may result in 'cyberbalkanisation', a form of social insularity in which people become inward-looking and pursue only their own narrow interests.

Advantages of the internet

◆ It is inexpensive and convenient (compared with more conventional forms of communication).

◆ It unites individuals who are physically remote and allows them to act as a virtual community.

◆ It rapidly provides huge quantities of up-to-date political, economic and social information.

◆ It allows political campaigners to publicise their successes so that others can replicate them.

◆ Individuals can choose what use to make of it for themselves – to access information, post comments, sign petitions, or organise political activity.

◆ It helps individuals and groups to promote their causes and campaigns, and to stimulate wider public debate.

◆ It is probably more suitable for loosely organised movements than for more formal organisations.

Disadvantages of the internet

◆ It cannot be relied upon as the sole source of information, since it may be affected by human and technical failings.

◆ Opponents of a cause may use it to try to undermine or sabotage that cause.

◆ It is not well regulated or policed, so it may be used irresponsibly by political activists.

◆ It is not equally accessible to everyone and this may exaggerate inequalities.

◆ It is merely a communication tool and is no substitute for more conventional human interaction.

(Source: adapted from Danitz and Strobel, 1999, pp.158–168)

Activity 3

Using the Burma case study and other information above, consider the advantages and disadvantages of cybernetworking in the sphere of postmodern politics. Copy and complete a table like the one below to write brief notes about six advantages and six disadvantages. If you cannot think of that many, refer to the notes above.

Advantages	Disadvantages

Section summary

Use the following words to write a paragraph explaining the key themes of this section.

- Alienation
- Legitimate
- Pressure groups
- New Social Movements
- Direct action
- Strikes
- Political terrorism
- Riots

Stretch and Challenge Activity

What sorts of policies do you think would appeal to people in the UK? Construct your own manifesto of ten key policies in as much detail as you can. Then find the manifestos of the main political parties to compare with your list of policies – which party has policies closest to the ones you selected?

Exam practice

1   Outline and assess the ways in which the political activities of new social movements differ from those of pressure groups. (50 marks)

2   Outline and assess sociological explanations for the emergence of global social movements. (50 marks)

(ii) Participation in and emergence of new social movements

Pause for thought

- Is it true that 'united we stand, divided we fall'?

- Have you ever supported any sort of social movement?

- Do only certain types of people join 'new' social movements?

Activity 4

As the inhabitants of the first country in the world to undergo an industrial revolution, the British people experienced both its positive and negative effects. The use of machines in the textile industry increased production and reduced costs, but also left workers facing lower wages and job losses. They petitioned Parliament for help but to no avail, so a destructive campaign followed, organised by men called Luddites – named after their legendary (and probably non-existent) leader 'King' Ned Ludd, who allegedly lived in Sherwood Forest. In 1811, they smashed textile machinery across the industrial Midlands; in 1812, they attacked textile mills in Lancashire and Yorkshire. At first there was no stopping them, but the government called in troops to put them down – 17 were hanged and scores deported. The Luddite movement collapsed.

1 How did economic and political conditions give rise to the Luddite movement?

2 Why did the Luddites resort to such a violent campaign of direct action?

3 How do the Luddites' actions compare with other historical examples?

4 What similarities and differences are there between the government response to the Luddites and government responses to direct action today?

Beginnings of social movements

Although popular discontent and campaigns to resolve it have existed for centuries, what sociologists now think of as **'social movements' (SMs)** only began to form from the late eighteenth century. The term itself seems to have been first used in 1850 in a book by von Stein, a German sociologist. The US sociologist Tilly (2004) argues that (as with the Luddites) early social movements emerged in response to economic and political changes in society during the first decades of the nineteenth century. Furthermore, he suggests that British campaigns to abolish the slave trade could be regarded as the first-ever social movement.

Social movements have been defined in various ways. One definition is proposed by Wilson (1971), who says that they are organised attempts to either block or promote social change using conscious, collective and non-institutional methods. This definition sees social movements as either fighting for or against change, but places them firmly in the realm of *extra*-Parliamentary politics – for example, the early trade unions often used strikes to try to achieve their goals. The trade unions – as a part of the labour movement – were then by definition generally working class. Thus social movements can be seen as concerned with issues of social class and economic inequality and their members as having similar backgrounds.

Such social movements were once regarded as class-based organisations fighting to secure economic and political rights – either through the labour movement (as in the UK) or by means of violent revolution (as in Russia). Indeed, this view remained largely true until the mid-twentieth century when, beginning in Europe and North America, structural changes in society were evidently bringing about changes in social movements. This gave rise to a new paradigm (way of thinking) of social movements, or what some writers call the 'New social movement' paradigm.

New social movements (NSMs) are regarded by most commentators as different from 'old' social movements. They emerged in Western societies in the years after the Second World War. They owe much to social and economic changes such as the spread of higher education and shifts in employment from the manufacturing to the service sectors, the rise of the welfare state and the increased influence exerted on people's lives by government and big business. Through NSMs, ordinary people challenge 'taken-for-granted' attitudes and try to create more individual and less class-based identities.

The emergence of NSMs can be seen as a challenge to representative democracy and the restricted notion of politics with which it is associated. Sociologists have always conceived of 'politics' in a wider sense than this, seeing it in terms of how power is used throughout social life. Sociologically, it is no coincidence that NSMs have flourished as trust in traditional party politics has declined. In the late twentieth century, too, traditional ideas about social class began to be challenged, and the processes of partisan dealignment and of class dealignment in politics and voting behaviour gathered pace. Politics is today seen not just in economic terms but much more widely.

Who gets involved?

NSMs are usually *non*-institutional – unlike conventional pressure groups, which come within the sphere of institutionalised politics – and often lack the bureaucratic structure of most pressure groups (they may not even have defined leaders as such). NSMs typically have supporters rather than members (unlike pressure groups and most traditional social movements). Supporters of NSMs do not come from any specific social class (unlike old social movements), but include students, retired and unemployed people as well as people in helping professions and new middle-class occupations.

In the pursuit of their cause, NSMs frequently attract a wide range of supporters who have nothing in common except what they are campaigning for – perhaps a single issue. Such campaigns are often coalitions of people from a variety of backgrounds and with different political interpretations beyond their central project, argues Scott (1999). He points to the women's movement as an obvious example: whereas socialist feminists believe that women's demands are part of a wider left-wing movement, the liberal and radical feminists reject this link between feminism and socialism.

Gender, ethnicity, religion and nationality are as central to NSMs as class was to older social movements. In the post-war years, NSMs dedicated to issues as diverse as anti-sexism, anti-racism, anti-war and anti-globalisation have been joined by those promoting women's rights, gay rights, civil rights and animal rights, along with others seeking to protect the environment and the planet itself. The watershed in the shift from traditional politics is usually thought of as the mid-1960s: student protests in the UK, France, Italy and Germany between 1967 and 1969 were accompanied by the rise of the Civil Rights movement in the USA and the spread of women's liberation.

A study of Edinburgh's 'Make Poverty History' (MPH) demonstration in July 2005 by Gorringe and Rosier (2008) analysed the composition of the marchers. Of 225,000 people who joined in this peaceful protest, over a third were from Edinburgh itself and another fifth from elsewhere in lowland Scotland. The rest were mostly from northern England and London. The marchers came from diverse backgrounds, including members of the National Union of Teachers, Socialist Workers' Party, and Christian and Muslim religions. However, only a third of the total admitted to being members of any sort of campaigning or protest organisation as such. Just 6 per cent said they supported a political party – twice as many claimed a Christian affiliation of some sort. Overall, MPH support was worldwide, from student groups and trade unions, all religious groups and none.

As a result, it is not easy to generalise about the 'sociological profile' of the people involved in NSMs today, according to Scott (1999). Different types of NSMs have different types of supporters – for example, anti-road-building protesters are often 'out of the labour market'; animal welfare campaigners tend to be middle-aged and in

Figure 4.1

work or retired; **ecologists** are usually educated and middle class. Smith (1997) argues that studies of the green movement indicate that it is predominantly middle class, but he notes that green campaigns involve both residents directly affected by new developments and also non-residents committed to the cause.

Can NSMs be labelled?

Confronted with such a plethora of NSMs, one of the first tasks of political sociologists was to attempt some sort of classification by type (or typology). In fact, several classifications exist; some, like Smelser's 'Norm-oriented/Value-oriented' category and Habermas's 'Defensive/Offensive' category, have parallels with existing categories into which pressure groups have been placed. It is important to point out that few social movements fit neatly into any of these categories (perhaps not even into the classification 'new' and 'old' social movements).

◆ *Old* social movements are (working-)class based and concerned with 'instrumental' issues (wages, working conditions, economic inequality), such as the labour movement; *New* social movements are socially diverse/non-class-based and concerned with 'moral' issues (rights, individuality, environmentalism, etc.), such as the feminist movement.

◆ *Single-issue* NSMs concentrate on one specific aim and work towards that, like Jubilee 2000 which aimed to cancel Third World debt by the millennium; *Multi-issue* NSMs deal with a number of related objectives and spread their efforts across all of them, such as the range of environmental issues pursued by Earth First.

◆ *Defensive* NSMs seek to protect a (romanticised) traditional aspect of life that they see as threatened, such as the New Age Traveller movement; *Offensive* NSMs instead promote a (utopian) liberated lifestyle free from existing constraints, like those that advocate the decriminalisation of cannabis and other illegal drugs.

◆ *Norm-oriented* NSMs seek only to change some social mechanism and to do so in legal ways, such as the movement opposed to the export of live animals; *Value-oriented* NSMs go further, trying (illegally if necessary) to change the value system of society, such as the Black Power movement in the USA.

◆ *Local* NSMs, as their name indicates, operate at a restricted geographical level, such as the direct-action group 'Reclaim the Streets' which began as a London-based movement; *Global* NSMs, again self-evidently, operate at a worldwide level, such as the international Anti-Globalisation movement.

Activity 5

Greenpeace was founded in Canada in 1971 to oppose US nuclear weapons-testing in Alaska. Today it is an international organisation with offices in over 50 countries and some three million supporters worldwide. It now campaigns on a range of environmental issues, and is opposed to whaling, nuclear power and global warming whilst trying to promote sustainable agriculture and world peace.

1 For each typology listed in the section 'Can NSMs be labelled?', decide which *term* in the pairing best fits Greenpeace.

2 Now place the five *typologies* in order of priority, according to how well overall each sums up the distinguishing features of Greenpeace.

3 In your own words, explain what conclusion you would draw about attempts to categorise social movements into typologies.

Theoretical explanations

If classifying social movements is no easy task, an even more complicated task facing political sociologists is that of developing theoretical explanations for the emergence of NSMs in the modern world. These go beyond the descriptive accounts of social change in various ways, and have their origins in different schools of sociological thought. Again, the difficulty sociologists face is coming up with a satisfactory theory to explain the rise of each NSM, something that no single theory may be able to do.

Collective Behaviour Theory was a product of the USA in the 1950s and adopted a negative view of social movements, associating them with riots and other types of crowd behaviour. It owed much to functionalist theory and was exemplified in the writing of Smelser (1962). Social movements were viewed as dangerous and irrational responses to abnormal social conditions. From this perspective, the formation of social movements is seen as dysfunctional behaviour resulting from strains in society. In a healthy society, political participation through traditional political channels is adequate, so social movements are unnecessary.

Whilst functionalist theory is no longer fashionable in sociology, there are politicians who still regard more extreme social movements as the politics of anarchy. But the real problem with the collective behaviour explanation of social movements is its static view of society. It assumes a normal social state in which political institutions are able to meet the demands of the people and maintain the status quo. Social change is undesirable and a source of problems; social movements that develop in response to social change are therefore seen as irrational and psychopathological. This outdated explanation of social movements has now been superseded by more detailed explanations.

Since the 1960s, an alternative explanation of social movements appeared in the USA and became known as Resource Mobilisation Theory (RMT). It adopts the opposite view from functionalism and sees social movements as highly rational responses to social change. RMT argues that social movements emerge when individuals make rational choices in pursuit of instrumental gain – that is, they are in it to see what they can get out of it. It sees social movements as shaped by and working within the limits set by the available economic, political and communication resources. This explanation sees people's actions in terms of selfish behaviour rather than belief in a cause – the cause is 'sold' to the public in a cynical way as a product.

According to McCarthy and Zald (1987), political grievances are always present in society, but social movements only emerge in particular circumstances – that is, when some individuals see that there are personal gains to be had from joining them. Social movement organisations (SMOs) afford resources such as status and career development to individuals. This approach is particularly concerned with the impact of movements on political issues and tries to gauge in a direct and measurable fashion how far individuals are able to make effective use of their leadership skills in pursuit of their goals.

In a critique of RMT, however, Beuchler (1993) highlights some of the problems with this explanation. Its focus on SMOs is the key problem: not all social movements actually have any formal organisation with status and career opportunities – they are communities of equals. Social movements try to avoid becoming institutionalised groups – supporters tend to be motivated by idealism, not materialism. RMT focuses on the organisation of a social movement rather than its collective identity, so does not see the whole picture. This is why it provides only a generalised explanation and cannot explain differences between social movements, including those which are revolutionary and anarchic.

Marxism

What is certainly clear is that classical Marxism is unable to explain the rise of NSMs. It *was* able to explain the emergence of traditional social movements: industrial societies were based on social inequality and **class conflict**; social movements grew out of the need for working-class people to voice their common concerns and to try to improve their lot as a group with shared economic interests. The explanation worked well until the character of social movements began to change in the post-war years. When they ceased to be mainly working-class movements interested in economic matters and instead gained support from university students and focused on quality-of-life issues, for instance, then other explanations had to be found for NSMs.

In Europe, more than in the USA, explanations for the emergence of social movements have sometimes developed from Marxist theories and built on notions such as the 'crisis of capitalism'. For instance, German critical theory argues that new sources of conflict have replaced economic conflict in society. A crisis of legitimacy has arisen from the state's attempts to control people's ways of life by imposing its own interpretations on events (**hegemony**). Habermas (1981) views government and big business intrusions into individuals' everyday affairs as an attempt to take over their lives. In contemporary life, contradictions give rise to conflicts that are not economic but cultural.

According to this approach, social movements are defensive reactions by ordinary people to reassert control over their threatened lifestyles. It is supported by Offe (1985) who argues that NSMs are best understood as responses to the growing dominance of the capitalist state. In modern capitalist societies, more areas of private life than ever become subject to state regulation by means of legal, media, educational, medical and psychiatric technologies. People's deprivations are no longer just work-related, but affect all aspects of their lives, says Offe, so NSMs emerge to reverse them.

Postmodern views

Also in a European context, another explanation of NSMs owing much to Marxism grew out of the work of the French sociologist Touraine (1981), who suggests that membership of NSMs helps individuals to create their identities. He claims that NSMs prevent social stagnation and are the fabric of social life. In post-industrial society, cultural conflicts have replaced economic conflicts – what is important now is the production of symbolic goods (knowledge and meaning). In post-industrial society, a technocracy (new dominant class) controls the production of knowledge and meaning, so NSMs provide outlets for the organised collective actions of individuals struggling to assert their own identities.

By way of evaluation, it is worth noting that if things are bad in capitalist societies, they are even worse in communist societies. For instance, the Russian sociologist Mamay (2002) points out that the political regime in the former Soviet Union was severely repressive both of actions against the state and modes of thinking that differed from the official one. Under communism, social relations ranging from jobs to sexual relations were under strict ideological control and people's consciousness of their self-interest was ideologically repressed. In these conditions, it is not surprising that social movements did not develop at all (although some have emerged since the fall of communism).

Nevertheless, sociologists on both sides of the Atlantic today acknowledge the core idea in Touraine's theory. For example, the Canadian commentator Klein (2000) also uses ideas from critical theory to develop her argument that in postmodern society, diversity and choice are crushed as big business imposes its culture on society. Since the 1980s, big business has invested in image-creation, using advertising campaigns to market brands more than products, in order to persuade consumers that such brands are an important part of their lives. Companies use strategies such as logo identification, event sponsorship and commodity branding – which she sees as social 'viruses'.

- Harriet Ritvo's account of the Thirlmere campaign viewed as the 'Roots of Environmentalism'
- Friends of the Earth website with links to environmental campaign information
- Information and activities exploring issues surrounding New Age Travellers
- The UK's 'best online coverage of human rights and sustainable development information', with various links
- How the Black Power movement was different from the Civil Rights movement
- Discussion forum with video links: the Animal Liberation Front – are they terrorists?
- Videos of actions of and interviews with Animal Liberation Front militant activists.

(See 'Websites', page ii.)

Globalisation

Big business is able to spread its 'viruses' more easily in postindustrial society because of the rise of multinational and transnational corporations (MNCs and TNCs). They have become powerful cultural influences as a result of **globalisation**: corporations like Disney, McDonald's, Nike, Coca-Cola and Pepsi are accused of corporate censorship, choice limitation and restrictive employment opportunities worldwide. Thus anti-corporate movements can be understood as an attempted counter-attack by consumers. Young people in particular are disillusioned with modern capitalism because they realise that youth culture is shaped by corporate branding rather than their own free choice.

To resist the influence of MNCs and TNCs, people are now supporting what Cohen and Kennedy (2000) refer to as transnational social movements (TSMs). In this way, they are bypassing state-centric (national) politics, and are assisted by improved communications technology like the internet. International problems can now be confronted worldwide by ordinary people in a virtual community: TSMs unite not just the citizens of postindustrial societies but also the dispossessed and exploited living in less democratic countries. Indeed, people in developing countries need TSMs most

and try hardest to gain support from them, often with the aid of activists in the West.

Today, as cultural, ethnic and national identities are undermined by global capitalism, protest movements are supported by individuals who want a citizen-centred alternative to the international rule of the brands and global corporations' control over their lives. They are of all ages and backgrounds; they may be schoolchildren or parents concerned about their children; they may be college students or educated professionals – all are worried about the declining quality of life. They are no longer just consumers, concludes Klein – they are individuals in search of their own identity. In this sense, NSMs are genuine movements of the people.

Whilst they do seem to be of increasing importance in politics today, the majority of social movements are not easy to classify or explain. Some sociologists point out that they have existed for over two centuries and are essentially similar in form and function. Others dismiss the distinction between old and new, and suggest that both types may be located on a continuum. Others think that social movements are so varied that any attempt to explain their emergence with a single theory is impossible – rival explanations may all contain a degree of truth, given that social movements arise at different times and in different contexts. What cannot be denied, however, is that populist politics now play a significant part in the lives of a growing number of people worldwide.

The Animal Liberation Front – a case study

What became the Animal Liberation Front (ALF) was formed at a meeting in London in 1973 by a small group led by Ronnie Lee, a solicitor's clerk. As a law student in 1971, he had founded a local group of the Hunt Saboteurs Association (HSA) in Luton, but had become impatient with the organisation's efforts.

The HSA itself had been founded ten years earlier by John Prestige, a Devon journalist, who had witnessed the chase and killing of a pregnant deer. The organisation used groups of volunteers all over England to obstruct hunts by blowing horns and laying false scents to throw the hounds off the trail.

Lee and his friends – all vegetarians or vegans – embarked on acts of destruction of property for which two of them – including Lee – were imprisoned. Upon his release, he was more militant than ever and in 1976 changed the name of his group to the ALF. It has supporters, not members, and operates in 'cells' that are independent of one another. It has since spread to many other countries and its name is used by activists who participate in animal-liberation activities. It claims to be non-violent but its activities have attracted criticism – its successful campaign against the fur trade resulted in several department stores that sold fur coats being fire-bombed.

According to its Press Office, ALF activists can come from all walks of life, all ages, all beliefs and none. Hundreds of them have spent time in prison as a result of their activities, but are often viewed as the 'Robin Hoods of the animal welfare world'. It has been claimed that this perception attracted a new type of activist to the ALF – younger, unemployed and more interested in anarchism than animal liberation as such, and less likely to believe in non-violence. Many supporters are university academics.

The ALF emerged in the USA within a few years of doing so in the UK and achieved some notable successes against abuses of animals used in research, but its activities earned it a reputation in some quarters as an extremist organisation, as a result of which some of its supporters have been refused entry to the UK to attend conferences. However, today the ALF has active 'cells' in some forty countries worldwide and continues to try and support animal liberation activists to protect animals' welfare.

Activity 6

Using the case study and other information above, analyse the character of the different participants involved in animal welfare movements in the UK and USA. Construct a Venn diagram (three overlapping circles) on a sheet of A4 paper: locate a participant in each circle (newspaper journalist/ solicitor's clerk/university professor) and write brief notes in each circle about their motivations, beliefs, actions and effectiveness. In what ways do they overlap – is there anything they all have in common, at the overlap of all three circles? (Use the internet to research and analyse other examples in the same way.)

Section summary

The most relevant theories to consider in this section are Collective Behaviour Theory, Marxism, neo-Marxism, postmodern views and globalisation.

Use the following words to write a paragraph explaining the key themes of this section.

- Social movement
- Non-institutional
- Defensive
- Offensive
- Resource mobilisation
- Hegemony
- Postmodern
- Globalisation

Weblink

Have a look at the official website of the Hunt Saboteurs' Association (see 'Websites', page ii).

Stretch and Challenge Activity

How do particular social movements emerge and who supports them? Create a 1000-word case study of a movement such as the Hunt Saboteurs' Association.

Exam practice

1 Outline and assess the view that the growth of new social movements is a result of a decline in support for institutional politics. (50 marks)

2 Outline and assess the relationship between the social characteristics of members of old social movements and new social movements. (50 marks)

(iii) The changing patterns of political action

Pause for thought

- Do Members of Parliament carry out the wishes of those who elect them?
- Would you/have you ever joined in any sort of political demonstration?
- Is the use of violence in pursuit of a political cause ever justified?

Figure 4.2: Greenpeace activists boarding the Shell Brent Spar oil rig in the North Sea, 1995

U3

4

Sociology of power and politics

Activity 7

Direct political action gets publicity for social movements and may result in economic problems for businesses. One famous case was Greenpeace's 1995 campaign against Shell's plan to dump its redundant Brent Spar oil rig at the bottom of the Atlantic Ocean to save money. Whilst the rig was anchored in the North Sea awaiting towing to the Atlantic, Greenpeace activists boarded it. They were removed, but got back on board. Ashore, Shell petrol stations were boycotted on an international scale – some were fire-bombed, though Greenpeace condemned the violence. Under pressure from falling revenue, Shell eventually gave way – the rig was dismantled and recycled at a cost of over £40 million (ten times the cost of dumping it).

1 How can direct action affect the decisions big businesses make?

2 Why did Greenpeace resort to direct action in this particular case?

3 What evidence is there to suggest that Greenpeace did not support all of the direct action taken in its name?

4 Why did Shell eventually do something that cost ten times what it planned to spend?

The decline of the ballot box

The emergence of new social movements has brought with it changing patterns of political action. Conventional politics – defined in terms of representative democracy – is based on the notion of political action through the ballot box. However, there is evidence that faith in this declined during the second half of the twentieth century: for instance, the turnout at the 2001 general election was only 59 per cent compared with 83 per cent 50 years earlier. Hallsworth (1994) argues that NSMs offer an alternative political order based on forms of mass participation in which people become more engaged with the decisions that affect them and which goes further than putting a cross on a ballot paper.

Thus patterns of political action are changing and are increasingly moving beyond the institutional framework of representative democracy based on political parties and voting every five years. Groups often find that they are unable to secure their objectives through established **political action** and turn instead to non-institutional forms of political action. This includes NSMs, which Giddens (2006) describes as collective attempts to pursue a shared interest or to achieve a shared goal by means of political action outside the sphere of established institutions. In modern societies, he says, there is a wide variety of social movements, many of which are today international in scale.

The types of political action deployed by NSMs differ accordingly. Even more than pressure groups and old social movements, NSMs are likely to resort to direct action. Whilst the former groups usually limited themselves to institutional methods and resorted to direct action – such as strikes – only when all else failed, NSMs readily adopt direct action methods. These range from demonstrations and sit-ins to mass trespass and fire-bombing. Hallsworth (1994, page 10) places them on what he calls a 'continuum of legality' and cites CND cutting the perimeter wire of a nuclear base as an example of mild **civil disobedience** and the ALF fire-bombing department stores selling fur coats as an example of more violent direct action – both are illegal.

The actions of contemporary social movements have been facilitated by technological developments such as satellite broadcasting, mobile phones and the internet. Giddens (2006) points out how – at the press of a button – grass-roots activists across the world can meet online to exchange information and coordinate action. He suggests that it is the ability of supporters of NSMs to work together in the pursuit of international political campaigns that most undermines institutional politics at the same time as it promotes non-institutional politics. Giddens cites the example of the worldwide protest movement against the Iraq war in 2003 as clear evidence of the ability of NSMs to mobilise instantly when an event occurs and to respond with concerted political action.

Activity 8

Because it thought existing environmental groups were not doing enough, Earth First! introduced civil disobedience campaigns to the USA in 1979. To block logging activities, its members invented 'tree-sitting' – anarchist members held flag-burnings and 'puke-ins' at shopping malls, although older members disliked this. In 1992 more militant members broke away and formed the Earth Liberation Front, which used criminal tactics including sabotage, such as the destruction of logging machinery.

1 Why did Earth First! supporters introduce new methods of campaigning to their organisation in 1979?

2 How have supporters within Earth First! displayed differences in terms of the methods they have used in pursuit of their environmental aims?

3 Which sort of methods (minor civil disobedience or militant criminal tactics) are more likely to help a social movement to succeed in its aims?

Theoretical explanations of political action

In their attempts to move beyond descriptive accounts, sociologists again confront a number of difficulties in developing theoretical explanations for changing patterns of political action. As with attempts to account for the emergence of, and participation in, NSMs, the same schools of sociological thought have attempted to come up with theories to account for changing patterns of political action, but social movements are so diverse that it may be impossible to come up with a single theory that will do so.

Marxism

Classical Marxist theory has tried to explain the political actions of social movements. The Marxist sociologist Castells (1983) was inspired by the protest movements in European cities in 1967–9 and originally argued that these resulted primarily from the same class conflict – between capital (bosses) and labour (workers) – as earlier protests. However, the fact that the student movement played a large part in these events made him modify his explanation, and he later suggested that such **urban social movements** were caused by a new source of inequality based less on production and more on consumption. In the final version of his theory, he admitted that such political action owed little to class as such and was a result of community-based urban social movements.

Many of the urban riots of the late twentieth century might indeed be explained using Castells' approach. According to him, urban social movements united those people who wished either to defend or challenge their local environment and public-service provision. As such they were made up of consumers of varied class backgrounds who were united by their **collective consumption**; they were capable of acting together to support a local hospital or oppose a new road scheme. Although Castells focused on urban movements, he believed they could also arise in other areas and posed a serious threat to the capitalist social order if they escalated from riots into revolution.

However, even in its developed form, Castells' theory has its shortcomings. His notion of collective consumption cannot explain all forms of non-institutional political action; different sections of the community depend on public-service provision to varying degrees. Saunders (1983) criticises Castells for overestimating the radical nature of urban social movements, claiming that middle-class people are better able to protect their interests and Urry (1990) plays down the radical nature of urban social movements by pointing out that they are as likely to be made up of middle-class NIMBYs ('not-in-my-backyard') as of radical protesters intent on drastic social change.

Feminism

Feminist criticisms of Marxist accounts of social movements are encompassed within those made about the political sphere in general – politics seems to be a male domain in which women are not fully included. In spite of the existence of Marxist feminism, feminist critics argue that the role of women in political action is conspicuous by its absence. The Marxist theorist Habermas is taken to task by feminists for the fact that his major study of communicative action says next to nothing about gender – he discusses politics as if it is gender neutral. Feminists believe that as in other spheres of life, **gender identity** has not been given due credit in the sociological analysis of political action.

Whilst many feminists campaign for equality between the sexes, others assert that it is more important to emphasise gender difference. Gilligan (1982), for example, argues that because men and women are different, the feminist movement should concentrate on the things that make women special. Indeed, because women are not a homogeneous type themselves but are divided by class, ethnicity and so on, Butler (1990) goes on to assert that the umbrella term 'women' should be abandoned. Women's identities are manifold but only specific actions are able to highlight the differences.

A notable instance of political action that did highlight one such identity was the peace camp at Greenham Common – set up and run by women to protest against the installation of nuclear weapons. The camp symbolised an explicitly feminist stance and would never have happened if life had not moved on from private to public patriarchy, according to Roseneil (1995). She argues that because women had gained certain freedoms in terms of (public) employment and welfare opportunities, they were also freed from (private) family ties. They now had the financial freedom to live at the camp, where – for the first time in their lives – they had a sense of real participation in decision-making and gained a new consciousness of men's domination of political and social life.

Figure 4.3: Protesters outisde the military base at Greenham Common, 1982

As well as being a community of women, the peace camp was (partly) a community of lesbians, which leads on to the issue of **sexual identity** in social movements. This is seen clearly in the gay movement Queer Nation, set up in Greenwich Village, New York, in 1990. Its aim was to eliminate homophobia through a variety of tactics including direct action: one tactic was to subvert of the language of its 'oppressors', as in reclaiming the word 'queer' as positive rather than negative in the name it adopted for itself. Following a bomb attack on a gay bar in New York, the movement mobilised a thousand protesters in a few hours; it soon spread across the USA and began a campaign of outing closet gays in positions of influence to end what it saw as hypocrisy in society.

Mirroring the feminist movement, some in the gay movement wanted to abandon the simple straight/gay distinction and instead view sexual identities as manifold and equally acceptable. As far as any social movement is concerned, however, such a tactic raises the danger of **fragmentation**: Nash (2000) warns that this action may divide a movement and prevent it from

gaining wider recognition in society. If the aim of political action is to generate solidarity within a social movement so that it can achieve its goal, dividing it to recognise manifold identities is not the best way to go about this.

Pluralism

Some of the harshest critics of NSMs attack them for precisely this reason. Sociologists who adopt a pluralist view (and believe the range of political parties and pressure groups in modern societies is accepted by the majority as legitimate) see no place for NSMs. For example, Hirst (1993) dismisses them as such fragmented and loose associations as to be relatively powerless in relation to governments. He doubts that their political actions will ever bring about radical change – if anything, they are only capable of making changes at the edge of society. In his view, NSMs have nothing worthwhile to offer society.

Postmodern views

Nevertheless, many people today do not accept the legitimacy of the existing political institutions

– far from it, they are deeply suspicious of the actions of governments. Many people have little trust in what they are told by government and scientific experts. Today, life seems more uncertain and public awareness of this has grown – the age of reflective modernity has arrived. Where industrialisation and capitalist production were once taken for granted, they are now subject to **reflexivity** (they are thought about and reflected upon). Thus the German sociologist Beck (1992) suggests that in what he calls a **risk society**, people are more likely to adopt political actions associated with NSMs. Environmental movements can be understood as a response to this perception of risk.

Collective Identity Theory

A growing number of sociologists believe that the world has moved on from modernity to postmodernity. In what has become known as Collective Identity Theory, social movements are not so much a response to coping with risk but instead a way for members to develop a self-image. For example, the Italian sociologist Melucci (1989) suggests that for supporters of NSMs, the issue they are campaigning for matters less than participation in the lifestyle that goes with it – this serves as a sign to others and is a mark of identity.

Moreover, the political action NSMs engage in is only superficial in relation to involvement in the organisations – which he refers to as **social movement networks**.

Being a member of an NSM helps an individual to develop a collective identity, and the movement itself develops a group self-image as a result. However, collective identities are not fixed but fluid – groups with positive self-images confer high self-esteem on their members (although 'stigmatised' groups can have the opposite effect). For Melucci, collective identity is a two-way process that is constructed and negotiated in the course of an individual's membership of an NSM. By way of evaluation, Collective Identity Theory can be seen as an advance on earlier social movement theories, because it fills the gaps in Resource Mobilisation Theory and others that focus more on political action.

Melucci's view of social movements is both **postindustrial** and postmodern, in that he emphasises the way they have moved on

from material to cultural concerns as central to understanding them as forms of political action. In this respect, his ideas are supported by Touraine, who also believes that in order for political action by social movements to be effective it is necessary for their supporters to develop a collective identity and alternative lifestyle. They differ in that Touraine also believes that social movements should aim for a takeover of the state; Melucci only regards them as informal networks of individuals linked by cultural contact but not by shared interests or ideologies.

Globalisation

From a different theoretical perspective, Fukuyama (1992) would agree with Melucci that shared ideology is unimportant – but only because he believes that 'ideology is dead'. Like others before him, Fukuyama holds that with the arrival of globalisation comes the end of ideology and a worldwide system of politics based on liberal democracy. Class is also dead from this perspective, but other sociologists do not accept this – Marxist theorists see plenty of evidence of continued class differences in postmodern society. A number, for instance, see class conflict continuing but on a global scale. Globalisation is simply another name for Americanisation and the **global imperialism** that goes with it.

Lash and Urry (1987) argue that nation states are now threatened by global capitalism (in the form of multinational and transnational corporations). These companies contract out their production to countries where labour costs are lowest, usually in the developing world, where national governments are so desperate for economic investment that they offer little protection to their factory workers, who often earn below subsistence wages. Klein (2000) uses the term 'sweatshops' to describe the factories where branded goods are made cheaply for sale in the West. In the West too, working conditions have declined in the pursuit of profit – Ritzer (1996) uses the term 'McJobs' to describe the growth in low-paid and insecure employment which is becoming the norm here.

The threat posed by global capitalism spawned the anti-capitalist or anti-globalisation movement, although the former name is more appropriate: the movement is only opposed to the negative features of globalisation and actually builds on some of the positive ones, particularly the growth in global communication. The movement is made up of a diverse range of supporters with wide-ranging concerns but a shared belief that the problems the world faces are caused by global capitalism. Callinicos (2003) believes that they are all motivated by a feeling that the world's problems are linked in some way to capitalism. Most supporters have some sympathy with green movements and movements of indigenous people, with socialism and even anarchism.

Weblinks

You might find the following websites interesting:

- Website featuring information about the historical Luddites and 'new Luddites' with links to various other sites
- A US organisation dedicated to investigating and exposing corporate crime
- Website of an anti-capitalist and anti-war organisation that aims to build a better world
- Website of an organisation campaigning against sweatshops in solidarity with workers worldwide.

(See 'Websites', page ii.)

In the fight against TNCs, social movements have extended their repertoire of political actions. Along with mass protests, campaigns and boycotts, the anti-corporate movement uses the internet in varied ways: Klein believes it is the most potent weapon available to the 'hacktivists' who infiltrate the internet to subvert corporate websites. This novel form of political action is now known as **culture jamming** – the act of subverting (changing) the advertisements produced by companies to promote their products. For example, Nike's 'swoosh' logo has been subverted as the 'Swooshtika' by activists, and is used to represent the poor pay and working conditions typical of sweatshop factories in the developing world.

Some corporations have tried to defend their products, such as McDonald's attempt to sue two protestors who had campaigned against it, but even this backfired and was itself subverted. What became known as the 'McLibel' case simply served to draw attention to the anti-McDonald's campaign. Klein concludes that culture jamming

is a valuable way for campaigners to publicise the deeper problems associated with global capitalism, such as worker exploitation and political repression. Culture jamming alone only inconveniences individual corporations, but Klein is hopeful that a global and coordinated movement may one day become as effective in its opposition as the corporations its political actions are trying to subvert.

On a related theme, Klein also draws attention to the anti-capitalist protests that have coincided with meetings of world leaders, such as the G8 (Group of 8) meeting in Genoa in 2001 where there was a violent protest which included a fatal shooting. The anti-capitalist movement also opposes international institutions which it thinks support global capitalism, such as the World Bank, the International Monetary Fund (IMF) and the World Trade Organisation (WTO). In 1999 in the USA, 40,000 demonstrators turned a WTO meeting into the 'Battle of Seattle' – the internet was used to coordinate protests in cities worldwide, including London. Other global protests have taken place since.

In conclusion, it would seem reasonable to suggest that changing patterns of political action are shaped by technological and economic change (the internet and globalisation). The development of global capitalism is certainly a factor in the emergence of worldwide groupings of campaigners – **transnational social movements**. How far these are based on class remains a matter of debate: right-wing commentators may well be right in asserting that capitalism will dominate the globe, but that may explain why some features of class analysis still seem relevant in explaining changing patterns of political action. As faith in institutional political action wanes, the rise of non-institutional political action may serve to reinvigorate democracy in the twenty-first century world.

'Reclaim the Streets' – a case study

Carmageddon! That's the threat that first prompted Reclaim the Streets (RTS) to fight back and try to stem the spread of cars and road-building schemes. RTS was formed in London in 1991, when anti-road-building campaigns were still a novelty. The campaign to prevent the destruction of Twyford Down near Winchester (to construct the M3 motorway) had already started and inspired people to take action elsewhere. In the capital, individuals formed small groups

Sociology of power and politics

to fight traffic congestion by taking direct action against the motor car, initially on their own streets.

Their avowed aim (according to the environmentalist publication *Do or Die!*) was to promote walking, cycling and cheap, or free, public transport and to oppose cars, roads and the system that encourages their use. Their direct action methods included DIY cycle lanes painted by night on the capital's streets, leaving a wrecked car in Park Lane to symbolise Carmageddon, vandalising ('subvertising') billboard car advertisements and disrupting the 1993 Earls Court Motor Show. However, they were galvanised into direct action of a more disruptive kind by a road-building scheme in East London.

In 1995, construction commenced on a long-planned M11 link road – ancient woodland and hundreds of homes lay in its path. 'No M11' campaigners had protested against it for years – using conventional methods such as lobbying and petitions – to no avail, but they were now joined by RTS activists. More direct methods were deployed: computers, video cameras, performance art and street parties, in spite of the fact that the 1994 Criminal Justice and Public Order Act made such civil protesting a criminal offence.

A coalition of environmentalists, socialists and anarchists formed, shaping RTS into a radical new movement. Increasingly, it resorted to the formation of what have become known as Temporary Autonomous Zones (TAZs) – sections of a busy road occupied by protesters – intent on stopping the traffic by partying, complete with scaffold towers and speaker systems. In July 1996, a street party held on the elevated M41 motorway in West London attracted a crowd of 8000 people who partied and danced as they dodged arrest by the police – whilst some drilled up the tarmac to plant trees.

It is significant that thousands of people can be united by a social movement *without* a leader, a hierarchy, a bureaucracy, an official membership or 'party policy'. Reclaiming a street by creating a TAZ may seem utopian, but RTS supporters (many middle class and university educated) see the movement as a radical new way of battling the forces intent on destroying the planet. For example, they have attacked oil and finance companies by printing a spoof 32-page *Evading Standards* newspaper (culture-jamming the *Evening Standard*). As the RTS website says, 'The streets are as full of capitalism as of cars'.

Figure 4.4: Reclaim the Streets aim to oppose cars and roads

Today, RTS groups exist throughout the world, based on the London model – the first street party outside the UK was held in Finland in May 1997, while others have since been held across North America, Australia and Africa. In many instances, street parties have become institutionalised and increasingly resemble more conventional forms of protest insofar as they are arranged in advance with the legal authorities. Nevertheless, to most participants, RTS is widely recognised as a new movement of non-violent direct action.

Stretch and Challenge Activity ➤

Why do some social movements resort to civil disobedience? Undertake a balanced evaluation of the direct action methods of a movement such as Fathers 4 Justice, using newspaper and magazine articles (and websites too if you have access) to produce a 'For' and 'Against' review. Which of the two sides has most points? (Is your evaluation the same as other students' in this respect?)

Section summary

The most relevant theories to consider in this section are Marxism, feminism, pluralism, collective identity, postmodernism and global imperialism.

Use the following words to write a paragraph explaining the key themes of this section.

- Political action
- Civil disobedience
- Urban Social Movement
- Gender identity
- Sexual identity
- Postindustrial
- Global imperialism
- Culture jamming

Exam practice

1   Outline and assess sociological explanations of changing patterns of political action. (50 marks)

2   Outline and assess the view that the growing support for the activities for new social movements indicates the end of class politics. (50 marks)

U3

4

Sociology of power and politics

Activity 9

Using the case study and other information above, analyse the changing objectives and methods of Reclaim the Streets before and after 1995. Draw up a table like the one below and write brief notes in each cell. What does your analysis of RTS tell you about the evolution of the movement? How typical is this of all NSMs? (You can use the internet to research and analyse other examples in the same way.)

	Aims	Methods
Up to 1995		
After 1995		

(iv) Political ideologies and their relationship to political action

Pause for thought

- Do any sorts of political beliefs make more sense to you than others?
- Why should people's lives be guided by sets of shared political beliefs?
- Where do individuals get their political beliefs from in society today?

Activity 10

In a workshop, five engineers were examining a machine. The first said the machine was no good because only half the population could use it. The second said that although the machine was okay, it should only be used when necessary and people should not come to rely on it. The third said there was nothing at all wrong with the machine and as it wasn't broken, nothing should be done to try and fix it. The fourth said the machine was only of use to a few people so it should be smashed up and a new one built. The fifth said he wasn't remotely interested in the rotten machine and left the workshop.

Suppose the machine was actually the machinery of state (government) and the five engineers were an anarchist, a conservative, a feminist, a liberal and a Marxist.

1 Try to pair up each engineer with one of the five views of what should be done with the machine. (If it helps, work in a pair with another student.)

2 How would you line up the engineers side by side, according to the strength of their different views of what should be done with the machine?

3 Which solution about what to do with the machine do you think most of the population would be likely to go along with? (Why?)

4 If you had to deal with a machine that was in working order but not catering for the needs of the population as a whole, what would your solution be?

Ideologies

In a way, the relationship between political ideologies and political action is a bit like the engineers and the machine – what people think about politics influences what action they take about it. When groups of people come together, whether in political parties or looser social movements, and share meaningful ideas about what the world is like – and even more so, what it *ought* to be like – it can be said that these people have adopted a political ideology. This will guide their beliefs and behaviour in the political sphere of life and have a direct effect on their pursuit of political action.

A **political ideology**, according to Heywood (2002), is a set of logical political ideas that provide a plan of action, whether that action is intended to preserve, modify or overthrow an existing political system. The concept of ideology is controversial in sociology, but all ideologies offer a way of viewing society as it *is*, and of how it *should be*, plus some notion of how change can be brought about to make it a better place to live in. For example, an ideology may suggest ways in which power can be re-allocated in society.

The US sociologist Bell (1960) says that the term 'ideology' was first used over two centuries ago by the French philosopher de Tracy, who was looking for a way to discover the real truth, beyond that handed down by the Church and the State. De Tracy felt that this could be done by purifying ideas by eliminating any bias within them and so making them objective. Thus he proposed a new science of ideas, which he called 'ideology', by means of which the correct ideas could be arrived at: in this sense, de Tracy's view of ideology is usually described as a neutral one.

However, later commentators challenged the notion that a science of ideas would lead to the 'truth'. In his book *The German Ideology*, Marx (1968) argued that ideas do not exist independently: instead they are created by people with particular points of view and their own vested interests. For this reason, Marx claimed that ideologies do not provide 'truth' but reflect the needs of specific groups – and because they mask these particular interests, ideologies are actually false. Marx turns de Tracy's argument on its head: therefore, the Marxist view of ideology is usually referred to as a negative one.

Bell draws out the relationship between ideologies and political actions with his phrase 'Ideology is the conversion of ideas into social levers', echoing the notion that ideas are weapons. What gives ideology its force is its passion, he goes on: ideology has the ability not only to transform ideas, it can also transform people. Political and social movements use ideology to 'rouse' people in three ways. First, ideology simplifies ideas; second, it lays claim to the truth; and third, it requires commitment to political action from supporters. This, then, is the relationship between ideology and political action.

Throughout the nineteenth and the first half of the twentieth centuries, ideologies – from Marxism on the political left to Fascism on the political right – did indeed inspire a commitment which led to political actions such as the Russian Revolution and the rise of the Third Reich. However, after the Second World War these ideologies were exhausted, according to Bell; they were driven by demands for social equality which was eventually achieved with economic development – indeed, the latter became a new ideology which washed away the memory of old disillusionments and discontent.

The post-war years were a time of **political pluralism** in which (in the Western world at least) the ideological age had ended. Bell concludes his book by warning against ideology and its effects – he thinks ideology is like a trap. Ideologists, he believes, simplify the truth and ideology makes it unnecessary for people to face up to particular issues – instead, people turn on an 'ideological vending machine' (page 405) and out comes an answer to any problem. When an ideology is backed by passion and people use its ideas as weapons, the political actions based on an ideology can have dreadful results.

Activity 11

Think about Bell's argument, then answer the following questions in your own words.

1 How are de Tracy's and Marx's views of ideology different from one another?

2 What three things does a social movement have to do to rouse people to action?

3 Why does Bell believe that political ideologies are not really good for people?

Nevertheless, since Bell made his prediction about the end of ideology half a century ago, it is evident that ideologies continue to play a major part in political life throughout the world. Older ideologies persist and newer ideologies have emerged, such as feminism and ecologism. Greater recognition is now accorded to a wider range of ideologies, such as fundamentalism and Islamism – indeed, the list of '-isms' seems endless. Modern sociologists are more interested than ever in examining how ideologies may shape political action, as can be seen in the following examples.

Liberalism

Any account of political ideologies should start with **liberalism**, according to Heywood (2002). It emerged at the end of the Middle Ages, with the decline of the feudal system, although it was not until the early nineteenth century that it became a 'creed' as such. It is associated with industrialisation and the rise of capitalism: classical liberalism favoured a laissez-faire economic system (opposed to government intervention) but in the nineteenth century this hard line softened with the growth of progressive liberalism (tolerating some degree of government intervention in the provision of social welfare).

Central to the liberal ideology is a belief in individualism – societies should recognise the uniqueness of individuals and develop policies that allow people to develop in their own way. However, individual freedom is tempered with a recognition that people should be free 'under the law', so that freedom for some is not a threat to others. Liberals believe in human reason and think that everyone has the right to exercise the maximum freedom possible, based on making their own moral decisions, provided that in doing so no one else is prevented from exercising that very same right for themselves.

Liberalism places more value on the notion of individuality than on equality as such. Of course, everyone should be free to develop their talents as fully as possible, but people do not have equal talents. While individuals should be accorded equality of opportunity, it has to be recognised that they have unequal talents and therefore unequal potential. Thus, according to liberal ideology, societies should be organised as meritocracies in which the individuals with the most talent are most rewarded.

For liberalism, the task of government is to balance the rights and responsibilities of individuals. To achieve this, government must be founded on the consent of the governed and this is most likely to be secured through representative democracy. The liberal view of government is 'bottom-up', and this is what legitimises it; any 'top-down' government is likely to be authoritarian. Liberals believe in limited government alongside a plurality of political organisations as the basis of a liberal democracy.

Classical liberalism places more emphasis on limited government than does progressive liberalism – this is especially apparent in economics. For example, the eighteenth-century economist Adam Smith used the metaphor of an 'invisible hand' to explain how markets are regulated simply by the self-interested actions of buyers and sellers without the need for any government intervention. From Smith onwards, this ideology praised the way in which markets contribute to the achievement of 'greater human prosperity' (Hinchliffe and Woodward, 2000). Regulation can be left to the price mechanism.

Progressive liberalism acknowledged the fact that leaving individuals to the ups and downs of the market created social problems that only a degree of state intervention could solve. It was a Liberal government that introduced the first welfare state provisions in the UK in the early twentieth century, and it was liberal-minded academics (such as Beveridge and Keynes) who advocated the extension of the provision after the Second World War. Only through a system of managed or regulated capitalism, says Heywood (2002), could individuals be responsible for their own circumstances and make moral choices.

A new classical liberal ideology appeared in the UK from 1980, following the election of Thatcher's government. Economists such as Friedman and Hayek advocated 'free market' ideas: the market, it was argued, is a form of spontaneous social order with no need of government intervention – what holds society together are the two-way links between self-interested individuals. Hayek also attacks trade unions because he believes their activities interfere with the price mechanism in the market.

Liberal ideology may well have a central concern with protecting individual rights from interference by others, but there is clearly room for differences within it. Liberalism is not like a club requiring its members to stick to a rigid set of rules, suggests Dawson (2000): it is more like an extended family of political theorists who share common concerns, values and a vision of an ideal community. For these reasons, Liberalism is, in his view, one of the most important ideologies in the contemporary world.

The fact that a Conservative government's political action was shaped by neo-classical liberal economic ideology may be a source of some confusion. In an essay entitled 'Why I am not a Conservative', Hayek tried to clarify matters: for him, the problem was that the word 'liberal' had been taken over by socialists for their own ideology and so lost its true meaning; all he had done was to reassert what classical liberalism really stood for. Hayek claimed that he could not be a conservative because he was a liberal – which then raises the question of precisely what it is to be a conservative.

Conservatism

Conservative ideology was formulated in the years after the French Revolution (1789) and was a reaction to the rapid political and social changes that followed. Conservatives looked back fondly to the *ancien régime* (old order) and dedicated themselves to trying to resist change – to conserve political order and social stability. Over the centuries, the ideology of **conservatism** has itself been modified and some conservative thinkers are less resistant to change, but they still argue that if change must occur, it should be gradual and built on tradition.

Central to the conservative ideology is a belief in tradition – societies should recognise the value of tried and tested customs and institutions from the past and use them as guides to the here and now. In the view of conservatives, tradition provides stability and security, which is all the more important given that their view of human nature is pessimistic: they believe that individuals are innately insecure, selfish and greedy. For this reason, people need security and order, which conservative ideology says is best achieved by a strong state, strict laws, and stiff penalties (Heywood, 2002).

The conservative view of society as a whole parallels that of functionalist sociology. It is based on an organic analogy, whereby society is thought of as an **organic whole** (that is, a living thing) – and this 'whole' is more than simply the individuals within it. People are members of social groups which have evolved naturally and are vital to maintaining a sense of solidarity (families, communities, nations). The family is of primary importance because it teaches individuals shared beliefs and behaviour: it is for this reason that many Conservative politicians emphasise Victorian and family values.

Linked to this is a belief in authority – which conservatives always see as top-down – and therefore of hierarchy – within families, education, employment and society overall: both are regarded as natural and essential. It is the ordered social roles that arise with authority and hierarchy that give people a sense of place and belonging. **Exteriorisation** of people's personalities is also encouraged by property ownership, a key component of conservative ideology (but something that is a taboo to others).

Heywood (2002) points out that there are significant divisions in conservative ideology. Authoritarian conservatism is the most reactionary and dictatorial form and was typified by Russia under tsarist rule. Paternalistic conservatism is still top-down but stresses the social obligations of the rich and powerful to those below them: it owes much to the thinking of the nineteenth-century Tory leader Benjamin Disraeli, but was still evident in Conservative governments in the mid-twentieth century. Libertarian conservatism was the basis of Thatcher's government, with its New Right, free-market ideology.

Neo-Conservatism

Neo-Conservatism is one of the divisions in conservative ideology noted by Heywood. It is a potentially confusing mixture of traditional conservative and neo-liberal ideology, and finds its clearest expression in the new right ideology associated with Thatcherism in the UK and Reaganism in the USA. It brings together beliefs in economic freedoms (market mechanisms) and strong social order. For this reason, some commentators see it as very different from traditional conservatism and more like classical liberalism – the idea that there is no such thing as society is the way Thatcher showed her individualism.

The ideology emerged in the 1980s, largely as a reaction to the permissiveness of the 1960s. The **moral pluralism** of the permissive society was deplored by neo-conservatism – as Heywood notes, the latter has a significant religious element, particularly in the USA. Here, the new right and the New Christian Right go hand-in-hand. In national politics, this is most evident in the conservative wing of the Republican Party, whose policies and rhetoric were influenced by fundamentalist religious organisations, according to Giddens (2006). For example, lawmakers were lobbied to overturn the ban on prayers in schools and to restrict women's legal right to abortion.

Religious fundamentalism and conservative political views often go together. Indeed, Keddie (1999) argues that fundamentalism can be regarded as a new religious politics. She views fundamentalism positively and suggests that it may be a focus for resistance to racism and discrimination. However, it can be seen negatively – when religious teachings are taken literally and moral crusades conducted against anyone perceived as 'different', the outcome may be repression and disempowerment for large sections of the population. By undermining liberalism and pluralism, neo-conservatism and fundamentalism display signs of authoritarianism and intolerance that suggest they are far from new.

In spite of its efforts to adapt and keep up with the times, conservative ideology always attracts criticism on the grounds that – with its belief in authority, hierarchy and the status quo – it is simply a mask for ruling-class ideology. Whereas conservatives are located to the right of the political spectrum, their critics are located to the left. Chief among these are the Marxists, whose ideology is diametrically opposed to conservative ideology. Marxism has its own divisions, and the political actions that have been undertaken around the world in its name have also muddied the waters.

Marxism

Marx wrote extensively about the emergence of modern capitalism in the nineteenth century. At the time he was writing, Europe was undergoing an Industrial Revolution which caused an economic and social transformation. The growth of industrialisation resulted in a migration of population to towns and cities, as a consequence of which living conditions changed and there were struggles for power – working-class demands for political representation were a key feature of this period of upheaval and conflict.

Central to Marxist ideology is a concern with the means of production – machinery, factories, raw materials – because it is this that shapes the relationships of individuals and groups in society. The factory system created the financial wealth of the new capitalist class (the bourgeoisie) but only at the expense of the property-less working class (the proletariat). Although the workers were paid, their labours made a profit for the ruling class in a process that Marx termed 'exploitation'. In this way, capitalism resulted in what Marx (1968) described as 'two great hostile camps'.

There is clearly much more to Marxist ideology than this, but Mackintosh and Mooney (2000) emphasise three crucial themes:

Figure 4.5

n/a

1. The way an individual's position in the system of production is the source of their social class.

2. The way a division into two hostile camps is a potential source of class conflict.

3. The way class conflict may give rise to class consciousness.

When the workers become class conscious (aware of their shared identity and interests), there is the possibility of collective political action through the experience of organisation and class struggle.

Marx predicted a proletarian revolution in which workers would seize power from the bourgeoisie and create a communist society in which wealth would be owned in common by everyone – there would be no private property. Although he died before it happened, it was in Russia in 1917 that the first such revolution occurred, when the tsarist regime was overthrown by Lenin's Bolsheviks, who led the working class in that country and helped it to achieve a **class consciousness** and take action. Since then, revolutions claiming to be inspired by Marxist ideology have occurred around the world.

Today, several different Marxist ideologies have developed. Heywood (2002) discusses three:

◆ Classical Marxism is that produced by Marx himself, which he thought of as a new type of 'scientific socialism', a socialism based on the new scientific thinking of the age.

◆ Orthodox Marxism is the way its founder's ideas were put into practice in Russia as Marxism–Leninism (or vulgar Marxism).

◆ Modern Marxism is the way its founder's ideas have been modified by academics in Western Europe in recent times as neo-Marxism.

Neo-Marxism

Neo-Marxists pay much attention to the ways in which the ruling class continues to be able to promote false consciousness.

For instance, the Italian political activist Gramsci (1971) broadened the definition of 'political' to include institutions such as religion, mass media and the workplace. Through these institutions, ruling-class ideas spread into the everyday lives of ordinary people, shaping their thoughts and influencing their behaviour. In this way, the ideas of the ruling-class become the dominant ideas accepted throughout society and so thoughts of revolutionary political action never even occur in the minds of the masses. (See also page 176.) This approach has been adopted by later neo-Marxists.

For example, Westergaard and Resler (1976) discuss the way liberal and conservative ideologies stress meritocratic inequality, market mechanisms, profit and private property. These things are presented as natural and legitimate, but this only serves to block criticism of them and ensure that ruling-class ideology goes unchallenged by the working class. If this is the case, it is no wonder that no opposition to it ever arises and that capitalism is so dominant. They conclude that the most effective form of control of the working class is that which 'embraces the minds and wills of its subjects so successfully' (page 41).

Feminism

The notions of exploitation and struggle evident in Marxist ideology are also found in feminist ideology (indeed, there is a Marxist–feminist ideology). Feminist ideology owes much to the eighteenth-century writer Wollstonecraft (1993): back in 1792, inspired by the French Revolution, she argued in her book *A Vindication of the Rights of Woman* for the proper education of women. Conservative ideologists opposed her 'revolutionary' demand at the time, but it was taken up by feminist ideologists in later years. Walby (1990), a modern feminist, describes two 'waves' of political action based on feminist ideology.

Central to feminist ideology is the concept of patriarchy (male dominance), which is indispensable to an analysis of gender inequality, according to Walby, who differentiates between private patriarchy (in the sphere of the home) and public patriarchy (in social life beyond it). She also distinguishes between first-wave feminism, which was focused on achieving certain political rights, and second-wave feminism, which campaigned on a broader range of social issues. Both waves held a common view of women as excluded citizens and shared a readiness to resort to direct action.

In the first wave, women were campaigning for suffrage (the right to vote) through an organisation called the Women's Social and Political Union (WSPU). They resorted to civil disobedience in the form of smashing windows, disrupting political meetings and being imprisoned for their cause. In the second wave, women demonstrated and protested in various ways through the wider Women's Liberation Movement (WLM).

Women workers at a Ford car factory came out on strike in 1968 and women protesters disrupted a live BBC broadcast of the Miss World contest in 1969. These two waves of feminism illustrate several of the types of political action mentioned in earlier sections.

Walby aimed to produce a theory of feminism that avoided existing classifications: liberal feminism had come to be seen as simply seeking equal rights for women; Marxist (or socialist) feminism was seen to treat women's subordination as a result of capitalism; and radical feminism was seen to be particularly opposed to 'male-stream' society and saw men as the enemy. Walby intended to unify these diverse theories with her own approach, but she has been criticised for treating gender, class and race as three separate but interactive systems of oppression when they are really one and the same.

In an article entitled 'Is feminism still important?', Jowett (2001) reviews the relevance of this ideology thirty years after the second wave and admits it is facing a real test today. The feminist movement today has become even more fragmented: now, there are black feminists, lesbian feminists, eco-feminists and postmodern feminists – the latter even doubt that 'woman' is a meaningful category. There has also been something of a reaction against feminism in recent years, and not just by men, but Jowett suggests that it is up to each generation of women to set their own agenda based on what is important to them.

Weblinks

You might find the following websites interesting:

- A definition of the term 'ideology' and much more from the Answers.com website
- Background information and three short quizzes to aid understanding of ideology
- An interactive test of knowledge of the rights of Victorian women – and other topics
- Access to the Anarchist Library, with biographies, essays and articles plus links.

(See 'Websites', page ii.)

Anarchism

A different political ideology contests how meaningful a more basic concept is – that of the state. This is **anarchism** (from the Greek for 'without rule'), which holds that societies could and should exist without the evil and coercive power of the state. The first person to call himself an anarchist was the Frenchman Proudhon in the nineteenth century, but as an ideology anarchy now has many forms, some of which pre-date him. Anarchism is usually seen as a radical left-wing ideology, but it may be translated into either individualist or collectivist lifestyles by those who subscribe to its principles.

Central to the anarchist ideology is a belief that all forms of compulsory government are unnecessary – people are capable of arranging their own affairs voluntarily and cooperatively without state control. Early individualist anarchists – who represented the minority view – believed that rational human beings can co-exist peacefully; modern individualists see a framework in market forces. Collectivist anarchists – a majority view following Proudhon's ideas – believe in **mutualism**, whereby groups of people living in communes exchange commodities without the use of money.

To Proudhon, property is theft and capitalism a source of injustice and exploitation. Anarchists see the state as corrupt and natural social order as spontaneous and harmonious. Their view of human nature is optimistic: they subscribe to social equality, common ownership and (mostly) non-violence. However, critics think of anarchism as a utopian ideology and – significantly – no large-scale society has ever been based on its principles. Indeed, because anarchist ideology rejects conventional means of political action, it seems unlikely that any society will ever develop it.

Activity 13

Using a textbook, journal article or the internet, find out about sociologist Catherine Hakim's 'Preference Theory'. How does her theory differ from all forms of feminist theory? If possible, organise a debate within your sociology group or sixth form – with male as well as female students – to consider the motion that 'Feminist ideology should take account of Preference Theory in its attempts to influence women's thinking'. (When voting on the motion, is there any gender difference within the group?)

Nevertheless, its influence cannot be dismissed entirely. Social movements have drawn on anarchist ideology in their challenges to state power: for example, in its creation of TAZs (Temporary Autonomous Zones), Reclaim the Streets has put into practice the idea of anarchist theorist Hakim Bey. Anarchism can be seen to have influenced other political actions in modern societies, even if it has not become a mass movement in its own right. It could be that in an increasingly fragmented and complex world its critics have missed the point, says Heywood (2002) – it may be mass politics itself that is dead. The Black Flag anarchist movement is opposed to all forms of government and state control, and instead campaigns for a social system based on mutual aid and voluntary cooperation.

In conclusion, it is obvious that there is some correlation between political ideologies and political action. From the conservative maintenance of the status quo and the liberal attitude of limited intervention, to the direct action of feminism, the non-violent isolation of individual anarchism and the direct action of collectivist anarchists through to the violent revolution of Marxism – ideology plays its part. Since Bell proclaimed the end of ideology half a century ago and Fukuyama more recently argued that ideology is dead, there have been many indications that – in spite of technological advances and globalisation – ideology is alive and well in society today.

Weblinks

Have a look at the following websites:

- An interactive quiz to find out if you're socialist, liberal, conservative or libertarian
- A wide-ranging selection of political quizzes – American, but worth trying by anyone
- Tests knowledge of key figures and ideas to do with political ideologies
- Find out your own political ideology by answering just 25 questions.

(See 'Websites', page ii.)

Section summary

Use the following words to write a paragraph explaining the key themes of this section.

- Political pluralism
- Organic whole
- Exteriorisation
- Moral pluralism
- Marxist
- Patriarchy
- Anarchism
- Mutualism

Stretch and Challenge Activity

Which political ideologies seem to have most relevance to political action today? In a 'raft debate', which *one* of the five main ideologies (liberalism, conservatism, Marxism, feminism or anarchism) should *not* be saved for twenty-first century society? (Discuss all five, giving clear and detailed written reasons for your choice.)

Activity 14

Using the information above, construct a set of summary notes of the five ideologies. Use five sheets of lined A4 paper, one per ideology. Use the following five sub-headings:

- Origins of the ideology
- Core beliefs of the ideology
- Variations within the ideology
- Political actions of the ideology
- Evaluation of the ideology

Write brief but clear notes about each aspect of each of the ideologies under all five of the sub-headings. Annotate each of your five summary sheets with comments to compare and contrast the ideologies' origins, beliefs and actions.

Exam practice

1 Outline and assess the relationship between political ideologies and political action with reference to any one political ideology with which you are familiar. (50 marks)

2 Outline and assess the view that ideology is dead. (50 marks)

(v) The nature and distribution of political power in society

Pause for thought

- Do you think it is fair that some people are more powerful than others?
- Is it always true that people with more money have more power than others?
- Why do most individuals do as they are told by those in positions of power?

Activity 15

In February 2006, the House of Commons voted 384–184 for a ban on smoking in pubs, clubs and workplaces. The director of the Tobacco Manufacturers' Association said he was disappointed at the decision, which went against the government's own manifesto. The spokesperson of the anti-smoking group ASH said she was amazed and delighted, given the parliamentary majority of 200 in a free vote. The National Health Service said smoking caused 1.5 million hospital admissions and 100,000 deaths a year. The spokesman of the pro-smoking group FOREST admitted that opponents had won the battle but not necessarily the war. The Free Society organisation said the ban was another attack on English freedoms by an intolerant, politically correct state.

1 For what reasons might it be 'amazing' that the government passed the smoking ban?

2 Why might it seem only to be expected that the government should pass a smoking ban?

3 If opponents thought the ban was only like winning a battle but not the war, how could they try to fight back?

4 What other examples are there of ways in which a 'politically correct state' might be seen as attacking English freedoms?

What is power?

Power is relatively easy to define – as the ability of a person/people to make others do something they want them to, even when those others may not themselves want to do it; however, the nature and distribution of political power in society is a more complex topic. Some sociologists suggest that part of the problem of discussing what power is and how it is distributed in society is to do with the fact that – in reality – power itself has been defined in many ways. Not only is it power over others, it can also be seen as the ability to 'realise certain objectives' – that is, to get things done.

For this reason, it may be that the different arguments and theories about power fail to realise that they are often dealing with different things. For instance, the two US sociologists Parsons (1951) and Mills (1956) disagree about the definition of power – the first uses power in the positive sense of getting things done, whilst the latter uses the term in the more negative sense of power being exercised over others; each theorist ignores the other's use of the term and so comes to a different conclusion about the nature of power – Parsons considers only the consequence, not the relationship, of power.

Power relationships may be based on different things, as Allen (2000) points out. They can be based on the use of coercion (force or threats) or subtle manipulation (cajoling and concealment). Power relationships may be based such things as domination (imposed by restricting choices), authority (expected by those with a superior position or knowledge), or persuasion (suggested by arguing the merits of a case). Given the different ways power works in society, says Allen, it is necessary to grasp not just what it is but also to examine it the way it has been used in sociology – as a theoretical construction.

Perhaps one of the best known ways is that of Lukes (1974), who adopts a radical view and argues that power has 'three faces'. The first is the obvious one, which sees political power in terms of the decision-making process whereby groups in society with opposing ideas about what they want done argue openly and seek to influence the outcome of any political debate in their favour. This first face is like Weber's idea of political power (see page 142), which accepts that it is evident in the outcomes achieved – but in Lukes' radical view it is only one-dimensional and so not an adequate explanation of power.

The second face sees power in terms of what is removed from the decision-making process – what is excluded from the political arena is just as significant as what is included. Power is involved in blocking off certain issues and debates from discussion and decision-making; limiting the political agenda has the effect of restricting choices and alternatives.

The third face sees power in terms of the ability of some to shape the thoughts and desires of others – so power is not about blocking consideration of alternatives, rather it is about creating acceptance in others of what the powerful want for themselves so there is no apparent need for debate.

The three-dimensional model of power put forward by Lukes has certainly opened up a wider discussion about the nature and distribution of political power in society. It reflects the interest of earlier writers in the concept of hegemony (the dominance of ruling-class ideas over those of the working class). Not surprisingly, therefore, his approach has found favour with neo-Marxist sociologists and all sociologists now consider the location of power through a wider range of examples of institutions and groups than previously. In particular, attention has been paid to the power held by the following participants in society.

The state

This has been defined in various ways but can be thought of as the Legislature (Parliament), Executive (government and Civil Service) and Judiciary (police, courts and prisons). Traditionally, power is seen to be held by the state, the institutions of which had a monopoly of power in making and enforcing laws – using state violence and coercion if necessary. As a 'nation-state', the state had sovereign (supreme) power to do so within its own demarcated (fixed) borders. Although nation-states only came into existence about three centuries ago, their powers are already being challenged by demands for devolution and the growth of globalisation – which is why sociologists now think of them 'too large to solve the small problems but too small to solve the big ones'. States retain considerable power but it is increasingly difficult to see them as being monopolistic.

Government

This is a key institution of the state and as such wields much power, but the development of democracy – even if only representative democracy – has had an effect on the power of government. For example, Hewitt (1974) researched 24 crisis issues in the UK's Parliament from 1944 to 1964 and discovered that governments responded to a diverse range of views in reaching their decisions. In spite of their powers, governments compromised on most issues: public opinion as measured in polls on eleven issues was only overridden once (on the abolition of capital punishment). Critics would point to other issues where public opinion has been overridden by government (a promised referendum on the UK's acceptance of the 'EU Treaty' in 2007), although this may serve to illustrate the extent to which national politics is subject to wider pressures.

The media

The media have been described as the 'fourth estate', suggesting that they have a power to rival the first three 'estates' (traditionally the church, the nobility and the people). Today, a global media market is dominated by ten worldwide corporations that are so huge that Mackay (2000) suggests that their influence surpasses that of the nation-state. The best-known in the UK is News Corporation – owner of the Sun newspaper – whose head, Rupert Murdoch, allegedly exercises direct control over much of the business it operates in nine different media across six continents. Critics point out how the media in general contributes to hegemony and agenda-setting in society, but they tend to underestimate the continuing power of the state to regulate it. In the UK, for example, News Corporation was excluded from the bidding for the Channel 5 licence and in the USA, Microsoft's activities were curtailed because of its monopolistic power.

Transnational corporations (TNCs)

TNCs are regarded by some writers as 'footloose capitalism' because their production is not based in, or subject to, a particular nation-state. TNCs can go where they like in pursuit of profit, with little regard for attempts by states to regulate their activities. Sklair (2003) argues that those who own and control TNCs wield most of the power in the world today: companies such as Coca-Cola, Pepsi, Nestlé and Sony have more economic power than most countries. The growing power of footloose capital has resulted in a reduction in the power of the state, although some states are more able to resist TNC power than others. Those with higher incomes, such as the USA, Japan, China and the EU, still have the political power to match TNCs, but smaller, developing states with low incomes are economically vulnerable to footloose capitalism.

Big business

Whether they are TNCs or MNCs, **big businesses** have the economic power to get their own way. Wealth brings power over the lives of others, claim Mackintosh and Mooney (2000). Today, wealthy people in the UK are a mix of those who have inherited money (landowners like the Duke of Westminster) and those whose wealth is self-made (such as Alan Sugar and Richard Branson). What they have in common is the possession of capital to use in any way they wish – and this provides the link between wealth and power. It is true that some wealth redistribution has taken place in the UK: in 1911, 69 per cent of all personal wealth was owned by 1 per cent of the population; in 2002 this was down to 23 per cent owned by 1 per cent. However, Urry and Wakeford (1973) say that in spite of attempts by successive governments to curb their powers, a small group of wealthy people in the UK are still a part of a dominant power group.

Individuals

On their own, ordinary people possess little real power, economic or otherwise. Three-quarters of the people in the UK own just one quarter of all the personal wealth in the country. Their only direct input to the process of government is to vote once every five years. Perhaps this is why they sometimes feel the need to take direct political action and exercise some power through social movements. For example, Allen (2000) describes how self-styled **eco-warriors** took on the likes of Monsanto, the US multinational corporation experimenting with genetically modified food in the 1990s. Calling it 'Frankenstein food', they dressed in protective clothing to destroy crops in fields and dressed as vegetables to protest outside supermarkets selling GM foods. The House of Commons barred GM food from its restaurants – a case of power to the people?

Figure 4.6: Anti-GM crop protesters ripping up crops from a field, 2002

It has been suggested that power may be based on coercion, manipulation, domination, authority and persuasion.

Decide which of these each of the following locations of power seem to use.

The state	Government	The media	TNCs	Businesses	Individuals

Weblinks

You might find the following sites interesting:

- Articles, videos and blogs on the website of a leading political author and commentator
- Public opinion data on political trends on the website of a polling organisation
- Political articles and video clips on the website of the US Media 'Watchdog'
- Articles and video clips on the website of the Organic Consumers' Association.

(See 'Websites', page ii.)

How is power distributed?

The matter of precisely how power is distributed across different locations continues to be hotly debated in sociology. The main theories are described below.

Weberian

Weber (unlike Marx) did not see power as class-based but argued that it was widely distributed across society – in the military, education and home as well as the market. To him, power was located in status groups and political parties as well as social classes – and political power counted for more than economic power – but it was a limited resource for which people competed. More power for some people meant less power for others, (this is known as a constant-sum approach to power).

In Weber's view, power is underpinned by three possible 'ideal types' of legitimate authority: 'charismatic' (strong leadership); 'traditional'

(established custom); or 'rational-legal' (bureaucratic procedures). In modern societies, Weber claimed authority inevitably became bureaucratic, which he believed was a technically superior form of organisation that would one day dominate industrial societies. Whilst he accepted a need for strong government, however, Weber was also in favour of democratic rule and a wide distribution of power.

The Weberian view of power has been criticised because it is developed in terms of ideal types – 'pure' forms which do not actually exist in reality. Those researchers who use ideal types have to do further work to find out to what extent real-life situations match up to them. Furthermore, critics such as Lukes (above) argue that Weber's view concerns itself only with the 'first face' of power and overlooks the other two faces of power.

Functionalist

Functionalist sociologists have extended this view of power. For Parsons (1951), power is not limited but can increase as a society develops. When the right to vote is granted to more people, there is more power in society as a whole (but at times of social breakdown it may decrease instead). This is known as a variable-sum approach to power and finds support in the work of more recent sociologists, who argue that the state today has greater powers than it had in the past. Parsons claimed that even the wider social roles of ordinary people in their everyday lives increased power within the social system.

The functionalist view of power has been criticised for its naive acceptance of arguments put forward by those in society who possess power. Critics claim that all functionalism does is to convert the ideas of the powerful into sociological theory and give them legitimacy. In particular, Parson's belief that power under capitalism works in a way that benefits everyone in society is attacked by Marxists for ignoring the fact that it serves the interests of some groups much more than others.

Neo-liberalist

Neo-liberalist sociologists take the functionalist view even further and argue that the state should empower its citizens by freeing them from state imposition, leaving them to shape their own lives. Writers such as Saunders (2002) see people's self-interested interaction in the market as enough to hold society together – spontaneous social order is thus established. The state is seen to have an essential but limited role to play – to let people live together and respect each other's rights. In an enterprise culture, power is diffused throughout a deregulated, privatised and marketised society in which the state itself is neutral.

The neo-liberalist view of power has been criticised for its blind faith in free market economics. By promoting a policy of non-interference in business matters, for example, this approach actually undermines democracy and equality. In the USA, for instance, it is accused of allowing the business lobby to exert more influence over government policy than ordinary citizens. In doing so, it reduces the power of the state to intervene to improve the lives of the majority of the population.

Pluralist

Pluralist sociologists have something in common with functionalists – both see power as widespread in society – although the former are more aware of conflicting interests in society. Pluralists adopt the Weberian constant-sum approach to power and see a range of interests in society competing for limited resources, with the state acting as honest broker (referee) in the competition which takes place. Given that power is widespread in society, rather than being in the hands of one or a few people, pluralists use the term 'polyarchy' (government by the many) to describe the distribution of power in society today.

The best-known study by a pluralist sociologist is that of Dahl (1961). He studied local politics in New Haven, USA: he was concerned to investigate precisely how decisions on matters to do with education, urban renewal and mayoral elections were taken. From his analysis of the decision-making process it was clear to Dahl that a range of interests was consulted and compromises made in reaching final decisions, and he concluded that no single group dominated local politics. However, critics would argue that Dahl's study only investigated the first face of power in New Haven politics.

Dahl later modified his view of the distribution of power to take account of criticisms: he has since acknowledged that the unequal distribution of wealth inevitably makes equal influence impossible – some individuals and groups have more say than others in political matters. For this reason, the approach Dahl originally supported (now known as classical pluralism) has given way to an alternative (now known as elite pluralism); typified by the work of Marsh (1985). He admits that some groups not only lack influence, they are not well represented politically. However, as voters, their views do carry some weight.

Elite theory

Elite theory sounds similar to elite pluralism, but it is in fact very different. It originated with Pareto (1935) and Mosca (1939), whose ideas are now termed classical elite theory. They believed that people with power possess superior personal qualities that make them best-suited to rule – they judged the masses to be inadequate for the task. Pareto argued that the ruling elites changed over time, alternating between individuals who were like 'lions' (strong) or like 'foxes' (cunning) – he called this the circulation of elites. Mosca claimed that ruling elites maintain stability and social order would collapse without them.

Classical elite theory is criticised for its lack of empirical evidence and undemocratic nature, but its general theme is supported by more recent studies, most notably the work of Mills (1956). In his book *The Power Elite*, he made a convincing case for the notion that in the post-war USA three elite groups – the political, business and military – were so interconnected as to form a single ruling group. Although there were different people in each group, they were sufficiently similar as to be of one mind; indeed, even the two main political parties – Democrat and Republican – did not offer real alternatives.

Mills's radical elite theory seemed to combine elements of Weberian theory with those of Pareto and Mosca. As such, it generated a powerful critique of pluralism – but only within the context of the post-war USA. In a counter-criticism, pluralists argue that Mills has only shown that the power elite has potential, not actual, control over society. Nevertheless, Mills's pioneering study is acknowledged as the inspiration for a similar one undertaken in the UK by Williams (2006), whose research led him to the conclusion that this country is dominated by financial and business elites (but less by political and military elites).

Marxist theory

Marxist theory goes further and does suggest that a single **ruling class** exercises power and those who control the means of production rule society. In a famous statement, Marx and Engels (1968) wrote that government rules on behalf of capitalism, saying 'The executive of the modern state is but a committee for managing the common affairs of the whole bourgeoisie' (page 37). Marxist sociologists take the same view: Miliband (1969) says that the state in the UK is made up of the government, the judiciary, police and military, and the top personnel in all of these institutions have similar backgrounds, outlooks and bourgeois interests.

Other Marxists take a different view, arguing that what matters is not the backgrounds of people (instrumental Marxism) but the structure of society (structural Marxism). This is the view taken by Poulantzas (1980), who argues that the state exists in its own right as a mechanism to support capitalism regardless of the individuals who run it. To Poulantzas, as well as the judiciary, police and military (repressive state apparatus) the state is made up of the church, media and education (ideological state apparatus). Thus the state is able to sustain capitalism not just by coercion but also by persuasion and manipulation.

Neo-Marxism

Neo-Marxists have taken this idea further and base their arguments on the concept of hegemony. Gramsci (1971), for example, says that for the ruling class to maintain its hold on society it must secure the consent of the masses by instilling in them its own ideas. He suggests that the power of the ruling class is based on its ability to use the state to instill a sort of **false consciousness** in the masses. This is done not by force (political society), but by persuasion (civil society) – the dominance of the ruling class is seen as legitimate by the masses because they have been persuaded to believe in its political ideology.

Marxist views on the distribution of power in society remain influential well over a century after they first appeared. A large body of evidence gives some support to Marxist theory, although it has to be said that where Marxism has been translated into action the outcomes are not at all as predicted. Classical Marxist theory is criticised for its emphasis on economic determinism (the influence of material factors in shaping society), although neo-Marxism has gone some way to correct that by stressing ideas and hegemony (the influence of cultural factors on the distribution of power).

Postmodern views

Postmodern views of power have their own version of something rather like cultural hegemony in the concept of discourses. A **discourse** is a taken-for-granted way of doing something, such as decision-making, which affects the exercise of power in any society. Through discourses, knowledge is power because some knowledge has superior status – these are 'expert discourses', which popular discourses (everyday knowledge) are unable to challenge effectively. So power in society operates through the discourses that restrict consideration by the masses of alternatives and so become a form of social control.

The best-known postmodernist in this respect is Foucault, who sees a direct relationship between power and knowledge. The modern state has more knowledge than ever at its disposal and so in his view is more powerful than ever. However, knowledge – and therefore power – is not the monopoly of the state and exists throughout society, but it exerts power over people because they internalise it. In this sense, says Allen (2000), power is an anonymous force provoking people to act in ways that make it difficult for them to do otherwise – people behave as they do because they see no alternative.

In Foucault's view, people are free to govern themselves but end up behaving in ways that have become institutionalised and accepted over time – they are dominated by the normal patterns of behaviour which most people rarely question. Thus power involves self-regulation of individual behaviour – even without the threat of sanctions most people govern themselves. The power of social institutions is not a top-down affair to Foucault: power circulates around people but its influence is random and it can be a negative or a positive force. When people exercise their power, they shape their own lives.

Postmodern views of power are complicated and not easy to understand. In some ways they resemble neo-Marxist views of power – discourses are a bit like hegemony and expert discourses can be thought of as little more than ideologies. Where postmodernists differ is in their rejection of the idea that any knowledge is ultimately 'true'. Extreme postmodernism rejects meta-narratives (all-embracing theories) and the very notion of politics itself; like all words, it has become detached from reality and politics is at an end – parties in modern democracies are all the same and not real alternatives.

Where does all the theorising lead in terms of helping with an understanding of the ways in which power is distributed in society? Without doubt, it contributes to a broader view of what political power is and where it resides, although it creates a diverse – and sometimes contradictory – range of ways in which political power can be seen to operate in society. Perhaps all theories of power distribution have something relevant to say about what is actually going on in world politics today, but to the question 'Which theory comes closest to the truth?' the answer must surely be that the jury is still out on that one.

Weblinks

Have a look at the following websites:

- A detailed account of theories of power in a two-part article
- Web pages examining the relevance to society of Power Elite and Pluralist theories
- An analysis of Foucault's theories of Power and Discourses, with links
- An analysis and comparison of Marx's and Foucault's theories of power.

(See 'Websites', page ii.)

Section summary

The most relevant theories to consider in this section are Weberian, functionalism, pluralism, elite theory, Marxism, neo-Marxism and postmodern views.

Use the following words to write a paragraph explaining the key themes of this section.

- The state
- Government
- The media
- TNCs
- Eco-warriors
- Neo-liberalist
- Pluralist
- Ruling class

Activity 17

Use the information in section v, plus the information in the weblinks above (and any other information that you can find about theories of political power) to produce a set of cards to aid your revision for this part of the topic. You will need at least seven cards, one for each theoretical explanation. On each card, use the following four sub-headings:

- Name of the theoretical perspective
- Sociologists associated with it
- Key arguments of the perspective
- Evaluation of the perspective

Write just enough detail so that you have an overview of each theoretical perspective. Work with another student in a question-and-answer session to test your knowledge – does your set of cards differ in any significant way(s) from your partner's cards?

Stretch and Challenge Activity

When has it perhaps been possible to see Lukes's three faces of power in action in political decision-making? Select a recent political event such as the war with Iraq and try to identify 'faces' one (clue: dictator), two (clue: oil) and three (clue: dossier) in reaching the final decision. Write a 1000-word analysis of the decision to go to war with Iraq, using Lukes's three-dimensional model of power.

Exam practice

1 Outline and assess sociological explanations of the distribution of power in society. (50 marks)

2 Outline and assess the view that the state only represents the interests of the ruling class in society. (50 marks)

Sociology of power and politics

Exam**Café**
Relax, refresh, result!

Exam question
Outline and assess the importance of direct action for new social movements.

(50 marks)

Relax and prepare

Hot tips

Stacey

I thought anything to do with politics might be boring, but the focus on social movements made it interesting and much more up-to-date than I expected. I need to make sure I use this focus in my answers.

Ryan

I found the weblinks really useful and I enjoyed doing my own internet research about a range of new social movements, including lots I had never heard of before.

Claire

We worked together on lots of the activities which helped us to understand the topics in the first place and has helped me to prepare my own revision notes.

Examiner's tip

One of the main differences between AS and A2 is the need to be able to write essay-style answers in response to open-ended questions. Fortunately, there is plenty of choice in the G673 exam paper – twelve questions to choose from, but only two to answer. They can both be chosen from any one of the four options, so specialising in just one topic like the sociology of power and politics means it is still possible to cover a range of material and yet find that it is all interconnected. This helps to make sense of it all and apply it as required to the actual exam questions set. Of course, there is no substitute for devising an effective plan of revision and practising writing exam-style answers beforehand: revision checklists like the following 'Refresh your memory' section are a good way of doing this.

Refresh your memory

Revision checklist

You might find it useful to use a table like the one below to check your knowledge, and record your own sources of information.

Theory of power	Do I know this?	Look here
Weberian		
Functionalist		
Neo-liberalist		
Pluralist		
Elite theory		
Marxist		
Neo-Marxist		
Postmodern		

Examiner's tip

- Remember the need for a sound style of essay-writing in response to open-ended exam questions. You need an introduction, body and conclusion.

- The introduction should link directly with the question set, perhaps by rephrasing it as an opening sentence. You may need to define key terms in the question, but there is no need for a lot of background information in the introduction – focus on the question set.

- In the body of your response, cover as much relevant ground as you can. Try to show as much knowledge and understanding as possible in relation to the question – use theories, concepts and studies (but avoid the 'shopping-list' approach to naming sociologists). Do remember that your response should show an awareness of any debates about the topic you're discussing – and try to show sustained evaluation throughout if you can.

- The conclusion is important and should again link back to the question set. This is where you make your final evaluation in relation to the question's requirement for you to assess what it asked you about. Offer a balanced and explicit evaluation of the topic.

Get the result!

Below is a student's response written under exam conditions to the following question:

Outline and assess the importance of direct action for new social movements.

(50 marks)

Examiner comment:

This is an effective introduction which establishes a good link with the question set.

Direct action is very important to new social movements. New Social Movements (or NSMs) can be defined in various ways but tend not to have links with institutionalised government. Instead, they can be seen as non-institutionalised organisations of people — a conscious and collective network of individuals united by a shared critique of the dominant values of society, which they may regard as repressive. In these circumstances, the political actions of NSMs are inevitably extra-Parliamentary — that is, outside usual channels of political behaviour. NSMs are therefore more likely than other political organisations to resort to forms of direct action.

Examiner comment:

This is useful background information to set the scene – but it does not need too much.

NSMs emerged in Western democracies in the years after the Second World War and benefited from social changes such as the declining importance of class divisions and the spread of higher education. Instead of members, NSMs tend to have supporters and these can come from many different walks of life — they are often young and educated people, such as students. Scott says that NSMs emerged in response to particular contemporary events, for example the student movement in the USA and Europe in the 1960s. Whereas certain issues — women's rights and black civil rights — were major concerns then, more recently animal rights and environmental issues have come to the fore.

Examiner comment:

These two paragraphs are valuable in explaining why NSMs resort to direct action – and the example shows that the student knows what forms direct action can take.

The emergence of NSMs brought with it a shift in the political arena. The concerns of NSMs are less conventional and so tended not to be taken up by politicians in mainstream channels, i.e. Parliament. Therefore the battles fought by NSMs take place in the wider world — on the streets, for example. Their aim is not so much to affect state legislation but rather to promote alternative politics and lifestyles. They promoted post-materialist issues to do with quality of life, freedom of expression and identity. So the location of conflict is within civil society rather than political society. Hallsworth believes it is significant that NSMs have emerged at a time when people's trust in party politics is falling.

Conflict and opposition are expressed in the form of direct action. For example, green campaigners lost faith in the ability — or will — of party politicians and big business to do the right thing when it came to disposing of the redundant Brent Spar oil rig. Shell wanted to save money by sinking it to the bottom of the Atlantic and was not opposed by party politicians. So Greenpeace activists got aboard it before it was towed out to sea, and got back aboard even after being removed the first time. Consumers boycotted Shell petrol and on the Continent some of its petrol stations were fire-bombed (this was not part of Greenpeace's action).

Examiner comment:

The next two paragraphs introduce some theoretical perspectives on NSMs – naming two sociologists as well – showing how cultural concerns have replaced economic concerns.

According to Touraine, NSMs are not concerned with economic issues because we now live in a post-industrial period. They focus on post-materialist affairs, and are often single-issue-oriented. Some aim to extend social rights to historically marginalised groups in society, where the state has ignored or repressed them. Outrage (a gay rights movement) and Black Power (an anti-racist group) are examples of this type of NSM. So cultural conflicts have replaced economic conflicts and NSMs give vent to the collective actions of previously excluded groups who are struggling to assert their identities. They may do this through non-violent protests or violent demonstrations.

Habermas, a sociologist of the Frankfurt School of sociology, saw new sources of conflict in society arising from attempts by government and big business to interfere in people's lives. This resulted in what he called a crisis of legitimacy, in which ordinary people fought back by taking political action through NSMs. Another German sociologist named Beck went further and said that we live in a risk society, where governments and businesses do things that endanger our environment and the planet itself. So NSMs are a response by some people to overcome uncertainty and risk in their lives. So-called eco-warriors turn to forms of terrorism in their battles against big business.

Anti-capitalist NSMs are helped by the internet to organise their supporters and fight back against international capitalism in the form of MNCs and TNCs. These companies go wherever they can to make the most profit, at the expense of workers in developing countries. Protesters have demonstrated at meetings of international banks, such as the battle of Seattle in 1999. But in this age of global communications, internet campaigns like culture-jamming are used too. So-called hacktivists get into companies' websites and change their advertising messages. Klein argues that this is the most powerful form of direct action they have.

Regardless of the specific issue under scrutiny, NSMs pose a great challenge to the established cultural, economic and political order of capitalist society. This is partly due to their alternative lifestyles. This alternative lifestyle includes a belief in their preferred form of political action (direct action). This is an important feature of NSMs. Supporters value the way of life that goes with it because it gives them autonomy. The example of the Greenham Peace Women illustrates how personal experiences can be made into the politics of difference. To them, the peace camp was a symbol of their feminist views and gave them the chance to gain a new consciousness of patriarchal domination.

Because they value freedom, NSMs reject authoritarianism as a way of organising the movement. They object to the idea of the officials and bureaucrats found in institutional organisations (such as in political parties and old social movements). NSMs usually lack a bureaucratic structure and may not even have leaders at all. They have social networks which reflect their ideology of equal and active participation. Their use of direct action is the preferred form of action and takes place outside of the formal political system. It can take peaceful, legal forms such as demonstrations, protests, strikes and lobbying, or it can use more violent and illegal forms of action such as symbolic attacks.

These forms of direct action have great significance. Not only are the issues under consideration by NSMs critical of our capitalist society, but the direct action taken is also challenging in itself. The adoption of alternative lifestyles is both a rejection of capitalism as a system and a search for an alternative lifestyle. This can only be found by rejecting a way of life based on institutionalised politics and turning instead to non-institutionalised forms of politics. In doing so, supporters of NSMs find conventional methods of political action lacking and have to turn instead to unconventional forms of political action. This is why direct action is so important to new social movements today.

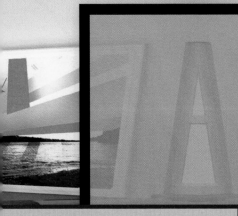

Examiner comment:

This paragraph brings in the global dimension to the debate about NSMs – again with a named sociologist. It allows the student to discuss further types of direct action.

Examiner comment:

In two more paragraphs, the student is able to discuss the politics of difference, lifestyle politics and single-issue-based politics. No theories or actual sociologists are identified but there are some concepts – and the examples are useful in highlighting direct action.

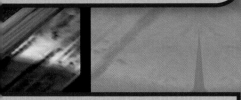

Examiner comment:

The student draws the argument together with a clear and concise concluding paragraph which links the points made back to the question set. There could be more evaluation in the body of the response, but there is explicit evaluation here in relation to the question. Overall, this is a very clear, focused and effective response to the question set – it would be given a high mark and achieve a good grade.

Unit 4

Exploring social inequality and difference

- Patterns, trends and sociological explanations of inequality and difference related to social class, gender, ethnicity and age
- Exploring sociological research on social inequality and difference

Guidance on answering questions in Unit 4 (G674)

The examination lasts for two hours, is worth 25 per cent of your A Level, and is marked out of 100. The question will be based on a piece of source material. You must read the source material fully, as you have to include it in your response. The first two questions will be based on methodology and related to the source material in some way.

You then select either Option 1, question 3(a) and (b) or Option 2, question 4(a) and (b). You must answer both questions in the option you choose. These questions assess the issues of social inequality and difference in the UK.

Remember that as an A2 exam it is synoptic – you should be looking to draw on and use your knowledge from throughout your two years of study. If you can put knowledge from other units to good use, you will be rewarded for doing so. Being synoptic also means that you should try to answer the questions thinking holistically as a sociologist, drawing on your knowledge and understanding of theory and methods.

The following provides guidance on answering each part.

1   These questions will always focus on the source material and your wider methodological understanding. Ten of the marks are for AO1, therefore you must display your knowledge of what is asked. Five of the marks are awarded for your application and interpretation of material, which means you must relate/locate it within the source material. If you don't do both, you will not be answering the question. There are 15 marks available.

2   This question requires you to display knowledge of the methodological issue being asked, interpret and apply it to the research context and crucially to evaluate. There are most marks available for evaluation and analysis. There are 25 marks available.

3   This question assesses your knowledge of social inequalities. You should aim to include as much empirical evidence as you can (named studies, data). You may want to refer to theories, which is fine, but your answer should not be entirely theoretical. Aim to display what you know from throughout the course, drawing on your AS material too. There are 20 marks available.

4   This question is the theoretical one, and you must include perspectives in your response. Aim to focus on the most relevant theories relating to the question and then use the others to evaluate the view in the question. This question will assess all three AOs, with the majority of the marks available for knowledge and your evaluation. There are 40 marks available.

5   The Exam Café on pages 253–258 shows an example of a Unit 4-type question, candidate response and examiner commentary.

Introduction to Unit 4

This unit will focus on the range, extent and sociological explanations of social inequalities and difference in the contemporary UK. The sociological theories and the methodology used in researching social inequality are also important parts of this unit and of your examination at the end of it.

Individuals and social groups in the contemporary UK can be defined by the social similarities and differences they share; these may be based on material or cultural factors. Material factors relate to goods, economic resources and money, cultural factors relate to norms, values and culture.

Of course, social differences do not necessarily lead to inequalities. People may be socially different, but this does not mean they will inevitably have unequal chances in life. A social difference could relate to a person's sexuality, which does not necessarily create a social inequality, though of course where sexuality becomes a barrier to social participation, it could be argued that sexuality is a site of social inequality. A social difference could relate to ethnicity, and the norms and values that form part of an individual's or group's identity, such as language, food, religion or dress codes. Different ethnicities do not in themselves create social inequalities, unless they become a barrier to social participation. Therefore social differences do not necessarily lead to social inequalities, but the two are often related.

For Payne (2006), social inequalities involve an element of social advantage or disadvantage for some groups or individuals over others. He argues that social inequalities refer to differences in people's share of material and cultural resources.

Weblink

The national statistics website is a good source of data (see 'Websites', page ii).

Activity 1

1 Two examples of social inequalities in the UK are income (earnings) and access to healthcare. Try to think of eight more.

2 Carry out some research into the extent of these inequalities in the UK today. Aim to find at least five pieces of data relating to inequality.

3 Share your findings with others in your group/class and make a montage/collage of facts to display in your classroom.

Cooke and Oppenheim (2008) claim that the UK remains one of the most unequal societies in the developed world. Despite a recent narrowing of the gap between rich and poor (especially if you ignore the super-rich at one end and the underclass at the other), they pose the question of whether the British public really want to eradicate inequality and the extent to which they are prepared to support measures to reduce it.

Activity 2

1 Devise a set of questions (not more than ten) to ask a sample of people about their views of inequality in the UK and whose responsibility it is to tackle such problems.

2 Carry out your research on a small sample of people and report on your findings.

The previous two activities require you to think about and carry out your own small-scale research into social inequality and differences in the UK. This focus on research methodology forms a crucial part of this unit and Section 2 is devoted to exploring how sociologists research social inequality and difference. As you work through Section 1 you should keep this focus on methodology in mind. The methods icons will help you to do this.

Patterns, trends and sociological explanations of inequality and difference related to social class, gender, ethnicity and age

Pause for thought

1   Do you think the contemporary UK can be most accurately described as an equal or an unequal society?

2   Would you prefer to live in a society based on equality or a society based on inequality. Why?

3   Who do you think holds power in the contemporary UK?

Sociological theories of social inequality

First, we will consider six key theories that you need to be familiar with:

◆ functionalist

◆ Marxist

◆ neo-Marxist

◆ Weberian

◆ feminist

◆ postmodern.

Additional theories associated more specifically with gender, ethnicity and age will be covered in those sections.

You should be familiar with some of these theories already, depending on which topics you have studied. This section will locate each theory within the context of the sociology of inequality and difference. This section forms a crucial introduction to understanding the key ideas, concepts, thinkers and criticisms of each theoretical perspective, which will be drawn on throughout this unit.

Functionalism

Functionalism is a structural theory that seeks to explain the social world with reference to the main structures, systems and institutions in existence. Functionalism is a consensus theory arguing that the structures, systems and institutions all serve a useful function in maintaining the healthy cohesion of society. A strong collective conscience exists in society which binds individuals and groups together for the sake of the common good.

Functionalist thought was particularly prolific in the USA in the 1940s and 1950s, but its ideas became well established throughout sociology and have been applied to the UK. Two key functionalists were Durkheim and Parsons, both of whom saw society as based on meritocracy. Durkheim's main contribution to sociological thought was in explaining the development of societies, from small-scale agrarian-based communities that functioned by sharing and trading resources and labour power, to the emergence of complex industrial societies with highly specialised divisions of labour, hospitals,

schools, churches. Within these complex societies social inequality and social difference were an inevitable and important part of maintaining social order and preventing a state of 'anomie' or chaos (Durkheim, 1944).

For Parsons, social inequality and difference are functional and an inevitable features of social systems. Social systems need to be hierarchical to accomplish order and ranking, both key elements of a maintaining a healthy functional society to meet the needs of its members (Parsons, 1940).

Marxism

Marxism is a structural theory based on the writings of Marx and Engels, who were writing in the nineteenth century in a context of rapid industrialisation; where the growth of factories and mass production was bringing a range of social and economic changes.

Marxism seeks to explain the existence and persistence of social inequalities around economic inequalities and the relationship of individuals to the economic structure of society. Through history, societies develop through different 'modes of production' or phases of development, and most of Marx's writings were based around the phase of capitalism, where the privileged in society owned the capital and everyone else owned only their 'labour power'.

Marx argued that within capitalism there are two main social classes, the bourgeoisie and the proletariat. The bourgeoisie are defined as the ruling class; although small in number they own and control the means of production (factories, land and businesses). This gives them a vested interest in making money and profit as they effectively control the lives of the other social class, the proletariat.

The proletariat can be defined as the workers; they own nothing but their own labour, which they sell to the bourgeoisie in return for wages. However, the wages are negligible because the bourgeoisie want to make more profit for themselves. The relationship between the proletariat and the bourgeoisie is exploitative: the workers are used by their bosses and treated as wage slaves. The proletariat are oppressed in that they cannot adequately exercise their dissatisfaction with the relations of production for fear of being sacked and because their ideas are being controlled by the state, through control of the superstructure.

The capitalist system is legitimised by the state, which intervenes in the media (it owns some of them), in religion (the Church of England, of which the Queen is the head), and the education system (which is subject to central state control through the operation of laws and national frameworks within which schools must operate). These all form part of what Althusser (1977), a neo-Marxist, called the the ideological state apparatus (ISA) – the ways in which the state tries to control our thoughts.

Activity 4

Consider the following quotations from Marx. What do you think each one means?

1 'Workers of the world unite, you have nothing to lose but your chains.'

2 'The ruling ideas of every age have been the ideas of its ruling class.'

3 'Religion is the opium of the masses.'

4 'Philosophers seek to explain the world, the point is to change it.'

Stretch and Challenge Activity

Do some research to find out about the cultural Marxists. What do they add to Marxist theory?

Marx argued that over time, the two classes would polarise and move further apart. The proletariat would develop a full awareness of their oppression and exploitation; they would become fully 'class conscious' and this would enable them to rise up against the bourgeoisie, challenge their economic dominance and force a proletarian revolution. Following the revolution, capitalism would be replaced by communism: a society free of oppression, exploitation and inequality. In effect, Marx argues that the proletariat would change from being a 'class in itself' to a 'class for itself'. This **polarisation** was crucial in the proletarian revolutions.

Marxists have been criticised on a number of grounds.

1 They are accused as being 'one dimensional' and trying to explain all inequality in terms of economic differences. This is also known as 'economic reductionism', tracing social inequality back to the ownership/non-ownership of capital/means of production.

2 The failure of the proletarian revolution to take place and the emergence in most industrialised societies of a growing middle class, who appear unlikely to challenge the most privileged in society.

However, Marxism should be credited as providing a systematic account of class divisions and Marx's legacy should not be ignored.

Neo-Marxism

Neo-Marxists have adopted the core principles of traditional Marxism and relate them to contemporary societies, where it has become increasingly clear that the proletarian revolution is unlikely to take place. Neo-Marxists agree with traditional Marxists that the principles of exploitation, oppression, class conflict and class struggle remain highly relevant in understanding and explaining social inequality in contemporary societies.

Neo-Marxist thinking is focused largely on explaining the growth of the middle classes and the changing nature of the class structure, which seemed to have stripped the proletariat of its revolutionary potential. They argue that society does not have two basic social classes existing in an exploitative relationship; the picture is more complex and draws on economic, cultural and social differences between different groups. In some respects the different modes of 'capital' (economic, social, cultural) and ownership of them illustrates the more multi-dimensional nature of neo-Marxism.

1 Give examples of the three types of capital: economic, cultural, social.

2 Who has access to them?

3 In what ways do they advantage some social groups over others?

Weberianism

Max Weber has been described as the 'ghost of Marx'. He agreed with Marx that the ownership of property and capital were important dimensions of privilege within society, however not the only dimensions.

Weber argued that social inequality was largely a product of three dimensions: class, status and party.

◆ By 'class', Weber referred to economic conditions such as a person's income, wealth, and occupation. Class was based on economic dimensions.

◆ By 'status', he meant a person's social standing within a society or community. Status was therefore connected to social dimensions.

◆ By 'party', he was referring to political dimensions and issues of power.

Sometimes class, status and party co-exist in the same individuals; the prime minister, for example, or the chief executive officer of a large multinational company could be used to illustrate possession of all three dimensions.

Feminism

Feminism can be described as a movement that seeks social, economic and political equality between men and women. Feminism has a long history in the UK, although as a theory it can be traced back to two particular 'waves'.

◆ First-wave feminism is associated with the women's suffrage movement in the early twentieth century, where campaigners fought for equality through accessing the vote for women in the UK.

◆ Second-wave feminism is associated with the radical 1960s/1970s, where it had become obvious that securing the right to vote had not brought the necessary social, economic and political changes that many wanted.

Copy and complete the table, stating whether each person in the list below would occupy a high or low class, status and party position. Compare your answers with others and be prepared to justify your ideas:

• a black female MP in the UK

• a white working-class plumber who spends his spare time running the local boys' football team

• a 35-year-old lottery winner (won £35 million) who becomes a property tycoon

• an elderly man who lives on a state pension and enjoys daily walks in the countryside.

	Class	Status	Party
MP			
Plumber			
Lottery winner			
Pensioner			

This activity should illustrate that Weberian theory is more applicable to a range of dimensions and may therefore be better placed to explain social inequality and difference than traditional Marxist theory. Weberian theory is multi-dimensional and Marxist theory is not, as it sticks rigidly to the importance of economic gain over social or political gain.

Feminist theory has many strands. Indeed, some have argued that there is a lack of coherence to the feminist movement and that feminists themselves are unsure what they actually want and how society should operate. Principally, there are three main strands to second-wave feminism.

◆ Liberal feminists asked for equality of opportunity between men and women. They wanted to remove the barriers to achieving equality and called for equal rights in the workplace and in the public arena. They were highly supportive of the Sex Discrimination Act (1975) and the Equal Pay Act (1970).

◆ Marxist feminists were interested in the economic aspects of gender inequality, particularly how women's role as primary carers and housewives helped to sustain the development of capitalism. They focused on women's economic role in society and the exploitation that women faced in the home, reliant on their husband's wage, cooking, cleaning and looking after children without a wage.

◆ Radical feminists were more interested in **patriarchy** and explained how society operates for the benefit of men, controlled by and in the interests of men. Credited with challenging conventional thinking and assumptions, some radical feminists really were radical and suggested that through artificial insemination the population could grow without the need for sexual relationships and in theory without the need for men. Writings such as these provided challenging ideas on the nature of female experience in contemporary societies.

Activity 7

Devise a questionnaire of not more than eight questions to access the views of young people today on feminism. Try to find out:

• What they think feminism is

• What they think of a movement that seeks to establish equality between the sexes

• Whether they think males can be feminists.

Analyse your results and write a brief report on the questions you asked, your sample and your findings.

Feminism is both a social and a political theory that tries to explain social inequality by focusing on gender relations. This places it in stark contrast to Marxism and Weberianism, both of which focus primarily on economic dimensions. There are also groups of black feminists who focus on ethnicity and gender as key dimensions in explaining social inequality, and post-feminists who respond to what second-wave feminism achieved.

Postmodern views

There is no one single postmodern view on social inequality and social difference, and therefore no clear explanations of structural inequalities from a postmodern viewpoint. Postmodern views do, however, question the relevance of sociological theories that try to explain diverse contemporary societies.

Some postmodern writers such as Jameson (1991) have sympathy with Marxist theory and argue that the divisions in society are a product of 'late capitalism' but cannot be explained by economic dimensions alone. Other writers focus on the place of consumption and style in the contemporary UK, along the lines of the pick-and-mix society (Polemus, 1997) where the existence of multiple identities means that the old social class, gender, ethnicity and age dimensions of identity and inequality are no longer meaningful in a postmodern world where the **fragmentation** of society has led to greater individualisation.

Structure and agency

The six theories introduced in this sub-section form the basis of a sociological understanding of social inequality and you will be using them throughout this unit. One of the key issues in explaining social inequality is whether you think society's inequalities are caused by the structure of society or by individuals' actions and decisions. Marxists, functionalists and feminists place the blame for inequality on the structure of society, but for very different reasons. Postmodern writers argue that there is no single overriding explanation for inequality; it will not always be due to structural factors, nor will it always be due to individual factors. Weberian sociology tends to see inequality as more of a combination; structural constraints impact on choices and decisions, but individuals are also active agents of their own future. Remembering this distinction between structure and agency will be helpful to your understanding of issues in this section.

Having been introduced to the main sociological theories, we are now in a position to consider evidence of social inequalities with regard to social class, gender, ethnicity and age. We will consider each in turn.

1 Read the two case studies below and think about the social disadvantages they illustrate.

2 Write down the factors that might explain these disadvantages.

3 Which of the theories in this section would account for these disadvantages?

4 How can the concepts of structure and agency help our analysis of each case study, and in what ways?

Suzy

Suzy is 15 years old and lives with her family in rented accommodation on a housing estate in the Midlands. She lives with her mum, who has been disabled since a car crash five years ago, her two sisters, aged 10 and 8, and her dad, who has been the main carer for the whole family since his wife's accident. Suzy realises that her life is different from that of many of her peers. Her family live on a low income and rely on state benefits, and she misses out on many school activities because she either can't afford to do them or is needed at home to help her dad. Suzy is underachieving at school and intends to leave as soon as she can to get paid employment.

Sean

Sean is 19 years old and lives in a hostel for young homeless men provided by a national charity. Sean lived in a care home from the age of ten when his parents were deemed unable to look after him satisfactorily. He left the care home aged 17 and enrolled on a course at a local college; he was given accommodation paid for by social security benefits and a weekly allowance from the state. However, he disliked the college, missed lots of days, lost access to his EMA (educational maintenance allowance) and his accommodation because of it. Sean felt he was in a spiral of despair with nobody to help him out of it. Since then he has worked in a range of jobs in the informal economy (washing/valeting cars and distributing fliers). Sean is keen to gain training that will give him qualifications to get a job and get himself out of the hostel.

Section summary

The most relevant theories to consider in this section are functionalism, Marxism, neo-Marxism, Weberianism, Feminism and postmodern views.

Use the following words to write a paragraph explaining the key themes of this section.

- Polarisation
- Meritocracy
- Fragmentation
- Individualisation
- Structure
- Agency

Stretch and Challenge Activity

Which theory or theories best explain the existence of a growing middle class in the UK? Justify your choice, giving reasons for its suitability.

Pause for thought

- To what extent are social inequalities and differences reflected by different occupations?

Before we consider the range of evidence of social class inequalities and difference in the UK, we need to consider the definition and measurement of social class. You will notice that evidence in this section uses differing criteria for measurement purposes. These can cause problems for sociologists as they are not always working with consistent data, which makes comparisons difficult. The different measurement criteria reflect the changing ways in which the government has approached the research and study of social class.

Defining and measuring social class

The government currently uses the National Statistics Socio-Economic Classification (NS-SEC) scheme when producing official data on social class. This is an occupationally based classification that uses households as the main unit of analysis. Each household is considered as having a nominal 'head', chosen on the basis of the highest income. In the case of dual-income households where the incomes are equal, age becomes a discriminating factor, with the older person becoming the sole indicator of socio-economic position of the household. The NS-SEC provides an objective measurement of occupational level (and hence class position). This is different from subjective measurements that ask people to place themselves in terms of class position and how they define themselves. This may be based on occupation, but is likely to be based on a number of factors (housing, parents, education, consumption patterns etc.).

Sometimes the objective and subjective class identities coincide, however, in many cases the class you identify yourself with will be different from that in which an objective measure places you. For this reason it important when assessing research on social class to be clear on the methodology used, and particularly whether objective or subjective indicators are used.

The basic divisions used in the NS-SEC are shown in Table 1.1. This shows that the status of different occupations and the employer/employee position are important considerations in the scheme. In this sense, sociologically it embraces elements both of Marxist theory (ownership of means of production) and Weberian theory (status of employment, work and market situation). In dividing the scheme into eight strata, the NS-SEC is moving away from the tri-level class structure of upper, middle and working class. Notice however that category eight accommodates those at the bottom of the social structure, arguably the 'underclass'.

1	Higher managerial and professional occupations. Split into: 1.1 Large employers and higher managerial occupations 1.2 Higher professionals
2	Lower managerial and professional occupations
3	Intermediate occupations
4	Small employers
5	Lower supervisors and technical occupations
6	Semi-routine occupations
7	Routine occupations
8	Never worked or long-term unemployed

Table 1.1: The National Statistics Socio-Economic Classification Scheme (Source: Office for National Statistics)

1 Using Table 1.1, say which social classes (1–8) you think the following occupations would be based in:

- car mechanic (employer)
- self-employed builder
- teacher
- solicitor
- headteacher
- waiter/waitress.

2 What difficulties did you face in allocating each one?

Prior to the NS-SEC, the government used a variety of schemes to group social classes, and some of these appear in the data that follows. We are now able to look at the patterns and trends in relation to social class inequalities in the UK.

Housing

In relation to housing there are clear patterns of ownership, with a stark distinction between ownership (with or without a mortgage) and renting in the UK. Patterns of home ownership are likely to reflect patterns of income differentials, see Table 1.2.

Income and expenditure

Evidence shows marked variation in the annual salaries earned by different occupational groupings (see Table 1.3). You will note that these differences do not align themselves with the average number of hours worked per week.

Occupational group	Average gross annual pay	Average total weekly hours
Managers and senior officials	£42,164	39.0
Professional occupations	£33,741	36.3
Associated professionals and technical occupations	£27,627	38.5
Administrative and secretarial occupations	£17,560	37.5
Skilled trades occupations	£21,060	42.6
Sales and customer service occupations	£14,912	38.8
Process, plant and machinery operatives	£19,113	44.8

Table 1.3: Pay and hours by major occupational group, 2006 (Source: Focus on Social Inequalities, Office for National Statistics)

	Owned outright (%)	Owned with mortgage (%)	Rented from social sector (%)	Rented privately (%)
Large employers and higher managerial occupations	14	77	2	6
Higher professional occupations	20	65	1	14
Lower managerial and professional occupations	14	68	6	12
Intermediate occupations	17	59	13	11
Small employers	26	54	7	13
Semi-routine occupations	17	38	30	16
Routine occupations	16	43	27	14
Never worked/long-term unemployed	12	2	73	13

Table 1.2: Socio-economic classification: by housing tenure, 2004 (Source: adapted from Social Trends, Office for National Statistics)

U4

1

Patterns, trends and sociological explanations

Item of expenditure	Occupational groupings			
	Managerial and professional	Intermediate	Routine and manual	Never worked and long-term unemployed
Food and non-alcoholic drinks	£56.70	£49.49	£45.99	£38.05
Alcohol, tobacco and narcotics	£12.86	£12.69	£13.11	£8.79
Clothing and footwear	£35.25	£25.45	£22.44	£25.98
Housing: fuel and power	£56.04	£51.83	£50.03	£63.51
Household goods and services	£44.99	£32.49	£24.99	£16.43
Health	£7.32	£4.31	£4.52	£1.37
Transport	£100.81	£70.18	£52.49	£41.76
Communication	£14.81	£14.69	£12.13	£11.72
Recreation and culture	£82.65	£67.35	£54.46	£31.95

Table 1.4: Expenditure and Food Survey 2008 (Source: adapted from: Social Trends, Office for National Statistics; Department for Environment, Food and Rural Affairs

Evidence from the Expenditure and Food Survey shows marked differences in terms of the amount of money spent on essential and non-essential goods per week. This is likely to reflect the varying incomes associated with each occupational group (see Table 1.3).

Education

Evidence from education shows a marked difference in the percentage of students attaining five or more GCSE grades A* to C by social class/NS-SEC. In 1992, 60 per cent of students from managerial/professional backgrounds achieved five or more GCSEs, by 2002 that figure had risen to 77 per cent. For those from an unskilled manual background in 1992, 16 per cent achieved five or more, by 2002 the figure was 32 per cent (Office for National Statistics). The gap between the higher and lower social classes at GCSE certainly remains significant. Education is a powerful lever in determining income and occupational groupings. Data show that those from the higher social classes are more likely to continue their education past the age of 18 and study at the most prestigious universities. Economic, cultural and social capital are all important markers of difference.

Health

Social class matters in relation to quality of life, too. Evidence from the Healthcare Commission shows:

◆ 2.6 million children live in households with below 60 per cent of the median household income (the official measure of poverty)

(one of the worst figures in Europe) and 2.1 million pensioners live in poverty.

◆ Life expectancy data for 1997/99 show that men in the highest social class live 7.4 years longer than men in the lowest social class, the difference for women being 5.7 years. Men in East Dorset live 8.3 years longer than men in Manchester, and women in Kensington and Chelsea live 7.2 years longer than women in Blackburn.

◆ People in routine occupations have the worst self-reported health among people in employment, with rates more than double those for people in higher managerial and professional occupations.

◆ Cancer mortality and cancer survival rates show strong gradients by social class and deprivation. For instance, five-year survival from breast cancer is higher among women in affluent areas than among women in deprived areas (71 per cent compared with 63 per cent).

◆ Teenage motherhood is seven times as common amongst those from manual social backgrounds as among those from professional backgrounds.

Politics

◆ Overall, almost one-third (32 per cent) of current MPs attended independent schools, which educate just 7 per cent of the population; 72 per cent went to university, including 43 per cent who attended one of 13 leading universities and over a quarter (27 per cent) who went to Oxbridge.

- Broken down by political party, Conservative MPs were most likely to have attended private schools (59 per cent having done so), while Labour MPs were the least likely (18 per cent).

- Less than half (42 per cent) of MPs were educated in comprehensive schools, with the remainder having attended either state grammar schools (25 per cent) or independent schools (32 per cent), many of which are also academically selective.

Activity 10

Further evidence on social class inequalities and differences can be found on pages 10, 65–67 and 119 of this book. Using a selection of this data, produce an account of the patterns and trends of inequality in relation to social class in the UK.

You may find it helpful to work in small groups to produce the evidence and then write it up individually. As a class, you could produce a montage of images/data related to this topic to display as a poster or a blog.

Weblink

Focus on Social Inequalities contains a vast amount of evidence relating to social inequalities in the UK (see 'Websites', page ii).

Theoretical explanations of patterns and trends in social class inequality and difference

All six of the theories introduced at the beginning of this section (pages 186–190) can be used to explain patterns and trends. You should refer to that material to supplement and expand the key points made below.

Functionalism

Social class inequality and difference are inevitable features of a healthy contemporary society where talent and hard work are rewarded. The functionalists view society as a meritocracy, with the most talented and able justifiably reaping the highest rewards. Competition is considered healthy and social inequality between groups is an inevitable and positive feature of a healthy society. Economic inequalities ensure that the most qualified people will secure the most functionally important jobs in society.

Davis and Moore (1945) suggest that pay is related to talent, and that there is a general consensus that the most important jobs are secured by the most able individuals, who are paid appropriately high wages. This enables the legitimisation of the system of inequality. These ideas in turn lead to the concept of the meritocracy, which is associated with functionalist theory; a meritocracy is a society where access to social rewards is determined by talent and achievement rather than social background.

Activity 11

On your own, write down your answers to the following three questions.

1 Which three jobs are the most functionally important in society and why?

2 Do these jobs attract the highest rates of pay?

3 Do you think the contemporary UK needs social inequality in order to function effectively?

Now share your answers with others in your class. To what extent do you agree with each other and what does this suggest about functionalist ideas?

Criticisms of functionalist explanations of social inequality:

1 Marxist writers argue that they underplay the importance of social class divisions and class conflict.

2 The degree of social harmony and consensus in society is also questionable.

3 Tumin (1963) raises questions about what is meant by 'functionally important' roles within a social system.

Saunders (1994), a new right theorist, restored interest in functionalist ideas in the 1990s when he controversially suggested that an individual's class position was largely a product of their talent and hard work. Locating his argument around the concept of the meritocracy, he argued that an individual's class position and class inequalities were a product of that individual's characteristics such as talent, hard work and motivation. Saunders rejected the SAD thesis – the idea that that social advantages and disadvantages (SAD) explained the strong relationship between an individual's social class origin and destination. However, Breen and Goldthorpe (1999) suggested that Saunders' work was both misleading and biased, a claim that Saunders rejects.

Marxist

Marxists view the exploitation of the proletariat by the bourgeoisie as a stage in the historical development of society, with capitalism as the precursor to the communist revolution. The bourgeoisie control the proletariat, and the source of control is economics. Exploitation, oppression and ideological control are all connected to the development of a full class consciousness.

The middle class is a transitory class that will disappear in time as society further polarises into rich and poor; rulers and the ruled. The middle class will either rise or fall. Most will fall into the proletariat as their jobs become deskilled (Braverman, 1974). See pages 186–187 for more details and a critique.

Neo-Marxist

For these theorists economic, cultural and social factors explain patterns and trends of social class inequality. The middle class is a permanent feature of society and enables its members to be at once the controlled and the controllers. Wright (1997) argues that the middle classes are a permanent feature of the social structure, occupying a contradictory class position, as both the exploiters (of those below) and the exploited (by those above).

Neo-Marxists argue that the working class is changing and being remade.

Sorenson (2000) writing from a neo-Marxist position, argues that the proletariat no longer 'sell' their labour to the bourgeoisie. They now 'rent it out', which means that wages can fluctuate depending on the skills of the worker and the economic climate. It is no longer the case of two social classes. Seabrook (1988) calls the proletariat the 'new servant class', serving middle- and upper-class taste and lifestyle. See pages 187 and 188 for more details and a critique.

Weberian

Weber argued that social classes exist in society and that some had significantly better life chances (health, education, income prospects etc.) than others. He argued that a social class is made up of people who share a similar market situation and work situation. Both these concepts are linked to occupational positions, which Weber considered crucial in explaining social inequality.

◆ A person's market situation comes from the amount of money they receive, so is largely income related.

◆ A person's work situation comes from the conditions of service the person enjoys in their work, such as hours worked, perks, additional entitlements, company car, status of employment.

These two dimensions of work and market situation combine to gel people to a particular social class. However, people are able to move between social classes, which prevents rigid classes from forming. For Weber, social mobility (movement between social classes) is a genuine feature of contemporary life and helps to explain why those at the bottom of the class structure are unlikely to rebel; as social improvement is always possible.

The divisions between those who own property and those who do not are important in Weberian theory, but equally important are the distinctions between those working in non-manual (office, administrative) employment and those in manual work, with non-manual employment generally occupying a higher status. In this sense Weber predicted that society would become more fragmented than polarised.

Service class	Managers, administrators, professionals	Strong work and market situation
Intermediate groups	Small owners, routine non-manual workers, service workers	Average work and market situations
Working class	Manual workers, long-term unemployed	Weak work and market situations

Table 1.5: Goldthorpe's main social class groupings

For Weberians, patterns and trends of social class inequality reflect real differences in the work and market situation of different occupational groups. These differences are not static; they will change with the economic and social climate.

Goldthorpe and Heath (1992) were writing from a Weberian perspective when they suggested that society could be divided into three main social groups, the key point of division being the different work and market situations each group shared.

Activity 12

1 How do you think functionalists and Marxists may criticise Weberian ideas?

2 There are similarities between neo-Marxists and Weberians. What do you think they are?

Feminists

Feminists do provide analysis of social class inequalities and differences, but also relate these to gender differences. For feminists, social class cannot be treated separately from other dimensions of inequality, particularly gender. Marxist feminists in particular pay close attention to the relationship between social class and gender. See pages 188 and 189 for more details and a critique.

Postmodern

Pakulski and Waters (1996) have been described as postmodern sociologists. They formulate the argument that class is dead, that profound social changes such as globalisation mean that class divisions are now essentially status divisions. They go on to argue that we live in an 'individualised'

society where people no longer see themselves in social class terms. Consumption means that people can buy the image they want to portray. However, it should be noted that Pakulski and Waters have relatively little empirical evidence to back up their claims that class is dead.

Activity 13

1 If you wanted to find out whether social class is dead in the UK, how would you go about it?

2 What methods would you use, and why?

3 Think of three difficulties you would have to overcome.

The changing nature of the class structure

The UK has traditionally been associated with a three-level class structure: the upper, middle and working classes. However, many sociologists, such as Payne (2006) argue that the UK has witnessed a movement away from this tri-level model. This section begins by outlining the traditional class structure, before considering what has happened to each of these social classes. It ends by considering a range of sociological explanations of what is happening to the class structure in the contemporary UK.

The traditional class structure can be linked to the work of both Marx and Weber, based on the ownership/non-ownership of property/capital (Marxist based) and the status divisions between different social groups and particularly between different occupational groups (Weberian based).

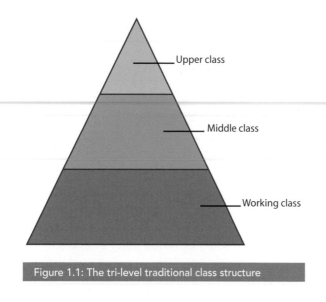

Figure 1.1: The tri-level traditional class structure

◆ The upper class was the smallest social class and comprised the aristocracy and people with an ascribed status largely through wealth (what they own) in the form of land or private ownership of property/goods. The upper class operated a system of social closure where they sought to protect their privileged status by operating an 'old boys' network', making sure they looked after people from their own social background and ensuring what is known as 'elite self-recruitment' where those occupying/born into elite positions favoured giving jobs to their own kind (Scott, 1991).

◆ The middle class traditionally consisted of professionals such as teachers, solicitors and doctors. Again, an element of elite self-recruitment was evident, with those born into middle-class families being most likely to gain a university education and secure leading high-status occupations that produced healthy incomes (earnings). Also nestling within the middle classes were the petite bourgeoisie (small business owners) and those in relatively high-status non-manual jobs also stake a claim to occupy a middle-class position in that their work and market situation were superior to those of manual workers.

◆ The working class comprised the largest social grouping and consisted of manual workers, usually employed in the heavy industries (coal, shipbuilding, steelworks) and increasingly in the twentieth century the manufacturing industries (factories) and latterly the relatively low-paid non-manual workers.

Below the working class, arguably there has always been an underclass or what Marx termed the lumpen proletariat: the long-term unemployed or unemployable.

Until the mid-twentieth century, evidence would suggest that this **tri-level class structure** was in operation in the UK, with relatively little social mobility between the classes. Social mobility was possible, but most people stayed in a social class position the same as or similar to the one they were born into. For Marxists this indicated **'cultural reproduction'**, where the advantaged in society could safeguard their position as the disadvantaged could not break free from oppression and exploitation.

A number of social changes in the twentieth century suggest that this model has now become less applicable to the UK. Some commentators suggest that the UK has moved from an industrial society, which operated a three-class basic class structure, to a post-industrial society, where knowledge and information technology in a global context have become important dimensions of society (Bell, 1973). For these writers, post-industrial societies have witnessed the growth of the **knowledge class**, where what you know determines more than who you know, and has contributed to a blurring of the class boundaries and increased social mobility. Others, such as Mount (2004) argue that the divide between rich and poor has grown, and suggests that the 'Uppers' have gained substantially while the 'Downers' have been left to suffer. Cannadine (1999) argues that in the UK social classes were never culturally homogenous, and that the tri-level class structure and clear class cultures as described above are historically inaccurate. Pakulski and Waters (1996) argue that although social inequalities remain, the concept of social class is no longer relevant in contemporary societies.

We will now explore each social class in turn.

Figure 1.2: Social inequality in the UK

Look at Figure 1.2 and think about the following:

1 Do you think the UK is a class-based society?

2 Do you think that social class in the UK is more or less important than it used to be?

3 In what ways does social class matter in the UK?

What has happened to the upper class?

The traditional upper class may still exist; there remains an aristocratic class in the UK to which many older people show deference. Inter-marriage and the existence of economic partnerships between rich families complement the argument that a distinct upper class exists in the UK, which is probably impossible to break into. Data on the ownership of wealth in the UK shown in Table 1.6 suggest that a distinct upper class may exist, and indicates the vast gulf between rich and poor in the contemporary UK.

	1976	1986	1996	2003
Most wealthy 1%	21	18	20	21
Most wealthy 25%	71	73	74	72
Most wealthy 50%	92	90	93	93

Table 1.6: Percentage of wealth owned by different groups over time in the UK (Source: Focus on Social Inequalities, Office for National Statistics)

Patterns, trends and sociological explanations

Summarise what the data in Table 1.6 show about the ownership of wealth over time and what they suggest about the existence of an upper class.

Scott (1991) argues that the UK still has a ruling class, but that it has changed and is divided into a number of fractions. An important division is between those with large economic holdings and the directorships of multi-national companies compared to those with small economic holdings or a small stake through shareholding. Those with large economic holdings can exercise considerable hegemonic power and have the ability to legitimate the views of the state. This view is largely supportive of the Marxist position that the state is a tool of the ruling class, used to control ideas in society (Miliband, 1969). For Scott the upper class still exists but it is changing in line with the growth of multinational and corporate conglomerates.

However, Goldthorpe et al. (1980) writing from a Weberian perspective, disagree. They argue that the 'old rich' who gain their wealth and status from property are so insignificant in number that they should not be considered as a meaningful category in their own right. For Goldthorpe et al., the upper class has changed and its power and prestige have been diluted.

Weblink

Find out who are the richest people in the UK, and how rich they are (see 'Websites', page ii)

The emergence of the super-rich in society complicates the picture further. Little research has been conducted into this group, although they clearly figure in *The Times* Rich List. However, they are unlikely to operate the same control as their aristocratic counterparts, largely because they are not 'insiders' and while they may have considerable economic capital, they do not wield the same type of cultural or social capital

as the true 'blue bloods'. The super-rich serve a crucial role in the class structure as representing the meritocratic and open nature of the class system in the UK. Some postmodern sociologists describe them as being 'media created'. There is no doubt that they serve an important cultural role, arguably deflecting interest from the real problems of the day towards trivia/gossip. In this sense they may serve an important ideological role. Individuals such as Roman Abramovich (owner of Chelsea Football Club) symbolise much of the super-rich, as he is a highly successful businessman on a global scale yet uses some of his money in a playful way.

To conclude, it would seem that the upper class still exists in the contemporary UK, although it is a matter of debate as to whether it is divided or homogenous. The relationship between the upper class and the state is also contested. Most of the evidence would suggest that the upper class does still exist in the UK, but that it is split into the old and the new (super) rich, that it has grown in size and plays important cultural, political and economic roles in society.

Make a list of the cultural, political and economic roles played by the upper class in the contemporary UK. Think of examples to illustrate each point you make.

Find out how the richest people in the UK achieved their wealth.

What has happened to the middle class?

The middle class can perhaps be more accurately described as the middle classes. Many commentators suggest that they form the majority in the contemporary UK, a view supported by evidence such as: the growth of non-manual work, rising living standards for many in society and claims by politicians in the 1990s that we are 'all middle class now'.

However, there is sociological evidence that the UK is not at ease with a middle-class identity. Devine (2005) carried out 50 unstructured in-depth interviews with a sample of doctors and teachers in Manchester, focusing on social divisions. Both these professions would be considered middle class, yet most of the sample did not refer to the concept of social class in their interviews. Devine suggests that they felt uneasy using the label of class, as they feared being perceived as feeling themselves to be superior to others.

The Future Foundation (2006) carried out a study focusing on class membership in the UK. Using statistical data collected as part of the British Household Panel Survey and their own questionnaires, they asked respondents the question 'Which social class do you belong to?' They found that 43 per cent felt they belonged to the middle class, 53 per cent to the working class and 1 per cent to the upper class. They predicted that by 2020 the UK will be a predominantly middle-class society, however they suggest that in many ways the UK is already middle class, they cite factors such as:

◆ mass affluence (more people getting richer)

◆ changing distribution of wealth through property ownership

◆ changing nature of employment (growth of the service sector)

◆ individuality and an ethic supporting social mobility.

These all indicate that the UK is perhaps already middle class, but is just not comfortable with identifying itself as such. They argue that the picture in the UK is one of being 'muddle class', with the boundaries between the classes increasingly blurred and a reluctance of people to label themselves as middle class. Table 1.7 shows data from the study, and matches occupation with the respondents' self-defined class identity (where they subjectively felt they belonged).

Activity 17

Study Table 1.7. To what extent do the findings surprise you and what factors might explain the data?

2 Do you think that social class in the UK is more or less important than it used to be?

3 In what ways does social class matter in the UK?

Occupation	Working class	Middle class	Other/refused to answer
University teacher	4	79	17
Solicitor	18	65	18
Secondary school teacher	20	65	15
Primary school teacher	27	67	6
Secretary	34	58	9
Waiter / waitress	31	48	21
Accountant	43	57	0
Security guard	44	41	15
Electrician	65	27	8
Lorry driver	68	23	9

Table 1.7: Self-defined class membership of selected occupations in the UK, 2005 (Source: Future Foundation, 2006, pp 12–13)

Patterns, trends and sociological explanations

Clearly the Future Foundation study conflicts with traditional Marxist theory, which viewed the middle class as transitory in nature, predicting that it would disappear as the proletariat and bourgeoisie polarised into extreme positions in the class structure. However, the existence of employees in the service class; (higher and lower grade) professionals in health, education and welfare and the growth in the number of intermediate occupations such as routine managerial and white-collar jobs suggest strongly that Marx was incorrect in his prediction for the middle class (Goldthorpe et al., 1980). Furthermore, in 2005 the UK average earnings were £22,900, for those in the working class they were £20,500 and those in the middle class they were £25,500 (Future Foundation, 2006, page 14). This is a 24 per cent difference in annual income, suggesting that on income alone, real divisions do exist between the middle and working classes in the UK.

Neo-Marxists such as Wright (1997) have argued that the middle class occupy a contradictory class location; tied simultaneously to the bourgeoisie and the proletariat, they are able to exercise some control over production but ultimately are not involved in key decision-making processes; they are at once the controlled and the controllers.

Weberian theory has perhaps been most influential in explaining the changing nature of the middle class(es). Roberts et al. (1977) showed how the middle classes have splintered into different groups/strata. Roberts uses the concept of fragmentation to describe the divisions within the middle class into different sections; some clearly holding a middle-class image of themselves alongside routine white-collar workers, who are more likely to define themselves as working class despite different objective occupational schemas such as the NS-SEC placing them in the middle ranks.

Following a similar argument, Savage et al. (1992) distinguished between different types of middle-class identities and lifestyles. This led them to conclude that the middle class is separated into public sector professionals (working in health, education, welfare) and private-sector entrepreneurs whose incomes were considerably higher than their public-sector counterparts.

It seems therefore that the neo-Marxist- and Weberian-inspired studies have as much in common as they have differences, both suggesting that a middle class exists in some form or other. The neo-Marxist studies locate economic position as crucial in distinguishing between the different strands of the middle class, and the Weberian studies are more likely to focus on status divisions between different occupations. Some commentators call these approaches hybrid explanations, as they appear to fuse class and status arguments.

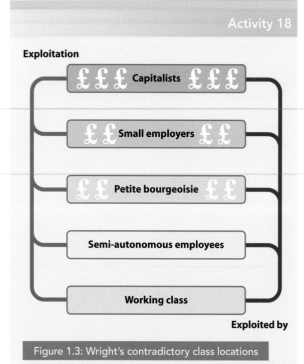

Activity 18

Exploitation

Figure 1.3: Wright's contradictory class locations

With reference to Figure 1.3, which groups are exploited and which are the exploiters?

Activity 19

Using the information in this section and your wider sociological knowledge, answer the following question.

To what extent does sociological evidence support the view that the UK is a middle-class society?

What has happened to the working class?

Tradition would dictate that the UK is a working-class society, with a long history of manual workers employed in the heavy and manufacturing industries.

The following films all show examples of the traditional working class in the UK.

- *Kes*
- *Billy Elliott*
- *Brassed Off*

Watching one or two of them would provide excellent background information. Look for evidence of employment, the role of women, attitudes to education, norms and values.

However, as the UK is no longer dominated by heavy industries and factories, it could be argued that in the post-industrial information age (Castells,1998), high-tech non-manual work has replaced coalmining and shipbuilding as the major employers in the UK. Educational opportunities have widened for young people and traditional gender roles are less rigidly adhered to. In the course of these changes the question has to be asked: what has happened to the working class?

Many traditional sociological studies explored working-class culture. Studies such as Willis's (1977) *Learning to Labour* portray life in traditional working-class communities based around a shared culture where jobs were based in manual and unskilled labour. Families were based largely around traditional gender roles and children were encouraged to follow in their parents' footsteps, indicating a form of cultural reproduction. This led to strong communities based on unity, solidarity and togetherness, where a 'them and us' attitude to management existed, with workers distrusting their employers' intentions.

Changes within the working class during the last twenty years have resulted in changing cultures. Observations of the changing working class could highlight the following: lives becoming more privatised, individualised and home-based, resulting in a loss of community; employment based on occupations in the service sector and intermediate occupations, more likely to be in non-manual work; shared responsibilities between men and women in the household and along with the rise of dual-income families increasing affluence, with more money to spend and a choice of consumer goods to spend it on.

This change from the traditional working class to the new more privatised working class is generally accepted as a valid reflection of social change. However, recent sociological evidence suggests that this may not be accurate.

Savage et al. (2005) carried out 50 unstructured in-depth interviews with people who lived in Cheadle in Manchester. They found a strong culture of manual labour. The area had a 'practical flavour': many of the men were employed in physical or manual jobs. Half the men interviewed belonged to a local social club, which formed the basis of their social life and leisure activities, showing a culture of collectivism. The women organised their social lives around local families or contacts in the area. However, most of the interviewees did not work locally and had to travel to work. Most were home owners, owned cars and had access to consumer durables. This study suggests that the working class may have changed, but it probably has not disappeared.

There is a classic sociological debate regarding what has happened to the boundary between the working and the middle classes. Although the studies involved are dated, the debate remains relevant to understanding the changing nature of the class structure, it is based around two theories: embourgeoisement (Weberian based) and proletarianisation (Marxist based).

Embourgeoisement theory

Embourgeoisement is a Weberian-based theory associated with Goldthorpe (1968) in which he tried to find out whether a new affluent (rich) worker had emerged in the UK. The research was based on finding out the social class position of a group of manual workers who lived and worked in Luton in the 1960s. The findings were then compared to the class position of a group of routine white-collar workers living in the same area at the same time. Goldthorpe argued that if the class position of the manual workers compared favourably to that of the non-manual workers, it could be deduced that Britain had a growing middle class; with evidence of embourgeoisement taking place.

The research found that the manual workers were not clones of the middle class; they had an instrumental attitude to work where work was a means to an end rather than an end in itself, and they were leading increasingly privatised lifestyles where the solidarity (unity/togetherness) of the working-class past was being replaced by a culture of individualism. They shared a similar work situation to the non-manual workers, but did not have a comparable market situation. Goldthorpe concluded that the process of embourgeoisement was not occurring in the UK, although there was evidence of an emerging affluent worker who may be part of a changing working class.

The embourgeoisement theory has been criticised in a number of ways.

1   Devine (1992) repeated the study in a different area of the south east and found even less evidence of embourgeoisement than Goldthorpe. The manual workers in her study were not leading privatised lives but were becoming more consumer conscious. They still displayed collectivist values and believed that society should be run along more egalitarian, meaning equal, lines.

2   Marxists argue that both manual and non-manual workers are part of the same oppressed working class, with no class consciousness.

3   It is a dated theory and questions have been asked about whether generalisations to other similar socio-economic areas (in different decades) can really be made.

4   The Future Foundation (2006) study suggests a more muddled picture with the boundaries between working and middle class being blurred.

5   The opposing theory of proletarianisation suggests that far from the working class becoming more middle class, the middle class is actually becoming more working class, and it is to this that we now turn.

Proletarianisation

Proletarianisation is a Marxist-based theory associated with Braverman (1974) who argued that many jobs in a capitalist economy, especially routine white-collar jobs, were subject to a process of 'deskilling', where specialist knowledge becomes replaced by machines and automation. Computers and information technology in particular were replacing skilled manpower and the working class were being denied any degree of control in their work. In such a situation Marxists argued that workers become alienated, dissatisfied and disaffected from their work. In this sense proletarianisation was a stage closer to the development of a full class consciousness en route to the proletarian revolution, as the more disaffected the workers become, the more likely they are to rebel.

The proletaratianisaton thesis has been criticised on a number of grounds:

1   It ignores the growing group of seemingly middle-class workers in the UK.

2   It assumes that the deskilling of a job effectively rules out the possibility of reskilling or what Gallie (1994) called upskilling, which appears to be a product of the information age. Machines may have been replaced by computers, but people still need training in these new developments.

3   The Future Foundation (2006) study predicts that by 2020 the UK will be a predominantly middle-class society; both subjectively and objectively.

It would seem that the traditional working class in the UK is changing and declining in numbers. However, a study of subjective class analysis in 2007 shows that a clear sense of 'working-class belonging' in the UK, which brings with it a sense of class opposition, between 'them' (managers) and 'us' (workers). This suggests elements of a class consciousness related to workplace attitudes and practices (Surridge, 2007).

One final point related to the working class in the UK is the extent to which they have become 'invisible' to politicians and to researchers. Very few recent studies have focused on the working class, either culturally or in terms of their structural position. Class is considered as a dimension of inequality in the work of some sociologists, but studies focusing solely on class are difficult to find. One example of a recent study by Thiel (2007) shows how the dimensions of class and gender need to be considered together.

Thiel (2007) spent a year carrying out a participant observation study of builders on a construction site in central London. He found masculine practices that were very similar to the 'shop-floor culture' observed in many earlier sociological studies of working-class life. The builders' informal workplace practices were characterised by general game-playing, 'having a crack', 'piss-taking' and conflict with those in authority. It was a culture that spread out from the workplace into leisure activities where talk of working hard, playing hard, drinking hard and fighting hard were dominant in the men's conversations. Thiel shows how class and gender cannot be separated when exploring social behaviour.

Weblink
You might be interested to find out whether the white working class in the UK are becoming invisible (see 'Websites', page ii).

Activity 21

Using the information in this section, and your wider sociological knowledge, answer the following question.

To what extent does sociological evidence support the view that the UK remains a working-class society?

What has happened to the underclass?

The **underclass** is a contested concept with no uniform meaning. Some sociologists suggest that it should not be used as it has negative connotations which lead to the labelling of some groups in society; a derogatory label that leads to the further alienation and marginalisation in society. The concept of the underclass was widely used in the USA in the 1980s but found its way into mainstream British sociology in the 1990s. Broadly speaking, there are two theoretical explanations for the emergence of the underclass: cultural theories associated with the new right and structural theories associated with Marxist and Weberian theory. First, however, we need to consider who the underclass are and what are their defining characteristics.

Runciman (1990) argues that a clearly defined underclass does exist in the UK, made up of those people unable to participate in the labour market. Roberts (1997) offers a more precise definition, arguing that the underclass occupies a structural position at the bottom of the class system with the following characteristics:

◆ long-term unemployed

◆ specific social and cultural outlooks

◆ economically excluded.

Clearly definitions of the underclass contain strands of economic disadvantage and social exclusion. However, the underclass should not be confused with the concept of social exclusion. Social exclusion is a concept associated with New Labour, it refers to social groups existing on the margins of society. These people have little or no employment history, rely on state benefits for survival and often have relatively high rates of crime. Concerned that the modern UK could become characterised by riots, disaffection and urban social problems, the government set up the Social Exclusion Unit in 1997 to tackle problems of economic, social and cultural deprivation.

The concept of social exclusion shares a number of common features with the underclass, however explanations of the underclass suggest that this group forms a concrete part of the social class structure. Although social mobility is possible, once individuals are positioned in the underclass it is extremely difficult for them to break out of it. On the other hand, the government's concept of social exclusion assumes that social mobility is possible.

Sociological explanations of the underclass tend to focus on either structural or individual (cultural) factors.

Cultural explanations

These explanations are associated with the sociologists of the new right. They argue that individuals operate in terms of economic rationality, capable of and willing to balance the economic benefits and costs of different actions. Therefore, people will only take up employment if the economic benefits/income they receive make it worth their while. If they can be economically better off living on the state, they will choose that option.

Murray (1994), a new right thinker, is the most controversial contributor to the underclass debate. He argues that the UK provides incentives that encourage failure and

Patterns, trends and sociological explanations

marginalisation from society. Murray presented his observations on the British underclass in the 1990s, he himself is American and had witnessed the growth of an American, largely black urban underclass and argued that the UK would follow the American way due to factors such as:

◆ rising unemployment

◆ rising crime rates

◆ increasing rates of illegitimacy

◆ a growing number of people with low intelligence.

He was particularly critical of single mothers, who played a pivotal role in the creation of what he termed the 'new rabble'. For Murray, illegitimacy, crime, single motherhood and unemployment bound together to produce a social group whose cultural outlook included reliance on state benefits, absentee fathers and engagement with crime. Furthermore, these underclass values were likely to be passed on from generation to generation.

Murray's work was understandably controversial and was subject to criticism from many sociologists, who argued that structural factors and not individual choice explained the emergence of the underclass. The point was also made that Murray's research in the UK was limited and hardly extensive enough to support his radical and extensive claims. Furthermore, it has been stated that rates of teenage pregnancies and what would once have been termed 'illegitimate' children were actually declining in the UK during the period of Murray's claims.

Figure 1.4: Young single mothers – part of the underclass?

Weblink

You can access Murray's article and a reply from the journalist Melanie Phillips (see 'Websites', page ii).

Activity 22

1 Explain how the following four factors could *bind together* (work together) to produce a distinct social group.

  • rising unemployment

  • rising crime rates

  • increasing rates of illegitimacy

  • a growing number of people with low intelligence (Murray added this feature at a later date).

2 What criticisms can you make of Murray's work?

Marsland (1996) expanded this line of thought, which placed the blame for the underclass at the door of the individual and welfare state provision, when he argued that the underclass were 'culturally dependant' on the state and were not encouraged to be self-supporting as state benefits were too high for those who were actually able to work, but chose not to.

The new right explanations of the underclass have been criticised by a range of structural explanations which show that the underclass do not constitute a sub-section of society with different norms and values from the majority, in fact the underclass is formed by those who fall into the category due to factors beyond their control. Furthermore, many studies show that members of the supposed underclass share the same basic norms and values as the majority population; most want to work and be self-dependent, however they face situational constraints which keep them in a lowly position they find it difficult to break out of.

Structural explanations

Traditional Marxist theory referred to the 'lumpen proletariat', the group at the base of the class structure who lack the necessary engagement with work in order to establish them as members of the proletariat. The lumpen proletariat were made up of what Marx described as 'the refuse of all classes', they were an unproductive part of society, as opposed to the proletariat, who were actively involved in making profit for the bourgeoisie. Westergaard and Resler (1974) argue that the lumpen proletariat were positioned at the base of the working class, a part of it but a sub-section or rather a sub-stratum. However, in 1992 Westergaard revisited his analysis of the lumpen proletariat and argued that a structurally dislocated underclass may well have emerged in the UK, but he warned against making that assumption without carrying out clear and well planned research. Hence the Marxists have not ruled out a structurally isolated underclass, but they are guarded in their claims of how it relates to the proletariat.

Weberian-inspired explanations are more precise in their agreement that an underclass has emerged in the UK. Field (1989) argues that the underclass is made up of: the long-term unemployed, single parents (who are disproportionately represented) and the elderly who are reliant on state pensions. For Field these three social groups are particularly susceptible to the underclass due to circumstances (largely to do with a weak economic position and low status) beyond their control.

Dahrendorf (1987) presents an explanation based more on economic than social or political factors. For him the British underclass emerged in the 1980s when mass unemployment under the Thatcher government created a periphery of underemployed workers in the part-time and casual-based economy. Over time these workers would become economically, socially and politically excluded and would form a British underclass, the primary cause of which was economic.

Wilson (1987) ties the underclass to social class disadvantage and race, although he emphasises social class inequalities as the primary cause of its emergence. He also suggests that the political and social connotations of the concept of the underclass are good reasons for replacing it with the concept of the 'ghetto poor', who are there through no fault of their own. Class inequalities and racism explain the creation of the ghetto poor, who fall into extreme poverty and have no way out of it.

Jones (1997) used questionnaires and qualitative interviews in her mixed methods research into the structural causes of the underclass, focusing on the experiences of young homeless people in the UK. She found a mixed picture, that individual choice and structural inequalities both played a part in explaining homelessness, and that family circumstances were crucial in explaining the vulnerability of most individuals to the underclass.

There is no agreement over the existence and class position of the underclass in the contemporary UK. The debate between the cultural explanations of the new right and the structural explanations indicates a dichotomy of views and the ones you have most sympathy with are likely to be a reflection of your own theoretical positioning: structure or agency.

Activity 23

Consider the following case study.

Connor is 36 years old and lives in social housing. He has never been formally employed. He left school at 15 without any qualifications and has lived on state benefits all of his adult life. He has lost contact with his family. He has friends at a local snooker club where he occasionally helps out serving behind the bar, being paid cash in hand. He has tried to find full-time employment but without a reference from work and with no employment history he has never been offered a job. He has very little money and a poor quality of life.

Who or what factors would you blame for Connor's situation and who/what should be looking after his needs?

Sociological explanations of the changing nature of the class structure

This section has considered what has happened to specific social classes; we now need to bring these together and consider a range of sociological explanations of the changing nature of the class structure. In doing this we must remember the importance of globalisation and that we are arguably living in the post-industrial society where the holders of information and knowledge become ever more prominent in society.

Each of the four boxes on this page contains a different explanation. In each one, the main focus of the explanation is noted and the key theories broadly associated with each.

Fragmentation: the view that the traditional class structure has split, divided and is no longer coherent. There is no coherence/unity in the upper, middle or working classes and one consequence of this is the blurring of class boundaries. Social inequality remains a feature but the class structure has fragmented.

Broadly associated with Weberians

Divided/meritocracy: the view that society remains unequal and that the most talented rise and the least talented fall, a 'survival of the fittest' analogy. Social classes remain intact as society as a whole benefits from competition and rewards hard work and talent.

Broadly associated with functionalists and the new right

Polarisation: the view that the gap between the rich and the poor has widened in society and the middle classes have either been stretched out or have polarised into different camps too.

Broadly associated with Marxists, neo-Marxists

Class is dead/irrelevant: the view that class divisions are not useful or applicable descriptions in a contemporary society with so many ways of identifying ourselves and others.

Broadly associated with some social commentators and occasional post modern writers such as Pakulski and Waters (1996)

Activity 24

For each of the explanations in the boxes above, find at least one study to support the view and at least two points of evaluation.

Copy and complete the table below as a way of structuring your work.

The view	Studies/evidence to support	Points of evaluation
Classes have polarised		
Classes have fragmented		
Classes are divided: the meritocracy		
Class is dead		

Position	Description	Examples
30% disadvantaged	Unemployed, economically inactive and marginalised in society	Unemployed

Casual workers, sometimes seasonal with no trade-union protection, often working for wages below the minimum |
| 30% newly insecure | In work but structurally insecure | Part-time, temporary, short-term contracts |
| 40% advantaged | In secure work and protected by trade unions if they want to be | Employed and with permanent contracts |

Table 1.8: Hutton's 30/30/40 society (Source: Hutton, 1995)

Some social commentators have offered their own analysis of what is happening to the class structure in the UK. To end this section we will consider two: the 30/30/40 society and the Uppers and the Downers.

Hutton (1995) described British society as the 30/30/40 society and argued that the development of the labour market had led to a situation where the UK was divided according to the position in the labour market. Table 1.8 shows how this works.

Mount (2004) argues that British society has failed the poor and that society has seen a deepening divide between rich and poor, between what he terms the 'Uppers' and the 'Downers'. Mount himself is a member of the British aristocracy, and does not claim to present a sociological analysis of the class structure, however in his book *Mind the Gap*, he presents the argument that a growing group of Uppers have essentially looked after their own interests, bought property and become socially mobile, leaving the Downers to become marginalised and fatally to become invisible. Mount claims that the UK is unique in allowing this gap to develop to the extremes it has been allowed to.

Section summary

The key theories to consider in this section are functionalism, Marxism, neo-Marxism, Weberianism, feminism and postmodern views.

Use the following words to write a paragraph explaining the key themes of this section.

- Tri-level class structure
- Cultural reproduction
- Knowledge class
- Fragmentation
- Polarisation
- Underclass

Stretch and Challenge Activity

Using the information you have covered so far, answer this essay question:

Assess sociological explanations of the changing nature of the class structure in the contemporary UK.

Exam practice

1   Outline the evidence that a distinct upper class exists in the contemporary UK. (20 marks)

2   Assess functionalist explanations of social inequality. (40 marks)

Patterns, trends and sociological explanations

Pause for thought

- Are any social roles more suited to men than to women?

- Do you think that men or women face more disadvantages in the contemporary UK?

Gender is considered a main site of social inequality in the contemporary UK. In both public and private domains there are social differences between men and women, many of which become social inequalities. The extent and causes of inequalities form the focus of this section, which will begin by considering data relating to the extent of inequality between men and women. It will then consider a range of theoretical explanations, focusing on feminism.

Workplace

One of the main sites of inequality is the workplace, yet significant pieces of legislation are in place to protect people from sexual discrimination and to try to bring equity to the workplace. In 1970 the Equal Pay Act made it illegal to pay men and women different rates for the same job. In 1975 the Sex Discrimination Act made it illegal to discriminate against an applicant for a job on the basis of their sex – unless it could be shown that a job required a person of a specific sex. More recent legislation has increased women's statutory right to maternity leave from 14 weeks to 18 weeks, and men have had a right to two weeks' paid paternity leave since 2003. The current Labour government has been looking at introducing legislation to make 'positive action' in recruitment processes much easier, to bolster the numbers of women and members of ethnic-minority groups in certain posts.

Activity 1

The table below lists areas of life in the contemporary UK where either men or women could be seen as being advantaged. Remember, of course, that it is difficult to generalise and that there may be more than one way of seeing each topic. Copy and complete the table, giving reasons for your views.

Share your ideas as a class and see to what extent there is a consensus of opinion.

	Female advantage	Male advantage	No difference
Home life			
Workplace			
Health			
Media representations			
Crime			
Education			
Political life			

Activity 2

Discuss the following questions and then write down your views.

- Do any jobs specifically require a man or a woman to carry them out, and if so what are the reasons for that?

- Should a woman have the right to 18 weeks' maternity leave, regardless of the impact it has on her workplace?

- What are your views on taking 'positive action' to get more men or women into jobs where they are under-represented? (All-women shortlists for MPs are a good example of this.)

Men are significantly more likely than women to work full time and to be self-employed, although as Table 1.9 shows, the differences in employment status over time may be reducing. Men have also been shown to work longer hours than women, regardless of their status as fathers (Dermott, 2006).

When women do work full time, they are less likely than men to achieve positions of authority. Data shows that female directors of FTSE 100 companies lag significantly behind male appointments.

The concept of the **glass ceiling** has been used to describe how women can reach a certain position but find it difficult to break through to the top jobs – a ceiling prevents them from accessing them. The concept of the leaky pipeline has been used, referring to the steady attrition of females from Science and Technology posts which are associated with the higher-paid jobs in society. Conversely, women are more likely than men to be employed in the areas of education, health and welfare – traditionally not the highest-paid occupational areas.

	1992			2007		
	Men	Women	All	Men	Women	All
Full-time employees	10.6	5.9	16.5	11.6	7.1	18.7
Part-time employees	0.6	4.5	5.1	1.3	5.1	6.3
Self-employed	2.6	0.9	3.5	2.8	1.0	3.8
Unemployed	1.8	0.9	2.8	0.9	0.7	1.7

Table 1.9: Economic activity by employment status and sex (of all economically active people, figures in millions) (Source: Social Trends, Office for National Statistics)

Female FTSE 100 (in numbers)	2001	2002	2003	2004	2005	2006	2007
Number of new female appointments	15	13	20	24	30	23	30
Number of new male appointments	113	111	129	117	149	181	152
Female % of new appointments	12	11	13	17	17	13	20

Table 1.10: Appointment years of FTSE 100 directors 2001–2007, by gender (Source: Sealy et al., 2007)

In pairs, think of what barriers prevent women from reaching the top positions in the workplace. Present your findings in a diagram like the one below.

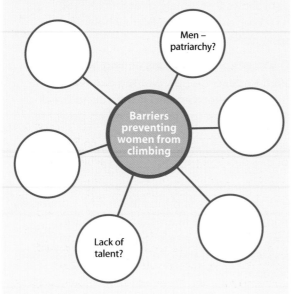

remains, the overall picture is one of convergence rather than divergence.

These patterns and trends are part of the reason why incomes differ between men and women. According to the Annual Survey of Hours and Earnings (Office for National Statistics, 2007), the average earnings of all full-time employees were £457.00 per week. The figure for men was £496, and for women it was £394. The peak earning age group for men was the 40–49 sector, for women it was 30–39. These figures suggest that men and women have differing life courses in relation to the workplace and income. Different earning levels throughout life will impact on the ability to buy into a private pension scheme, which women are less likely than men to do.

Women are more likely than men to live in low-income households, linking with what has been termed the feminisation of poverty. However the gap between male and female earning has reduced over the past twenty years. In 1994, 20 per cent of men lived in low-income households, compared to 24 per cent of women. In 2005, the figure remained at 20 per cent for men but had reduced to 22 per cent of women (Palmer et al. 2007, pages 42, 47). These data suggest that the inequalities between men and women may be diminishing, however the economic well-being of most women is weaker than that of men. One reason for this is differing roles carried out in the private sphere – the home.

There are also differences in relation to working patterns: women are significantly more likely to have flexible working patterns. This flexibility would of course fit with the domestic homemaker role. Again however, this is changing and men are increasingly being given access to flexible working patterns. Although a gender divide

	Men (%)	Women (%)	All (%)
Full-time employees			
Flexible working hours	10.1	14.9	12.0
Annualised working hours	5.2	5.2	5.1
Term-time only working	1.1	6.1	3.0
Any flexible working pattern	18.3	27.4	21.8
Part-time employees			
Flexible working hours	7.4	9.2	8.9
Annualised working hours	3.1	4.2	4.0
Term-time only working	4.5	11.4	10.0
Job-share	1.0	2.4	2.1
Any flexible working pattern	17.8	28.0	26.0

Table 1.11: Employment with flexible working patterns: by sex and type of employment, 2007 (Source: Social Trends, Office for National Statistics)

Home

Despite the fact that women are more likely to be in paid employment than they were 50 years ago, their entry into the labour market has not seen the end of their role as homemakers. Part-time work and flexible working arrangements can complement the role of homemaker. Some sociologists have referred to this as the dual role: women play an active role in the public *and* the private domestic spheres. However, men are increasingly playing a greater role in domestic life. Data from the organisation Carers UK (2007) show that there are almost as many male carers in society as there are female carers.

Seager (1997) used time diaries as a way of researching the number of hours men and women used per weekly on different tasks; home and work related. Women spent more time each week on domestic activities and men spent more time on paid work. Men had more leisure and rest time than women.

Politics

Although the number of female MPs has grown during the last 100 years, women are still grossly unrepresented in Parliament. In October 2008 there were only 126 female MPs out of 646.

Weblink

You can find out more about women's role in politics in the UK (see 'Websites', page ii).

Activity 4

Why do you think so few women are MPs?

List the possible reasons and write a paragraph explaining the one(s) you think are the most likely causes of female under representation in politics.

Education

Education is an area where males seem to experience more disadvantage than females. On average, females achieve better results in SATs at all Key Stages, in GCSEs, A Levels/Diplomas and degrees. There are differences in relation to subject choice, with Maths, Physics and ICT being male-dominated and English, modern languages and Biology being female-dominated. Truancy rates show that males are more likely to truant from school and significantly more likely to be excluded than females.

Data from the Department for Children, Schools and Families (DCSF, 2006/7) shows 65.5 per cent of girls and 56.4 per cent of boys achieved five or more grades A*–C at GCSE. This pattern is reflected over time in performance data. At degree level 56.6 per cent of all first degrees awarded in 2007 were to women and 43.4 per cent awarded to men (Office for National Statistics). It would seem that education favours females in the contemporary UK, however some studies suggest that girls have a harder time in the classroom and in school than boys, that they receive less attention from the teacher than the boys, who dominate space both in the classroom and outside.

Activity 5

If women are achieving stronger examination results, why are they not improving their position in the workplace at a similar rate? Copy and complete this spider diagram illustrating factors that may explain the relationship between education and work.

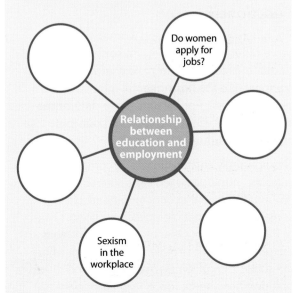

Health

Theoretical explanations of gender inequalities

Functionalist

For functionalists, men and women naturally serve different social roles. Parsons (1955) refers to the 'expressive' caring role that women play, compared to the 'instrumental' practical role played by men. For Parsons these differences are innate, ascribed at birth, and contribute to a healthy, smooth-running society.

Unsurprisingly, the functionalist argument has been criticised, not least by feminists such as Oakley (1974) who argue that gender roles are socially constructed and not biologically ascribed. Critics of Parsons point out that his theory is written from the point of view of a male academic – for whom the social roles of female homemaker and male breadwinner were probably very convenient.

Human capital theory is related to the idea that men and women serve different roles and purposes in society. Human capital theorists argue that many women choose to prioritise their role as homemaker, fitting with their maternal instincts, they are therefore the architects of their own position. Critics, however, point out that this view ignores the structural constraints in society which many argue disadvantage women.

Marxist

Marx himself wrote very little about gender; his interest was in economic disadvantage. However, the concept of the reserve army of labour has been applied to women in capitalist society. As a social group they have been easy to hire and fire and could be seen as useful to the workings of a capitalist economy. According to Beechey (1976), women are less likely to join trade unions and more likely to accept low wages as their income is frequently supplementary to that of the male breadwinner. However, in the twenty-first century, jobs are less likely to be unionised and women are increasingly the main wage-earner or in dual-income households. To consider women as a reserve army of labour is probably over-generalising.

Figure 1.5: Structure or agency?

Engels (1972) did write on the subject of gender and women's role in society. For Engels, the subordinate position of women was a result of historical development and the growth of private property and accompanying laws of hereditary rights. Keen to pass on their property, it became important for men to establish their rightful heirs, hence the development of monogamous relationships. For Engels, men gained control over women through their initial acquisition of private property. Many Marxists agree with this basic argument, however it does not explain why it was men, and not women, who gained control of private property. The whole explanation has been accused of prioritising class and economic differences over sex differences without any real supporting evidence.

Weberian

Men and women are thought to occupy differential positions in the workplace in terms of position they reach and the area they are employed in. Horizontal and vertical segregation have been used as metaphors to describe women's position in the workplace. Horizontal segregation refers to the different types of jobs women and men hold; vertical segregation refers to the different levels they reach within the workplace – in effect, status.

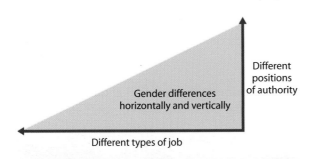

Figure 1.6: Horizontal and vertical segregation

Barron and Norris' (1976) dual labour market theory has been applied to women's employment patterns. There are two labour markets: the primary, characterised by high pay, secure jobs with good promotion prospects and the secondary labour market with low pay, poor promotion prospects and poor job security. They suggested that women were more likely than men to be in the secondary labour market.

Feminism

Most of the prominent literature on gender inequalities is associated with second-wave feminism and the 1960s and 1970s.

Activity 8

Using pages 188–189, remind yourself what first- and second-wave feminism are.

Different groups of thinkers have been identified within second-wave feminism; liberal, Marxist and radical feminists, and this section will look at each in turn before moving onto third-wave/post-feminist thought. You will need to be familiar with a range of different types (sometimes called strands and faces) of feminism, criticisms of each and consider the contribution of feminism as a whole to understanding gender inequality in the contemporary UK. Beware, however, that there is as much disagreement within feminism as between feminism and other sociological theories. Generally however, feminists are united in the belief that aspects of gender inequality need to be the focus of their work.

Activity 9

How does the key focus of feminism differ from Marxism, Weberianism and functionalism? What does each of these theories focus its explanations of inequality on?

Liberal feminism

Liberal feminists such as Friedan (1963) are associated with the belief that gender inequality is a product of general inequality in society which has been allowed to proceed unchallenged for centuries. They do not blame anyone or anything in particular for this, and tackle reform by removing the barriers blocking equality of opportunity between men and women. They were supportive of legislation such as the Equal Pay Act, Sex Discrimination Act, and Education Reform Act (1988). They would be largely supportive of ideas such as positive discrimination, but would not seek to extend women's rights beyond those of men. Their ideas were massively influential in challenging male dominance in society from the 1960s onwards, however most commentators would agree that legal changes do not go far enough in developing equality of opportunity between men and women.

Activity 10

Despite the Equal Pay Act, men's and women's earnings are not equal. What other factors may explain this?

Marxist feminism

Marxist feminism built on the work of liberal thought and argued that deeper and more fundamental changes were needed in society to tackle gender inequality. They positioned most of their explanations within the contribution of gender differences (and inequalities) to explaining the rise of capitalism. Writers such as Benston (1972) focused on the economic aspects of gender inequality: women as a reserve army of labour, the contribution of domestic labour to capitalism and the ideology of the nuclear family used by the state. In short, they argued that women are used to benefit the operation of the capitalist economy and Marxist feminists can be seen as fusing Marxist thinking with gender inequality.

However, critics are keen to question who, or what, was being blamed here: was it the economy as in classic Marxist theory, or patriarchy and male dominance? Was Marxist feminism signifying a unified system of society or a dual system where patriarchy and economics were interlinked? The relationship between Marxism and feminism has been described by Hartmann (1981) as an *unhappy marriage*, as the focus of the two strands are difficult to mould into a coherent theory.

Hartmann (1981) argued that patriarchy and economic both a play a crucial role in explaining and understanding gender equality. She argued that historically men have controlled women for many reasons, and key among these is the control of 'labour power'. This can come through legislation that operates economically to the benefit of men in society, for example laws on maternity and paternity rights, or through purely economic differences in terms of access to income and wealth. Hartmann's work begins to explore the idea that neither patriarchy nor economics alone can explain gender inequality. Her work is an example of a **dual systems theory**.

Marxist feminism is a complicated theory which has many divisions regarding what to foreground: economics, patriarchy or an intertwined approach to explaining gender inequality. It did, however, move the feminist argument into new terrain by asking searching questions for its day.

Activity 11

Copy and complete the table below, showing how women could be seen as contributing to the development of capitalism and any solutions that could be put in place to combat this.

Women assist capitalism by:	Possible solutions	Potential problems
Providing free housework	Pay women for carrying out housework	How much, and where would the money come from?
Providing free childcare		
Promoting an ideology of the nuclear family		
Beautifying themselves		
Working for lower wages than men		

Radical feminism

Radical feminists foreground patriarchy in explaining gender inequality between men and women. In short, society is patriarchal, men have been allowed to control women in both the personal and the public spheres, and hence a situation of extreme inequality has arisen between them. Some radical feminists argue that the source of patriarchy lies in biological differences between men and women, women's ability to give birth resulting in patriarchal dominance (Firestone, 1971). Millet (1971) disagreed with this biological argument and argued that patriarchy was not ascribed but rather socially created and therefore capable of being challenged and deconstructed.

Activity 12

1 If patriarchy has a social cause, what solutions could be offered?

2 If patriarchy has a biological cause, what solutions could be offered?

Radical feminists are associated with the slogan 'the personal is the political,' and their work moved the feminist debate into the role played by patriarchy in the private and public arenas. Radical feminism is characterised by the concept of patriarchy, but internal disagreements are evident in terms of what causes patriarchy and how it could be challenged. Radical feminism has been associated with a number of controversial ideas.

Activity 13

Here are three slogans associated with radical feminism. Discuss what they mean and where you think they originated.

1 All feminists are lesbians.

2 All men are rapists.

3 Marriage makes women 'sick'.

Walby (1990) has made an important contribution to our understanding of patriarchy in recent years. Although not accurately described as a radical feminist, she suggests that patriarchy is not a universal term which is true in one form at all times and in places. At one level, patriarchy exists as a social system built on the assumption that men will try to oppress women, but they do not and cannot always do this in the same way and with success. For Walby there are a number of patriarchal relations in operation in paid work, the state and cultural institutions such as the media and education.

This section has outlined the main ideas associated with different feminists in the second-wave phase. It is worth noting that these labels have been ascribed to the writers and that many feminists see them as unhelpful as they stereotype their thinking. However, they do provide a useful way of analysing the work of a group of sociologists who have as many differences as they do things in common. We now turn to focus on more recent feminist work.

Black feminism

A group of black feminists have developed, whose work raises the profile of race and ethnicity as hidden dimensions of inequality. They argue that much feminist thought was based on the experiences of white, middle-class women writing about their own lives. Far from being a source of oppression, some black feminists argued that the family was frequently a source of solidarity and support for them. Black feminists began to question the notion of 'womanhood' and what it meant – perhaps there were different ways and pressures of experiencing it – and that ethnicity, class and age were neglected areas of feminist research.

Stretch and Challenge Activity

Research the work and writings of bell hooks.

Third-wave feminism

Feminist thought has moved on since the second wave and some argue that it has entered a third wave or post-feminist stage. However, there is no agreement as to what characterises the third stage. For some writers the battle between men and women has moved on and changed, while others raise questions about whether women can have it all, and whether they want to have their place as primary carers *and* the right to equality in the workplace. Others say that feminism has simply gone too far and that men are as disadvantaged as women in many ways. There is no doubt that third-wave feminism is as divided as second-wave feminist thought. However that is not to overlook its contribution. Asking questions and offering commentary help to ensure a healthy debate about gender inequality.

This is not to suggest that feminism is dead, but it is changing. Increasingly, feminist groups use new technology to convey their messages and set up cybernetworks.

choice which they exercise, and acknowledge that many are happy with their position in society. Her typology is useful for beginning to understand the differences between groups of women. However, it has been stated that exercising choice/agency is never really free from structure/circumstance. In this sense although preference theory contributes a great deal to the patriarchy/biology/economic debate that characterised second-wave feminism, it still fails to capture the variety of women's experiences.

Weblink

Finn MacKay is a leading feminist in the contemporary UK. To look at some of her ideas, see 'Websites', page ii.

Preference theory

One of the most comprehensive challenges to all modes of feminist thought comes from Hakim (2000), who argued that not all women are disadvantaged. Employing concepts from rational choice theory, she proposed what is known as **preference theory**, that women do exercise choice in relation to their position in the home and workplace. Her research identified three groups of women, characterised by their relationship to their domestic roles and workplace.

The adaptive group constitute the largest percentage of women, with approximately 60 per cent, compared to 20 per cent each for the other two groups. For Hakim, feminism must move on and accept that women have

Activity 14

Carry out some research into how much choice women of different generations feel they have/had in their lives.

You could repeat the exercise with men.

A questionnaire or an interview would be the most useful method to use.

Collate your results and see if any patterns emerge.

Stretch and Challenge Activity

Find out more about the following contemporary writers and their views of feminism.

- Camille Paglia
- Naomi Walters
- Finn MacKay

	Work-centred	Adaptive	Home-centred
Key characteristics	• Career-orientated • Often single • If with partners, in egalitarian relationships	• No clear preference for main role • The drifters • Lack clear economic use of qualifications	• Wives and/or mothers • Work flexibly or part-time

Table 1.13: Hakim's three groups of women (Source: Hakim, 2000, p. 6. Reproduced with the permission of Oxford University Press)

Patterns, trends and sociological explanations

This section on feminism has introduced a variety of different feminist writers and approaches. Many commentators ask whether there is any such thing as feminism – and point out that feminist thought has as many divisions within at as it has similarities to the feminist cause. While feminism may be characterised by diversity, all feminists share a common cause in wanting to eradicate sexual discrimination – they differ in what they see as its cause and crucially in what its solution is.

Stretch and Challenge Activity

Write an essay on the following:

'Feminism is characterised more by disagreement than by agreement.' Discuss.

Section summary

The key theories to consider in this section are functionalism, Marxism, neo-Marxism, Weberianism, feminism and preference theory.

Use the following words to write a paragraph explaining the key themes of this section.

- Patriarchy
- Dual systems
- Glass ceiling
- Preference theory

Exam practice

1 Outline the evidence to show how women face both advantages and disadvantages in the contemporary UK. (20 marks)

3 Assess sociological explanations of gender inequality in the contemporary UK. (40 marks)

(iii) Inequalities relating to ethnicity

Pause for thought

- Are some ethnic-minority groups more advantaged than others in the contemporary UK?
- Do you think that ethnic inequalities are changing in society?

Differences between and within ethnic groups provide a rich source of data for sociologists studying social inequalities and differences. The workplace in particular provides evidence that some ethnic groups are distinctly advantaged over others in terms of their potential work and market situations. These differences correspond to some degree with differential patterns of educational achievement. In this section we will consider a range of data in relation to social inequalities between ethnic groups. First, however, we will take a brief look at the issues of terminology and classification systems.

Ethnic classification

As you will recall from the AS Sociology course, the concept of 'ethnicity' refers to cultural differences and 'race' refers to biological ones. Everyone belongs to at least one ethnic group. The majority ethnic group in the contemporary UK could be described as white British, although what it means culturally to be white British is a matter of debate. British sociologists are more likely to use the term 'ethnic differences' than American sociologists, who tend to use the concept of race. Throughout this section we use ethnicity as a concept.

The government uses a classification scheme that identifies groups sharing a common ethnic background. The scheme used in the 2001 Census is outlined in Table 1.14. This is the most recent nationwide database available on numbers belonging to different ethnic groups.

Ethnic group	Number	Percentage of the population
White	54,153,898	92.1
Mixed	67,117	1.2
Indian	1,053,411	1.8
Pakistani	747,285	1.3
Bangladeshi	283,063	0.5
Other Asian	247,664	0.4
All Asian or Asian British	2,331,423	4.0
Black Caribbean	565,876	1.0
Black African	485,277	0.8
Black other	97,585	0.2
All black or black British	1,148,738	2.0
Chinese	247,403	0.4
Other ethnic groups	23,615	0.4
All minority ethnic population	4,635,296	7.9
All population	58,789,194	100

Table 1.14: Population of the UK by ethnic group, 2001 (Source: Social Trends, Office for National Statistics)

Classification schemes are useful for monitoring purposes and in helping to target and eradicate ethnic disadvantage where necessary. Critics, however, point out that some of the groups are more heterogeneous than homogenous, having as many differences within them as similarities. The government has recently updated its classification schema to include some sub-categories, such as South Asians. Critics also point out that most new immigrants to the UK are not from the Asian subcontinent, that the truly multicultural nature of the UK is under-researched due to the difficulty of conducting research on such a wide variety of groups.

Verotec (2007) notes that there is now a far greater variety of groups and individuals living in the UK, from more places around the world. Alongside the UK's well-established African-Caribbean and Asian communities, there are relatively new, small, scattered groups of Romanians, Ghanaians, mainland Chinese, Afghans, Japanese, Kurds, Zimbabweans, Iraqis and numerous others. These new immigrant groups are highly diverse, and range from the highest-flying professionals to those with little education or training. Many hope to remain in the UK and become citizens, while others plan to stay for only a short period. Verotec uses the term **'super-diversity'** to describe this situation.

Activity 15

1 What is the problem with using the following concepts:
 • White
 • Black
 • Mixed
 • South Asian?

2 How reliable would the Census data in Table 1.14 be?

3 Why do you think researching super-diversity is so difficult?

Despite the objections to classification schemes, they are widely used in the contemporary UK and form the basis of much of the quantifiable evidence in this area. Before we consider some of this evidence, we need to look at one other concept: racism.

Weblink
You might be interested to find out about the 2011 Census (see 'Websites', page ii).

Racism

Racism is a contested concept. Broadly speaking, it is concerned with negativity regarding a racial or ethnic group. However, there can be racism

Patterns, trends and sociological explanations

U4

1

with intent and racism without intent. Intentional racism is overt and conscious. An example would be not offering work to a black British man because of his skin colour. Unintentional racism is more hidden and covert. It could include, for example, the existence of an **ethnocentric** curriculum in schools, which may be racist but without anyone intentionally making it so.

Racial prejudice is when people hold racist beliefs and values; racial discrimination is based on action that goes beyond beliefs (Cashmore, 1984). It is therefore possible to be racially prejudiced without discriminating against any one person or group. Racial prejudice is very difficult to prove, discrimination is more easily demonstrated.

Cultural racism refers to the negativity relating to the attitudes and attributes associated with groups rather than with individuals. A good example of cultural racism is **Islamophobia**. Islamophobia refers to hostility towards Islam, and a distrust and dislike of Muslims. Islamophobia has clearly increased in the UK since 9/11. A report for the Runnymede Trust (1997) identified four aspects of it:

◆ Prejudice – for example, in media coverage of Muslim culture

◆ Discrimination – for example, in employment practices, health and education

◆ Exclusion – from positions of authority in employment, politics and government

◆ Violence – physical and verbal abuse against Muslims.

The Runnymede report was subject to criticism for its assumptions about Muslim culture. However, evidence bears out the fact that British Muslims suffer disadvantage: 31 per cent working in the UK have no formal qualifications, there is a high unemployment rate among British Muslims and they are the most likely group to be employed in poorly paid, low-skilled jobs (Office for National Statistics).

Institutional racism is different: it is thought to pervade society and organisations within it. It can be intentional or unintentional, but the result is the same, perpetuating the disadvantage felt by some in comparison with others. The case of Stephen Lawrence, the black teenager murdered in 1994, resulted in the Metropolitan Police being branded 'institutionally racist' for its handling of the murder inquiry.

The extent to which the contemporary UK is racist is a thorny issue, due to different definitions of racism and the difficulty of researching whether society is racist or not.

The concepts and ideas covered in this section will be useful as we consider the evidence relating to ethnic disadvantage in the contemporary UK.

Data on ethnic inequalities

Workplace

Some ethnic groups are much more likely to be employed than others, and gender is a crucial variable here too. There are also noticeable differences in relation to earnings for different ethnic groups (see Table 1.15).

	Full-time employment	Part-time employment
White	91	9
Mixed	85	15
Indian	91	9
Pakistani	80	20
Bangladeshi	61	39
Black Caribbean	87	13
Black African	78	22
Chinese	82	18

Table 1.15: Male employment rate (%) by ethnic group in the UK, 2005 (Source: Equality and Human Rights Commission, 2006, p. 14)

The fourth Policy Studies Institute (PSI) survey (Modood and Berthoud, 1997) carried out an analysis of household income by ethnic group; this was the first time such data had been collected. A key finding was the extent of poverty among Pakistani and Bangladeshi households. Caribbean, Indian and African Asian households were all more likely than whites to experience poverty; Chinese households were close to white households in terms of experience of poverty. The data led Berthoud (1997) to name Pakistani and Bangladeshi households as among the social groups most likely to experience poverty. However, such findings need be treated with caution, as the recent changes in the educational success of groups suggests that this pattern is likely to alter.

Heath and Yi Cheung (2006) carried out statistical analysis to find out the extent of the ethnic penalty in the contemporary UK. The **ethnic penalty** is defined as the disadvantage that ethnic minorities face in the labour market compared with British whites of the same age and similar human capital. They concluded that some ethnic minority groups were more likely than others to experience the ethnic penalty: Pakistanis and Bangladeshis appeared again, alongside Caribbean men and women. They also concluded that first-generation migrants may have experienced a greater ethnic penalty than second-generation groups. Particularly

interesting was their finding that the patterns of disadvantage could not be explained by factors such as age, education or foreign birthplace and, although the research does not state discriminatory practices as a finding, there is a clear feeling that the weight of sociological evidence, both quantitative and qualitative, points in the direction of discrimination within the workplace.

Following an analysis of research in this area spanning many decades, Mason (2003) stated that it is difficult to argue against the fact that members of some ethnic groups are severely disadvantaged in the labour market, and one reason for this may be employers' attitudes. For this reason it is not surprising that ethnic minorities figure prominently in entrepreneurial activities in the UK.

Evidence from Business in the Community included the following:

- Black Caribbean men have the highest unemployment rate of all ethnic groups: 14 per cent

- 75 per cent of working-age Bangladeshi women and 69 per cent of working-age Pakistani women are not working or seeking employment

- 10 per cent of all business start-ups in the UK are by individuals from minority ethnic groups

- Chinese and Indian men are the most likely of all ethnic groups to be in the professional and managerial social classes

- Young people from minority ethnic groups are more likely in be in full-time education aged 18

- South Asian minority groups own a quarter of the UK's small businesses, they have been dubbed the 'new middle class'.

Figure 1.7: The new middle class?

Diverse experiences according to ethnic group and generation are supported by evidence from Iganski and Payne (1999), whose research on social mobility suggested that while first-generation immigrants were disadvantaged by the decline of a manufacturing-based economy in the UK, second-generation immigrants may have gained from the move to a service-sector economy. However, this social mobility is not true for all ethnic-minority groups.

Ginn and Arber (2001) argued that ethnic-minority groups, especially women, are disproportionately dependent on state pensions later in life. Having earned less throughout their working life, they have been unable to pay as much into private pension schemes and as government policy shifts further towards private provision this situation is likely to result in disproportionately more women from ethnic-minority groups ending up in poverty.

Education

Some ethnic groups are more likely to be educationally successful than others, and some groups are more likely to experience truancy and display anti-school and anti-education cultures. The blame for this has been placed with schools – through, for example, the existence of an ethnocentric curriculum – and with the cultural background of the ethnic group(s) themselves.

Activity 17

Using pages 75–79, produce evidence to show which ethnic groups over- and under-perform in education.

Crime

Some ethnic groups are more likely than others to be stopped and searched by the police in the UK, and to spend time in prison. Again, the blame for this has been attributed to structural and cultural factors.

Activity 18

Using pages 27–30, produce evidence to show which ethnic groups are advantaged/disadvantaged in the British justice system.

Media

Some ethnic groups and individuals are misrepresented in the media. Whether it is overexposure or underexposure, there is evidence that media representations of ethnicity are frequently distorted. Sections of the media could be accused of cultural bias or cultural racism.

Activity 19

Using pages 117–119, produce evidence to show which ethnic groups are advantaged/disadvantaged by the British media.

Politics

Dawn Butler is one of the few black women MPs in the UK, and has documented frequent racism experienced from politicians throughout her career. In her personal reflections, she describes many instances of direct and non-direct prejudice during her political career and her rise as a Labour MP (Mossa, 2008). Her stories form part of a personal study of racism in British politics.

Activity 20

1 Find out how many black and Asian MPs there currently are in the House of Commons.

2 Find out how many members of the Cabinet are from minority ethnic groups.

3 Compare these figures with the official national percentage of ethnic minorities in the UK (9 per cent). What conclusions would you make about the political representativeness of the UK Parliament?

This section has highlighted evidence relating to ethnic disadvantage in the contemporary UK, and you should be able to add to it from your AS notes and the A2 Power and control topic. We will now look at the ways in which sociologists have explained these patterns.

Theoretical explanations of ethnic inequalities

Functionalist

Functionalists explain ethnic inequalities with reference to the common value system. Ethnic differences and inequalities are temporary and based on cultural differences between minority or immigrant groups and their host nation. Such differences are inevitable for a period of time, but functionalists argue that the maintenance of social order and the collective solidarity meant that minority groups slowly adapt to the majority culture over time. This process is sometimes referred to as **assimilation**, where a group gives up its own cultural values and adopts those of the ethnic majority – a kind of cultural melting pot. Assimilation was considered as a positive outcome of racial and ethnic inequality and a means of preventing a state of anomie. Writing in 1966 in the USA, Parsons argued that the 'American Negro' was a second-class citizen. At that time skin colour symbolised inferiority and was used as a justification for placing black Americans at the bottom of the social ladder (Parsons, 1966). However, Parsons argued that over time the common value would change: minority ethnic groups would either become assimilated or integrated into an emerging shared value system and would play a full role in the meritocratic society.

The functionalist approach has been subject to criticism. First, there is no agreement as to what constitutes the common value system. Is it in fact the white, middle-class, male perspective? Secondly, there is no evidence that minority ethnic groups assimilate into mainstream culture, the multicultural UK is a good example of diversity over time. Finally, the persistence of racism against the same minority groups and between minority groups would suggest that long-term evolution cannot explain inequalities between different ethnic groups. The functionalist approach also treats societies as though they are homogenous entities, whereas evidence suggests that inequalities experienced by different ethnic groups are based on the area/region they live in. The experience of a minority ethnic worker in multiethnic London may differ vastly from life in rural Scotland.

Weblink

You can access and read the article 'Ethnic middle classes join the "white flight"' (see 'Websites', page ii).

Stretch and Challenge Activity

Read extracts from Monica Ali's novel, *Brick Lane* (2003) and consider what it suggests about the process of ethnic assimilation.

Closely related to the functionalists' views are those of the new right, where attempts have been made to foster assimilation and ethnic integration. In the UK, for example, there have been attempts to legislate that the English language must form part of compulsory training for minority groups at risk of marginalisation and ethnic separatism. Such approaches have been blamed for fuelling ethnic conflict in some parts of the UK, where uneasy relationships exist between and within all cultures.

Marxist

For traditional Marxists, racism and ethnic inequality play an important role in the capitalist economic system. One of the earliest Marxist writers, Cox (1948), proposed that racial differences and racism itself had been the creation of the economic system – that racism was created and sustained by capitalism. Racism helped to maintain a false class-consciousness by using a divide-and-rule tactic: by creating divisions within the working class itself, there is less opportunity for the working class to unite in revolt.

Marxist sociologists such as Castles and Kosack (1973) have argued that ethnic-minority groups could also be used as part of a reserve army of labour, supporting the capitalist system while providing an illusion of meritocracy. These workers are forced to work for lower wages than their white counterparts in order to survive. For these Marxist writers, minority ethnic groups form a sub-section of the working class and prevent the development of *a class in itself* to a *class for itself*, a key process in Marx's theory of class development. Westergaard and Resler

(1976) disagree with this analysis and argue that minority groups form part of a unified working class, not a divided one.

These economic arguments are powerful, however historical evidence shows that racism precedes the development of capitalism (Solomos, 1986) and most neo-Marxists would reject Cox's over-simplistic argument that capitalism created racism. They have developed the economic position and blended it with some cultural arguments. Similarly, it is perhaps over-simplistic to argue that ethnic-minority groups form part of a united working class.

Neo-Marxist

Neo-Marxist writers on ethnicity have combined elements of the economic arguments with work on cultural differences, and acknowledge that ethnic differences cannot adequately be explained in such a deterministic manner as they had been by traditional Marxists. Miles (1980) made an important contribution when he argued that minority ethnic groups are part of the same class structure as the majority group; however, they form a **racialised** part of it. By this he meant that ethnic minorities may always be treated or perceived as being different, because of racial factors. This does not, of course, imply direct racism, but may be a form of cultural racism. Miles used the concept of *racialised class fractions* to explain the existence of ethnic minorities in the petite bourgeoisie, or middle classes (which do exist, as the neo-Marxists argue). In short, ethnic minorities can be found in all social classes, but their ethnicity means they will be subject to differential treatment.

Other neo-Marxist writers have developed the traditional economic arguments and shown how ethnic minorities can be scapegoated by the ideological state apparatus. Hall (1979) made an important contribution when he argued that ethnic relations are historically specific and subject to change over time. His work highlights the immigration problems of the 1970s, which he argues were used by the media to divert attention away from the economic recession facing the government of the day.

The neo-Marxist studies begin to fuse economic and cultural arguments in explaining inequalities. They could be well applied to the position of Polish migrant workers in recent times, who enter the UK legally as members of the European Union, but who face difficulties fitting into British society as they are perceived by some to be 'taking jobs' and by others to be culturally different and therefore troublesome. The fusion of economic and cultural arguments is a powerful force in explaining ethnic inequalities in the UK.

However, neo-Marxists have still not tackled the formation of racist attitudes themselves, which does not fit with the growth of capitalism. There is also a strong argument put forward by Weberian-based sociologists that ethnic/racial differences override economic differences in explaining inequality.

Weberian

Weberian-based explanations differ from the Marxist ones in suggesting that ethnic differences may be viewed as more important than economic differences in explaining inequalities. In this sense Weberian explanations are more flexible and multi-dimensional, certainly than traditional Marxist ones. Some sociologists have suggested that the neo-Marxists actually use a great deal of Weberian theory in their work.

Parkin (1968) terms minority ethnic groups as 'negatively privileged status groups'. He uses the concept of social closure to argue that the more privileged groups can operate a system of social segregation and keep minority groups out of positions of authority. The concept of the glass ceiling can be used here, although some have suggested that for minority workers the ceiling is actually concrete as they are denied vision of the white male-dominated boardrooms.

Rex and Moore (1967) argued that minority groups were severely disadvantaged in the labour market, that they formed part of the dual labour market, being placed in the secondary labour market. Their life chances and market position were noticeably weaker than their white counterparts; they were marginalised and risked forming an underclass in society. It was racial differences rather than economic differences that had created this situation.

Questions have been asked about the difference between these approaches and the neo-Marxist idea of racialisation and class fractions. There are clear overlaps, but the Weberian explanations probably do give more credibility to ethnic differences than to economic ones, and for Marxist writers the opposite is true. The main criticism against them comes from the postmodern views, but these can be taken as a critique against all of the classic sociological theorists.

Postmodern

Postmodern sociologists in this area are keen to extend the analysis of ethnicity beyond that of recalling disadvantage and offering structural solutions. In a world characterised by diversity, fluidity and fragmentation, postmodern writers have engaged with the concept of super-diversity and are producing work which documents the range of diversity within the UK. They are working to bring about lasting change, not only in material circumstances but also in seeking to ensure that grand themes and analyses are no longer applied to whole ethnic groups – who are, they argue, not all experiencing the same advantages and disadvantages and who are as diverse as they are common.

Modood leads the way here in wanting to develop a more plural approach to ethnic relations that will extend into the future, rather than looking backwards. His work stresses difference and diversity of experience rather than commonality, and is critical of the portrayal of ethnic-minority groups as being victims (Modood and Berthoud, 1997). Work on hybrid identities and code-switching also form part of the postmodern contribution. You should be familiar with these from the AS course.

Section summary

The key theories to consider in this section are functionalism, Marxism, neo-Marxism, Weberianism and postmodernism.

Use the following words to write a paragraph explaining the key themes of this section.

- Super-diversity
- Assimilation
- Racialised
- Ethnocentric
- Islamophobia
- Ethnic penalty

Stretch and Challenge Activity

Create a log of evidence relating to ethnic disadvantage in the contemporary UK. Look for evidence relating to specific ethnic groups and gender divisions. Following the media closely will be helpful in this task.

Exam practice

1   Outline the evidence that ethnic disadvantage is a feature of life in the contemporary UK. (20 marks)

2   Assess Weberian explanations of ethnic inequality in the contemporary UK. (40 marks)

(iv) Inequalities relating to age

Pause for thought

- What age groups do you think are most disadvantaged in the UK, and why?

- At what age should people stop 'working'?

- What are your views on having a minimum wage law that does not cover people under the age of 17?

You should recall from your AS course that the older age categories are the fastest growing in the UK, where increasing life expectancy and a falling birth rate have resulted in changing **demographic** patterns. You may also remember examples of age-related restrictions in the UK. Schools are based on chronological age, and the right to vote, to learn to drive, buy alcohol and be eligible for a state pension are all age related. In this section we will focus on evidence of social inequalities relating to age and the sociological explanations for this.

The main site of disadvantage is related to the workplace and incomes, which evidence suggests shows examples of discrimination and ageism. Bytheway (1995) however explains how **ageism** is a misleading concept as age is experienced so differently by sections of the population. Age discrimination may be prevalent in the UK, but finding evidence of shared experiences can be difficult.

Workplace

Age disadvantage in the workplace is complex. Increasingly, people are experiencing compulsory early retirement, where they lose their once-secure employment and may find themselves unemployable, many years short of state retirement age. The phrase 'too old to employ' is frequently related to this growing group of workers, and the cost of the economically inactive over-fifties is a considerable drain on government resources. However, other people choose to work past the state retirement age, not wanting to lose their employee status. Others are in a position of relying on part-time work in retirement to maintain their standard of living. There are no clear patterns of age-related behaviour in the workplace. Featherstone and Hepworth (1999) argue from a postmodern perspective that this is an example of how individual life-courses are becoming destructured and fragmented.

European legislation passed in 2006 made age discrimination illegal, however legislation often takes time to have the desired effect and loopholes are often present. One in five workers from all age sectors told a MORI survey that they had experienced discrimination at work, with 38 per cent citing ageism as the cause (MORI, 2002).

However, for employers there are often benefits associated with employing workers from particular age-related categories. Younger people are often cheaper to employ as they have not accumulated years of experience to justify higher wages; they are also likely to be easier to train and mould. Middle-age categories are associated with higher earners and those seeking career progression. Employing older people can be costly, as they are likely to remain in that employment until retirement, and if their skills are no longer required this can result in costly redundancy or retraining packages. While the idea of age-diverse workplaces is an inclusive one, in reality they are not always easy to find.

Economically and culturally, old age is experienced differently by different people (Vincent, 2006). Life expectancy favours women, hence the concept of the 'feminisation' of later life. Many women have been the most affected by material disadvantage during their lives. Material disadvantage in youth and middle age is structured around class, gender and ethnicity; in old age this becomes more pronounced and can be related to the issue of pensions.

Patterns, trends and sociological explanations

227

Figure 1.8: Examples of age-diverse workplaces can be difficult to find

Pensions

Traditionally, receiving the state pension has been considered as a marker of old age. However, with life expectancy increasing; it is becoming common for society to think about pensions and old age in different ways. McKingsley (2001) refers to people aged 85 and over as the 'oldest old', therefore implying that there is a stage of being 'young elderly'. Milne and Harding (1999) researched the lifestyles of over 1000 older people in the UK and found evidence of two worlds. One was made up of people in the early years of retirement, often practising active ageing. The other was made up of over-eighties, increasingly likely to be living alone, with few savings and increasingly isolated. These different experiences mean that old age is not a universal category with shared social, cultural and economic experiences. However, there is evidence to suggest that the elderly are disadvantaged in the contemporary UK.

Individuals in the UK are eligible to receive state pensions when they reach a certain age, soon to be 65 for both men and women. Like Child Benefit, the pension is not means tested – it is a universal benefit available to everyone legitimately residing in the UK. In recent years, studies have shown that pensioners are more prone to poverty than those in the working population; between 1998 and 2001, 18 per cent of pensioners lived in poverty compared to only

7 per cent of the working population (Giddens, 2006, page 352). Pensioners (along with children) in the UK are among the most likely social groups to live in low-income households. Single female pensioners and older pensioner couples are the most likely to live in low-income households (JRF, 2007). Despite this universal benefit, there are huge discrepancies in the standard of living for older people, and this is related to social class, gender and ethnicity as much as to age.

Many older people have contributed to private pension schemes during their lives, and reap the benefit of this in later years. However, those groups who are materially disadvantaged during their working lives are unable to buy into the private schemes or to pay as much into them. For them, older age brings increased deprivation and disadvantage (Vincent, 2006). Ginn and Arber (1992) examined the extent of disadvantage in private pension scheme arrangements and analysed the results according to gender and ethnicity: Pakistani and Bangladeshi women were particularly disadvantaged compared to their white British counterparts – reflecting patterns of disadvantage in the workplace.

The issue of pensions, rights and responsibilities is a thorny one. Being the main pension provider places a huge financial burden on the state, and there is increasing criticism that provision is insufficient. The likelihood in the future is for pension provision to be modelled as it is in the

USA – based much more on private and personal financial contributions – and this will inevitably favour the higher earners in stable employment, who are able to contribute the most to their individual pension plans. Johnson (1995) argued that contributing to state pension funds would disadvantage the younger age groups, who were unlikely to receive the same level of pay-outs as the older people now do. Provision for the elderly also has social costs for families and carers. The concept of the 'sandwich generation' has been used to refer to those carers caught in the middle of young and older generations – caring at both ends of the spectrum.

Activity 21

1 Why do you think there is frequent discussion about raising the age of entitlement to the state pension?

2 What are the social implications of abolishing state pensions and telling everyone they have to finance their own retirement through private schemes?

Age disadvantage in other areas

The optimum age for committing crimes in the UK has been linked to age and gender in particular. Girls are likely to deviate at a younger age than boys and to engage in criminal activity for a shorter period of time. Young males are most at risk of being the victim of a crime, yet amongst the least likely to fear crime. Older people living alone fear crime the most, yet are unlikely to experience it. The media could be accused of creating moral panics about old age and crime in the UK.

It could be argued that older age groups are better represented in the political system than younger ones. However, the age composition of British politicians cannot be expected to be representative. Furthermore, older people are more likely than younger ones to know and understand how to use the political system to meet their needs. Groups such as Age Concern wield considerable power in Parliament, as they are well known and well connected, with high levels of social capital. Younger people tend not to have these links and are more likely to be marginalised by the political system.

Clearly patterns of ill-health are age-related. Children, young people and the elderly suffer most frequently, for obvious reasons. However, there is evidence that age discrimination occurs in healthcare provision in the UK, which often goes unnoticed. For example, there are upper age limits for breast-cancer screening which seem to go unopposed.

The representation of older age groups in the media has been described as stereotypical, focusing on dependency and ill-health. Positive representations of active ageing are difficult to come by in the media. Carrigan and Szmigin (2000) argue that the advertising industry either ignores older people or stereotypes them as caricatures who are decrepit, withering, physically ugly or losing their mind. In this way advertisers fail to reflect the reality of life for older people.

Activity 22

Carry out an analysis of advertising on either the television or print media. Collect images of older people and categorise them according to the roles they portray.

There seems to be considerable evidence which indicates that age is a site of social disadvantage for some social groups in the contemporary UK, and we will now consider how sociologists have explained these patterns. As we proceed through the next section, please keep an important point in mind: age is a relatively new emerging area of social research, which has not received the same degree of treatment (or interest?) as class, ethnicity or gender. One reason for this is the complexity of isolating age from any other social category. When considering sociological explanations of the patterns, we will draw on sociological concepts already covered as well as introducing some new ideas.

Sociological explanations

Functionalism

Functionalists have viewed age stratification in terms of modernisation and social roles. The development of a modern industrial economy brought with it inevitable changes for the young and old. Laws restricting the employment of children and laws bringing in a retirement age and universal state pension provision meant that socially and economically, conditions would change in the name of modernisation and progress. Some functionalist writings associated old age with the concept of **disengagement**, where age brings with it a movement from the mainstream to the periphery of society. Disengagement concerns itself with the role old age plays within the social system, rather than at an individual level. Individuals become aware of the ageing process and actively seek to abandon some social roles, leaving them for younger generations to pick up. Such a process serves to maintain the social order, a key component of functionalist theory.

Arguably, functionalism has offered more insight into age difference than any other sociological theory. Critics, however, point out that disengagement does not align itself particularly easily with the concepts of social solidarity or the collective conscience.

Parsons (1954) concentrated on the important role that age played in the acquisition of social roles. He viewed teenage culture as a transitional stage between childhood and adulthood, associating it with issues of transition and insecurity as young people sought to fulfil their social roles. Old age was considered as a time of isolation and loneliness. Receiving a pension created a dependency and with it came a drop in status. The social roles of old people changed as they became increasingly cut off from mainstream society. In a similar way Eisenstadt (1956) argued that differential age groups (youth, middle age, old age) enable individuals to learn and acquire new social roles and therefore contribute to social cohesion and solidarity.

There are many criticisms of the functionalist approach to age stratification. First, it assumes homogeneity of experience, whereas in reality age is characterised by diversity of experience. Secondly, it neglects the issues of class, gender and ethnicity which intersect with age to create disadvantage. However, Parsons did consider the issue of gender in his work, and class differences are alluded to in some functionalist writings. Finally, the functionalist work was researched by middle-class American males in their own communities and hence could be accused of lacking generalisability.

Marxism

Marxist theory can provide answers to some of these failings, yet they themselves do not provide a convincing account of age disadvantage in the UK.

The reserve army of labour could be applied to age groups at both ends of the spectrum. Those under 14 provide cheap labour in the informal economy in jobs such as newspaper delivery. Equally those over 65 are increasingly seeking to extend their working lives with part-time work for financial and social reasons. Both groups can meet the needs of an economy which experiences boom and bust, as both can be easily hired and fired. However, the reserve army of labour can be applied to many other sectors of the workplace too, and it fails to explain the breadth of experience that age disadvantage begs.

State provision for the young and old through Child Benefit and pensions also raises the question that the state wants to create dependent groups who legitimate the position of the powerful as the rule-makers in society. Laws created by the state serve the needs of a capitalist economy, and it could be argued that in the past, older age groups may have drained the economic resources of private companies by demanding higher wages to match their levels of skill. In establishing universal state pension provision, the state may have been seeking to divert such costs, and few could have predicted the increase in life expectancy during recent decades, which may result in a reversal of the universal benefits for older age groups. In this sense, welfare provision may be a part of the ideological state apparatus.

Weberian

The ageing process can clearly be associated with issues of status and power in the UK. Old age and indeed retirement can be construed as triggers for a loss of status (McKingsley, 2001) and this is as much cultural as it is economic. Without a strong market and work situation there will inevitably be a weakening of status and power. Youth groups could also be explained with adherence to these concepts.

Parkin (1968) used the concept of negatively privileged status groups in his work on ethnicity, a concept which could be applied to older people who have lost their position in the labour market, kept out by younger workers keen to work their way up the occupational ladder. Related to this is the idea of the glass ceiling, that some people quite simply become too old to promote, regardless of their credentials. The dual labour market theory could be applied to older and young groups in the workplace. However, as with Marxist concepts and ideas, these could all apply equally well to an array of social groups, they are not particular to age, so where does this leave us?

It is fair to say that theories of age disadvantage and difference are in the process of developing, that economic rewards and status are linked to participation in the productive capitalist system, and that this is governed to a large extent by the activities of the state. Whether discussing state retirement, Child Benefit or the existence of Educational Maintenance Allowance (EMA), the state does play a key role in establishing and maintaining age differentials in the contemporary UK. Marxist and Weberian concepts can help to explain some of the reasons for this, however the diversity of age experiences can probably be explained most readily with reference to postmodern concepts.

Postmodern views

The concept of individualisation has been applied with some accuracy to an individual's life trajectory – which is highly unlikely to follow a common course or theme (Everingham, 2003). Individual choice and a destructuring of society has made age an increasingly fragmented and diverse social category (Featherstone and Hepworth, 1999). Individuals such as Mick Jagger and Helen Mirren are good examples of older people who do not adhere to the typical expectations of how older people should look or think.

However, to argue that age is too heterogeneous to make sense of, falls into the trap of ignoring crucial social divisions. Evidence from earlier in this section shows that older people, particularly women, do appear to be amongst the groups most likely to experience poverty. For this reason, sociological research that focuses on the intersection of age with other social divisions needs to become the norm, and this is the focus of the next section.

Stretch and Challenge Activity

Research examples of age discrimination in the UK and compare them to the numbers of cases of ethnic and gender discrimination.

Weblink

You can read more about the inequalities faced by older people on the Help the Aged website (see 'Websites', page ii).

Section summary

The key theories to consider in this section are functionalism, Marxism, Weberianism and postmodernism.

Use the following words to write a paragraph explaining the key themes of this section.

- Ageism
- Demographic
- Disengagement
- Functionalism
- Marxism
- Weberianism
- Postmodern

Exam practice

1 Outline the evidence to show that older people are disadvantaged in the UK. (20 marks)

2 Assess functionalist explanations of age differentiation. (40 marks)

The intersection of class, gender, ethnicity and age

One of the key themes of this section and your Sociology course is the extent to which any social category exists independently of the others. In the examples used throughout this section, people are never solely men or women, black or

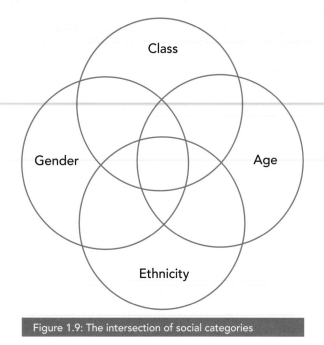

Figure 1.9: The intersection of social categories

white, young or old. Social categories interact and intersect with one another. This could be considered diagrammatically, as in Figure 1.9.

The social categories intersect and interact with one another, making social behaviour difficult to pin down to any one variable. Sociologists from different perspectives have looked at the issue of intersection, as the two examples below show. Although postmodern sociologists are perhaps the most keen to point out the importance of the intersection, the two examples considered in this section are not from postmodern work. Writers such as Anthias (2001) show how the material and cultural aspects of class, age, ethnicity and gender all need to be considered within quality theoretical work. This poses a huge challenge for sociologists trying to produce detailed research evidence. Many postmodern writers will argue that it is not possible to produce high-quality research that focuses on the intersection of class, gender, ethnicity and age, as the relationships are too complex and fragmented. If this is true then the explanations for the intersection are also going to be over-complex. Some sociologists have drawn on existing theories (Marxism, feminism, functionalism) to make sense of the relationships.

Example 1: 'Class in construction: London building workers, dirty work and physical cultures', by Thiel (2007)

Thiel studied a group of male builders working on a building site in London. This was an ethnographic study, using participant observation

and unstructured interviews. The men displayed a working-class and highly masculine culture. They had strong physical capital (their bodies) and social capital (their family and friends) and were embedded within local community networks. They learnt their trade skills informally, through on-the-job training, and had a 'them and us' attitude to management. The men did not, however, identify themselves as being part of the 'working class', their identities were fractured by their status as builders, and by ethnic and gender divisions.

Example 2: *Formation of Class and Gender*, by Skeggs (1997)

Skeggs studied a group of white working-class women in their twenties and thirties who had enrolled on Caring courses in an FE (Further Education) college. She gained access to the women as she was a lecturer on some of the courses. Her study was longitudinal, conducted over an eleven-year period as she sought to construct accounts of the women's lives and analyse the data. Skeggs was writing from a feminist perspective, using feminist methodology, and was clear in her view that she brought values to the research, from the lived experience of being a woman and sharing some features of the women's lives with them. Nevertheless, Skeggs argued that she was able to produce valid and authentic accounts from the women. Skeggs spent the first three years of the research 'doing ethnography' and spending as much time as possible with the women – in and out of the college environment. She remains in touch with some of the women today. Her research found that these working-class women could be defined by their desire to achieve 'respectability'. Respectability meant that the women were concerned to distance themselves from working-class women who lacked what they viewed as respectability – through factors such as what they wore, their employment and lifestyle.

Stretch and Challenge Activity

Assess the view that it is not possible or desirable for sociologists to consider social differences in isolation from each other.

In your answer you should include theoretical and methodological issues.

Exploring sociological research on social inequality and difference

Pause for thought

1   If you wanted to collect data on the extent of poverty in the UK, how would you do it?

2   If you wanted to collect data on the experiences of 16- to 19-year-olds in rural areas as they proceeded from education to employment, how would you do it?

3   What are the main problems you would face in both scenarios?

You should be familiar with the distinction between positivist and interpretivist approaches to sociological research. Positivists seek to generate quantifiable data in numerical form which can be tabulated and used to establish patterns, trends and generalised laws. Their preferred methods of data collection are questionnaires, structured interviews and statistical data. Interpretivists seek to generate qualitative data in textual form which can be used to describe and explain social phenomena rather than measuring it. Their favoured methods of data collection are unstructured interviews and observation. Your answers to the questions on the previous page are likely to be based to some extent on positivist thinking for question 1 and interpretivism for question 2.

This section will revisit the work on **methodology** covered at AS Level. It will extend it by introducing some new and more demanding methodological concepts and using examples of sociological research based around the topics of social inequality and difference. First, we will look at two different examples of research based on social inequality and difference, broadly associated with positivism and interpretivist research methodologies.

Example 1: *Monitoring Poverty and Social Exclusion*, by Palmer et al. (2006)

This is one of a series of annual reports which aims to provide data on the progress made in reducing poverty and eliminating social exclusion in the UK. The reports began in 1998 and are based around key indicators of poverty and social exclusion. An example of some of the 50 indicators used in the report are:

◆ number of households on low income (see below)
◆ numbers with low attainment at school at age 11 and 16
◆ numbers of teenage pregnancies
◆ numbers of premature deaths
◆ numbers of workless households
◆ numbers of households lacking essential items.

Selecting the key indicators of poverty/social exclusion is one task for the research team, but how each one is quantified and operationalised is also crucial. Low pay, for example, is defined

as an income that is 60 per cent or lower of the contemporary average household income after the deduction of housing costs; this is the standard definition used by the government.

The data from this report are taken from secondary sources; that is sources of data collected by other researchers. One of the issues connected to this report is that while it is an excellent source of data on poverty/social exclusion in the UK, there is no way of determining the validity and reliability of the secondary sources it uses. The links with quantitative data collection methods and positivism are evident from studies like this one.

Activity 1

1 Take each of the indicators listed above and think about how a sociologist would go about operationalising each.

2 What additional information would they need for each one and how might they access it?

3 Which indicators do you think would be especially problematic and why?

Weblink

You can access the whole report *Monitoring Poverty and Social Exclusion* (see 'Websites', page ii).

Example 2: *Should I Stay or Should I Go? Rural Youth Transitions*, by Midgely and Bradshaw (2006)

This research explores the experiences of young people not in education, employment or training (NEETs) aged between 16 and 19 living in rural areas in the north of England. It focuses on the options available to them as they move through the transitory phase of adolescence into adulthood. One of the key findings in the research was that many of these young people move in and out of education and training as they are unable to find a stable route to provide them with sustainable economic and social stability. Many of the participants found that they needed to move out of their local area to 'move on' in life, as they felt that their rural localities did not offer adequate access to the education, training and employment to meet their needs. Using a combination of focus-group interviews with the young people themselves and 24 semi-structured interviews with people working in organisations supporting the young people, the study aimed to present authentic accounts of the experiences and aspirations of these youngsters.

Activity 2

1 Where might a sociologist go to gain access to the views of 16- to 19-year-old NEETs?

2 The aim of the research was to access the experiences and aspirations of this group of people. What topics would you want to cover in the focus-group interviews?

3 What methodological difficulties might a sociologist face (a) in conducting the focus-group interviews, (b) in the data transcription and (c) in establishing an authentic and valid account from the research participants?

Both the examples above illustrate research with roots in particular methodologies, generating different types of data: quantitative in the poverty study and qualitative in the research on NEETs. Before we proceed to look at the methodologies in more depth, it is worth reminding ourselves that few sociologists label themselves as positivists or interpretivists: most researchers choose the methodology and research design that fit their purpose.

However, most sociological research can be placed to some degree as fitting into one of the following methodologies: positivist, interpretivist, feminist and realist. The remainder of this section will consider these in turn.

Research methodologies

Positivism

Positivism is an approach to social research which tries to apply the logic of natural sciences to investigations of the social world. It is based on the assumption that since there are patterns and regularities, causes and consequences in both the natural world and the social world, the same scientific principles of investigation can be applied to the study of both. Positivists view the world as made up of observable phenomena, which are causally related to one another and have a direct impact on how humans think and act. For example, positivist-based research may consider that the marital status of a child's parents (married/divorced/separated/cohabiting) is causally related to a child's educational under-achievement. A positivist-based research study may consider the extent to which these two phenomena are related.

Activity 3

1 How could a sociologist measure the extent of any causal relationships between any of the following: (a) divorce, (b) separation, (c) cohabitation and (d) educational under-achievement in the UK?

2 What problems might they encounter in their definitions of these terms?

The aim of positivist research is to produce an objective understanding of society by following the same principles of investigation used in natural science. Positivist research is therefore based around the generation of empirical, systematically generated quantifiable data, high in reliability. Positivists argue that sociology can be studied scientifically.

The origin of the word 'positivism' is attributed to one of the earliest sociologists: Comte in nineteenth-century France. Comte has been described as an independent scientist who believed that the development of a social science committed to social reform and reorganisation was necessary for society to become stable and equitable. He argued that sociological research should be confined to observable or directly measurable phenomena, the same core scientific principle on which natural science was based. Other core principles of this approach would be objectivity, verification and replication of empirical evidence. Through rigorous social scientific research it was argued that it was possible to discover the laws that govern people's behaviour in the social world.

Think about your experiences of studying Science at GCSE. In pairs or small groups, discuss whether you think science is based on:

- objectivity (non-bias)

- study of measurable and observable phenomena

- findings that can be replicated.

Durkheim is considered by many as a positivist sociologist. He developed the idea that there could be a social science, suggesting that rather than researching only observable and measurable phenomena, sociological research should base itself on the study of 'social facts'. For Durkheim (1970) social facts are things which are external to social actors. His definition of social facts included belief systems (including religious beliefs) and the norms and values of institutions and societies. In one of his major works he showed how the topic of suicide could be studied in social terms through the collection and analysis of statistical data on suicides (treated as social facts). Causes and correlations, patterns and regularities in suicide statistics across different nations and social groups were all established through the careful analysis of statistical data on suicide. His methodological approach was based on inductive positivism, where through the collection of data, theories are developed which can be tested and verified time and again in order to generate laws of human behaviour.

Weblinks

You can find out more about Durkheim's study *Suicide* and the important contribution it has made as the first empirical sociological study of its kind (see 'Websites', page ii).

You might like to look at a useful source of information on sociology and science (see 'Websites', page ii).

Positivism has developed since Durkheim, perhaps most notably through the work of the philosopher Popper (1959) who asked how a statement such as 'all swans are white' could ever be proven to be 100 per cent accurate, since we only what has happened up to this point, and future events may confound our expectations, that is, tomorrow we may see a swan that is not white. Popper put forward a deductive approach to research in the natural and social sciences, where a theory or hypothesis is stated, and data collected in an attempt to falsify the statement.

The distinction between inductive and deductive methodologies has led to the view that there is no single valid way of carrying out scientific research. This has led some commentators to question the extent to which science is indeed factual, objective, replicable and verifiable.

Stretch and Challenge Activity

Find out more about the nature of science and the extent to which sociology can be considered as scientific. Many general sociology texts have chapters on this topic. Useful names to research are Thomas Kuhn and Karl Popper.

Despite changes in the way that positivist sociological research has been understood and carried out, positivist-inspired sociological research remains popular in contemporary studies where key indicators are used in quantitative studies whose main aims are to establish patterns and regularities, as is the case on the example of poverty given on page 234. A study by Gartrell and Gartrell (2002) suggests that positivism is still influential in sociological research and that such research features some of the following features:

- generation of law-like statements

- operationalisation of definitions

- generation and testing of hypotheses

- empiricism

- use of statistical techniques.

However, positivism is not without its critics.

First, many sociologists argue that social reality cannot be studied in the same way as the natural world. People do not react to stimuli in the same way as phenomena do in the natural world. Laws of causation may be applicable in the natural world, but in the social world people choose to interpret situations in particular ways, which means you can never be certain that what you see/observe/measure is actually a valid/authentic account.

Secondly, it has been suggested that natural science is not itself based on the systematic generation of empirical evidence free from bias. It may be that scientists are as susceptible to the manipulation/interpretation of results as any researcher is. Science, it seems, may not be all it is assumed to be.

Thirdly, the subjective experiences of individuals cannot be ignored in social research; how people feel and act are crucial elements of sociological research and positivist-inspired research may find this data difficult to access.

Interpretivism

Interpretivism is an approach to social research which seeks to understand the subjective experiences of those being studied: how they think, feel and act. Interpretivist research gives priority to the subjective understandings of research participants. In this respect interpretivists offer an alternative approach to research sociological from that of positivists. Interpretivists try to understand social life from the point of view of those being studied and consider validity to be the most crucial element of quality research. An important concept in helping to achieve valid sociological data is verstehen.

Verstehen is related to the idea of empathy where the researchers place themselves in the position of those being studied, and try to understand how those people would see the world. If we take the example of divorce, interpretivists are unlikely to be interested in establishing causal links between parental divorce and a child's educational under-achievement, however they are likely to be interested in how a child copes with parental divorce, their thoughts and their actions, which may well impact on their educational achievement. Interpretivists do not believe that sociology can be studied in a scientific way, they are more interested in the collection and interpretation of qualitative rather than quantitative data.

Activity 5

1 If you were researching the effects of parental divorce on a 14-year-old's behaviour, what method/s would you use and why?

2 Which method/s would you reject and why?

Sociologists who take an interpretative approach to methodology are closely associated with a number of theories, most notably social action theory and symbolic interactionism.

Social action theory derives from the work of Weber (1968), who argued that we can only understand social action by interpreting the meanings that lie beneath it. In order to access those meanings, researchers need to collect data that are rich in detail and depth, textual data, sometimes in narrative form, that will help to explain the meanings and motives underlying the behaviour of individuals and social groups. It is the role of the sociologist to interpret and understand these actions, and one way of achieving this is through the concept of verstehen.

Symbolic interactionism is closely associated with the work of Blumer (1969) who argued that sociologists should seek to immerse themselves in the lives of those experiencing the phenomena they are trying to understand. As humans act on the basis of meanings, these meanings need to be understood. Only by trying to take on the actor's (another person's) viewpoint will the researcher begin to access how social actors understand and experience social reality.

Stretch and Challenge Activity

You can find out more about symbolic interactionism by researching the ideas of George H. Mead, Charles Cooley and Howard Becker.

Interpretivist sociologists seek the collection of qualitative data, rich in deep contextual detail. In order to gain access to these data, the researchers need to build a rapport with those being studied, however they need to remain sufficiently detached to be as objective as possible when carrying out the research.

Interpretivism is not without its critics.

First, positivists criticise it as it lacks scientific rigour. The scale and representativeness of their research have been criticised. Due to the depth of detail needed to understand motives and meanings, interpretivist research is inevitably carried out on a limited number of cases, on a micro scale.

This has led to the second criticism: that their research is based on such low numbers of participants that it becomes meaningless. In response, however, most interpretivist research does not claim to be representative or generalisable beyond the sample group. By providing rich contextualised accounts of social reality, the readers themselves can decide how far, if at all, the findings can be generalised to other groups (Schofield, 1973).

Thirdly, they have been accused of ignoring and playing down the role of social norms in society, even if the behaviour of individuals is not determined by social structure, there would seem to be a basic order in society which is largely ignored in favour of researching specific events or phenomena. In fact, symbolic interactionism, which forms the theoretical basis of much interpretivist research, has been described as concentrating on deviant minority groups in society, rather than non-deviant majority groups.

Finally, as they try to access subjective understandings, it has been suggested that interpretivist research lacks reliability; if another sociologist tried to replicate their studies they would be unlikely to achieve the same results, due to the depth and detail required.

Feminist methodology

As there is a lack of consensus on what constitutes feminist theory, it follows that the idea of a feminist methodology will be contested. Reinhartz (1992) argues that a feminist methodology is based around 'women's ways of knowing', which by implication suggests a difference from 'men's ways of knowing'. Feminist methodology (some suggest methodologies in the plural) seeks to represent and access the views of all people (regardless of gender), in an attempt to combat 'malestream' sociological research: research conduced by men for men. For Reinhartz, feminist methodology is based around some common features:

◆ being grounded in feminist theory

◆ aiming to bring about social change

◆ including the researcher as a participant and not as the separate 'other' (Fine, 1994)

◆ stressing the importance of the relationship and rapport between the researcher/ researched.

It would follow therefore, that feminist methodology is attractive to qualitative methods of data collection, showing close affinity with the interpretivist research tradition.

However, Ramazanoghlu (2002) and Reinhartz (1992) both argue that there is no reason why feminist methodology would not use quantitative methods if they fit the research purpose. It could be argued that feminist methodology seeks to give specific prominence to the female voice and concerns, more so than traditional sociological research. It is closely associated with some form of feminist theory and can use a range of methods depending on the purpose of the research.

Activity 6

Using the information in this section, copy and complete the following table, identifying the main uses and limitations of positivist and interpretivist research.

	Uses	Limitations
Positivist		
Interpretivist		

Using this information, and placing yourself in the role of a sociologist, would you be drawn to (a) positivist, (b) interpretivist or (c) both research methodologies? Explain your answer.

Skeggs (1997, see page 232) provides an example of feminist methodology. She argues that it was impossible to separate her values from the research process itself. Do you think this discredits the research or enhances it?

Critics of feminist research methodology raise concerns about the objectivity of the research, which is closely bound up with feminist theory. Feminist researchers, however, see this as a strength; in positioning their theoretical values so prominently within the methodology they seek to be as open as possible to the possibility of value judgements influencing the quality of the data collected. Feminists argue that research cannot be value free, **reflexivity** (see below) and the importance of achieving valid data are crucial within feminist methodology and the development of a rapport with their participants gives feminist methodology its character. Feminist researchers would argue that being aware of one's values does not make objectivity unattainable; Skeggs (1997) points out that having values can mean that the researcher is aware or becomes aware of issues that others cannot see. It has also been suggested that feminist methodologies have had their day and that in contemporary sociological research all voices are now represented, it is no longer malestream, so therefore feminist methodology has served its purpose.

Using the paragraph above, identify three criticisms of feminist methodology and explain how the feminists have responded to each one.

Realist methodology

In contrast to feminist and interpretivist methodologies, realists argue that sociological research can follow the logic and methods of the natural sciences, however they adopt and work with a different interpretation of science from the positivists. Realists distinguish between open and closed systems of science. The key difference between the natural and social worlds is that natural science generally operates within 'closed systems', where it is possible to generate hypotheses, make predictions and collect empirical data that support or reject the hypothesis. This is generally the case but not exclusively so; consider the work of meteorologists who study the weather: they are not always working within closed systems of science, they do not work with observable phenomena all the time, yet they can still make predictions (which are frequently wrong) and be considered as a science. Realists argue that social science operates within an 'open system' where causal mechanisms underlie regularities, yet these mechanisms are rarely observable and are subject to rapid and unpredictable change. An example would be the operation of the economy. Sociologists can study the effects of unemployment in a number of different ways (using quantitative and/or qualitative methods), yet lying beneath patterns and regularities of unemployment are causal mechanisms relating to the operation of the economy and capitalism.

Figure 2.1: Causal mechanisms, underlying patterns and trends

So, rather than viewing science as the systematic study of empirical evidence and accumulation and analysis of observable phenomena, the realists argue that there are causal mechanisms underlying patterns and regularities in both the natural and the social world.

1 Can you think of areas other than meteorology where natural scientists work with unobservable phenomena?

2 Think of examples of causal mechanisms that may lie beneath:

- the divorce rate

- the crime rate

- the child poverty rate.

Realists argue that sociological research is not and cannot be value free, it is always linked with theory to some extent. They argue that sociologists should be engaged in the systematic collection of evidence that is both reliable and transparent but capable of accessing and exploring the subjective dimensions of an individual's social experiences. Realists are not committed to quantitative or qualitative methods of data collection, they will use the methods that fit their purpose.

Realism is a contested concept in social research; it is used in relation to philosophical issues and has many different interpretations. It is sometimes used when a researcher is justifying the use of mixed-methods research. In some respects, realist-based methodology sees the fusion of the concepts of social structure and social action.

This section has introduced four main research methodologies which influence and underlie sociological research. Most research can be associated with one or more of these traditions. A key theme throughout these methodologies is value freedom and the position taken on whether value-free research is desirable or possible within sociological research. To end this section, we will explore the concept of value freedom and associated methodological implications.

Value freedom

Value freedom is concerned with the extent to which research can achieve **objectivity**, that is, be free from the bias/personal opinions of the researcher. **Subjectivity** is the opposing concept: the view that values and personal opinion pervade human consciousness and cannot be eliminated or suspended during social research.

The concept of **reflexivity** is associated with value freedom. Reflexivity is a form of self-evaluation, where researchers are constantly thinking about how far their decisions and presence in the research may influence the quality of the data collected. Reflexivity is especially relevant in qualitative research where the presence of the researcher (interviewer effect, socially desirable responses, etc.) has the potential to influence the shape of the research itself. The social characteristics of the researcher; their social class, age, gender and ethnicity may all influence the participants in the study, even if the researcher feels they are being objective. The concept of **researcher imposition** has been used to describe the various ways in which the researcher may influence and shape the study, without even being aware of it. The choice of topic, method, methodology and operationalisation of concepts all have the potential to impose values on the research process, which need to

Positivists argue that sociological research can be value free; that researchers can detach their own values from the research in a quest to gain objective data free of bias.

Interpretivists, on the other hand, argue that sociology cannot be value free, as it is impossible to detach one's values from the research itself. As interpretivist researchers are seeking to access the subjective understandings of social actors, they tend to be explicit about the values that may affect the quality of the data collected. Gouldner (1975) makes a powerful argument that even if the researcher suspends their values/ personal opinions and attempts to adopt a neutral position as researcher, isn't neutrality a value?

Feminists and realists agree with each other than value-free research is not possible or desirable, as theory is inevitably and rightly linked with methodological research questions, choice of method and the interpretation of the data.

Figure 2.2: Theories and value freedom

be limited or acknowledged. To be reflexive is therefore to be introspective in a quest to acknowledge and limit biases and values from the research process.

One means of achieving this is through using **respondent validation**. This is where the respondents are used to check that the data collected from the research are a valid, accurate account of the phenomena being studied. There are various means of doing this.

◆ Feeding the interview transcripts/field notes back to the respondents to read through and check.

◆ Sharing the data analysis with the respondents as a means of limiting misrepresentation.

◆ Using an additional method as a means of checking the validity of an account, for example using interviews alongside a diary.

◆ Some sociologists ask their colleagues to read through the field notes/transcripts to seek an expert opinion of whether the data seem credible as an additional means of validation.

Activity 10

Copy and complete the table below, using the information in this section. Some of the answers have been inserted to help you.

	Is sociology a science?	Can sociological research be value free?	Main uses of the methodology	Main limitations of the methodology
Positivist	Yes, it can and should follow the same procedures as natural science.			
Interpretivist				Limited scale. Lacks scientific rigour and reliability. Too subjective and based on values of the researcher.
Feminist		No, the values of the researcher cannot be ignored or suspended. They need to be built in at every stage.		
Realist				A contested concept used in different ways. Complexities of what an open system is.

The next section looks at the research process itself; reminding us of the main stages in research design, the main methods of data collection studied at AS Level and introducing some new methods and concepts.

Stages in research design

Sociologists do not collect their data by following exactly the same processes and procedures, such is the nature of conducting research on the social world where nothing is predictable and concrete. However, it is possible to say that sociological research covers the same important stages but not necessarily in the same order. Figure 2.3 illustrates the different stages with a basic procedure.

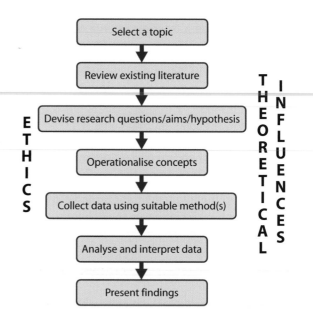

Figure 2.3: Stages in the research process. You will notice that ethical considerations and theoretical influences (positivist, interpretivist, feminist, realist) are placed as free floating; this is because they inform and pervade at all stages

Activity 11

Answer the following questions. You may want to use your notes from AS Sociology, Table 2.1 and the Glossary to help you.

1 List three factors a sociologist would consider when choosing a topic to research.

2 What are the differences between a research question, a hypothesis and research aims?

3 What is meant by the term 'operationalisation' and why is this a crucial part of sociological research?

4 What is the difference between primary and secondary data?

5 List three methods useful for the collection of qualitative data and three methods useful for collecting quantitative data.

6 What is meant by the term 'mixed methods research', and why is the interpretation of this type of research considered to be difficult?

7 Define each of the following concepts and state why they are considered important in achieving high-quality sociological research: validity, reliability, representativeness and generalisability.

In carrying out this activity you will have covered some of the work from AS Level. It is important that you revisit the concepts listed in the AS specification; Table 2.1 lists some of these concepts and offers brief definitions of each.

Concept	Definition
Research questions/ aims/ hypothesis	These determine what the research is trying to find out; they are used to give the research a focus and are usually stated at the beginning of a study
Operationalisation	A process that defines and puts into operation the key terms and concepts, so that readers know exactly what was meant by each key idea
Primary data	Data collected by the sociologist first-hand, using methods such as questionnaires
Secondary data	Data that already exist and were collected by another researcher/ organisation. Texts and statistical data are usually secondary data
Sampling	A smaller group of a larger target population, used because time and money constraints prohibit accessing a whole target population
Access	Used in relation to gaining access to the sample, often through a **gatekeeper**
Ethics	Procedures for ensuring that research participants are guaranteed anonymity, privacy and confidentiality. The process for gaining the consent to carry out the research
Pilot study	A test or pre-run of the research
Interpretation of data	The process of deciding what the data collected actually show; a very skilled process
Validity	The extent to which the research provides a true picture of the social reality of those being studied
Reliability	The extent to which the data are consistent and capable of verification by another researcher
Representativeness	The extent to which the sample is representative of the wide target population
Generalisability	The extent to which it is possible to apply the findings to the wider target group
Triangulation	Allowing findings to be cross-checked using more than one method, often to enhance the credibility of the findings
Methodological pluralism	Using more than one method to build a more coherent and fuller set of data

Table 2.1: Definitions of a selection of key methodological concepts from the AS specification

In small groups, select one of the following research aims, and devise a research strategy for achieving it (remember, you are designing it, not carrying it out).

- To find out the ways in which middle-aged people are represented in the media.

- To find out the extent to which working-class children are disadvantaged in the education system.

- To find out whether men are disadvantaged by the Criminal Justice System.

- To find out the influence pressure groups have on decision-making processes in the UK.

You should cover the following headings, but may want to change the order:

- method/s
- operationalisation of concepts
- sample/selection of participants
- ethics
- theoretical influences
- processes of data interpretation
- presentations
- findings.

When you have designed your project, make a short presentation to your class and ask them to evaluate it, specifying three aspects that they think will work and three potential problems.

The remainder of this section deals with the advantages and disadvantages of different methods of data-collection, before proceeding to consider some new methodological concepts you need to be familiar with at A Level.

Quantitative data-collection methods

Quantitative data-collection methods are the favoured choice of positivist researchers. They are useful in creating numerical data through standardised measurement devices that can be replicated when dealing with large sample sizes and data sets. The interpretation of quantitative data is generally based on statistical analysis.

Questionnaires

Questionnaires are designed for self-completion, and can be administered in many ways: face to face, by post or increasingly via the internet. Some of the advantages and disadvantages of using questionnaires are listed below.

Advantages of questionnaires

- Economical, relatively easy to administer, relatively low-cost, less time-consuming than other methods.

- No chance of face-to-face researcher influence.

- Relatively high in reliability.

- Can be used with large sample sizes from which generalisations can be made.

- Can be administered and returned in various formats: post, internet.

- Standardised responses to standardised questions: all respondents are faced with the same questions in the same order and format.

- Potential to pre-code the answers and the availability of software packages such as SPSS makes data analysis potentially more straightforward.

Disadvantages of questionnaires

- A questionnaire is only as good as the questions it contains. If the questions are misinterpreted then the data will be low in validity.

- Pre-coded, standardised questions can be off-putting to respondents, resulting in a low response rate.

- No chance to check the truthfulness of the answer, again affecting the validity of the research findings.

- Postal questionnaires can be expensive and have low response rates; accessing a representative sample can therefore be difficult.

The Future Foundation (2006, see page 201) used questionnaires as part of its study into middle-class belonging and lifestyle in the UK. Why do you think it did this? Why would questionnaires be useful in dealing with a large sample size?

Weblink

Questions from the British Crime Survey, which uses structured interviews, can be read at The Question Bank (see 'Websites', page ii).

What does the range of questions suggest about the task of data interpretation?

Structured interviews

> *Advantages of structured interviews*
>
> - Standardised answers to standardised questions: all respondents are faced with the same questions in the same order and format.
>
> - Potential to pre-code the answers and the availability of computer software make data analysis potentially more straightforward.
>
> - High response rate as new respondents can be accessed if sample size drops.
>
> - The presence of the interviewer to explain any question (if allowed).

> *Disadvantages of structured interviews*
>
> - An interview is only as good as the questions it contains. If the questions are misinterpreted then the data will be low in validity.
>
> - Pre-coded, standardised questions can be off-putting to respondents, resulting in lower validity or non-completion of the interview.
>
> - Potential for some interviewer effect through body language and tone of questioning. The social characteristics of the researcher (age, gender, ethnicity etc.) may influence the responses.
>
> - Interviews are time-consuming and the cost of paying the interviewers has to be allowed for.

Semi-structured interviews

In a semi-structured interview the interviewer is present and has a clear list of issues to be addressed and questions to be answered. The questions are generally open-ended and can be asked in any order. Due to the flexible nature of the interview, quantitative data could be collected (which is why this method has been included here).

Statistical data

Official statistics are compiled and owned by the government (under Crown copyright) but are available for use by anyone, for no fee. The largest survey is the Census, which is conducted by the government every ten years. Non-official statistics are also used by sociologists, these are collected by researchers who are not working for the government. The study looking at the causes of poverty on page 234 is an example of a study using statistical data from both official and non-official sources. The Future Foundation study (2006) on the future of the middle class used data from its own questionnaire research and statistical data from the British Household Panel Survey.

> *Advantages of statistical data*
>
> - As secondary data they are cheap, usually free (official statistics) and relatively easy to access.
>
> - Patterns and trends can be clearly visible.
>
> - They deal with large sample sizes and are considered as representative.
>
> - They can be used and re-used to test different variables.
>
> - They are considered reliable as the data generated can be checked year on year.

U4

2

Exploring sociological research

Disadvantages of statistical data

- Statistical data are open to misuse; they can be manipulated to show what the researcher wants them to show.

- There is potential for misuse by the government or organisation compiling them, in order to show what they want them to show.

- Some researchers use statistical data but do not understand them, meaning they can be misinterpreted.

- They cannot express reasons for trends, and reduce everything to a number, therefore they are criticised for being low in validity.

- They are secondary data, which makes it difficult to verify the data.

Activity 14

Statistics compiled by others are an example of secondary data. Give three reasons why sociologists may want to use these and three potential problems with them.

Content analysis

Advantages of content analysis

- It quantifies the meaning of text. It can uncover the terminology/ideas being used and the frequency with which they occur.

- It is relatively high in reliability and as it follows systematic procedures it should be replicable.

- It is relatively cheap.

- It can be used on words, images or sound and is of major importance in studying the mass media.

- On straightforward pieces it can yield useful results.

Disadvantages of content analysis

- The initial coding of texts is crucial in establishing the categories to be analysed.

- If the coding is inaccurate then the findings will be considered invalid.

- It could be accused of analysing text out of context.

- It is not considered as a valid method on its own for complex textual analysis.

Activity 15

Using pages 116–124, make notes on the use of content analysis.

Qualitative data-collection methods

Qualitative data-collection methods are the favoured choice of interpretivists and most feminist researchers. They are useful in creating rich, valid, deep textual data that can explore meanings and motives. The interpretation of qualitative data is a lengthy and complex process based on the analysis of transcripts/field notes. It often uses an inductive process known as grounded theory (Strauss and Corbin, 1998) where the researcher reads and transcribes the data in an ongoing process until they are confident that the emerging thematic analysis is a valid interpretation of the data.

Observation

Observation is a useful technique for many research topics, and there are different types of observation: participant/non-participant, and structured/unstructured. The differences are based around the extent to which the researcher immerses themselves within the lives of the group being studied and the extent to which the researcher identifies what they are observing in advance of the study.

Activity 16

Structured non-participant observation is often chosen as a suitable method of data collection for researching classroom interactions in schools. Can you think why?

Advantages of participant observation

- Limited changes in behaviour/Hawthorne effect gloss.

- Data collected are high in ecological validity gloss.

- Provision of a holistic account, focused on the individual's own point of view.

- Strong in accessing the subjective experiences of social actors.

- Limitation on equipment needed.

- Data collected should be valid and achieve verstehen of social reality.

Disadvantages of participant observation

- Gaining access to the group.

- Going native.

- Difficulty in taking notes.

- Ethical issues.

- Commitment and time.

- Whether the data are representative.

- Whether the data are reliable.

- Risk to the observer, particularly if the observation involves groups who use drugs or violence.

- Social characteristics of the researcher are crucial to its success.

Ethnography

Ethnographic studies use participant observation and often unstructured interviews to provide an in-depth account and analysis of a social group or culture.

Advantages of ethnographic studies

- Direct observation of the people under study.

- Detailed and rich data can be collected over time, increasing validity.

- Strong in ecological validity.

- Provide a holistic understanding.

- Good for achieving empathy/verstehen.

Disadvantages of ethnographic studies

- Lack of reliability as the research is difficult to repeat.

- Ethical issues relating to consent in observation.

- Problems of gaining access.

- Insider knowledge/status may be required for access and can lead to problems in gaining objective data.

- Tendency for ethnographic accounts to become based on stories and perceived as such.

- Small scale and lacking generalisability.

Activity 17

Thiel (2007, see page 232) used participant observation in his ethnographic study of builders' workplace practices in London. Why would this method be a suitable choice for his research and what difficulties might it lead to?

Interviews

Qualitative data can be generated by unstructured interviews and by focus-group interviews, both explored in this section. Semi-structured interviews can provide qualitative and/or quantitative data depending on how they are designed.

Exploring sociological research

Advantages of unstructured interviews

- Ability to gain empathy and insight, achieving an understanding through asking questions and responding to answers.
- Flexibility to deviate from the topic under discussion.
- Rapport can be created and sustained through the conversational basis of the interview.
- The potential for rich valid data from a small group of people.
- High response rate as interviews are pre-arranged.
- Greater depth of information as interviewer can probe and prompt for further data.
- Additional questions can be asked when they need to be, placing less pressure on the interview schedule. This also allows for questions to check the accuracy and plausibility of respondents' answers.

Disadvantages of unstructured interviews

- Time-consuming to conduct and analyse.
- Interviewer effect – whether respondents answer truthfully or in the way they think the interviewer wants them to.
- Difficulty in data analysis due to length and complexity of transcripts.
- The social characteristics of the researcher are crucial in accessing valid data.
- Lack of reliability – whether the interviews could be repeated by another sociologist.
- Whether they are representative because time constraints usually restrict the interview to a small number of people.
- Skill of the interviewer in accessing the information without digressing onto different topics.
- Importance of interview setting for achieving ecological validity.

Studies by Devine (2005) and Savage et al. (2005) both used unstructured interviews in studies that aimed to gain access and understanding of social class cultures and belonging in the north of England. Can you think why this method would be useful for the research aims?

Semi-structured interviews

These contain some pre-set standardised questions or topic areas and the opportunity for additional questions to be asked when necessary.

Focus-group interviews

These are used to access attitudes, feelings, beliefs, expressions and experiences from a small group of respondents at the same time. Their main use is in the insight and data produced by interaction between the participants. In this sense they are a more collaborative research method than most others.

Advantages of focus groups

- They enable issues to be explored which might otherwise remain unknown.
- They can encourage a wider range of respondents to be involved because of the group basis.
- They can be tailored around specific groups' needs.
- The group facilitator can promote debate within the group.
- They have the potential to empower the participants.

Disadvantages of focus groups

- It can be difficult to record and transcribe the data.
- Respondents may not disclose sensitive material.
- The interviewer effect is not eliminated.
- The discussions can become dominated by specific individuals.

Personal documents

Different types of documents can be used in sociological research; these can be in written or visual form. Personal documents include letters, diaries and photographs.

Advantages of personal documents

- They are cheap and can be easy to access.
- They are permanent.
- Their interpretation could be checked by another researcher.

Disadvantages of personal documents

- Whether they are credible and authentic – in other words, can we trust them?
- How representative they are.
- Problems in interpreting their meaning.

Activity 18

Personal accounts of racism within the House of Commons (see page 223) would be considered as personal documents, as they are based on personal stories/memoirs (Mossa, 2008).

How useful do you think sociologists would find such documents? In your answer, consider the validity of the data and whether data like that could be achieved through any other method?

Mixed methodology

Some studies use a combination of methods to access the data they require. This can be in the form of qualitative and/or quantitative data-collection methods. This approach is used as a way of building up a more complete and accurate account (methodological pluralism) or as a means of cross-checking the quality of the data collected, possibly to enhance the validity or reliability of the study (triangulation).

Activity 19

Jones (1997, see page 207) used a mixed-methods approach in a study on the underclass. Can you offer reasons for this choice of methods? What problems might it lead to?

Having explored the research methods you studied at AS Level, you are now in a position to add to your understanding of the research process. The remainder of this section introduces some new and concepts and ideas.

Longitudinal studies

A **longitudinal study** is a piece of research carried out over a prolonged period of time, with a key focus on researching the process of change over time. As the data are collected in time sequence, this enables changes and connections to be established. Some longitudinal studies have taken years to complete, often in an ongoing ethnographic form (see Skeggs, 1997). Others have been in operation for a number of years but focus on research at specific times; analysing cases at specific time periods. An example of a longitudinal study is the West of Scotland 11–16 Study, which focused on the health and health behaviours of children aged 11, 13 and 15 (West and Sweeting, 2001). Longitudinal studies often used panels of respondents who are contacted at key intervals.

However, they are expensive to undertake and suffer from the problem of attrition, where respondents may drop out or withdraw from the research before it is completed. It has also been suggested that some longitudinal studies provide little more than snapshots of events carried out at predetermined moments in time, and lacking validity.

Activity 20

An example of a longitudinal study is the television documentary *7UP*, which followed a group of children from the age of seven into adulthood, studying the progress in their lives every seven years. Based on the Jesuit saying 'Give me a child until he is seven, and I will show you the man', the documentary tracks the lives of a group of children through life. In September 2005, *49UP* was screened on television. If your teacher can access this or any of the other programmes, they provide excellent viewing on social inequality, differences and the issue of attrition in longitudinal studies.

Watch an episode and identify examples of social inequality and difference illustrated.

Case studies

Case studies have been defined in various ways. Some sociologists use them as a research method that focuses on the exploration of a 'case' in depth. For example, some ethnographic studies can be seen as case studies of a particular location/event. Other researchers use case studies as a research strategy that focuses on a specific event/place/social group in depth while using other research methods to access the data required. Thus you could have a case study of a whole school that uses questionnaires and interviews as the methods of research, equally a case study of one class in a school could be used.

The key issue in a case study is what constitutes the unit of analysis. In a study of a school, the unit of analysis may be four teachers, it may be a group of students, or the senior leadership/management team. Case studies are generally used to produce data that are high in validity, but they have been accused of lacking representativeness and often generalisability. However, case studies do not claim to achieve representativeness: they are often carried out to focus on typical or indeed atypical cases in depth.

Pilot studies

A **pilot study** serves the purpose of a test run, a first time through a particular research method to check that the research design/method meets the needs of the research question/aims/hypothesis. For example, if a researcher was using a questionnaire they would first construct the questionnaire and pilot it on a small sample to check that the questions worked. Pilot studies form important stages of most research strategies, especially with questionnaires and structured interviews, where standardised measurement tools need to be created prior to the full-blown study itself. Pilot studies enable any obvious problems to be detected and corrected. They also enable the feasibility of the research strategy to be checked, and can allow for the collection of some preliminary data which can be used to fine-tune other aspects of the research design, such as interpretation of results, ethics.

However, it has been suggested that conducting a pilot study in qualitative research may be undesirable. In qualitative interviewing and ethnographic research, the data collection methods are often fined tuned as part of the full-blown study itself. It has also been suggested

that conducting pilot studies may lead to the contamination of the research process, as the preliminary findings from any pilot study may be inaccurate and if these are used to justify changes to the research design, this can impact on the validity of the data collected.

Activity 21

Select a topic relevant to your school/college on which you know most people will have an opinion. Devise a list of not more than ten questions to explore the views and feelings of a sample of respondents on that topic.

Pilot the questions on a small sample of people, and evaluate your design of the questions. What worked and what would you need to change?

Sampling

Sampling is the process of selecting a group of respondents from the **target population** on which to conduct the research. Some samples are representative and some non-representative, depending on the needs of the research. A representative sample usually involves a sample frame: a list of the whole target population from which a sample may be selected. School registers, the postcode address file and telephone directories are all examples of sampling frames.

Activity 22

1 For some studies a sampling frame of the target population is not available. Think of three social groups for which a sampling frame would not be available.

2 What are the problems of using a telephone directory as a sampling frame?

There are three main sampling techniques for achieving a probability/random sample, often conceptualised as names out of a hat.

1　Simple **random sampling** involves selecting a number of sampling units (individuals/groups) from the sampling frame.

2　Systematic random sampling is a variation on the above and involves picking one unit from the sampling frame and then choosing every *n*th name after that.

3 **Stratified random sampling** involves dividing the population according to the numbers of people with the social characteristics required, for example gender or age, and then making a random selection within those groups. This type has the greatest probability of achieving representativeness, as the social characteristics of the sample form a key part of the selection process.

The main techniques for achieving a non-random, non-probability sample are as follows:

1 **Quota sampling**, where the sociologist makes a decision about the numbers of people they want from certain social characteristics and then selects them to fit their purpose. The sample should match the needs of the research directly, however the sample may well be biased.

2 **Snowball sampling**, which involves a sociologist finding one person they are interested in and then asking them if they know anyone else who might be willing to take part, hence the snowball effect of rolling growth. This approach is used when trying to access a difficult sample.

3 **Purposeful sampling**, which involves focusing the research specifically on the type(s) of people needed and seeking them out. This is similar to a quota sample but perhaps less rigorous.

4 Volunteer sampling where, as the name suggests, a sample comes from those volunteering to take part in a study. This can sometimes come from advertisements in local newspapers or local shops where particular types of people are required.

5 Opportunity sampling, when the researcher uses people who happen to be around at the time and place of the study.

Access

Different sampling techniques involve different issues of **access**. Access can be gained through putting advertisements in local newspapers or shops. Bhopal (2000) gained access to her sample of South Asian women living in East London through a snowball technique and placing an advertisement in a local shop window asking for volunteers to take part. Some studies require a **gatekeeper**: someone who knows the people and is able to provide the sociologist with initial access to the group. If you were conducting research in a school, the gatekeeper may well occupy a formal role such as the head teacher, research in a workplace would involve the employer/manager.

Some social groups, however, are more difficult to gain access to and rely on 'insiders', people who have links with the group and who are willing help, insiders could also be called informal gatekeepers (Patton, 2002). If a researcher wanted to conduct research on a group of homeless men in a city centre, they would be likely to need the help of an 'insider' who may be a voluntary worker or friend of the group.

Activity 23

Read the boxed text below and answer the questions that follow.

Taylor and Kearney (2005) conducted a study that involved accessing drug-using parents, in seeking to explore the impact of drug use on the day-to-day lives of parents and children. Drug-using parents are a hidden population, very difficult to gain access to. Contact with users were made through a Project Advisory Group, which included a number of specialist agencies. Three drug users (one of whom was a parent) volunteered to participate in the study and underwent training in interviewing skills, with a view to gaining access to a wider group through their insider status. Using a snowball sample these interviewers built up a rapport with the participants based on trust and mutual respect; which led to the accumulation of high-level insightful data. The researchers argued that this data could not have been accessed without the help of this insider group. The insider group were not paid for their role in the research.

1 Why are drug-using parents a hidden population, difficult to access?

2 Why do you think the insiders were able to build up a rapport and level of trust more easily than the university researchers?

3 Do you think this study illustrates any ethical concerns?

Ethics

Sociological research is governed by codes of practice to ensure that research is conducted in an ethical manner. Ethical concerns include gaining informed consent from the participants, the right to anonymity, confidentiality and the right to withdraw from the research at any point. Research into social inequality and difference inevitably means that some participants are drawn from vulnerable sections of the population: children, young people, older people and those on the margins of society at risk of social exclusion. Gaining informed consent from vulnerable groups can be particularly difficult and research suggests that such groups are often very willing to participate without considering what is involved. Constraints on time, emotions, and the fact that most participants are not paid for their involvement are all part of gaining informed consent.

Section summary

The main methodological approaches are: positivist, interpretivist, realist and feminist.

Use the following words to write a paragraph explaining the key themes of this section.

- Methodology
- Value freedom
- Gatekeeper
- Longitudinal study
- Reflexivity
- Researcher imposition

Stretch and Challenge Activity

Devise a research strategy to answer the following research question:

What are the causes of social exclusion in the contemporary UK?

Exam practice

These questions will be based on a piece of source material. See the Exam Café on page 255 for an example.

1   Outline and explain the advantages of using semi-structured interviews in sociological research. (15 marks)

2   Assess the usefulness of using feminist methodology to research the experiences of female professionals in the workplace. (25 marks)

ExamCafé
Relax, refresh, result!

Hot tips

Carlos

I'm confident that I know the material – it's just using the source material that concerns me. I must remember to refer to it directly in parts (a) and (b), but not in (c) and (d).

Tash

I really didn't want to answer a question on age, but I should remember what my teacher and the examiners say – to apply the theories to it. It's a newer area of research.

Joe

This is OK – I know my stuff but should remember to read the source material through at least twice before writing the answer, as I know I should refer to it in (a) and (b) to improve my marks.

Revision checklist

You might find it helpful to make some notes on the topics below, to check your knowledge and record your own sources of information.

Topic	Studies	Do I know this?	Look here
The uses of questionnaires.			
The uses and potential difficulties of mixed-methods research.			
Evidence of social class inequalities: • workplace • education • health.			
Sociological explanations of age disadvantage: • functionalist • postmodern • Weberian • feminist.			

Get the result!

West and Sweeting, The West of Scotland 11–16 Study

This was a longitudinal school-based study, focusing on the health and health behaviours of a range of children from different social class backgrounds .The children were surveyed at the ages of 11, 13 and 15, using a mixed-methods approach which combined self-completion questionnaires with mini-interviews. One of the aims of the research was to find out the extent to which children and young people can provide accurate, reliable data on their parents' occupation and other status characteristics.

At the first stage of the research the children, aged 11, and were given self-completion questionnaires to complete at school. Due to the difficulties some 11-year-olds face in answering questionnaires, researchers were on hand to provide motivation, answer queries and in some cases to offer help (reading out questions, etc). On completion of the questionnaire the children's responses were checked through by one of the research team. This level of help was considered particularly important at the age of 11, when children needed help of various kinds.

The questionnaire contained questions on a wide range of topics, including physical and mental health, health behaviours, lifestyles, school and family life, and the future. One of the questions at the end of the survey referred to job aspirations and read: 'What job do you want to hold when you grow up?' A mini-interview was conducted with each child as they completed the questionnaire. During the interview the researcher asked the child how they had responded to that particular question. This in turn eased the discussion into talking about aspects of their parents' situation; including parental occupation/s.

Parents were also given a questionnaire to complete at home. This was returned in a sealed envelope to the research team via the school. One of the findings of the research was the high level of agreement between children/young people and parents in their accounts of their parent's economic status. The researchers thought that the link between the questionnaire response and mini-interview was a key reason for the success of the research.

(a) Using the item and your own sociological knowledge, explain the ways in which questionnaires are used in sociological research. **(15 marks)**

(b) Outline **and** assess the usefulness of adopting a mixed-methods approach in sociological research. **(25 marks)**

(c) Outline the evidence that social class inequalities exist in the contemporary UK. **(20 marks)**

(d) Assess sociological explanations of age disadvantage in the contemporary UK. **(40 marks)**

Student answer

Examiner comment:

A good point, but the answer needs to explain why. Make slightly more use of the item here; in relation to the children and the parents, why would questionnaires be used?

(a) Questionnaires are designed to be completed by individuals without the face-to-face influence of a researcher. They are particularly useful for researching potentially sensitive topics, such as health behaviour and lifestyle as in the West and Sweeting study.

Examiner comment:

A good point, but again the student should say why, and needs to show some knowledge of **generalisability** or representativeness.

As the researcher is not present, the potential for interviewer effect is ruled out, although participants may still give socially desirable responses. Questionnaires which use closed-ended questions can produce quantifiable data from a large sample, making the data easier to generalise from.

As the questions and possible responses are standardised, these can be designed around key ideas or indicators, which should improve the quality of the data collected. The Future Foundation used questionnaires when researching the changing nature of the class structure in the UK, reaching a large sample and able to produce statistical data to show patterns and make predictions. Questionnaires can be used as a single method or as part of a mixed method approach as in the study above.

Examiner comment:

A good link to the item, but the student needs to discuss how questionnaires are used in this study, i.e. as a way into accessing qualitative data on a difficult topic.

They are the favoured method of positivists, who believe that the study of society should follow the same procedures used in natural science: quantifiable data, high in reliability and able to be verified. Questionnaires that use closed-ended questions are an ideal way of accessing this kind of data.

Examiner comment:

The student is right to make a link to theory, but this could be expanded to open-ended questions too, which don't fit the needs of postivists so well. Overall a good response, but it falls short of being excellent. More use should be made of the item, as it is there to help more than this student has used it. Open-ended questions and methods of questionnaire administration could also be included.

(b) Mixed-methods research involves using more than one method of data collection in a study. It is used when sociologists want to build up a more coherent, fuller account of an issue, or if they want to use different methods to cross-check the validity and reliablity of their findings. West and Sweeting use interviews and questionnaires in their mixed methods approach, but as a way of accessing difficult data from the children (aged 11). They seem to use questionnaires as a way of initiating a conversation (mini-interview) with the child and then focusing on the key questions they want to ask. In this way mixed methods are used as a way of planning the research in different stages as part of a progression which uses different methods for their strengths and weaknesses.

Examiner comment:

This is very good, with clear definitions and an excellent interpretation of the item, well contextualised.

Triangulation is achieved when sociologists use different methods to cross-check the accuracy and consistency of their data, for example, using interviews as a way of following up questionnaire responses. The sociologist could ask the same sorts of questions by as part of a conversation to check that the participant is telling the truth, or as a form of respondent validation. Alternatively, methodological pluralism is used when sociologists want to build up a fuller, more complete picture. For example, using participant observation and in-depth interviewing as part of an ethnographic study to gain a greater quantity and quality of data. The greatest use of mixed methods is that it can fit the research purpose.

Examiner comment:

This student is making good points here, with relevant concepts and definitions, but needs to be sure to explain these points. What is fitness for purpose, and how does it relate to mixed methods? Another technique would be to use a study to illustrate the point/s.

Mixed-methods research has many strengths but it also has weaknesses; it is time-consuming and can lead to over-complicated studies. However it is obvious why sociologists are attracted to it, as it overcomes so many potential barriers and can be a way of combining the strengths of quantitative and qualitative data.

Examiner comment:

This is evaluation and would score some marks, but it needs to be more detailed. In particular the issues of time and complication need explanation, but most importantly the issue of data analysis is missing. What happens when the findings do not fit together and show contradictory results?

(c) The UK is a class-ridden society. It always has been and despite claims from some postmodern sociologists that 'class is dead', the wealth of evidence showing class inequalities is too great to argue otherwise. In this answer I will illustrate some of these differences focusing on topics I have studied.

Examiner comment:

This is a good start as it focuses the answer.

There is a clearly defined upper class in the UK, defined by its aristocratic blue blood. Operating high degrees of social closure, this group is literally out of reach of the rest of the population, as marrying outside the inner circle is frowned on. There is also a visible underclass in the UK, defined by their marginalisation and insecurity. The fact that such stark distinctions and divisions are visible in the UK illustrates that inequality is evident.

Examiner comment:

Again a good point made here. It would be improved with some names of sociologists or evidence – Scott? Murray?

Examiner comment:

Some excellent data in here and clear links to lifetime differences. Again high quality work. The use of Weberian concepts and evidence will always improve your work and mark.

Examiner comment:

This point is good but could be developed. How does this show a class inequality?

Examiner comment:

Evidence on educational attainment would improve this answer.

Examiner comment:

This is a potentially strong answer. It needs a bit more depth and evidence, but is clearly strong on concepts and evidence in a number of places.

Examiner comment:

This is a good introduction, setting the scene for what will follow. The student needs to say something about the type of disadvantages.

Examiner comment:

The paragraph focuses on functionalism and touches on the young and old. It should have included a paragraph prior to this on the types of disadvantage faced by different ages in the UK.

In the workplace the working classes are much more likely to occupy jobs in the secondary labour market – with weak work and market situations. The middle class can access employment in the growing service economy or the professions, with stronger work and market positions. This leads to differences in income and earnings. The Future Foundation Report found that the average annual income in the UK was £22,900; for the working class it was £20,500; for the middle class it was £25,500. This is clear evidence of social class inequality. These differences in earnings manifest themselves in many ways, the ownership of wealth being very divided and also the ability to pay into private pension schemes (Ginn and Arber).

Differences in income may affect a person's potential to buy services, goods and even a lifestyle. The middle and upper classes are much more likely to attend private schools than the working class, 32 per cent of current MPs attended independent/private schools, which educate 7 per cent of young people nationally. This has been described as an 'old boys' network' – people with strong degrees of social capital who look after themselves and represent the views of the majority.

Away from politics young people who are educated privately are best placed to achieve the most in terms of educational attainment. With high levels of economic and cultural capital (Bourdieu) they are well placed to take advantage of their parents' social capital and networking potential. Compare these people to the life chances of the builders in Thiel's study and you will see differences and inequalities. Thiel studied working-class builders in London and argued that they had high levels of social capital within working-class communities, fuelled with high levels of physical capital (strength).

The middle and upper classes are also likely to be able to buy private healthcare and insurance. Teenage mums are seven times more likely to come from manual working backgrounds than from professional backgrounds. This again shows a social difference and an implied social inequality

(d) Age disadvantage is one of the less well researched areas in sociology. Nevertheless, sociologists have attempted to explain the causes of age disadvantage through their existing theories. Functionalists and postmodernists have probably been the most successful in doing this.

Functionalists argue that the ageing process is part of a process of social disengagement, where older people begin to lose their different social roles and prepare for the latter stages of their life, almost making way for younger people to take their place in the social hierarchy. Having a compulsory state retirement age is one way in which older people begin the process of disengagement, as they leave the workplace and enter a phase of life associated with ageing. At the other extreme, the beginning of compulsory formal education at the age of five can be viewed as a starting point for social inclusion, almost as a way of engaging with society. Parsons focuses on age and social roles and argues that old people lose their roles and experience feelings

of isolation and loneliness. For younger people the teenage years begin to build a bridge between childhood and adulthood, and enable young people to take on more responsibility stage by stage. For both the young and old, age directly influences the roles they are playing in life.

Functionalism did contribute heavily to the age disadvantage debate, despite being accused of having been written by white middle-class Americans, writing about their own closeted communities. As with functionalism in general, it assumes that age disadvantage is a collective experience and fails to differentiate between men and women, different social classes or ethnic groups. It assumes there is a homogenous collective disadvantage experienced by the 'old' and the 'young', whereas more recent research has shown this is not the case.

Women are more likely to be disadvantaged in later life than men. They tend to live longer and having earned less during their working lives, to be much less likely to have private pension provision. The term 'feminisation of poverty' has been used to describe this situation. Radical feminists might argue that this is a result of patriarchy: another way in which men dominate women. Marxist feminists are more likely to explain this by referring to the operation of the capitalist system and women's position in it.

Marxist concepts such as the reserve army of labour could be applied to explain the disadvantage faced by older and younger people in the labour market.

Weberian sociologists would use the concept of the glass ceiling to explain how older people are systematically disadvantaged in the labour market. Older people become too expensive to employ, and as a result they face ageism. Old people and younger age groups could also be considered as status groups. The older people are a negatively privileged group (Parkin), the younger ones are a positively privileged group.

Ginn and Arber researched private pension provision by age, ethnicity and gender. They found strong links between the three variables, and social class too. Pakistani and Bangladeshi women were the most disadvantaged in the private pensions market and this reflects their weak work and market situation. They have earned less and are less likely to be able to contribute to a private scheme, becoming the most likely social group to suffer economically. When you think about the cause of this, it is both cultural and structural. Structurally, this group of women occupy a marginal position, based on a combination of factors: their age, gender, ethnicity and social class — this disadvantage perpetuates inequality which no economic system can address through government support (Welfare State). Culturally however, it could be argued that the UK allows such dependency to exist through accommodating a liberal approach to work and social security provision. Ginn and Arber's work shows how age alone cannot be the sole disadvantage faced by a social group. Individuals have a gender, social class and ethnicity too.

Postmodernsists argue that the diversity of experience makes it meaningless to carry out first-hand research on age disadvantage. It is experienced by different people in different ways.

Examiner comment:

This is a good evaluative paragraph, displaying understanding of functionalism in general and in relation to age disadvantage.

Examiner comment:

Yes, but how?

Examiner comment:

A good point but again how, and what is a privileged status group? The student needs to explain these points more fully.

Examiner comment:

This is a good example to use as it focuses on a piece of research and helps to raise the evaluative point of the intersection. It is good practice to incorporate the structure/culture distinction in any answer where it is relevant.

Examiner comment:

Overall, the answer lacks a conclusion, it lacks a full exploration of what age disadvantage is, but it does attempt to deal with different explanations. It is stronger on evaluation than on knowledge.

Glossary

The glossary includes terms that may be of value in further reading, in addition to those terms that have been highlighted in the text.

access how to get in touch with the target population or a sample of the target population

age (1) a person's chronological age; (2) a stage in life

ageism discrimination and/or prejudice based on age

agenda-setting a process that involves shaping a news story and focusing on particular issues within it, thereby deciding what issues should be brought to the attention of the public and which should not

alienation an individual's feeling that things are beyond their control

amplification an idea linked to labelling theory, which believes that the reaction of the police, courts and media can make an initial act of deviance greater than it originally was

anarchism (literally 'without rule') an ideology that believes that all forms of compulsory government are unnecessary

anomie a concept developed by Durkheim and used by other writers such as Merton. It refers to a sense of normlessness, whereby people feel separated from the values of society and the people around them. It is seen to produce crime, as those who are unconnected to society's values will be more likely to be unconstrained by them

assimilation giving up one's own ethnic culture and adopting that of the mainstream

big business the generic term for all companies, whether multi-national or trans-national corporations, which operate on a large scale in the modern world

broken windows a theory that if minor types of disorder like vandalism are stopped, then larger crimes will be stopped too. It is associated with zero tolerance

case study method or approach that looks at a case in depth

censorship regulating and controlling the media by preventing material from reaching its audience or by restricting the audience being reached

cheap labour with regard to vocational education, the accusation that employers get young people onto vocational schemes just to carry out essential tasks for low pay, but without actually learning anything. In addition, employers may receive government subsidies to take these trainees on, and thus get workers virtually for free. Some employers promise jobs after the training period to get workers to work hard, but these jobs never materialise

chivalry thesis the idea that the police and courts will treat women leniently and be less likely to impose punishment on them than they would on men, as women are believed to be more vulnerable and more likely to suffer from punishment

civil disobedience actions in pursuit of political goals which involve (usually minor) law-breaking

civil rights the rights of ordinary citizens to freedom and equality under the law of the land

class conflict the struggle between groups with different economic interests in society

class consciousness an awareness amongst a class of people that they share common interests

collective behaviour the unified behaviour patterns resulting from membership of groups, in which individuals can be influenced by those around them to take part in actions such as riots and crowd violence

collective consumption the shared use of public services by particular groups in society

collective identity the unified belief patterns resulting from membership of groups, in which individuals have a mutual influence on one another in the development of a shared sense of purpose and self-image

compensatory education the idea that extra help should be given to those social groups who underperform in education. It has traditionally been associated with the working class and ethnic minorities. This form of education has been associated with positive discrimination

competitiveness in this context, the ability of the economy to produce high-quality goods or services for a relatively low price, so that British goods will be bought at home and abroad and employers will need workers

comprehensive school a secondary school that educates all children together under one roof, regardless of ability, social class, gender and ethnicity

concentration in the media, a trend whereby ownership becomes concentrated in the hands of a small number of powerful individuals or organisations

conservatism an ideology that believes in tradition and supports tried and tested institutions and customs

content analysis a research method used to quantify a particular aspect of media content by counting or measuring it

corporate crime crime committed by an organisation for its own benefit. It is distinct from white-collar crime, which can be committed by middle-class individuals for their own personal gain

crime an activity that breaks the law

crime prevention usually, situational crime-prevention measures, but some would argue that wider measures like reducing poverty are crime-prevention measures

criminal iceberg the idea that a vast number of crimes do not appear in the official statistics. It implies that the statistics lack validity

criminalisation a process whereby people or their actions become defined as criminal. This has the consequence of those people being treated as criminals and has the potential to push them further into criminality

cultural capital the cultural advantages possessed by the middle and upper classes. These mean that the educational system will favour these groups while appearing to treat everyone equally. Values, norms and linguistic skills are a way in which wealth and privilege are passed from one generation to another

cultural deprivation a lack of values, norms and linguistic skills that are seen as essential for educational success. It is argued that the working class lack these things due to inadequate socialisation. This concept is normally employed by functionalist and new right sociologists; in some models of cultural deprivation the family transmits a subculture of criminality and deviance

cultural reproduction the process of passing on the norms and values of social groups between generations, associated with Marxism

culture jamming changing and undermining the advertisements used by companies to promote their products

cybernetworking the use of the internet to develop global networks of individuals with shared concerns

cyberocracy internet democracy

defensive concerned with protecting/defending a particular state of affairs

democracy literally, 'rule by the people', which in modern societies usually takes the form of all adults voting every few years to elect people to govern on their behalf, (i.e. representative democracy)

demographic concerned with the study of population patterns and trends

demonstration an attempt by a large group of people to express particular views (usually peacefully)

determinism a view that sees human behaviour as the fixed result of particular influences, events or experiences and does not acknowledge the possibility of a different result

deviance an action that is thought to be abnormal

deviancy amplification the theory that the role of the media is to strengthen and magnify deviance, or the appearance of deviance, in society

direct action attempts by ordinary people to influence political decisions by taking matters into their own hands

direct theories views on media effects that see the media as having an immediate and powerful influence on an audience

discourse a set of ideas that people believe in to make sense of the world but which has built-in assumptions of power and control (after Foucault)

disengagement movement from the mainstream to the periphery of society

diversification in the media, a trend towards companies owning a variety of media sectors or even branching out to take over businesses outside of the media

dual systems theory an approach that combines elements of different theories, often associated with feminism and Marxism

dysfunctional causing problems and having negative effects on something

ecologists individuals concerned with the relationships between all living things and their environments

eco-warriors individuals whose ecological concerns lead them to resort to direct action methods of political protest

editor a media professional who supervises journalists' work and can select, make changes to and rewrite stories

Educational Maintenance Allowance (EMA) money given to 16- to 19-year-old students from low-income families, provided they attend college and are successful. The system is designed to encourage low-income students to attend college or sixth form

elite theory the belief that power is rightly in the hands of those best equipped to exercise it for the benefit of society as a whole

ethnic penalty a disadvantage experienced by ethnic minorities in the workplace compared with white British workers

ethnicity a shared identity founded on cultural and religious factors. These might be language, food, dress and religion. It is distinct from the term 'race', which implies biological differences

ethnocentric a view of the world dominated by one ethnic group and based on that group's values, beliefs and traditions

experiment a research method used under controlled conditions

exteriorisation the outward signs (such as possessions) of an individual's nature and personality

false consciousness the state of mind of the working class when it accepts the ideas of the ruling class, (according to Marxism)

feminism a sociological theory that foregrounds women's rights. There are many different types of feminism

folk devil the idea that a group or individual can be defined by the media as a threat to society's values and best interests. The folk devil is presented in a stereotypical manner by the media

Fourth Estate a name for the media that sees them as having power and political influence in society

fragmentation the breakdown and splitting up of established social groups, such as social classes

functionalist a view that sees power as an inevitable and positive feature of any society

gatekeeper a media professional who has the power to select the news stories that will be included in print and broadcast media *or* someone who is able to provide access to a sample for a study

gender society's expectations about how males and females should behave

gender identity the range of behaviours and roles adopted by men and women in specific cultures around the world

glass ceiling the barriers that prevent women from reaching to positions in society

global imperialism a new form of global domination and empire-building (compare Americanisation)

globalisation the growth of interdependence between countries, resulting in a form of worldwide society

government a key institution of the state, comprising the Prime Minister, the Cabinet and front-line politicians from the leading political party

hegemony a dominant set of ideas in society, and the power of a dominant group in society to impose its ideas on others

hidden curriculum a set of values, norms and attitudes which are not formally stated but are transmitted by schools. It can be created through practices like requiring pupils to stand up when teachers enter a room, or dividing the school day. Writers from a feminist perspective would argue that the hidden curriculum transmits patriarchal ideologies

horizontal integration in the media, a trend towards companies in the same sector being taken over by, or merged into, larger companies

ideological state apparatus (ISA) the means by which the state controls people's ideas, particularly through education, religion and the media; associated with Marxism

incarceration imprisonment. Rates of incarceration vary around the world: the USA has the highest. Europe generally has low rates and Britain has the highest rate in Europe. Over the last few years, more and more people have been imprisoned. Over the next few years the state will be building Titan prisons which will hold many more prisoners; there are fears that they will act as warehouses rather than places where prisoners will be reformed

indirect action political action that comes about through an intermediary, for example lobbying MPs to represent your views

indirect theories views on media effects that see effect as the product of interaction between different factors, such as the role of opinion leaders or the social class, gender, ethnicity or age of the audience

industrialisation a process whereby the production of goods moves from the land into factories and there is increasing use of machinery. In Britain it began around 1750 and ended towards the beginning of the twentieth century. The results of this process were felt in many areas of social life

institutional racism the collective failure of an organisation to provide an appropriate service to a group because of its specific needs. Discrimination emerges through unwitting prejudice which disadvantages minority ethnic groups

instrumental serving a purpose and bringing about some sort of specific outcome

interpretivism a sociological view that sees people as active participants in society and seeks to understand the meaning of people's actions

Islamophobia dislike and distrust of Muslims

journalist a media professional who writes news stories or articles for print or broadcast media

knowledge class the contemporary term for people who hold knowledge which brings with it power; often associated with the information age and technological understanding

knowledge economy an economy based on producing things through the work of the mind rather than manual work. It is the belief that knowledge and information, rather than land, labour, or energy are the main ways of creating wealth. Education is vital to success in the knowledge economy

label a classification of someone or something. It comes to define that person and they are treated on the basis of the label. Labels can be positive (e.g. 'clever') or negative (e.g. 'stupid'). Individuals are judged on the basis of the label given to a particular group and it may be argued that a label is a stereotype. Hargreaves argues that teachers initially speculate about students based on things like appearance. Initial assumptions gradually become more fixed as teachers get to know their students. Eventually the actions that students engage in are judged in terms of the label and it becomes difficult for someone labelled as deviant to be seen positively, regardless of their actions

labelling theory the belief that labels have a direct effect on action. There are two main variants: one argues that labels create a self-fulfilling prophecy, while the other claims that it affects the classifications of those with power to define actions in a particular way

legitimate accepted as right and just

liberalism an ideology that stresses individualism and the rights of individuals to do anything they wish (within the law)

lobbying organised attempts by individuals or groups to influence MPs to vote in particular ways

longitudinal studies studies carried out over a period of time, usually to focus on a process of change over time

Marxism a sociological theory based on the writings of Karl Marx that see inequality and conflict between social classes as the defining characteristics of society. It tends to focus on the economy as the controlling feature of society

mass media ways of communicating to large audiences that involve cinema, magazines, newspapers and radio as well as new forms of media like satellite television and the internet

material deprivation a lack of money and closely associated with poverty. It means that people cannot afford the things that are regarded as essentials, such as housing, clothing and books. This term is normally employed by those on the left

meritocracy a system of inequality based on talent and ability: those at the top of the social system deserve their wealth because they have worked for it. It also implies that there are equal opportunities: those at the top have the most talent and have worked the hardest, while those who have little ability and/or are lazy will be found at the bottom of the system. It also implies that a person's position in the structure is based on their achievement

meta-narrative one overarching story that explains all other beliefs about the world. This is a central concept of postmodernism, which argues that in modern societies people believed in a big story, primarily science, that explained how the world operated. This single story is now eroding as we enter a new era of human history – the postmodern age – where people are more sceptical and willing to question the 'truths' they are given

methodology theory and methods associated with a piece of research on a research tradition

moral panic widespread public concern, fuelled by the media, about an event or social group that is seen as a threat to society's norms and values

moral pluralism the existence of a number of different moral codes in a society, none of which is believed to be better that the rest

mutualism a way of life in which individuals co-exist and are dependent on one another

neo-conservatism an ideology that merges liberal and conservative beliefs (compare new right)

neo-liberalist a view that argues that the state's role is simply to empower its citizens

neo-Marxism a sociological theory that updates Marxism and looks at a wider range of inequalities and conflicts in society, including those based on gender, ethnicity and sexuality as well as social class. It sees the economy as an important influence in society, but also acknowledges the role of culture in shaping ideas

New Deal a scheme designed by New Labour, which aimed to solve the problem of long-term unemployed youth, by creating either training or work

new right a political philosophy associated with the Conservative party. It has two elements: a neo-liberal element which stresses the need for more individual freedom from state control as well as more individual responsibility in the field of economics, and a 'moral' view that the role of the state is to control and curtail freedom

new social movements organisations that act outside the realms of established political activity

news values values concerning the beliefs and attitudes that media professionals hold, which shape the way they select and construct the news stories they write

non-institutionalised methods methods of political action that bypass parliamentary and/or institutional channels

norm-oriented focused on particular forms of behaviour and ways of doing things

objectivity research that is free from bias or personal opinion

offensive concerned with promoting/challenging a particular state of affairs

oligarchy literally, 'rule by the few', for example in social movements (like trade unions) characterised by full-time leaders who take day-to-day decisions on behalf of an organisation's mass membership

organic whole a social system composed of inter-related and inter-dependent parts, like a living thing

owner an individual who owns media companies and employs media professionals, including journalists and editors to write and report news stories

panopticon a model for a prison where all prisoners could be viewed from a central tower at any time without knowing they were being watched. It was designed to create discipline through self-control. CCTV may serve to control the whole population through this principle

parentocracy a system of education in which parents are given the power to choose which school to send their child to. It is argued that schools will be forced to compete with each other and that this will improve standards

patriarchy (literally 'rule by men') a system of male power and rule that implies the subordination of women. This is sometimes enforced using physical strength but it is also maintained by patriarchal ideology (a set of false beliefs designed to legitimate male power) and economic power. A second feature of patriarchy is the dominance of older men over younger men

personalisation an idea that has come to influence many elements of public service over the last few years. The central idea is that while the state should provide a high-quality service for everyone, it should also ensure that an individual's learning (or health, etc.) needs are met. The state should also adapt its provision to the needs of individual learners

pilot study a pre-run or test run for a research study or method

plea bargaining in the legal system, the dropping of a more serious charge in return for a guilty plea to a less serious charge. It means that prosecutors can be assured of a prosecution, the court process is speeded up and the defendant gains a reduced sentence. It also means that criminals are not always prosecuted for the crimes they have committed

pluralism the belief that a range of different views accepted as valid in society, and that power in society is dispersed amongst many different groups and individuals

polarisation a process where by indistinct groups become clearly separated. It indicates that society is divided into two (polar) opposites and suggests that each is partly defined by its opposition to the other

political action any action (direct or indirect) intended to have some influence on the exercise of political power

political ideology a set of ideas that become the basis for political action

political party a group of like-minded individuals who come together in an attempt to win elections and get into government

political pluralism the existence of a number of different political ideas, none of which is a dominant ideology

political terrorism the use of violence by groups that are opposed to an established government

politics the exercise of power in all its shapes and forms, but mostly 'legally'

post-industrial a stage of social development increasingly characterised by middle-class professional ways of life, according to Bell

postmodern a stage of social development beyond modern industrial society, in which existing certainties are challenged and rejected; postmodern views see society as being characterised by diversity and choice, and believe that the media play a central role in defining our identity and culture

power the ability of a person/group to make others do something they want them to, even when those others may not themselves want to do it

preference theory the theory, associated with Hakim, that women choose what to prioritise – they are not forced into domestic roles

pressure group group of like-minded individuals who come together not to win power but to influence it

purposeful sampling focusing specifically on the types of people needed for the study and selecting them out

quota sampling sampling that matches the needs of the research directly

racialised where race/ethnicity is seen as a key variable

racism the belief that human beings can be separated on the basis of biological differences, also that one race is superior to others and that different ethnic groups should be treated differently

radicalisation a process whereby individuals or groups develop political sympathies that challenge the existing society. Radicals thus challenge those who have power at the moment and seek a speedy transformation of the status quo. Radicalisation has been used to describe the emergence of strongly left-wing groups, but it could also imply a movement to the right

random sampling selecting a number of sampling units from the sampling frame

reflexivity the ability of individuals to think about their own beliefs and behaviours, a means of self-evaluation to ensure quality research

rehabilitation the idea that criminals can be reformed, the causes of their criminality addressed and their offending stopped. This idea was popular in the 1960s but has an impact on policy today

reintegrative shaming the idea that shaming can form part of an offender's reintegration. The offender is controlled by the stigma placed on them, but they must also be given the chance to get back into society, and the label should not be permanent

relativity the idea that there are no moral absolutes. Whether something is regarded as good or bad will vary from place to place and time to time

religious fundamentalism a belief in the literal teachings of a particular religious group

repressive state apparatus (RSA) the means by which the state enforces its ideas, through for example the police and the army; associated with Marxism

researcher imposition the ways in which a researcher shapes a study without necessarily being aware of it

resource mobilisation action intended to bring about certain gains and benefits

respondent validation a means of checking the quality and accuracy of data collection

retribution the idea that punishment should be based on the notion of vengeance. It means that society or the victim is able to get their own back on the offender for the crime they have committed. The function of punishment is not to rehabilitate or reform

riots acts of public disorder that involve crowd violence of some sort

risk society a society in which there are constant problems and dangers, according to Beck

ruling class the dominant group in society, exercising power over others, often by means of its wealth

sampling a process of selecting a group of respondents from the target population

semiology a research method that involves analysing the meaning of signs, symbols and codes

sexual identity the sexual preferences and orientations pursued by individuals

snowball sampling finding one person who puts the researcher in touch with others to form the sample

social class a social group with a shared culture and economic position

social closure associated with Weberian sociology and a means by which some groups retain power for themselves by excluding entry to the group; the 'old boys' network' is a good example

social construction the idea that society makes a person or thing what it is, by interpreting actions or events according to its own values and norms. Thus an individual does not become deviant or mentally ill until they have been defined as such

social movement (SM) an organised attempt to either block or promote social change by using non-institutionalised methods

social movement network the sense of involvement and community that people feel from belonging to social movements (according to Melucci)

state, the the machinery of government, consisting of parliament, the government, the civil service, the courts, the police and the military

stratified sampling dividing the population into categories and selecting from those

strike a temporary stoppage of work (or some other social input to society, such as payment of rent) in an attempt to secure a certain outcome

subjectivity research that is value laden or biased

super-diversity a mix of ethnicities in the UK, extending beyond multiculturalism

synergy a trend towards large media companies bringing together various aspects of their business to produce a range of connected products

target population the group(s) or people the sociologist would like to research

terrorism unlawful use, or threatened use, of force or violence by a person or an organised group, with the intention of intimidation and/or coercion of government or society

transnational corporations (TNCs) companies that carry on their business in several different countries around the world but don't necessarily have an established base in any of them

transnational ownership a media company owning media organisations that operate in a number of countries

transnational social movements worldwide groupings of campaigners which operate across national boundaries

trends and patterns in media and ownership and control in issues concerning who owns and controls the media, 'trends' refer to the general direction that ownership and control of the media is taking, 'patterns' refer to the particular way ownership and control of the media is organised

tri-level class structure a traditional idea of three levels: the working, middle and upper classes

tripartite system a system of education resulting from the 1944 Education Act. It provided three types of secondary school based on an IQ test at the age of 11 (the 11+ exam)

underclass a contested term related to the social and economic position of people at the very bottom of the class structure – or even beneath it

urban social movements social movements active in big cities and similar urban areas

value consensus agreement over what is important or desirable in a society. According to functionalist writers, it is the source of social harmony: if society is divided in its values there will be conflict, as different groups or individuals will desire different things

value freedom the extent to which research is free from bias

value-oriented focused on particular ideas or beliefs and ways of thinking about things

verstehen empathetic understanding, advocated by Weber. It implies that the sociologist should endeavour to see the world as the person they are studying sees it. A consequence of this is that sociologists need data on people's feelings and thoughts, and this implies the need for qualitative data

vertical integration a trend in media ownership towards all the stages in media production, distribution and consumption being owned by one company

victim-blaming the concept that a theory or view blames the victim of a crime. This is done in order to transfer blame from the real cause of crime. To blame women for rape (via dressing provocatively or behaving in a certain way) is a victim-blaming theory as it transfers accountability from the perpetrator to the victim

vocational education education geared towards the needs of the economy. It is aimed particularly at giving skills and knowledge for work rather than a more academic education that appears to have less relevance to the economy

Weberian a view that sees power based on a wider range of factors than just economic class (after Weber)

zemiology the argument that traditional criminology accepts the official definitions of crime and has a narrow view of the victims of crime: we should look at social harm rather than simply crime

References

Abbas, T. (ed.) (2005) *Muslim Britain: Communities under Pressure*. London: Zed Books.

Adler, F. (1975) *Sisters on Trial*. Maidenhead: McGraw-Hill.

Alexander, C. (2000) *The Asian Gang: Ethnicity, Identity, Masculinity*. Oxford: Berg.

Ali, M. (2003) *Brick Lane*. London: Doubleday.

Allen, J. (2000) 'Power: its institutional guises (and disguises)', in G. Hughes and R. Fergusson (eds) *Ordering Lives: Family, Work and Welfare*. London: Routledge.

Althusser, L. (1977) *'Lenin and Philosophy' and Other Essays*. London: New Left Books.

Anthias, F. (2001) 'The material and the symbolic in theorizing social stratification issues of gender, ethnicity and class', *British Journal of Sociology*, 52(3), 37–390.

Archer, L. and Francis, B. (2006) *Understanding Minority Ethnic Achievement: Race, Class, Gender and Success*. London: Routledge.

Archer, L., Halsall, A. and Hollingworth, S. (2007) 'Inner-city femininities and education: "race", class, gender and schooling in young women's lives', *Gender and Education*, 19(5), 549–568.

Atkinson, J. (1978) *Discovering Suicide*. London: Macmillan.

Bagdikian, B.H. (2000) *The Media Monopoly* (6th edn). Boston, MA: Beacon Press.

Baldwin, J. and Bottoms, A.E. (1976) *The Urban Criminal*. London: Tavistock.

Ball, S. (1990; 2006) *The Selected Works of Stephen J. Ball*. Abingdon: Routledge.

Ball, S. (2008) *The Education Debate*. Bristol: Policy Press.

Bandura, A., Ross, D., and Ross, S.A. (1963) 'The imitation of film-mediated aggressive models', *Journal of Abnormal and Social Psychology*, 66(1), 3–11.

Barker, C. (1999) *Television, Globalization and Cultural Identities*. Maidenhead: Open University Press.

Barlow, J., Dickens, P. and Fielding, T. (1992) *Property, Bureaucracy and Culture: Middle Class Formation in Contemporary Britain*. London: Routledge.

Barron, R.D. and Norris, G.M. (1976) 'Sexual divisions in the dual labour market', in D.L. Barker and S. Allen (eds) *Dependence and Exploitation in Work and Marriage*. London: Longman.

Baudrillard, J. (1988) *The Ecstasy of Communication*. New York: Semiotext.

Baudrillard, J. (1995) *The Gulf War did not Take Place*. Sydney: Power Publications.

BBC Royal Charter (2007) available at http://www.bbccharterreview.org.uk.

Beck, U. (1992) *Risk Society*. London: Sage.

Becker, H.S. (1963) *Outsiders*. New York: Free Press.

Becker, H.S. (1977) 'Social class variations in teacher–pupil relationship', in B.R. Cosin et al. *School and Society: a Reader*. Maidenhead: Open University Press.

Beechey, V. (1976) 'Women and employment in contemporary Britain', in V. Beechey and E. Whitelegg (eds) *Women in Britain Today*. Maidenhead: Open University Press.

Bell, D. (1960) *The End of Ideology: On the Exhaustion of Political Ideas in the Fifties*. New York: Free Press.

Bell, D. (1973) *The Coming of Post-Industrial Society*. New York: Basic Books.

Benston, M. (1972) 'The political economy of women's liberation', in N. Glaser-Malbin and H.Y. Waehrer (eds) *Women in a Man-Made World*. Chicago: Rand-McNally.

Bernard, J. (1976) *The Future of Marriage*. Harmondsworth: Penguin.

Bernstein, B. (1961) 'Social class and linguistic development: a theory of social learning', in A.H. Halsey et al. *Education, Economy and Society*. New York: Free Press.

Berthoud, R. (1997) 'Income and living standards', in T. Modood and I. Berthoud, *Ethnic Minorities in Britain*. London: Policy Studies Institute.

Best, L. (1993) '"Dragons, dinner ladies and ferrets": sex roles in children's books', *Sociology Review*, February.

Beuchler, S.M. (1993) 'Beyond resource mobilization? Emerging trends in social movement theory', in S. M. Buechler and F.K. Cylke (eds) (1997) *Social Movements: Perspectives and Issues*. Mountain View, CA: Mayfield.

Bhopal, K. (2000) 'Gender, "race" and power in the research process: South Asian women in East London', in C. Truman (ed.) *Research and Inequality*. London: UCL Press.

Biggs, S. (1993) *Understanding Ageism*. Milton Keynes: Open University Press.

Blumer, H. (1969) *Symbolic Interactionism*. Englewood Cliffs, NJ: Prentice-Hall.

Bolognani, M. (2007) 'The myth of return: dismissal, survival or revival? A Bradford example of transnationalism as a political Instrument', *Journal of Ethnic and Migration Studies*, 1, 59–76.

Boudon, R. (1974) *Education, Opportunity and Social Inequality*. New York: John Wiley.

Bourdieu, P. (1973) 'Cultural reproduction and social reproduction', in R. Brown (ed.) *Knowledge, Education and Cultural* Change. London: Tavistock.

Bowles, S. and Gintis, H. (1976) *Schooling in Capitalist America*. London: Routledge & Kegan Paul.

Braverman, H. (1974) *Labor and Monopoly Capitalism*. New York: Monthly Review Press.

Breen, R. and Goldthorpe, J. (1999) 'Class inequality and meritocracy: a critique of Saunders', *British Journal of Sociology*, 50(1), 1–27.

Bridges, G. and Brunt, R. (eds) (1981) *Silver Linings: Some Strategies for the Eighties*. London: Lawrence & Wishart.

Briggs, A., Burgess, S.M. and Wilson, D. (2006) *The Dynamics of School Attainment of England's Ethnic Minorities*. London: London School of Economics.

Briggs, A. and Cobley, P. (eds) (2002) *The Media: An Introduction*. Harlow: Pearson.

Butler, J. (1990) *Gender Trouble: Feminism and the Subversion of Identity*. London: Routledge.

Bytheway, W. (1995) *Ageism*. Buckingham: Buckingham: Open University Press.

Callinicos, A. (2003) *An Anti-Capitalist Manifesto*. Cambridge: Polity Press.

Cannadine, D. (2000) *Class in Britain*. London: Penguin.

Carers UK (2007) *Facts about Carers, by Gender and Age*, available at http://www.carersuk.co.uk.

Carrabine, E., Iganski, P., Lee, M., Plummer, K. and South, N. (2004) *Criminology: A Sociological Introduction*. London: Routledge.

Carrigan, M. and Szmigin, I. (2000) 'Advertising in an ageing society', *Age and Society*, 20(2), 217–233.

Cashmore, E. (1984) *Dictionary of Race and Ethnic Relations*. London: Routledge & Kegan Paul.

Castells, M. (1983) *The City and the Grassroots*. London: Edward Arnold.

Castells, M. (1998) *End of Millennium*. Oxford: Blackwell.

Castles, S. and Kosack, G. (1973) *Immigrant Workers and Class Structure in Western Europe*. Oxford: Oxford University Press.

Chambliss, W. (1976) *Whose Law? What Order? A Conflict Approach to Criminology*. New York: John Wiley.

Cicourel, A.V. (1976) *The Social Organisation of Justice*. London: Heinemann.

Cicourel, A.V. and Kitsuse, J. (1963) *The Educational Decision Makers*. Indianapolis: Bobbs-Merill.

Coard, B. (1971; 2005) *How the West Indian Child is Made to Feel Educationally Sub-normal in the British School System*. New Beacon Books: London.

Cohen, A.K. (1955) *Delinquent Boys*. New York: Free Press.

Cohen, R. and Kennedy, P. (2000) *Global Sociology*. Basingstoke: Macmillan.

Cohen, S. (1972) *Folk Devils and Moral Panics*. London: MacGibbon & Kee.

Cohen, S. and Young, J. (eds) (1981) *The Manufacture of News: Deviance, Social Problems and the Mass Media*. London: Constable.

Collins, R. and Murroni, C. (1996) *New Media, New Policies*. Cambridge: Polity Press.

Commission for Racial Equality (1992) *Set to Fail? Setting and Banding in Secondary Schools*. London: Commission for Racial Equality.

Cooke, G. and Oppenheim, C. (2008) 'Unequal struggle', *Guardian*, 23 January.

Cox, O.C. (1948) *Caste, Class and Race: A Study in Social Dynamics*. New York: Modern Reader Paperbacks.

Cranfield Institute (2007) *Female FTSE Index and Report*. Cranfield: Cranfield Institute.

Curran, J. and Gurevitch, M. (eds) (2005) *Mass Media and Society*. London: Hodder Arnold.

Dahl, R.A. (1961) *Who Governs?* New Haven: Yale University Press.

Dahrendorf, R. (1987) 'The Underclass and the Future of Britain', 10th Annual Lecture, St George's House, Windsor.

Danitz, T. and Strobel, W.P. (1999) 'Networking dissent: cyber activists use the internet to promote democracy in Burma', in J. Arquilla and D. Ronfeldt (eds) (2001) *Networks and Netwars: The Future of Terror, Crime, and Militancy*. Santa Monica: Rand.

Davies, J. and Biesta, G.J.J. (2007) 'Coming to college or getting out of school? The experience of vocational learning of 14- to 16-year-olds in further education college', *Education*, 22(1), 23–41.

Davis, K. and Moore, W.E. (1945) 'Some principles of stratification', in J. Scott (ed.) (1996) *Class Critical Debates*. London: Routledge.

Dawson, G. (2000) 'Work: from certainty to flexibility', in G. Hughes and R. Fergusson (eds) *Ordering Lives: Family, Work and Welfare*. London: Routledge.

Department for Children, Schools and Families (2008) *Attainments and Outcomes at GCSE*, available at http://www.dcsf.gov.uk.

Department for Work and Pensions (2007) *Households Below Average Income*, available at http://www.dwp.gov.uk/.

Dermott, E. (2006) 'What's parenthood got to do with it? Men's hours of paid work', *British Journal of Sociology*, 57(4) 619–634.

Desai, P. (1999) 'Spaces of Identity, Cultures of Conflict: The Development of New British Asian Identities', PhD Thesis, Goldsmiths College, London.

Devereux, E. (2008) *Understanding the Media*. London: Sage.

Devine, F. (1992) *Affluent Worker Revisited*. Edinburgh: Edinburgh University Press.

Devine, F. et al. (2005) *Rethinking Class: Culture, Identities and Lifestyle*. Basingstoke: Palgrave.

de Waal, A. (2008) *School Improvement – or the 'Equivalent'*, available at http://www.civitas.org.uk/pdf/gcseequivalent.pdf.

Douglas, J.W.B. (1964) *The Home and the School*. London: Macgibbon & Kee.

Durkheim, E. (1893; 1964) *The Division of Labour in Modern Society*. New York: Free Press.

Durkheim, E. (1925; 1961) *Moral Education*. London: Free Press.

Durkheim, E. (1938) *The Rules of Sociological Method*. New York: Free Press.

Durkheim, E. (1938; 1970) *Suicide: A Study in Sociology*. New York: Free Press and London: Routledge & Kegan Paul.

Eisenstadt, S. (1956) *From Generation to Generation: Age Groups and Social Structure*. New York: Free Press.

Engels, F. (1972) *The Origin of the Family, Private Property and the State*. London: Lawrence & Wishart.

Equal Opportunities Commission (2006) *Facts about Women and Men in Great Britain*, available at http://www.eoc.org.uk.

Evans, H. (1983) *Good Times, Bad Times*. London: Weidenfeld & Nicholson.

Everingham, C. (2003) 'Self-actualisation and the ageing process from an inter-generational life-course perspective', *Ageing and Society*, 23, 243–253.

Fairclough, N. (1995) *Media Discourse*. London: Arnold.

Fawbert, J. 'Boys n the hoodie', *Guardian*, 3 March 2008, available at http://www.guardian.co.uk/society/2008/mar/03/hoodie.comment.

Featherstone, M. and Hepworth, M. (1989) 'Ageing and old age: reflections on the postmodern life course', in W. Bytheway (ed.) *Becoming and Being Old: Sociological Approaches to Later Life*. London: Sage.

Feinstein, L. (2003) 'Very early evidence: how can we predict future educational achievement?' *Centerpiece*, 8(2).

Feshbach, S. and Singer, R.D. (1971) *Television and Aggression: An Experimental Field Study*, San Francisco: Jossey-Bass.

Field, F. (1989) *Losing Out: The Emergence of the British Underclass*. Oxford: Blackwell.

Fine, M. (1994) 'Working with hyphens; reinventing self and other in qualitative research', in N.K. Denzin and Y.S. Lincoln (eds) *Handbook of Qualitative Research*. Thousand Oaks: Sage.

Firestone, S. (1971) *The Dialectic of Sex*. London: Jonathan Cape.

Fiske, J. (1989) *Understanding Popular Culture*. London: Unwin Hyman.

Flood-Page, G. (2000) *Youth Lifestyles Survey.* Home Office Research Study No. 209. London: Home Office.

Frazer, E. (1987) 'Teenage girls reading *Jackie*', *Media, Culture and Society*, 9, 407–425.

Friedan, B. (1963) *The Feminine Mystique.* New York: W.W. Norton.

Fukuyama, F. (1992) *The End of History and the Last Man.* Harmondsworth: Penguin.

Fuller, M. (1984) 'Black girls in a London comprehensive school', in M. Hammersley and P. Woods (eds) *Life in Schools: The Sociology of Pupil Culture.* Milton Keynes: Open University.

Future Foundation (2006) *Middle Britain: Summary Report, Class Membership and Money in the 21st Century.* London: Liverpool Victoria.

Gallie, D. (1994) 'Patterns of skill change, upskilling, skilling or polarisation?' in R. Penn et al. (eds) *Skill and Occupational Change.* Oxford: Oxford University Press.

Gamson, W. (1992) *Talking Politics.* Cambridge: Cambridge University Press.

Gartrell, C. and Gartrell, J. (2002) 'Positivism in sociological research: USA and UK', *British Journal of Sociology*, 53(4), 639–657.

Gauntlett, D. (1995) *Moving Experiences: Understanding Television's Influences and Effects*, Academia Research Monograph 13. London: John Libbey.

Gauntlett, D. (2007) *Creative Explorations: New Approaches to Identities and Audiences.* London: Routledge.

Gauntlett, D. (2008) *Media, Gender and Identity: An Introduction* (2nd edn). London: Routledge.

Gerth, H.H. and Mills, C.W. (1948) *From Max Weber: Essays in Sociology.* London: Routledge & Kegan Paul.

Gewirtz, S., Ball, S.J. and Bowe, R. (1995) *Markets, Choice and Equity in Education.* Maidenhead: Open University Press.

Giddens, A. (2006) *Sociology* (5th edn). Cambridge: Polity Press.

Gilborn, D. and Mirza, H.S. (2000) *Educational Inequality: Mapping Race, Gender and Class. A Synthesis of Research.* London: Ofsted.

Gilborn, D. and Youdell, D. (2000) *Rationing Education: Policy, Practice, Reform and Equity.* Maidenhead: Open University Press.

Gilborn, D. and Youdell, D. (2001) 'The new IQism: intelligence, "ability" and the rationing of education', in D. Youdell (ed.) *Sociology of Education Today.* Basingstoke: Palgrave.

Gilligan, C. (1982) *In a Different Voice: Essays on Psychological Theory and Women's Development.* Cambridge, MA: Harvard University Press.

Gilroy, P. (1983) 'Police and thieves', in Centre for Contemporary Studies (ed.) *The Empire Strikes Back.* London: Hutchinson.

Ginn, J. and Arber, S. (2001) 'Pension prospects of minority ethnic groups: inequality by gender and ethnicity', *British Journal of Sociology*, 50(2), 195–215.

Goldthorpe, J.H. (1968) *The Affluent Worker: Political Attitudes and Behaviour.* Cambridge: Cambridge University Press.

Goldthorpe, J.H. and Heath, A. (1992) 'Revised class schema', *Joint Unit for the Study of Social Trends*, working paper 13.

Goldthorpe, J.H., Llewellyn, C. and Payne, C. (1980) *Social Mobility and Class Structure in Modern Britain.* Oxford: Clarendon Press.

Goode, E. and Ben-Yehuda, N. (1994) *Moral Panics: The Social Construction of Deviance.* Oxford: Blackwell.

Gorard, S. (2008) 'Who is missing from higher education?' *Cambridge Journal of Education*, 38, 421–437.

Gouldner, A.W. (1975) *For Sociology: Renewal and Critique in Sociology Today.* Harmondsworth: Penguin.

Gramsci, A. (1971) *Selections from Prison Notebooks.* London: Lawrence & Wishart.

Gray, J. and McLellan, R. (2006) 'A matter of attitude? Developing a profile of boys' and girls' responses to primary schooling', *Gender and Education*, 18(6), 651–672.

Griffith, J.A.G. (1997) *The Politics of the Judiciary* (5th edn). London: Fontana Press.

Gurevitch, M., Bennett, T., Curran, J. and Woollacott, J. (eds) (1982) *Culture, Society and the Media.* London: Methuen.

Habermas, J. (1981) 'New Social Movements', *Teleos*, 49 (Autumn).

Hakim, C. (1995) 'Five feminist myths about women's employment', *British Journal of Sociology*, 46(4), 424–455.

Hakim, C. (2000) *Work–Lifestyle Choices in the 21st Century: Preference Theory*. Oxford: Oxford University Press.

Hall, S. (1973) 'The determination of news photographs', in S. Cohen and J. Young (eds) *The Manufacture of News: A Reader*. Beverly Hills: Sage.

Hall, S. (1980) 'Encoding and decoding', in S. Hall, D. Hobson, A. Lowe and P. Willis (eds) *Culture, Media and Society*. London: Hutchinson.

Hall, S. (1981) 'The whites of their eyes: racist ideologies and the media', in G. Bridges and R. Brunt (eds) *Silver Linings: Some Strategies for the Eighties*. London: Lawrence & Wishart.

Hall, S., Critcher, C., Jefferson, T., Clark, J. and Roberts, B. (1978) *Policing the Crisis*. London: Macmillan.

Hallsworth, S. (1994) 'Understanding New Social Movements', *Sociology Review*, 4(1), 7–10.

Haralambos, M. and Holborn, M. (2008) *Sociology: Themes and Perspectives*. London: Collins.

Harcup, T. and O'Neill, D. (2001) 'What is news? Galtung and Ruge re-visited', *Journalism Studies*, 2(2), 261–280.

Hargreaves, H.D. (1967) *Social Relations in a Secondary School*. London: Routledge & Kegan Paul.

Hartmann, H. (1981) 'The unhappy marriage of Marxism and feminism; towards a more progressive union', in L. Sargent (ed.) *Women and Revolution: The Unhappy Marriage of Marxism and Feminism*. London: Pluto.

Haynes, T. and Cabellero, C. (2006) 'The barriers to achievement for white/black Caribbean pupils in English schools', *British Journal of Sociology of Education*, 27, 569–583.

Healthcare Commission (2007) *Evidence of Health Inequalities*, available at http://www.healthcarecommission.org.uk/_db/_documents/04017601.pdf.

Heath, A. and Yi Cheung, S. (2006) *Ethnic Penalties in the Labour Market: Employers and Discrimination*, Department for Work and Pensions, available at http://www.dwp.gov.uk/asd/asd5/rports2005-2006rrep341pdf.

Hebdige, D. (1988) *Hiding in the Light: On Images and Things*. London: Routledge.

Hebdige, D. (1988) *Subculture: The Meaning of Style*. London: Routledge.

Heidensohn, F. (2002) 'Gender and crime', in M. Maguire, R. Morgan and R. Reiner (eds) *Oxford Handbook of Criminology*. Oxford: Oxford University Press.

Hewitt, C.J. (1974) 'Elites and the distribution of power in British society', in P. Stanworth and A. Giddens (eds) *Elites and Power in British Society*. Cambridge: Cambridge University Press.

Heywood, A. (2002) *Politics* (2nd edn). Basingstoke: Palgrave.

Himmelweit, S. and Simonetti, R. (2000) 'Nature for sale', in S. Hinchliffe and K. Woodward (eds) *The Natural and the Social: Uncertainty, Risk, Change*. London: Routledge.

Hirst, P. (1993) *Representative Democracy and its Limits*. Cambridge: Polity Press.

Hoelscher, M., Hayward, G., Hubert, E. and Dunbar-Goddet, H. (2008) 'The transition from vocational education and training to higher education: a successful pathway?' *Research Papers in Education*, 23, 139–151.

Hofstede, H.G. and Werfhorst, S. (2007) 'Cultural capital or relative risk aversion? Two mechanisms for educational inequality compared', *British Journal of Sociology*, 58, 391–415.

Holborn, M. (2005) *Developments in Sociology*, 21. Ormskirk: Causeway Press.

Hood, R. (1992) *Race and Sentencing*. Oxford: Clarendon Press.

Hutton, W. (1995) *The 30/30/40 Labour Market*, available at http://www.jobsletter.org.nz/jbl03010.htm.

Hyman, H. (1967) 'The value systems of different classes', in R. Bendix and S.M. Lipset (eds) *Class, Status and Power*. London: Routledge & Kegan Paul.

Iganski, P. and Payne, G. (1999) 'Socio-economic restructuring and employment: the case of minority ethnic groups', *British Journal of Sociology*, 52(3), 519–539.

Jackson, C. (2006) *Lads and Ladettes in School: Gender and a Fear of Failure*. Maidenhead: Open University Press.

Jameson, F. (1991) *Postmodernism, or the Cultural Logic of Late Capitalism*. Verso: London.

Jamieson, R. and McEvoy, K. (April 2005) 'State crime by proxy and judicial othering', *British Journal of Criminology*, 45, 504–527.

Jewkes, Y. (2004) *Media and Crime*. London: Sage.

Johnson, M. (1995) 'Interdepency and generational impact', *Ageing and Society*, 15, 234–265.

Jones, G. (1997) 'Youth homelessness and the underclass', in R. MacDonald (ed.) *Youth, The 'Underclass' and Social Exclusion*. London: Routledge.

Jowett, M. (2001) 'Is feminism still important?' *Sociology Review*, 11(1), 16–18.

JRF (2007) *Monitoring Poverty and Social Exclusion*, available at http://www.poverty.org.uk.

Kane, J. (2006) 'School exclusions and masculine, working-class identities', *Gender and Education*, 18(6), 673–685.

Karmen, A. (1990) *Crime Victims: An Introduction to Victimology*. Pacific Grove, CA: Brooks Cole.

Katz, E. and Lazarsfeld, P. (1955) *Personal Influence*. New York: Free Press.

Keddie, N. (1999) 'The new religious politics and women worldwide: a comparative study', *Journal of Women's History*, Winter (February).

Kitzinger, J. (2002) '"Impacts and influences": media influence revisited: an introduction to the "new effects research"', in A. Briggs and P. Cobley (eds) *The Media: An Introduction*. Harlow: Pearson.

Klapper, J.T. (1960) *The Effects of Mass Communication*. New York: Free Press.

Klein, N. (2000) *No Logo*. Toronto: A.A. Knopf Canada.

Kosak, C.A. (1973) *Immigrant Workers and Class Structure in Western Europe*. Oxford: Oxford University Press.

Labov, W. (1973) 'The logic of non-standard English', in N. Keddie (ed.) *Tinker, Tailor … The Myth of Cultural Deprivation*. Harmondsworth: Penguin.

Lash, S. and Urry, J. (1987) *The End of Organised Capitalism*. Cambridge: Polity Press.

Lea, J. and Young, J. (1984) *What is to be Done about Law and Order?* Harmondsworth: Penguin.

Lee, D., Marsden, D., Rickman, P. and Dunscombe, J. (1990) *Scheming for Youth: a Study of YTS in the Entrerprise Culture*. Milton Keynes: Open University.

Lemert, E.M. (1972) *Human Deviance, Social Problems and Social Control*. Englewood Cliffs, NJ: Prentice-Hall.

Lewis, O. (1959) *Five Families*. New York: Basic Books.

Lobban, G. (1974) 'Data report on British reading schemes', *Times Educational Supplement*, 1 March.

Lukes, S. (1974) *Power: A Radical View*. London: Macmillan.

Machin, S. and McNally, S. (2004) *The Literacy Hour*. London: London School of Economics, Centre for Economics of Education.

Machin, S. and Vignoles, A. (2006) *Education Policy in the UK*. London: London School of Economics, Centre for the Economics of Education.

Mackay, H. (2000) 'The globalization of culture?', in D. Held (ed.) *A Globalizing World? Culture, Economics*, Politics. London: Routledge.

Mackintosh, M. and Mooney, G. (2000) 'Identity, inequality and social class', in K. Woodward (ed.) *Questioning Identity: Gender, Class, Ethnicity*. London: Routledge.

Macpherson, W. (1999) *The Stephen Lawrence Inquiry*. London: HMSO.

Malik, S. (2002) 'Race and ethnicity', in A. Briggs and P. Cobley (eds) *The Media: An Introduction*. Harlow: Pearson.

Mamay, S. (2002) *Theories of Social Movements and their Current Development in Soviet Society*, available at http://lucy.ukc.ac.uk/czacpub/russian/mamay.html.

Marsh, D. (1985) 'Power and politics', in M. Haralambos (ed.) *Developments in Sociology*, 1. Ormskirk: Causeway Press.

Marshall, G. (1998) *A Dictionary of Sociology*. Oxford: Oxford University Press.

Marsland, D. (1992) 'The roots and consequences of paternalistic collectivsm', *Social Policy and Administration*, 26(2), 16.

Marsland, D. (1996) *Welfare, or Welfare State? Contradictions and Dilemmas in Social Policy*. London: Macmillan.

Marx, K. (1968 edn) *Karl Marx and Friedrich Engels: Selected Works in One Volume*. London: Lawrence & Wishart.

Mason, D. (2003) 'Ethnicity', in G. Payne (ed.) *Social Divisions*. Basingstoke: Palgrave Macmillan.

Matza, D. (1964) *Delinquency and Drift*. New York: Wiley.

McCarthy, J.D. and Zald, M.N. (1987) 'Resource mobilization and social movements: a partial theory', in S.M. Buechler and F.K. Cylke (eds) (1997) *Social Movements: Perspectives and Issues*. Mountain View, CA: Mayfield.

McCullagh, C. (2002) *Media Power*. Basingstoke: Palgrave.

McKingsley, E. (2001) *The Spiritual Dimensions of Ageing*. London: Jessica Kingsley Publishers.

McKnight, A., Glennerster, H. and Lupton, R. (2005) 'Education, education, education … an assessment of Labour's success in tackling educational inequalities', in H.A. Stewart (ed.) *A More Equal Society? New Labour, Poverty, Inequality and Exclusion*. Bristol: Policy Press.

McLuhan, M. (1964) *Understanding Media: The Extensions of Man*. New York: New American Library.

McLuhan, M. and Fiore, Q. (1971) *The Medium is the Massage*. Harmondsworth: Penguin Books.

McQuail, D. (1972) *The Sociology of Mass Communications*. Harmondsworth: Penguin.

McQuail, D. (2000) *McQuail's Mass Communication Theory*. London: Sage.

McRobbie, A. (2005) 'Cutting girls down to Victoria Beckham's size', *The Times Higher Educational Supplement*, 14 October.

Melucci, A. (1989) *Nomads of the Present: Social Movements and Individual Needs in Contemporary Society*. Philadelphia, PA: Temple University Press.

Merton, R.K. (1938) *Social Theory and Social Structure*. New York: Free Press.

Messerschmidt, J.W. (1993) *Masculinities and Crime: Critique and Reconceptualisation of Theory*. Lanham, MD: Rowman & Littlefield.

Mhlanga, B. (1999) *Race and Crown Prosecution Service Decisions*. London: HMSO.

Middle Britain: Summary Report, Class Membership and Money in the 21st Century. London: Liverpool Victoria.

Midgely, J. and Bradshaw, R. (2006) *Should I Stay or Should I Go? Rural Youth Transitions*, available at http://www.ippr.org/ipprnorth.

Miles, R. (1980) 'Class, race and ethnicity: a critique of Cox's theory', *Ethnic and Social Studies*, 3(3), 169–187.

Miliband, R. (1969) *The State in Capitalist Society*. London: Weidenfeld & Nicolson.

Miller, W. (1958) 'Lower-class culture as a generating milieu of gang delinquency', *Journal of Social Issues*, 14, 5–19.

Millet, K. (1971) *Sexual Politics*. London: Sphere.

Mills, C.W. (1956) *The Power Elite*. New York: Oxford University Press.

Milne, A.E.H. and Harding, T. (1999) *Later Lifestyles: A Survey by Help the Aged and Yours Magazine*. London: Help the Aged.

Modood, T. and Berthoud, I. (1997) *Ethnic Minorities in Britain*. London: Policy Studies Institute.

Moore, S., Aiken, D. and Chapman, S. (2005) *Sociology AS for OCR*. London: Harper Collins.

MORI (2002) summary available at http://news.bbc.co.uk/1/hi/business/2542313.stm

Mosca, G. (1939) *The Ruling Class*. New York: McGraw-Hill.

Mossa, Z. (2008) *Seeing Double: Race and Gender in Ethnic Minority Women's Lives*. London: Fawcett Society.

Mount, F. (2004) *Mind the Gap, The New Class Divide in Britain*. London: Short Books.

Murdock, G. (1982) 'Large corporations and the control of the communications industries', in M. Gurevitch, T. Bennett, J. Curran and J. Woollacott (eds) *Culture, Society and the Media*. London: Methuen.

Murray, C. (1994) *Underclass: The Crisis Deepens*. London: Institute of Education.

Nash, K. (2000) *Contemporary Political Sociology*. Oxford: Blackwell.

National Statistics Online available at http://www.statistics.gov.uk/.

Negrine, R. (1989) *Politics and the Mass Media in Britain*. London: Sage.

Newburn, T. (2007) *Criminology*. Cullompton: Willan.

NS-SEC (2001) available at http://www.statistics.gov.uk/methods_quality/ns_sec/.

Oakley, A. (1974) *Housewife*. London: Allen Lane.

Offe, C. (1985) 'New Social Movements: challenging the boundaries of institutional politics', *Social Research*, 52(4), 846.

Office for National Statistics (2001) *Population of the UK by Ethnic Group*, available at http://www.statistics.gov.uk.

Office for National Statistics (2004) *Focus on Ethnicity: Employment Patterns*, available at http://www.statistics.gov.uk.

Office for National Statistics (2004) *Focus on Social Inequalities*, available at http://www.statistics.gov.uk.

Office for National Statistics (2004) *Government Actuary's Department*. London: HMSO.

Office for National Statistics (2006) *General Household Survey*, available at http://www.statistics.gov.uk.

Office for National Statistics (2007) *Annual Survey of Hours and Earnings*. London: HMSO.

Office for National Statistics (2007) *Labour Force Survey*. London: HMSO.

Office for National Statistics (2008) *Expenditure and Food Survey*, Social Trends 38, available at http://www.statistics.gov.uk.

Osgerby, B. (2002) 'The good, the bad and the ugly: post-war media representations of youth', in A. Briggs and P. Cobley (eds) *The Media: An Introduction*, Harlow: Pearson.

Packard, V. (1957) *The Hidden Persuaders*. Harlow: Longman.

Pakulski, J. and Waters, M. (1996) *The Death of Class*. London: Sage.

Palmer, G., MacInnes. T. and Kenway. P. (2006) *Monitoring Poverty and Social Exclusion*, available at http://www.poverty.org.uk/socialexclusion.

Palmer, G., MacInnes. T. and Kenway. P. (2007) *Monitoring Poverty and Social Exclusion, 2007*. London: Joseph Rowntree Foundation and New Policy Institute.

Pareto, V. (1935) *The Mind and Society*. New York: Harcourt-Brace.

Park, R. (1950) *Race and Culture*. New York: Free Press.

Parkin, F. (1968) *Middle Class Racialism*. Manchester: Manchester University Press.

Parry, G. (1969) *Political Elites*. London: George Allen & Unwin.

Parsons, T. (1940) 'An analytical approach to the theory of social stratification', in J. Scott (ed.) (1996) *Class Critical Debates*. London: Routledge.

Parsons, T. (1951) *The Social System*. New York: Free Press.

Parsons, T. (1954) *Essays in sociological theory*. Glencoe, IL: Free Press.

Parsons, T. (1955) *Families, Socialisation and Interaction Process*. Glencoe, IL: Free Press.

Parsons, T. (1961) 'The school class as a social system', in A.H. Halsey et al. *Education, Economy and Society*. New York: Free Press.

Parsons, T. (1966) *The Negro American*. London: Routledge.

Patton, M.Q. (2002) *Qualitative Evaluation and Research Methods*. London: Sage.

Payne, G. (2006) *Social Divisions* (2nd edn). Basingstoke: Palgrave Macmillan.

Phillips, C. and Bowling, B. (2002) 'Racism, ethnicity, crime and criminal justice', in M. Maguire, R. Morgan and R. Reiner (eds) *The Oxford Handbook of Criminology* (3rd edn). Oxford: Oxford University Press.

Philo, G. (ed.) (1999) *Message Received*. Harlow: Longman.

Philo, G. and Miller, D. (2005) 'Communication and power: production, consumption and reproduction', in M. Holborn (ed.) *Developments in Sociology*, 21. Ormskirk: Causeway Press.

Platt, L. (2007) *Poverty and Ethnicity in the UK*. Bristol: Policy Press.

Polemus, T. (1997) 'In the supermarket of style', in S. Redhead, D. Wynne and J. O'Connor (eds) *The Clubcultures Reader: Readings in Popular Cultural Studies*. Oxford: Blackwell.

Pollack, O. (1950) *The Criminality of Women*. Philadelphia, PA: University of Philadelphia Press.

Popper, K. (1959) *The Logic of Scientific Discovery*. London: Hutchinson.

Poulantzas, N. (1980) *State, Power, Socialism*. London: Verso.

Putnam, R.D. (2000) *Bowling Alone: The Collapse and Revival of American Community*. New York: Simon & Schuster.

Ramazanoghlu, C. (2002) *Feminist Methodology: Challenges and Choices*. London: Sage.

Reinhartz, S. (1992) *Feminist Methods in Social Research*. New York: Oxford University Press.

Rex, J. and Moore, R. (1967) *Race, Community and Conflict*. Oxford: Oxford University Press.

Ritzer, G. (1996) *The McDonaldization of Society*. London: Pine Forge Press.

Roberts, K. (1997) 'Is there an emerging British "underclass"? The evidence from youth research', in R. MacDonald (ed.) *Youth, the 'Underclass' and Social Exclusion*. London: Routledge.

Roberts, K., Cook, F.G., Clark, S.C. and Semeonoff, E. (1977) *The Fragmentary Class Structure*. London: Heinemann.

Ronfeldt, D. (1992) 'Cyberocracy is coming', *The Information Society Journal*, 8(4), 243–296.

Roseneil, S. (1995) *Disarming Patriarchy: Feminism and Political Action at Greenham*. Buckingham: Open University Press.

Rosenthal, R. and Jacobsen, L. (1968) *Pygmalion in the Classroom*. New York: Holt, Rinehart & Winston.

Runciman, W.G. (1990) 'How many classes are there in contemporary British society?', *Sociology*, 24(3), 378–396.

Runnymede Trust (1997) *Islamophobia*. London: Runnymede Trust.

Sampson, R.J., Raudenbush, S.W. and Earls, F. (1997) 'Neighbourhoods and violent crime: a multi-level study of collective efficacy', *Science*, 277, 918–924.

Saunders, P. (1983) *Urban Politics: A Sociological Interpretation*. London: Hutchinson.

Saunders, P. (1994) 'Is Britain a meritocracy?', in R. Blackburn (ed.) *Social Inequality in a Changing World*. Cambridge: Cambridge University Press.

Saunders, P. (2002) *Roots of the Neoliberal Revolution*. Cambridge: Cambridge University Press.

Savage, M., Barlow, T., Dickens, P. and Fielding, T. (1992) *Property, Bureacracy and Culture: Middle Class Formation in Contemporary Britain*. London: Routledge.

Savage, M. et al. (2005) 'Local habitus and working-class culture', in F. Devine et al. (eds) *Rethinking Class: Culture, Identities and Lifestyle*. London: Palgrave.

Schlesinger, P. (1987) *Putting 'Reality' Together* (2nd edn). London: Methuen.

Schofield, J.W. (1973) 'Learning through interviewing', in T. Logan and J.F. Schostak (eds) *Pupil Experience*. London: Croom Helm.

Scott, A. (1999) 'Social and political movements', *Sociology Review*, 2–5.

Scott, J. (1991) *Who Rules Britain?* Polity: Cambridge.

Seabrook, J. (1988) *The Leisure Society*. Oxford: Blackwell.

Seager, J. (1997) *The State of Women in the World Atlas*. Harmondsworth: Penguin.

Sewell, T. (1997) *Black Masculinities and Schooling*. Stoke-on-Trent: Trentham.

Sharpe, S. (1976) *Just Like a Girl: How Girls Learn to Become Women* (2nd edn 1994). Harmondsworth: Penguin.

Shaw, C.R. and McKay, H.D. (1942) *Juvenile Delinquency and Urban Areas*. Chicago: University of Chicago Press.

Skeggs, B. (1997) *Formation of Class and Gender*. London: Sage.

Sklair, L. (2003) 'Globalisation, capitalism and power', in M. Holborn (ed.) *Developments in Sociology*, 19. Ormskirk: Causeway Press.

Smart, C. (1979) *Women, Crime and Criminology*. London: Routledge & Kegan Paul.

Smelser, N. (1962) *Theory of Collective Behaviour*. London: Routledge & Kegan Paul.

Smith, M.J. (1997) 'Green sociology', *Sociology Review*, 29–33.

Smith, T. and Noble, M. (1995) *Education Divides: Poverty and Schooling in the 1990s*. London: CPAG.

Solomos, J. (1986) 'Varieties of Marxist conceptions of "race", class and state: a critical analysis', in J. Rex (ed.) *Theories of Race and Ethnic Relations*. Cambridge: Polity Press.

Sorenson, A. (2000) 'Employment relations and class structure', in R. Crompton, F. Devine, M. Savage and J. Scott (eds) *Renewing Class Analysis*. Oxford: Blackwell.

Stack, S. (2000) 'Blues fans and suicide acceptability', *Death Studies*, 24(3), 223–231.

Stack, S., Gundlach, J., and Reeves, J.L. (1994) 'The heavy-metal subculture and suicide', *Suicide and Life-Threatening Behavior*, 24(1), 15–23.

Strand, S. (2008) *Minority Ethnic Pupils in the Longitudinal Study of Young People in England*. University of Warwick.

Strauss, A. and Corbin, J. (1998) *Basics of Qualitative Research*. Thousand Oaks: Sage.

Strauss, A. and Corbin, J. (1998) *Grounded Theory in Practice*. Thousand Oaks: Sage.

Sugarman, B. (1970) 'Social class, values and behaviour in schools', in M. Craft (ed.) *Family, Class and Education*. London: Longman.

Sullivan, A. (2001) 'Cultural capital and educational attainment', *Sociology*, 35(4), 893–914.

Sumpter, R.S. (2000) 'Daily newspaper editors' audience construction routines: a case study', *Critical Studies in Mass Communications*, 17, 334–46.

Surridge, P. (2007) 'Class belonging: a quantitative exploration of identity and consciousness', *British Journal of Sociology*, 58(2), 207–226.

Sutton Trust (2008) *Wasted Talent*. London: Sutton Trust.

Taylor, N. and Kearney, J. (2005) *Researching Hard to Reach Populations: Privileged Access Interviews and Drug-Using Parents*, available at http://www.socresonline.org.uk/10/2/taylor.html.

Taylor, I., Walton, P. and Young, J. (1973) *The New Criminology: For a Social Theory of Deviance*. London: Routledge.

The National Evaluation of Sure Start Team (2008) *The Impact of Sure Start Local Programmes on Three-Year-Olds and their Families*. London: HMSO.

Thiel, D. (2007) 'Class in construction: London building workers, dirty work and physical cultures', *British Journal of Sociology*, 58(2), 227–251.

Thussu, D.K. (2007) 'The "Murdochization" of news? The case of Star TV in India', *Media, Culture and Society*, 29(4), 593–611.

Tilly, C. (2004) *Social Movements, 1768–2004*. Boulder, CO: Paradigm.

Tombs, S.A. (1999) *Corporate Crime*. Harlow: Longman.

Tomlinson, S. (2005) *Education in a Post-Welfare Society* (2nd edn). Maidenhead: Open University Press.

Touraine, A. (1981) *The Voice and the Eye: An Analysis of Social Movements*. Cambridge: Cambridge University Press.

Tumin, M.M. (1963) 'On inequality', in J. Scott (ed.) (1996) *Class Critical Debates*. London: Routledge.

Tunstall, J. and Palmer, M. (1991) *Media Moguls*. London: Routledge.

Urry, J. (1990) 'Urban sociology', in M. Haralambos (ed.) *Developments in Sociology*, 6. Ormskirk: Causeway Press.

Urry, J. and Wakeford, J. (1973) *Power in Britain*. London: Heinemann Educational Books.

van Dijk, T. (1991) *Racism and the Press*. London: Routledge.

Vasterman, P. (1995) 'Media hype: self-reinforcing news waves, journalistic standards and the construction of social problems', *The European Journal of Communication*, 20(4), 508–530.

Vattimo, G. (1992) *The Transparent Society*. London: Polity.

Vertovec, S. (2007) 'New ethnic communities: from multi-culturalism to super-diversity', in *Britain in 2007*, London: Economic and Social Research Council.

Vincent, J. (2006) 'Age and old age', in G. Payne (ed.) *Social Divisions* (2nd edn). Basingstoke: Palgrave Macmillan.

Walby, S. (1990) *Theorising Patriarchy*. Oxford: Blackwell.

Walby, S. and Allen, J. (2004) *Domestic Violence, Sexual Assault and Stalking: Findings from the British Crime Survey*, Home Office Research Study No. 276. London: Home Office.

Walklate, S. (1998) *Understanding Criminology: Current Theoretical Debates*. Maidenhead: Open University Press.

Walklate, S. (2007) *Imagining the Victim of Crime*. Maidenhead: Open University Press.

Weber, M. (1968) *Economy and Society*. New York: Bedminster Press.

West, P. and Sweeting, H. (2001) 'We really do know what you do: a comparison of reports from 11-year-olds and their parents in respect of parental economic activity and occupation', *Sociology*, 35(2), 539–559.

Westergaard, J. (1992) 'About and beyond the underclass: some notes on influences of social climates in British sociology today', *Sociology*, 26(4), 575–587.

Westergaard, H. and Resler, H. (1976) *Class in a Capitalist Society*. Harmondsworth: Penguin.

Westergaard, J. and Resler, H. (1976) *Class in a Capitalist Society*. Harmondsworth: Penguin.

Whale, J. (1980) *Politics and the Mass Media*. London: Fontana.

Whelehan, I. (2000) *Overloaded: Popular Culture and the Future of Feminism*. London: Women's Press.

Williams, H. (2006) *Britain's Power Elites: The Rebirth of a Ruling Class*. London: Constable.

Williams, J. (2008) 'The seductions of crime', *Sociology Review*, 17(3), 28–30.

Williams, J. (2008) 'The victims of crime', *Sociology Review*, 17(4), 30–32.

Williams, K. (2003) *Understanding Media Theory*. London: Arnold.

Willis, P. (1977) *Learning to Labour*. Farnborough: Saxon House.

Wilson, J. (1971) *Introduction to Social Movements*. New York: Praeger.

Wilson, J. (1987) *The Truly Disadvantaged*. Chicago: Chicago University Press.

Wilson, J.Q. (1975) *Thinking about Crime*. New York: Basic Books.

Winlow, S. (2001) *Badfellas: Crime, Violence and New Masculinities*. Oxford: Berg.

Wolf, A. (2002) *Does Education Matter? Myths about Education and Economic Growth.* Harmondsworth: Penguin.

Wollstonecraft, M. (1993 edn) *A Vindication of the Rights of Woman.* London: Penguin Classics.

Wright, C. (1992) 'Early education: multiracial primary school classrooms', in D. Gill et al., *Racism in Education: Structures and Strategies.* London: Sage.

Wright, E.O. (1997) *Class Counts: Comparative Studies in Class Analysis.* Cambridge: Cambridge University Press.

Young, J. (1971) 'The role of the police as amplifiers of deviancy, negotiations of reality and translators of fantasy', in S. Cohen (ed.) *Images of Deviance.* Harmondsworth: Penguin.

Young, J. (2002) 'Crime and social exclusion', in M. Maguire, R. Morgan and R. Reiner (eds) *The Oxford Handbook of Criminology.* Oxford: Oxford University Press.

Young, J. (2007) *The Vertigo of Late Modernity.* London: Sage.

Index

Index

Index